1985

Readings in Latin American History

Volume I   The Formative Centuries

Readings in Latin American History

Volume I   The Formative Centuries

Edited by Peter J. Bakewell, John J. Johnson,

and Meredith D. Dodge

Duke University Press   Durham 1985

Contents

Preface

In choosing articles for our reader, we have applied several criteria. We have tried to give a representative sample of the best articles published on colonial and modern Latin America during the past fifteen years or so, showing at least some of the new approaches and concerns demonstrated by historians in that time. We have sought a balanced coverage of regions, topics, and broad historical periods. Above all, we have tried to avoid articles that are too narrow, technical, or complex for beginners in Latin American history. The use of these criteria in our selection, added to simple limits of space, has meant that many first-rate pieces have not found a place here.

Despite our concern with intellectual accessibility, it would be wrong to pretend that all the articles reprinted here are easy to absorb, in meaning and implication, at first reading. That this is so, is simply a reflection of the striking growth in sophistication that the historiography of Latin America has experienced in the past two decades. Nevertheless, we believe that if this collection is read in conjunction with a standard text on the history of Latin America, and if students have the benefit of a certain amount of interpretive explanation from their teachers, the articles will not be beyond the reach of people embarking on the study of Latin American history for the first time.

We have eliminated nearly all footnotes from our selections—partly for reasons of economy, and partly because most of the scholarly apparatus of the original articles will be of little concern to most of our readers. More advanced readers should, of course, go to the originals for bibliographical and archival references. The journals and multiauthor books from which our articles have been drawn are available in most university libraries. We have also lightly edited the texts, with various purposes in mind: to increase uniformity of style; to economize (for example, by cutting out some purely descriptive or anecdotal passages); and, in a very few cases, to bring articles into line with knowledge and concepts that have appeared since the original date of publication. Again, more advanced readers should refer to the original versions of these articles.

Peter J. Bakewell
John J. Johnson
Meredith D. Dodge

Part One ❖ Contact, Conquest, and Settlement

1 ❂

The Problem of Conflicting Spanish Imperial
Ideologies in the Sixteenth Century
JOHN LEDDY PHELAN (1924–76)

In building an empire in the New World, Spain exercised its conscience as well as its sword. As the conquest progressed, Spanish theologians and scholars attempted to define what means ought to be employed to secure the new empire and what ultimate purposes it ought to serve. Three principal approaches or patterns of ideas emerged. The work of Juan Ginés de Scpúlveda (1490–1573) is perhaps the outstanding example of one pattern, this-worldly humanism. Bartolomé de las Casas (1475–1566) expressed a second approach that was largely derived from Thomas Aquinas and Roman and canon law. A third pattern of ideas found its most eloquent spokesman in the Franciscan chronicler Friar Gerónimo de Mendieta (1525–1604), who was dazzled by the mystical idea that the Indians' conversion could begin the millennial kingdom preceding the end of the world.

Famous already as an Aristotelian scholar, Sepúlveda consistently based his vision of Spain's new empire on Aristotle's axiom that all lower forms of created life should be subject to higher forms. From this central premise of natural slavery, Sepúlveda took a metaphysical leap and concluded that the Indians as a race were grossly inferior to the Spaniards. The Indians were barbarians, not simply in the vulgar sense that their human sacrifices, cannibalism, and other practices were barbaric, but in the original Greco-Roman meaning of the word as well: They lacked the *humanitas* of the Christian and Roman civilization of Spain—that quality of mind and spirit that makes a given people competent to achieve civilization.

Several conclusions followed from these basic considerations. By

From *Latin American History: Select Problems,* edited by Frederick B. Pike, © 1969 by Harcourt Brace Jovanovich, Inc. Reprinted by permission of the publisher.

virtue of its cultural superiority, the Spanish nation had the right and the duty to assume the legal guardianship of the Indian race. The Spaniards were obligated not only to Christianize their wards, but also to hispanicize them. The Indians should be made to work for the Spaniards so that in time they might acquire the good customs and social organization of their guardians. The eventual goal of Spain's wardship was to raise the Indians gradually to the higher level of Spanish *humanitas*.

Sepúlveda seems ethnocentric today, but he was a passionate and sincere Spanish nationalist. Deeply moved by the glittering exploits of the Spain in which he lived, he was contemptuous of the cultural achievements of the Indians. He once observed that in wisdom, intelligence, virtue, and *humanitas* the Indians were as inferior to the Spaniards as infants were to adults and women were to men. Sepúlveda was one of the first defenders of modern imperialism. He invented a central justification for imperialism (reformulated by Rudyard Kipling as "taking up the white man's burden") that was to be invoked endlessly from the sixteenth to the twentieth centuries.

Both Las Casas and Mendieta challenged Sepúlveda's attempt to apply the Aristotelian doctrine of natural slavery to the Indians. In the course of a formal debate convoked in Valladolid in 1550–51 to advise the crown on Indian policy, Las Casas argued that the concept of natural slavery could not be applied to any race as such; it could be applied only to a few deformed individuals. Las Casas based himself squarely on Aquinas's interpretation of Aristotle; Sepúlveda, in contrast, followed the interpretation of the poet Dante. Fifty years after Aquinas, Dante had extended the category of natural slavery to include whole races in order to justify the right of the Roman people to rule the world. Sepúlveda's aim was to establish the right of the Spanish nation to govern the Indies, and he naturally followed Dante's lead. In fact, Sepúlveda saw the Spaniards as constituting a new Roman empire, an image that was congenial both to his classical tastes and to his militant Spanish nationalism.

Bartolomé de las Casas found his inspiration, not in classical antiquity or in Spanish nationalism, but in the ideological traditions of the Dominican order to which he belonged. Francisco de Vitoria, *prima* ("morning") professor of theology at the University of Salamanca and a somewhat older Dominican contemporary of Las Casas, was the first to articulate an essentially ecclesiastical and juridical justification of the conquest. His frame of reference was that all nations and all peoples belonged to one world community that was based on natural law and the law of nations, the jus gentium of Roman jurisprudence. The Spaniards might preach the gospel to the Indians, but they must also respect the political sovereignty and property rights that the Indian nations and their citizens possessed by virtue of their membership in the world community of peoples.

Vitoria and Las Casas were in fact endeavoring to replace an Augustinian with a Thomistic view. During the first decades of discovery and conquest, Spanish actions were largely inspired by the view, long identified with St. Augustine, that only membership in the church guaranteed the personal, political, and economic rights of individuals. The prevailing belief was that those who remained outside the pale of Christianity were without social rights when they came in contact with a Christian people. In the 1520s and 1530s, however, partly as a consequence of a drastic decline of the Indian population in the Antilles and partly as a reaction to the conquest of Mexico, a change of attitude occurred. The Dominicans and other members of the regular clergy vigorously protested the inhumane treatment accorded the Indians and attempted to awaken the conscience of the new imperialism. The most eloquent and tireless spokesman in this campaign of protest was Las Casas himself.

St. Thomas Aquinas, the great theologian of the Dominican order, had provided his sixteenth-century successors with a veritable arsenal of arguments with which to challenge the Augustinian view of the proper relation among the peoples of the world. Aquinas was emphatic in denying that the pope possessed temporal jurisdiction over infidels. Hence, mere infidelity was no justification for depriving pagans of their social rights, which were derived from natural law and the law of nations; the pope could exercise temporal sovereignty in pagan lands only in order to further strictly spiritual ends.

These Thomistic views were fundamental to the thinking of both Vitoria and Las Casas. Las Casas held that the preaching of the gospel was the sole basis of Spanish sovereignty; only after the Indians had been baptized could the Spanish crown begin to exercise some political jurisdiction over them. Furthermore, the Spaniards had no authority over the pagans unless they willfully obstructed the preaching of the gospel; accordingly, the Spaniards were constrained to choose a method to convert the Indians that would not alienate them. Las Casas was not a pacifist of the kind that opposes all war on principle, but he bitterly denounced Sepúlveda's use of the "just war" doctrine because he believed military action would prejudice the Indians against voluntary acceptance of the true faith. His ideal was conversion by means of persuasion and reason; warlike measures prevented the operation of free will and the use of reason.

Las Casas spent more than four decades tirelessly defending the principle that the personal, economic, and political rights of the Indians were founded in natural law and the law of nations and must be respected by the Spaniards. Yet he could not deny that the Spanish kings, to whom he directed his appeals, in fact exercised political jurisdiction over the Indies. He extricated himself from this dilemma by asserting that Pope Alexander VI in his celebrated donation had made the Spanish kings "emperors of the Indies" in order to promote the spiritual welfare of the natives.[1] The imperial authority granted did not conflict with local political jurisdictions of preconquest origins; rather, the two jurisdictions complemented each other. Las Casas had in mind the contemporary situation in Germany, where the sovereignty of the Holy Roman Emperor complemented, but did not eradicate the sovereignties of the secular and ecclesiastical princes of the separate German states. Las Casas's view of sovereignty in the Indies was pluralist, in short, while Sepúlveda's was unitary.

Gerónimo de Mendieta many years later challenged the Aristotelian theories of slavery Sepúlveda had expressed during the Valladolid debate. Whatever relevance the doctrine of the "gentile philosopher" may have had in antiquity, Mendieta contended, had disappeared with the coming of the Christian ideal of the equality of all men. Aristotle's natural slavery had given way to St. Paul's doctrine that Greek and Jew (and, Mendieta pointedly added, Spaniard and Indian) were equal in the sight of God.

Mendieta shared with Las Casas the conviction that Spanish rule in the New World flowed exclusively from Spain's evangelical obligation. But Mendieta's approach is more difficult to understand today than the legalism of Las Casas or the secular humanism of Sepúlveda. Mendieta was a Franciscan mystic, heir to a rich mystical tradition that went back to St. Francis himself. He thought in symbolic, figurative, and at times poetic terms, rather than in the more formal logical terms of his fellow

---

[1]   Shortly after Columbus's first voyage, Pope Alexander VI issued three bulls (usually referred to as the Donation of Alexander VI), in which he divided Africa, America, and Asia between Spain and Portugal. It is not at all clear from the text of the bulls whether the pope was merely dividing the world between the two Iberian powers for missionary purposes or actually transferring sovereignty of the newly discovered lands to the crowns of Spain and Portugal.

theologians. For Mendieta the Bible was to be interpreted symbolically through the ancient method of exegesis. Sepúlveda was a humanist scholar, Las Casas a lawyer-lobbyist at the royal court. Mendieta, who actually spent all of his adult life in Mexico, was a missionary caring for the souls of the Indians in his parish.

Mendieta was not alone in interpreting the discovery and conquest of the New World as an apocalyptic event: Columbus held the same view. Yet nowhere in the writings of Mendieta's contemporaries can we find a formulation of the proposition that the New World represented a specific step in mankind's passage to the end of the world that is as systematic or eloquent as his own. All Christians believed that before the Last Judgment there would be a millennial kingdom in which man would achieve angelic perfection. Mendieta passionately believed that together the Franciscan friars and the Indians could create the most perfect form of Christianity ever practiced on this earth and that this would be the millennial kingdom prophesied in the Apocalypse of St. John.

Mendieta idealized the Indians; more precisely, he "franciscanized" them, stressing their meekness, their docility, and their contentment with poverty. St. Francis and the Franciscans after him had regarded avarice as the deadliest of the seven deadly sins. They idealized the life of poverty, which they identified with the primitive apostolic church before the emperor Constantine (311–37), as the most perfect fulfillment of Christian asceticism. Thus, Mendieta naturally saw contentment with poverty as a common bond uniting Franciscan and Indian. The Indians became for him children of God who would inherit the earth.

The vineyard of terrestrial perfection that the friars and the Indians were beginning to build in the New World was ravished well before the end of the sixteenth century. Mendieta placed all the blame on the avarice of the Spanish colonists, whose only concern, he claimed, was to live off the sweat and blood of the Indians. He saw the colonists as the slaves of Mammon, literally engaged in a diabolical conspiracy. And Mendieta became overwhelmed by what he regarded as the parallels between the histories of the Old Testament Jews and the Indians. The preconquest period was the Egyptian slavery of the Indians, that is, the bondage of idolatry. Hernán Cortés was the new Moses who liberated the natives from slavery and led them to the promised land of the church. The period 1524–64 was the golden age of the Indian church, just as the time between Moses and the destruction of Jerusalem by the Babylonians was the golden age of the Jewish people. And the period between 1564 and 1596 was the Babylonian captivity of the Indian church or the great Time of Troubles before the end of the world prophesied in the Apocalypse. Likening himself to the prophet Jeremiah, Mendieta predicted the ultimate fall of Spain's monarchy if its kings did not deliver the Indians from bondage.

Mendieta's description of the Time of Troubles that had deluged the Indian church is a Franciscan image of the Apocalypse. It is the final battle between the city of God and the city of the Devil, between the lambs of poverty and the wolves of greed on the eve of the establishment of the millennial kingdom. His apocalyptic pessimism must be interpreted as a reflection of the larger crisis through which the Spanish empire was passing in the time of Philip II. Spain itself was beginning to show signs of collapsing under the strain of the herculean obligations that it had assumed. In Mexico, the Indian population was declining rapidly. The crown's partiality toward the secular clergy in Mexico over the regular clergy (to which branch Mendieta belonged) also contributed to his mood of gloom, for he was deeply moved by the misfortunes and sufferings of his Indian flock, whom he loved out of a sense of Christian compassion.

Conclusion

The conquests have always received a preponderant attention in the history of Spanish-Indian relations, and the presence or absence of conquest has emerged as a crucial point of distinction between Spanish and other European colonizations in America. Yet it is clear that Spanish-Indian relations were complicated by many factors besides conquest. The Indian societies that were wiped out were not directly destroyed by conquest. The attributes of the conquered societies that enabled them to survive were frequently the very attributes that had induced Spaniards to conquer them in the first place.

The pressures that the Spaniards brought to bear on the Indians varied from time to time and from place to place. Conquest, conversion, encomienda, repartimiento, and corregimiento rule brought institutionalized forms of stress, each making a distinct series of demands. Indian society confronted not one but many crises. We might emphasize the problems of the Indian community or village, because this was ordinarily the largest social unit that survived the conquest and the largest that was called upon to make an adjustment to Spanish colonization. The community struggled to preserve its lands, to maintain its government, to pay its tribute, to feed its people, to provide laborers, and to achieve other goals necessary for survival under colonial conditions. But the community was made up of lesser units, and the interests of the whole and the parts did not always correspond. Thus, an Indian governor might sell out independently to Spaniards who wanted more land or more tribute or more laborers. Indian classes, families, and individuals confronted separate situations. In an economy in which surpluses went to Spaniards, Indian society was disunited, and its parts, subjected to different kinds of choice, reacted differently. And community life was much weaker in some areas than in others.

It remains true that Indian society survived to a greater degree under Spanish colonial government than under the colonial government of any other European power in America. There can be no doubt that this survival was the result in part of the legislation of the crown and the labors of the missionary clergy. Both the church and the civil government acted in particular ways to reinforce and protect the Indian communities. But this is only a partial explanation. Ecclesiastical and civil authorities might themselves be exploitative. Protection and benevolence were limited in time, location, and applicability. Where Indian society survived, it perhaps did so more as a result of its internal structure and character than because of any external efforts to preserve it.

Suggested Further Reading

Friede, Juan, and Benjamin Keen. *Bartolomé de las Casas in History*. DeKalb, Ill., 1971.

Hanke, Lewis. *Aristotle and the American Indians: A Study of Race Prejudice in the Modern World*. 2d ed. Bloomington, Ind., 1970.

————. *The Spanish Struggle for Justice in the Conquest of America*. Philadelphia, 1949.

Pagden, Anthony. *The Fall of Natural Man: The American Indian and the Origins of Comparative Ethnology*. New York, 1980.

Phelan, John Leddy. *The Millennial Kingdom of the Franciscans in the New World*. 2d ed. Berkeley, 1970.

2 ✵

The Rise and Fall of Indian-White Alliances:
A Regional View of "Conquest" History
STEVE J. STERN

The colonial history of Latin America usually begins with the drama of conquest, and this is, by and large, appropriate. Yet anyone who has read Bernal Díaz del Castillo knows that beneath the broad outline of conquest exploits lies a more subtle history of Indian-white alliances. The assistance of powerful regional kingdoms like Tlaxcala in Mexico, or that of the Huanca people in Peru, proved critical to the Spanish conquest of the Aztec and Inca empires. Such alliances expressed the internal contradictions and discontents that plagued Aztec and Inca rule, and the failure of these empires to eradicate the independent military potential of resentful ethnic kingdoms. Yet we also know that mutually beneficial alliances between Spaniards and restive Indian peoples could prove short-lived. Spanish-Tlaxcalan relations soured after a "positive" early phase, and in 1564 the Huancas joined their former Inca enemies in a plot to throw off Spanish rule.

This article explores the early history of Indian-Spanish relations in Huamanga, a highland region in the heartland of the former Inca empire. The story focuses not on a major ethnic kingdom that emerged as a strategic power in its own right, but on the diverse region of Huamanga, which comprised numerous rival ethnic or tribal groups, whose desires to secure political autonomy and economic resources frequently pitted them against one another and against the Incas. To understand better how the societies of Huamanga responded to the presence of the Span-

Published originally in the *Hispanic American Historical Review*, 61:3 (August 1981).

iards, who founded the city of the same name in 1539–40, we turn briefly to pre-Columbian history and social structure.[1]

Among Huamanga's local peoples, relations of kinship and reciprocity defined boundaries of social identity and economic cooperation. An ethnic group viewed itself as a "family" of ayllu lineages, related to one another by descent from a common ancestor-god. Within such "families," exchanges of labor created bonds of mutual obligation by which households and ayllus gained access to resources and labor assistance. Such cooperation enabled kin units, as coproprietors of the ethnic domain, to work ecologically diverse lands and resources scattered "vertically" in the Andean highland environment. As an economic institution, therefore, reciprocal labor exchange among "relatives" was a fundamental social relationship, governing production and distribution of goods. As an ideology, moreover, reciprocity defined relations between ayllu or ethnic kurakas ("chiefs") and commoners. For the ethnic "family" as a whole, and for each of its many internal subdivisions, a kuraka symbolized the collective identity and interest of "his" people. In exchange for service as a guardian of local norms and interests, kurakas at the higher levels of social organization acquired special rights to labor services. A kuraka was expected, among other duties, to protect the group's domain against rivals, redistribute and enforce rights to land and other resources, organize work and ritual, and "generously" redistribute accumulated goods in the form of "gifts" from personal and community stores. In exchange, "his" people worked his fields, herded his animals, wove his cloth, and tended to household needs such as water and fuel. The exchange had to appear "balanced" to enjoy legitimacy.

Two consequences of this social and economic organization had important implications for the early colonial period. First, traditions of kinship and reciprocity imposed constraints on native "leadership." Only by building and maintaining a long-term exchange of mutual obligations, expectations, and loyalties did a kuraka acquire the prestige or "influence" that made ayllus or households responsive to his formal "requests" for labor services. Kurakas who failed to fulfill the expectations of kin, or who consistently violated local norms, risked an erosion of prestige that undermined their authority. Second, the local mode of production tended to divide producers into competing, self-sufficient groups.

---

1   The largest ethnic groups of Huamanga probably numbered no more than 30,000 individuals, or 5,000–6,000 domestic units. Even within these groups, social identification, economic claims, and political authority were significantly varied along lines of kinship and ethnicity.

The division of provincial society into autarkic, ethnically distinct networks of producer-relatives whose scattered properties often overlapped or were interspersed among the claims of other such networks, fostered fierce conflicts over lands and "strategic" ecological zones (coca fields, for example). Even within the bounds of an ethnic "family," decentralized networks of kinship and reciprocity bred competition between distinct kin groupings for self-sufficiency, prestige, and wealth. The very nature of local social and economic structure, therefore, tended to generate endemic rivalries between kindreds and ethnic groups.

The Incas conquered Huamanga around 1460. Their empire converted communities and ethnic groups into a peasantry whose surplus labors sustained an expansive state, but left intact traditional relations of production that assured local self-sufficiency. Despite the sophistication of Inca statecraft, loyalties remained fragile; local peoples proudly retained oral traditions of resistance to the invading Incas. To consolidate control over the region, the Incas implemented their standard policy of settling ethnic "outsiders" (*mitmaq*) in strategic zones of Huamanga. Inca domination thus left Huamanga a legacy of intensified ethnic fragmentation, together with anti-Inca politics and attitudes, and usurpations of local peoples' resources and labor, but without undermining the internal organization of local production and social identification. The disintegration of the Inca empire after 1532 brought a resurgence of small-scale community and ethnic societies whose economic vitality drew on centuries of local tradition and experience.

The confrontation of these peoples and the Spanish conquistadores gave rise to a complex pattern of alliances—negotiated primarily between encomenderos and Indian kurakas—in the new, post-Incaic era. As we shall see, both sides had good reasons to develop mutually acceptable relationships, but fundamental contradictions limited such relations to a transitory adaptation, and doomed the post-Incaic alliances to failure.

The Rise of Uneasy Alliances

The Europeans wanted riches and lordship. After the distribution of precious metals brought to Cajamarca to ransom the Inca Atahualpa, Francisco Pizarro and his fellow conquistadores set out southward to subjugate, plunder, and rule over an Andean colony. The European thirst for precious metals and the looting of religious shrines created the folk legend that Spaniards ate gold and silver for food. Pizarro distributed encomiendas of Indian peoples to his conquistador allies. The encomendero was charged with serving the crown's military and political needs in the colony, and attending to the material and spiritual well-being of the Indians "entrusted" to his care. In exchange, he was free to command tribute and labor from them. As the personal representative of the crown in the field, the encomendero could use his authority over "his" people to enrich himself, but he also carried the burden of forging colonial relationships with the new Indian subjects.

Military security quickly became a top priority, particularly after the puppet Inca emperor, Manco Inca, soured on his European friends and escaped to the montaña northwest of Cuzco in 1536. From his hidden jungle fortress, Manco organized raids that disrupted European commercial routes and harassed Indian societies allied to the Europeans. The resistance of Manco's "neo-Inca state" became so troublesome that Pizarro resolved to consolidate European control and expansion along the highland route between Jauja and Cuzco. The few Europeans who had set up a frontier town in Quinua (Huanta) held out precariously against Manco and the local groups who supported the Inca's cause. Pizarro sent Vasco de Guevara, a veteran of Nicaragua and Chile, and twenty-five Spaniards to the area in 1539, hoping to establish the Europeans more firmly in the region of Huamanga.

In the interests of security, the more than twenty encomenderos centered in Huamanga decided in 1540 to move south from Quinua to a more defensible site. The move was carried out under the leadership of Vasco de Guevara. Huamanga overlooked a strategic area west of the neo-Incas, and the conquistadores repeatedly sought to stabilize a European population in the new city to counter the threat of neo-Inca raids and local rebellions. Those who settled in Huamanga saw the local Indian communities as a source of labor and plunder. Spanish settlers required Indian labor and tribute for the most basic necessities—food; transport of water, wood, and merchandise; construction of houses and public works such as churches, roads, and bridges. Furthermore, the loyalty of the local Indians was essential to the Europeans if they were to resist Inca encroachments. The cabildo, a municipal council controlled by the European encomendero elite, sought to curb abuse of the natives in 1541 because it "would give the Indians reason to turn against us, killing Spaniards as they used to do."

Fortunately for the conquistadores, local Andean societies had good reason to ally themselves with Europeans. The military prowess of the Spaniards, skilled masters of horse and sword, impressed the kurakas who accompanied Atahualpa in Cajamarca in 1532. As is well known, peasant societies are remarkably sensitive to changes in power balances important to their survival, and the Lucanas peoples of Andamarcas and Laramati quickly recognized the Spaniards as new masters. The kurakas of the Lucanas Laramati peoples proclaimed themselves "friends of the Spaniards" when the victorious entourage passed through Vilcashuamán en route to its historic entry into Cuzco. Once the Spaniards broke the Inca siege of Cuzco in 1537, such proclamations acquired additional credibility.

Besides having a healthy respect for Spanish military skills, local societies of Huamanga saw positive benefits in an alliance with the Europeans. These local societies could finally break the yoke of Inca rule, and advance ethnic interests in a new, post-Incaic era. Some of the *mitmaq* populations settled in northern Huamanga by the Incas returned to their home communities. The Europeans were not the only people who plundered the Andean sierra in the early years. Local communities sacked warehouses once dedicated to the discredited Incas and major *huacas* ("deities") associated with the state, and a mushrooming population of yanaconas—individuals who left ayllu society to become dependent retainers of the Europeans—joined their masters in the hunt for precious metals.

Given these circumstances, the conquistadores got the help they needed, despite tenuous loyalties and occasional conflicts between Europeans and their native allies. Early in 1541, Indians from northeast Huanta, who bore the brunt of Manco Inca's assaults, came to Huamanga to warn of the Inca's plans to overrun the Spanish city. The cabildo sent Francisco de Cárdenas to lead an expedition of twenty Spaniards and "two thousand Indian friends" to forestall the attack and "to protect the natives." Through the early 1550s, the continual turbulence of civil war among the Spaniards and fights with the neo-Incas put local societies and their kurakas in a difficult position. Given the claims all sides made for logistic and military support, native peoples could not choose neutrality. They had to decide what kind of alliance would most benefit ethnic or communal interests. Robbed of the option of neutrality, local societies participated heavily in the early wars, which "[left] the Indians destroyed." While some Indians of Huamanga joined forces with the neo-Incas, most groups—including Incas settled in Huamanga— fought on the side of the Spanish crown. The strategic highway connecting Lima (founded in 1535), Huamanga, and Cuzco threw the burden of fighting upon the societies of the northern districts through which it passed—Huanta, Vilcashuamán, and Andahuaylas. In addition, Huanta and Andahuaylas bordered on the area controlled by the neo-Incas. A kuraka "guarding a pass out of fear of the Inca" sent urgent notice in 1544 that Manco Inca, with the help of dissident Spaniards, was planning an attack that threatened the encomienda Indians of Pedro Díaz de Rojas. But even the societies far to the south did not escape involvement. When Francisco Hernández Girón rebelled against the crown in the early 1550s, he raided the rich herds of the Soras and Lucanas peoples for supplies. The raids provoked Indian elites into supporting the royal campaign.

The encomenderos knew that they needed favorable working relationships with "their" kurakas; the shrewdest sought to cement alliances with favors and gifts. Encomenderos and other Spaniards frequently came before the cabildo in Huamanga's first decade to ask for land grants (mercedes) for estancias or farms. Percipient encomenderos encouraged the cabildo to grant mercedes to their kurakas as well. The kurakas of Juan de Berrio received ten *fanegadas* (nearly thirty hectares) in the fertile valley of Viñaca west of the city of Huamanga; one kuraka sponsored by Berrio received title to twenty *fanegadas*. Francisco de Balboa asked the cabildo to grant sixteen *fanegadas* in the rich Chupas plains south of Huamanga to his chief kuraka (kuraka principal). Diego Gavilán claimed twenty *fanegadas* for himself in the Chigua Valley, and then had the cabildo grant the rest of the valley to his kuraka. One of the most successful encomenderos, Diego Maldonado, showered gifts upon the kurakas of his Andahuaylas encomienda. The native elite received a Black slave, mules, horses, livestock, and fine Inca and Spanish cloths. In a later dispute, a kuraka pointed out that such gifts were given "because [Maldonado] owed it to them for the services they would render him."

Communities and ethnic groups hoped that alliances with Europeans would help them gain the upper hand in their own native rivalries. In 1557, for example, the Lucanas Laramati peoples complained that neighboring groups were intruding upon valuable hunting lands. With the help of their encomendero, Pedro de Avendaño, secretary of the viceroy and a resident of Lima, they obtained a viceregal ban on hunting directed against the Lucanas Andamarcas, Yauyos, Huancas, Parinacochas, and coastal peoples who surrounded the core settlement area of the Lucanas Laramati. The Chancas of Andahuaylas, traditionally bitter rivals of the Incas, used European power against their enemies. When the neo-Incas kidnapped the Chanca guardians of coca fields in

Mayomarca (between Huanta and Andahuaylas), ethnic groups from Huamanga threatened to take over the treasured fields. The Chancas solved their difficulty by persuading their encomendero to lead a military expedition to Mayomarca, which secured their control. Collaboration with Europeans, despite the tolls of war, tribute, and labor, brought its advantages.

A closer look at the Chancas of Andahuaylas shows how astute encomenderos cultivated working relationships with native elites and societies. Diego Maldonado, one of the richest and most successful encomenderos, preferred negotiating agreements with the kurakas to resorting to brute force. Through one such agreement, Maldonado persuaded some natives who had lived in distant valleys and punas to resettle in a valley nearer the royal highway to Cuzco. Maldonado also avoided usurping treasured Chanca resources. Instead, he carved out lands and herds for his hacienda from the vast holdings once dedicated to the support of the Inca state. Initially, at least, Maldonado settled personal yanaconas on his lands rather than demand encomienda labor. When Indians complained that his expansive herds damaged their crops, he (or his administrator) inspected the claims and distributed corn, potatoes, *ají* ("hot peppers"), and other products as compensation for damages incurred. Maldonado also negotiated agreements with the kurakas, specifying the tribute obligations of his encomienda. Maldonado customarily set aside a third of the tribute in foodstuffs for redistribution, and in lean agricultural years donated food and relieved his encomienda of various tribute obligations. He contributed the labor of African slaves and yanaconas to the construction of an *obraje* jointly owned by his Indians and a Spanish entrepreneur, and distributed European novelties such as scissors and glass cups. He preferred agreements to unsystematized plunder, and thus in a sense integrated himself into native society as a generous, "redistributive" patron, though Maldonado's son later exaggerated when he stated that his father's gifts were responsible for the kurakas' impressive wealth. Indian workers on his fields received, besides the customary payments, "gifts" of corn, coca, salt, *ají*, meat, sheep, and wool. During the twenty-two-day harvest of coca leaves, Maldonado would regale workers with eight baskets of coca. In his will, he donated thousands of cattle to his Indians. During his lifetime, Maldonado sometimes acted as if he were a shrewd ethnographer applying Andean rules of "generosity" to create dependencies and "reciprocal" exchange obligations.

Alliance did not, of course, imply that life was free of conflict or abuse. Behind the negotiations often lay violence and the respective power and needs of both sides. At one point, Indians killed an African slave of Maldonado, and the encomendero sometimes jailed the Chanca elites. A record of fines collected by Huamanga officials from 1559 on documents the rough, violent episodes that marred many relationships. Among the encomenderos themselves, gambling and fighting seemed to be a way of life. The Indians were subject to whippings, looting, and rape by Spaniards, Blacks, mestizos, and mulattoes. Labor conditions were crude and harsh. Construction of Huamanga in its original site cost the lives of many workers.

As conquerors and aspiring commanders of the labor of their Indians, encomenderos saw themselves as agents personally responsible for basic public tasks. To construct a church, they assessed themselves a labor draft of 510 Indian workers. Later, they assumed responsibility for supplying Indians to carry water to urban Huamanga's households. In general, encomenderos and masters of yanaconas tended to treat their wards as personal property. For the native workers, such a relationship imposed harsh demands. For example, a lively business flourished around the rental of Indian workers and sale of Indian subjects. Rental of Indian labor encouraged its exploiters, like some conquistadores bent on returning to Spain after a few years of plunder, to ignore the long-run survival of workers. The buyer of Indians who sought to squeeze out the most work in a short time period, as one observer put it, "enters like a hungry wolf."

These abuses should not blind us, however, to facts that were so obvious to the native peoples themselves. Cooperation or alliance with the conquerors of the Incas offered at least the possibility of protection against extreme violence. Significantly, most fines collected for personal abuse of Indians were not imposed on members of Huamanga's small circle of elite families, but on lesser Spanish, mixed-blood, and native residents. If alliance did not create an idyllic era, it nevertheless offered the advantages sketched above—continued freedom from Inca (or neo-Inca) rule, special privileges for the kuraka friends of the conquistadores, and valuable help in the endemic rivalries among local communities and ethnic groups.

Early relations, then, displayed an uneasy mixture of force, negotiation, and alliance. The parties to the post-Incaic alliances probed one another for weaknesses, testing the limits of the new relationships. In the early years, each encomendero—accompanied by soldiers if necessary—"asked his cacique [kuraka] for what he thought necessary, and [the chief] bargained about what he could give." Ill treatment and extortion varied "according to the care and greed of each [encomendero], and the skill that he had with his Indians."

Sheer ignorance of the true resources available to local societies handicapped the conquistadores. The first inspection of the Huamanga region, in 1549, turned up only 12,179 native males between the ages of fifteen and fifty; several years later, when population should have declined, Damián de la Bandera counted 21,771 tributaries. Despite his considerable skills and knowledge, Bandera had little choice but to rely on kurakas for much of his information. Felipe Guaman Poma de Ayala wrote a scathing indictment of the European colonials around 1600. Significantly, this bitter Indian critic from Huamanga praised the first generation of encomenderos. The conquistadores "used to sit down to eat and gave all the clothes and textiles the [Indian] notables wanted, and if the crops froze or were lost, they pardoned the poor Indians [their tribute]." Francisco de Cárdenas, who had led 2,000 Indians against the neo-Incas in 1541, left his Indians thousands of sheep on their punas in Chocorvos and Vilcashuamán. Don Pedro de Córdova, said Poma de Ayala, helped protect his Lucanas Laramati peoples from abusive priests and officials. The Lucanas Laramati, who had always sought to be "friends of the Spaniards," granted Córdova a huge ranching estate "for the many releases of taxes and tributes which, as encomendero, he made and pardoned them." The parties of the post-Incaic alliances understood very well that they needed one another.

The Early Commercial Economy

By securing cooperative relations with native elites and societies, an aspiring ruling class of encomenderos laid a foundation for the colonial economy and society in Huamanga. By the 1550s, Spanish-Indian relations entered a second phase as a corregidor and other appointed officials began to assume responsibility for many judicial and administrative tasks. The colonial state, centered in Lima, thereby began to intervene in a restricted way to limit the regional autonomy of Huamanga's leading families. Colonial officials, however, tended to enter into alliances with powerful local Spaniards, and, in the early years, the cabildo, dominated by encomenderos, had moved quickly to establish rules and guidelines for a colonial society. The cabildo, almost immediately, had taken on the task of assigning *solares* ("town lots") for homes, shops, gardens, and small farms, and of granting mercedes for farm and pasture lands. During the years 1540–43, the cabildo granted forty-two mercedes for estancias ("grazing sites") and farm lands to twenty residents. In 1546, the city appropriated common lands "that are around this town that are neither worked nor populated by Indians." It appears that eighteen notables of Huamanga received an average of eighty hectares each. Twelve years later, the cabildo distributed thousands of hectares in the irrigated Chaquibamba plains to more than sixty vecinos and other residents.

Leading citizens acquired lands and pastures for their own personal gain. Encomienda tributes already supplied Huamanga with food, cloth, artisan products, and precious metals. An encomendero who owned a fine home in the city and a productive encomienda had little reason to yearn for a huge estate to satisfy status pretensions. Commercial agriculture, however, offered lucrative possibilities. Lima, Cuzco, and the booming silver town of Potosí created markets for foodstuffs, cloth, wine, sugar, coca, tallow, hides, and artisanal items. Huamanga itself served as an economic pole attracting rural products. Corn and potatoes, for example, sold for twice the price in Huamanga that they fetched in faraway rural Lucanas. Through cabildo mercedes, sales by kurakas, negotiations, or force, encomenderos and lesser European residents began to claim lands. Rather than consolidate holdings in a single large estate, the Europeans commonly carved out multiple holdings—often small- or middle-sized—on lands whose fertility, suitability for marketable products such as coca or wine, or location near the city or major commercial routes (i.e., the main highway in Huanta and Vilcashuamán) promised material reward. Herds of cattle, sheep, and goats; irrigated patches of wheat, corn, vegetables, and alfalfa; groves of fruit trees and carefully kept vineyards and water-powered flour mills began to dot the valleys of Huatata, Yucay, and Viñaca near the city of Huamanga. Along the eastern edges of Huanta, aggressive entrepreneurs set up coca plantations.

Commercial capital, understood as buying or producing cheaply to sell dearly, thus structured early patterns of investment and initiative. The Europeans cast their entrepreneurial eyes not only toward agriculture, but also mining, manufactures, and trade itself. Already in 1541, Pedro Díaz de Rojas had uncovered rich gold mines in the coca montaña of Mayomarca (eastern Huanta). The gold mines attracted fortune-seekers fired with passion and dreams of glory; in 1545, the cabildo sent a leading citizen to restore order and authority to the violent, rough-and-tumble life of the mines. The discovery of major gold and silver deposits in Atunsulla (Angaraes) in 1560, and of mercury in Huancavelica in 1563, made Huamanga a major mining region in its own right. The royal accountant in Huamanga joined encomenderos rushing to Atunsulla to extract minerals worth tens of thousands of pesos. On January 1, 1564, the encomendero Amador de Cabrera registered the fabulous mercury deposits of Huancavelica. Mercury soon circulated as a regional medium of exchange, along with gold and silver. With the discovery of major mines, Huamanga's entrepreneurs began to build textile workshops and *obrajes*. Within fifteen years of Cabrera's discovery, encomenderos had established at least three major rural *obrajes* to supply the growing mining and commercial centers of Huamanga. In neighboring Andahuaylas, another *obraje* had been supplying the Cuzco market since the 1550s. Huamanga's encomenderos had established trading networks with Lima very early, and the Vilcashuamán *tambo* ("inn") on the Inca highway from Huamanga to Cuzco rapidly emerged as a major trading center.

The Indians, rather than isolate themselves from these economic developments, usually sought to take advantage of new trends and opportunities. Individually and collectively, Indians searched for money and commercial advantage. To be sure, native societies had to find ways to acquire money if they were to pay tributes owed to the encomenderos. The early documentation, however, offers evidence that belies the conclusion that native societies participated reluctantly in the commercial economy just to gather money needed for tribute. On the contrary, communities displayed an open, aggressive—even enthusiastic—attitude that rivaled the boldness of Diego Maldonado's amateur ethnography in Andahuaylas. Long before the Spaniards gained control of Atunsulla around 1560, communities well over a hundred kilometers away had sent *mitmaq* representatives to mine "the hill of gold" abandoned by the Incas. The Lucanas Indians worked local gold and silver mines for their own benefit, but complained bitterly about demands that they work Spanish mines in faraway sites. Kurakas in Andahuaylas sent natives to set up ethnic outposts in the distant silver mines of Potosí. Unhampered by Inca claims on coca fields, local societies expanded coca production and sales. One group used coca to pay "the tribute [they owed], and with what remained after paying tribute, they sustained themselves." Another group used the coca left after tribute to buy sheep and swine. By the 1550s, the Chancas and Adrián de Vargas, a Spanish entrepreneur, agreed to build an *obraje* half-owned by the Indians, who sold some of the finished textiles to their encomendero in Cuzco.

Individually, too, natives reacted innovatively to the new colonial economy. By 1547, Indian workers and traders captured an impressive share of the Mayomarca gold dust in exchange for their services and products. Native merchants flocked to supply the dynamic mines and commercial centers of Huamanga, and artisans left ayllus to find opportunities elsewhere. Silversmiths joined encomenderos in Huamanga, where their skills yielded handsome rewards. Stone masons earned money in colonial construction, and skilled native artisans became indispensable specialists in the Huancavelica mines. The brisk commerce in coca led Indian entrepreneurs, especially the kurakas, to join Spaniards in setting up private coca farms or plantations. Andean ethnic "families" had always been plagued by internal tension and stratification; now, colonial society offered new possibilities to dissatisfied individuals willing to abandon or loosen ties with ayllu society. Some looked for possibilities in the city of Huamanga. In the mines, the loyalties of ayllu Indians sent to work distant ore deposits on behalf of their ethnic groups sometimes abated.

The kurakas, in fact, were in some ways better equipped than the Spaniards to take advantage of new opportunities. The Europeans needed their cooperation to stabilize the early colony and to exact tribute and labor from ayllu society. The native elite, moreover, enjoyed special privileges precisely because their "kinfolk" recognized them as guardians of the collective welfare of their ayllus and communities. The long-run "reciprocal" exchange between peasant households and kurakas gave elites, as privileged leaders, the means to initiate rewarding activities in the colonial economy. One knowledgeable observer called the privately owned coca farms "their particular trade." The kurakas' power, complained the corregidor of Huamanga, allowed them "to rent [the natives] like beasts and to pocket the money themselves." It was true that a kuraka who consistently violated his kinfolk's sense of a fair reciprocal exchange ran the risk of encouraging emigration or disloyalty. In extreme cases, Indians even turned to colonial authorities or patrons to denounce a kuraka or to challenge his authority. In 1559, Huamanga's officials fined one such chief 250 pesos for "certain torments and deaths of Indians." In less extreme cases, however, or when native societies found alliance with European colonials beneficial to their interests, the kurakas' economic initiatives did not necessarily erode their traditional prestige or "influence" among ethnic "relatives."

Thus the Indians, impelled by the hunt for money and commercial profit, joined in the creation of a colonial economy. The native-white alliances did not only enhance the ability of Huamanga's colonials to create an impressive array of commercial production and relationships; they reinforced the natives' "open" attitude toward the newcomers, which focused on taking advantage of new opportunities rather than withdrawing sullenly from contact. The goals of Indians and Spaniards were different and ultimately in contradiction, but joint participation in the commercial economy was, nevertheless, quite real. The Indians embraced the entry of commercial capital on the Andean stage; only later would they discover that the embrace was deadly. The encomenderos saw that alliance with local elites and societies could lay a foundation for colonial extraction; only later would they discover that the foundation was unstable, and that it could crumble under pressure.

Labor and Tribute under the Alliances

The problem was that, under the terms of the early alliances, the colonial economy continued to depend for goods and labor almost wholly upon an Andean social system, managed and controlled by Andean social actors, relationships, and traditions. A colonial state apparatus had only partially rooted itself in Huamanga. Despite the presence of outside colonial officials and formal tribute lists by the 1550s, the colonials could not rely on the state to organize a new economic system that would funnel them native goods and labor. On the contrary, the natives went "over the heads" of local colonials to appeal for favorable rulings from metropolitan-oriented officials in Lima and Spain. The "state" in Huamanga in actuality remained the personal responsibility of about twenty-five encomenderos and a handful of cooperating officials who, as the king's representatives, sought to rule over the area. Under such conditions, it was difficult to reorder the native economy.

Instead, it seemed more feasible to base colonial extraction upon long-standing Andean traditions. The more formal lists by officials in the 1550s and 1560s specified a large variety of items far more impressive than the short lists after 1570. Aside from the gold and silver, food, animals, and cloth of the post-1570 lists, the early tributes included items such as wooden plates and vases, washtubs, chairs, footwear, horse and saddle gear, large sacks and ropes, cushions and rugs, whips, and so forth. The diversity not only attests to the capacity of native societies to incorporate new products and skills into their economic life, but it also dramatizes the dependence of Europeans upon indigenous communities, governed by Andean-style labor relations, for items that would later be supplied by a more hispanicized artisan and handicrafts economy. The documents also hint that early encomenderos—to obtain their tributes—had to respect at least some of the traditional rules governing Andean labor and "taxes." Households continued to retain exclusive rights to crops produced on ayllu lands for local use; to pay tribute, households and ayllus contributed labor time on other lands specifically designated to satisfy outside claimants. Traditionally, such practices protected ayllus and households from having to pay a tribute in goods from subsistence crops or from reserves in years when crops fared poorly. A shrewd observer of Andean life commented that Indians would rather go as a community to work fifteen days on other fields than give up for tribute a few potatoes grown by the family for its own use. Poma de Ayala's praise of Huamanga's early encomenderos for lightening the Indians' tribute burdens in bad years perhaps reflected the encomenderos' inability or unwillingness to overturn such cherished rules. In Andahuaylas, Diego Maldonado supplied the wool needed to make textiles the Indians "owed" him. Such practices respected the rule that peasants supplied labor to claimants rather than raw materials or local subsistence products. Ethnic groups and communities distributed tribute obligations—including money tributes—by ayllu, in accordance with traditional practices.

To obtain labor for public works, transport, and agriculture, the colonials had to pursue a similar policy. To replace worn fibrous cable bridges, the cabildo of Huamanga ordered "that all the caciques [kurakas] and Indians of this province come together [to say] who are obligated to make bridges . . . from old times, and their [European] masters are ordered to donate the Indians [thereby designated]." To "rent" Indians to transport wares or to work lands, a European often had to make the arrangement with kurakas rather than hire the laborers directly. A contract as late as 1577 shows that the prominent Cárdenas family could not independently hire the workers they needed on their estancia in Chocorvos. Instead, a kuraka loaned twenty-seven kinsmen to the family and received the 162 pesos owed them after six months of labor. (Presumably the chief then distributed six pesos to each worker.)

We should not exaggerate, of course, the dependence of the Europeans. They had alternatives and used them when they felt it necessary. Aside from an impressive population of yanaconas, they could draw on the services of slaves, mestizos and other mixed-blood dependents, or exploit individual natives directly by extortion or agreement. For ambitious enterprises, however, these alternatives could only supplement rather than replace the labor of ayllu-based encomienda Indians. In the case of the Cárdenas estancia, the twenty-seven encomienda herders far outnumbered the "five yanaconas and four Indian cowboys" on the spread. Furthermore, even if an encomendero wished to deal directly with individual natives to work various farms and estates, his ability to do so stemmed from a general spirit of cooperation with native societies as a whole, led by their chiefs. The Maldonados of Andahuaylas secured workers to tend to various herds, grow wheat and barley, harvest coca leaf, and so forth. Such relations sometimes carried the flavor of a direct interchange with native individuals, who earned food and money for their labors. Often, however, the Indians worked not to receive money, but to discharge collective tribute accounts settled upon with the kurakas. Even in the cases where encomienda Indians received individual payments in coin or in kind, Maldonado's access to their labors was facilitated by the kurakas' early approval, as spokesman for communities and ethnic groups, of such relations. In the first year, kurakas had given Diego Maldonado llamas and Indian workers to transport items to Potosí and Lima. A tribute list in 1552 probably systematized earlier rules on the number of workers kurakas could spare to help out on Maldonado's farms, orchards, ranches, and in domestic service. As we saw earlier, Maldonado's success was related directly to a shrewd amateur ethnography. He rewarded cooperation with "gifts" and favors, negotiated agreements with the kurakas, and tended to respect traditional Andean prerogatives.

It is perhaps not surprising that most of the agricultural and artisanal surplus, and a considerable amount of the precious metal tributes, funneled to the Europeans rested heavily on the kurakas' ability to mobilize the labor of kinfolk in accordance with traditional Andean norms and expectations. More dramatic, however, is that even in the most dynamic sectors of the colonial economy—mining and textile manufactures—the Europeans could not transcend their reliance upon the kurakas. The mines and *obrajes* were strategic nerve centers crucial to the growth of a thriving commercial economy. Yet the voluntary flow of individuals or families to work the mines was not enough to assure an adequate and regular labor force. In 1562 a special commission struggled unsuccessfully to reform Huamanga's mines and stabilize a labor force. Still, as late as 1569, Amador de Cabrera negotiated with the kurakas of his encomienda to contract Indians he needed to work the mines of Huancavelica. The corregidor complained that Huamanga's rich mine deposits were languishing "because of a lack of Indian workers."

Well into the 1570s—a transitional decade—European entrepreneurs depended upon the kurakas to supply workers for *obrajes*. In 1567, Hernán Guillén de Mendoza reached an agreement with the Tanquihuas Indians of his encomienda to rotate a force of sixty Indians for his *obraje* "Cacamarca" in Vilcashuamán. Ten years later, in Castrovirreyna, the kurakas of the Cárdenas family agreed to provide forty adults and fifty children to run a new *obraje*. Only an agreement among the chiefs of the various lineages—tied to one another and to their people by the long-standing expectations and interchanges of local kinship and reciprocity—could commit ayllu Indians to labor in the *obraje*. One Huamanga contract recorded the formal approval of seven different chiefs; a similar contract from another region recorded the unanimous agreement of sixteen kurakas and "notables" (*principales*). Significantly, the kurakas of Cárdenas sent a minor chief to oversee production in the new *obraje*. In the 1570s, though not in later years, Antonio de Oré appointed prominent encomienda Indians instead of Europeans or mestizos to manage his *obraje* in Canaria (Vilcashuamán). The native elites oversaw labor relations within the *obraje* and adapted traditional Andean techniques to the manufacture of textiles.

Excluded from the traditional web of reciprocities among "kinfolk," which mobilized labor and circulated goods in Andean ethnic "families," and unable to reorganize the native economy or control directly the basic elements of production, the colonials had little choice but to rely upon their alliance with the kurakas. Even if Europeans aspired to take on the precarious task of reordering internally the native economy, the limits of their position would force them to rely upon the kurakas' ability to persuade their kin to participate in this change. By cultivating working relationships with the managers of autonomous native economies, Huamanga's colonials could, at least, receive a portion of the wealth and labor available in dynamic local economies without having to try to organize a powerful state apparatus or reorder local society. Whether the alliance was more voluntary or forced in character, the chiefs would use their traditional prestige to mobilize a flow of labor and tribute to the colonial economy. Combined with an impressive show of Spanish military skill in Cajamarca and elsewhere, and some willingness to help local societies promote ethnic interests, such a strategy seemed sensible at first. It is no accident that the early decades produced figures like Juan Polo de Ondegardo and Domingo de Santo Tomás. Experienced and shrewd colonials, they urged the crown to base its exploitation of native economies upon a respect for the traditional relationships and prerogatives of Andean society. To the greatest extent consistent with crown interests, royal policy should siphon off surplus goods and labor from ongoing native economies rather than reorganize or control them directly.

Extracting a surplus by allying with the chiefs of autonomous and rather wealthy economic systems was for the conquistadores a realistic path of least resistance, but it soon led to a dead end. The kurakas controlled the basic processes of production and reproduction that sustained the colonials' economic, social, and political positions. If the kurakas were not at all "inferior" to the Europeans, but in fact directed the social relations and dynamic economies crucial to the survival of colonial enterprise, why should they accept a subordinate position in colonial society? On the contrary, their indispensable position tended to reinforce their posture as collaborating allies rather than dependent inferiors. The colonials remained foreign, extraneous elements superimposed upon an autonomous economy in which they served little purpose. Such a limitation did not augur well for an aspiring ruling class's hegemony, or for its long-run capacity to dominate a society and capture the wealth it produced. As soon as the specific advantages of the kurakas' alliance with the Spaniards began to run out—because the Europeans demanded too much or because Andean kinfolk reacted against the alliance—the early colonial system would enter a crisis. The dependence of Europeans upon native elites for access to exploitable labor in agriculture, transport, public works, manufactures, and mining exposed the artificial character of foreign hegemony. The economy erected by the post-Incaic alliances was deeply vulnerable to changes in the natives' cooperative policies. Disillusion with the Europeans could spell disaster.

Contradiction and Breakdown

To understand why disillusion set in, we should remember that the native-white alliances had always been uneasy and contradictory. The encomenderos cultivated working relations with local chiefs and societies in order to rule over the Andes and to extract as much wealth as possible. The natives accepted an alliance with the victorious foreigners as a way to advance local interests and to limit colonial demands and abuses. The contradictions of the post-Incaic alliances thus bore within them the seeds of severe disillusion. The violence and arrogance endemic in early relations warned of the limitations of such alliances for both sides.

In many ways, Huamanga's native societies had fared relatively well by allying with the Europeans. Their adaptations freed them of onerous bonds with the Incas, found them allies in ever-present struggles with rival native groups, and offered them the opportunity to accumulate wealth in the form of precious metals. The combined effects of epidemic disease, war, and emigration of yanaconas took their toll upon the several hundred thousand natives of Huamanga, but the decline was not as irrevocably devastating as that in other Andean areas. The Lucanas peoples, who in 1572 numbered about 25,000, claimed in the 1580s that their population had even increased since the turbulent reign of the Inca Huayna Capac (1493–1525). For Huamanga as a whole, a high birth rate, the relative immunity of people in high-altitude areas to disease, shrewd politics, and good luck helped cut net population decline to an average rate of perhaps 0.5 percent a year, or some 20 percent over the 1532–70 period. Such a loss posed hardships for a labor-intensive system of agriculture, but was not by itself disastrous. Indeed, the rich herding economies of the high punas of Lucanas, Chocorvos, and Vilcashuamán served as a kind of "insurance" against a decline of labor available for agriculture. Successful adaptation to colonial conditions had enabled Huamanga's Indians to maintain traditional relationships and economic productivity. Inspections of southern Huamanaga in the 1560s turned up many local *huacas,* presumably supported by retaining rights to lands, animals, and ayllu labor. Several years later, Viceroy Francisco de Toledo was so impressed with the wealth of the Lucanas Laramati peoples that he nearly tripled their tribute assessment. Huamanga's kurakas joined other Andean chiefs in offering King Philip II a dazzling bribe to end the encomienda system—100,000 ducats more than any offer by the Spanish encomenderos, who wished the system continued.

Nevertheless, the alliance with the Europeans had created ominous trends. First, even though Huamanga's rural societies weathered the effects of epidemic, war, emigration, and population decline relatively well, these were disturbing events. Economically, unpredictable drops in the population available for local tasks augured poorly for the long-run dynamisms of ayllu-based society. A certain expected level of available human energy was a prerequisite for the maintenance of the traditional economic prerogatives, relationships, and exchanges that tied producers together. Ideologically, Andean societies tended to interpret misfortune— especially disease or early death—as the result of poorly functioning, "imbalanced" social relationships within the community of kin groups and gods (many of them ancestor-gods). Disease was often considered the work of neglected or angry deities. War and epidemic disease raised the specter of fundamentally awry relationships, which could bring about a major catastrophe far more devastating than earlier trends.

Second, colonial relationships created humiliations and dependencies that undercut the ethnic freedom gained by liberation from Inca hegemony. Aside from the individual abuses and extortions that natives confronted everywhere, local societies found themselves relying upon colonial authority to defend their interests. Using an alliance with Europeans to protect against encroachments by outside ethnic groups was one matter, but dependence upon Europeans to settle internal disputes or to correct colonial abuses was quite another. Unfortunately, such a dependence grew increasingly frequent. Given the internal strife that plagued decentralized ethnic "families," it was difficult to avoid turning to Europeans as a source of power in local disputes over land rights, tribute-labor obligations, and chieftainships. By the 1550s, Huamanga's Indians commonly traveled as far away as Lima to redress local grievances.

Finally, the new relationships generated demands for labor that might go beyond what local societies were willing to offer in exchange for the benefit of alliance with the colonials. The number of Spaniards, of course, increased over the years. Moreover, the demands of any particular set of colonials did not necessarily remain static. Consider, for example, relations with Catholic priests. The rural priests (*doctrineros*) theoretically lived among ayllu Indians to indoctrinate them on behalf of the encomenderos; in practice, many were "priest-entrepreneurs" who sought to use their positions to promote commercial interests. At first, many communities probably accepted the necessity of an alliance with the priests. To ally with the Europeans without cooperating with their gods was senseless from the Indians' point of view. The powerful Christian deities had defeated the major Andean gods at Cajamarca, and, like the native gods, could improve or damage the material well-being of the living. Since the Catholic priests mediated relations with the pantheon of Christian divinities (including saints) who affected everyday welfare, Indians did not rebuff the priests or their demands lightly. By the 1550s, churches and crosses—however modest—dotted rural areas, and their priests demanded considerable labor services, including those for transport, construction, ranching, and household service. By 1564, the rural priests' ability to extract unpaid native labor inspired jealousy among the urban encomenderos. But as the priests' demands escalated, would native societies judge them far too excessive for the supposed advantages that favorable relations with Christian gods offered them?

The kurakas, as guardians and representatives of the community, could not ignore such evaluations of the relative advantages and disadvantages of cooperation with colonials. The kurakas who mobilized labor for European enterprise did not, in the long run, enjoy complete freedom to will the activities of their peoples. The chiefs bolstered their privileges and "influence" by fulfilling obligations to guard the communitarian unity and welfare. The traditional interchanges of reciprocities that enabled chiefs to mobilize the labors of kinfolk created expectations that might be difficult to reconcile with a unilateral flow of goods, labor, and advantages to European society. Traditional reciprocities also placed limitations upon the kinds of requests a kuraka could make of his ayllus and households. Production of textiles for the Europeans through a "putting-out" system similar to accepted Andean practices was one matter. As we shall see, sending workers to distant mines was quite another. Natives would be reluctant to comply, and once at the mines might never return to the domain of local society.

Evidence shows that labor demands became a matter provoking resentment among Indians, even when the labor was sought for activities superficially similar to traditional Andean practices. If labor demands were originally the price for the relative advantages of working relationships with the encomendero elite, the advantages could dwindle over time, and the price could rise unacceptably high. In local society, for example, canal cleaning had normally been an occasion for celebration on the agricultural and ceremonial calendars. In ritual led by the native elite, a community of "relatives" reaffirmed the importance of such tasks for the collective welfare of the group. But the same activity carried an onerous flavor if viewed as uncompensated labor to the exclusive benefit of others. The Huachos and Chocorvos Indians complained in 1557 that they were forced to sweep clean the great canal "with which the citizens [of Huamanga] irrigate their [farms]." The Indians did not benefit from or need the water. Under such conditions, kurakas could not transfer the celebratory aspect of Andean work to colonial canal cleaning even if they had so wished. A kuraka who felt compelled to satisfy colonial labor demands could not assume that his call for labor would be accepted as justified.

In the 1560s, the contradictions inherent in the post-Incaic alliances sharpened. The growing dependency of Indians upon Europeans to settle disputes; economic shortages or hardships imposed by colonial extraction, emigration, or population decline; the tendency of encomenderos, local priests, and officials to demand increasing shares of ayllu goods and labor—all these eventually would have provoked a reassessment of native policies toward the colonials. What made the need for a reevaluation urgent, however, was the above mentioned discovery in the 1560s of gold and silver at Atunsulla and mercury at Huancavelica. The discoveries fired Spanish dreams of a thriving regional economy whose mines would stimulate a boom in trade, textile manufactures, artisanal crafts, construction, agriculture, and ranching. The only obstacle or bottleneck would be labor. If European demands escalated far beyond the supply of individual laborers, or of contingents sent by kurakas, how would the colonials stabilize an adequate labor force?

By 1562, the labor problem merited an official inquiry by the distinguished jurist Juan Polo de Ondegardo. Polo investigated Indian complaints, set out to reform and regulate labor practices, and ordered native societies to turn over a rotating force of 700 weekly laborers for the Atunsulla mines. The labor regime imposed by the miners had been harsh. Miners sought to maximize their exploitation of native laborers. Natives personally hauled loads of fuel, salt, and other supplies from distant areas; in the mines themselves, laborers had to meet brutally taxing production quotas; after fulfilling their labor obligations, they faced a struggle to obtain their wages. Small wonder that the Indians asked a noted defender, Fray Domingo de Santo Tomás, to inspect the mines. Santo Tomás found that "until now the Indians have been paid so poorly, and treated worse . . . that even if they went voluntarily, [these abuses] would wipe out [their willingness]." Hopeful that Polo's reforms—boosted by higher salaries—could attract enough voluntary labor, Santo Tomás warned that the Indians and kurakas would resist attempts to force natives to work under the abusive conditions of the past, "even if they knew they would have to spend all their lives in jail." Santo Tomás found the Indians restless about demands for mine labor. The Soras and Lucanas peoples, farther away than other groups from Atunsulla, were particularly vexed about working under abusive conditions current in distant mines.

Polo's reforms changed little. The supply of native laborers forced or coaxed individually or through the kurakas remained irregular and insufficient. The corregidor of Huamanga complained in 1569 that work on the region's fabulous deposits faltered because of the labor shortage.

The mines made obvious the limitations of previous relationships to both sides. For the Europeans, driven by the international expansion of commercial capital, alliances with native societies meant little if they could not supply a dependable labor force for a growing mining economy. For the Indians—kurakas as well as their kinfolk—collaboration with the colonials offered few benefits if the Europeans insisted upon draining ayllu resources in a drive to develop a massive mining economy beyond the control of local society. The Europeans wanted favors that the kurakas could not or would not give them. Yet the colonials still lacked the organized state institutions and force that could compel the chiefs to turn over large contingents to the mines.

At this very moment, contradictions between metropolis and colony encouraged the Indians to rethink the necessity of cooperation with encomenderos. In Spain, the rulers had long debated whether to abolish the encomienda system and convert the Indians into direct vassals. By 1560, the crown had received impressive bribe offers from both encomenderos and the native kurakas, but had not reached a decision. A commission sent to report on the merits of the encomienda issue dispatched Polo de Ondegardo (proencomienda) and Santo Tomás (antiencomienda) to conduct an inquiry. The pair toured the Andean highlands in 1562. In Huamanga as elsewhere, they organized meetings of natives to participate in a public debate of the encomienda issue. The Indians sided with Santo Tomás. Royal interests and moral sensibilities, honed by frictions between encomenderos and the church, created a spectacular debate. In the very years when mine discoveries made the basic antagonisms between natives and whites ever more weighty and ominous, the crown's distinguished representatives advertised political instability, divisions among the elite, and a receptivity to the idea that the encomenderos were dispensable to crown and native alike.

If growing disillusion with labor demands prompted sabotaging or discarding colonial relationships, the apparent vulnerability of such relationships to reform imposed by the metropolis could only give further impetus to such urges. Soon after 1560, native discontent expressed itself in the number of broken alliances. In 1563, kurakas in seven different Huamanga encomiendas refused to send Indians to the city plaza for corvée duty. The mines continued to suffer from an irregular labor supply. Many of Huamanga's peoples, especially the Soras and Lucanas, confirmed Santo Tomás's warnings by openly rejecting calls for laborers to work the mines. Indian shepherds cost their encomendero, Diego Maldonado, a claimed 7,000 sheep through robbery or neglect. Encomenderos blamed priests for the natives' growing tendency to ignore previously accepted obligations; one observer placed the blame on popular rumors that the Spaniards would kill natives for medicinal ointments in their bodies. In an economy where the Europeans depended greatly upon alliances with native elites to gain access to exploitable labor, the spread of such disillusion and resistance poisoned enterprise. In a society where the neo-Incas maintained a military force in the montaña between Cuzco and Huamanga, and the colonials had not yet organized an impressive state apparatus, growing hostility posed strategic dangers as well. The corregidor of Huamanga warned the acting viceroy, Governor-General Lope García de Castro, that a rebellion might break out. In neighboring Jauja and in Andahuaylas, alarming discoveries of stored arms confirmed that Indian-white relations were in jeopardy.

Demands for mine labor on a new scale, the encomenderos' political vulnerability, and the neo-Incas' probable willingness to lead a revolt created a conjuncture that compelled second thoughts about the post-Incaic alliances. From the beginning, the inherent contradictions of the early alliances had created the likelihood of disenchantment. Despite the relative success of their adaptation to colonial conditions, Huamanga's native peoples confronted trends that threatened to undermine local autonomy, relationships, and production. Demographic decline and instability, humiliation and dependence, growing demands for labor—all tended to expose the erosive consequences of an alliance among partners whose fundamental interests clashed. The discovery of major gold, silver, and mercury mines brought such contradictions to a head. The Indians' severe disaffection expressed itself in a radical millenarian upheaval, "Taki Onqoy," which inflamed Huamanga. The sect preached pan-Andean unity, proclaimed an end to all contact with Hispanic society, and pressured kurakas to cut off cooperation with colonials. The movement had exceptional appeal to peoples ethnically divided against themselves, and deeply disillusioned by the consequences of cooperation with the Hispanic world. By the end of the decade, kurakas stubbornly refused to send Indians to the mines, and colonial relationships entered a crisis stage.

Conclusion

The rise and fall of Indian-white alliances in Huamanga yield broad implications for the study of early colonial history. First, the activities of local Andean peoples had a decisive impact upon the particular texture of early relations and institutions "imposed" by Hispanic society (encomienda, tribute, labor drafts, Christianization, and the like). Yet a deeper understanding of the interests and motives behind native activity is elusive unless informed by an awareness of preconquest history and social structure. In this perspective, the line between pre-Columbian and colonial history becomes, in many respects, artificial and misleading. Second, the kurakas' importance as strategic mediators singled out for special favors by Spanish allies, and the impact of Andean ethnic rivalries upon native-white relations, indicate that divisions and tensions internal to local Andean societies played key roles in European success and failure, and the colonial process in general. We would be well advised, therefore, not to homogenize the "Indians" into a seamless social category, thereby ignoring internal contradictions that shaped events. Third, the crisis of the 1560s and its link to the mining economy illuminate the fundamental contradictions of purpose and interest that marred early native-white alliances, and doomed them to failure. Indeed, the demise of the alliances meant that only a more effective, direct control of local native life and institutions, backed by a revitalized state, would truly serve Hispanic interests, and develop the mining economy. It is in this sense that massive reorganization of the Andean colony, like that led by Viceroy Francisco de Toledo (1569–81), was a historic necessity. Early alliances and cooperation represented not a "golden era" of native-white relations, but a transitory phase whose contradictions would eventually assert themselves with increasing force.

Finally, the Indian-white alliances might lead us to reassess the old distinction between sedentary native societies ruled by the Aztecs and Incas, and more independent or mobile peoples who had escaped subjugation by pre-Columbian empires. We normally observe that Europeans experienced little trouble dominating a sedentary peasantry already accustomed to rule from above, but encountered much more difficulty conquering stateless peoples undefeated by the Aztecs and Incas. There is merit in the distinction, and we may certainly contrast the options and "moral economy" of peasants and those of free and independent "savages." But the contrast misleads us in certain respects. It underestimates the degree to which stateless Indian peoples forged early alliances with Europeans, and the dynamics that drove such relations to disaster. It overestimates the power of "habits of obedience" among peasantries exploited by the Aztecs and Incas. We presume that such habits generated a passive posture toward the Europeans, who simply filled the void left by Aztecs and Incas. By this line of reasoning, colonizers commanded surplus labor and products of peasants not because the latter (and their chiefs) had reason to comply, but because tradition dictated obedience. If the birth, evolution, and final demise of Huamanga's post-Incaic alliances tell us anything, however, it is that sedentary peasantries actively assessed their alternatives and made choices within the confines of their interests and power, and that, like many human beings, they could even change their minds.

Suggested Further Reading

Kubler, George. "The Quechua in the Colonial World." In *Handbook of South American Indians,* vol. II, edited by Julian Steward. Washington, D.C., 1946–59.

Riley, James D. "Crown Law and Rural Labor in New Spain: The Status of *Gañanes* during the Eighteenth Century." *Hispanic American Historical Review* 64:2 (May 1984).

Schwartz, Stuart B. "Indian Labor and New World Plantations: European Demands and Indian Response in Northeastern Brazil." *American Historical Review* 83:1 (February 1978).

Stern, Steve J. *Peru's Indian Peoples and the Challenge of Spanish Conquest: Huamanga to 1640.* Madison, 1982.

Taylor, William B. *Drinking, Homicide, and Rebellion in Colonial Mexican Villages.* Stanford, 1979.

3

Conquistador y Pestilencia: The First New World
Pandemic and the Fall of the Great Indian Empires

ALFRED W. CROSBY

The most sensational military conquests in all history are probably those
of the Spanish conquistadores over the Aztec and Incan empires. Cortés
and Pizarro toppled the highest civilization of the New World in a few
months each. A few hundred Spaniards defeated populations containing
thousands of dedicated warriors, armed with a wide assembly of weapons from the stone and early metal ages. Societies that had created huge
empires through generations of fierce fighting collapsed at the touch of
the Castilian.

After four hundred years the Spanish feat still seems incredible.
Many explanations suggest themselves: the advantage of steel over
stone, of cannon and firearms over bows and arrows and slings; the
terrorizing effect of horses on foot soldiers who had never seen such
beasts before; the lack of unity in the Aztec and Incan empires; the
prophecies in Indian mythology about the arrival of white gods. All of
these elements combined to deal to the Indian a shock such as only
H. G. Wells's *War of the Worlds* can suggest to us. Each was undoubtedly worth many hundreds of soldiers to Cortés and Pizarro.

For all of that, one might have expected the highly organized,
militaristic societies of Mexico and the Andean highlands to survive
at least the initial contact with European societies. Thousands of Indian
warriors, even if confused and frightened and wielding only obsidian-
studded war clubs, should have been able to repel at least the first few
hundred Spaniards to arrive.

The Spaniard had a formidable ally to which neither he nor the
historian has given sufficient credit—disease. The arrival of Columbus

Published originally in the *Hispanic American Historical Review,* 47:3 (August
1967).

in the New World brought about one of the greatest population disasters in history. After the Spanish conquest an Indian of Yucatán wrote of his people in the happier days before the advent of the Spaniard:

> There was then no sickness; they had no aching bones; they had then no high fever; they had then no smallpox; they had then no burning chest; they had then no abdominal pain; they had then no consumption; they had then no headache. At that time the course of humanity was orderly. The foreigners made it otherwise when they arrived here.

It would be easy to attribute this lamentation to the nostalgia that the conquered always feel for the time before the conqueror appeared, but the statement is probably in part true. During the millennia before the European brought together the compass and the three-masted vessel to revolutionize world history, men at sea moved slowly, seldom over long distances, and across the great oceans hardly at all. Men lived at least in the same continents where their great-grandfathers had lived and rarely caused violent and rapid changes in the delicate balance between themselves and their environments. Diseases tended to be endemic rather than epidemic. It is true that man did not achieve perfect accommodation with his microscopic parasites. Mutation, ecological changes, and migration could bring the likes of the black death to Europe, and few men lived three score and ten without knowing epidemic disease. Yet ecological stability tended to create a crude kind of mutual toleration between human host and parasite. Most Europeans, for instance, survived measles and tuberculosis, and most West Africans survived yellow fever and malaria.

Migration of man and his maladies is the chief cause of epidemics. And when migration takes place, those creatures who have been longest in isolation suffer most, for their genetic material has been least tempered by the variety of world diseases. Among the major subdivisions of the species homo sapiens the American Indian probably had the dangerous privilege of longest isolation from the rest of mankind. The Indians appear to have lived, died, and bred without extra-American contacts for generation after generation, developing unique cultures and working out tolerances for a limited, native American selection of pathological microlife.[1] Medical historians guess that few of the first-rank

---

1 Solid scientific proof exists of this isolation. The physical anthropologist notes an amazingly high degree of physical uniformity among the Indians of the Americas, especially in blood type. Only in the Americas, and in no other large area,

killers among the diseases are native to the Americas. (A possible exception is syphilis. It may be true, as Gonzalo Fernández de Oviedo maintained four hundred years ago, that syphilis should not be called *mal francés* or *mal de Nápoles, but mal de las Indias.*)

When the isolation of the Americas was broken, and Columbus brought the two halves of this planet together, the American Indian met for the first time his most hideous enemy—not the white man or his Black servant, but the invisible killers these men brought in their blood and breath. The fatal diseases of the Old World killed more effectively in the New, and comparatively benign diseases of the Old World turned killers in the New. There is little exaggeration in the statement of a German missionary in 1699 that "the Indians die so easily that the bare look and smell of a Spaniard causes them to give up the ghost." The process is still going on in the twentieth century, as the last jungle tribes of South America lose their shield of isolation.

The most spectacular period of mortality among the American Indians occurred during the first century of contact with the Europeans and Africans. Almost all contemporary historians of the early settlements from Bartolomé de las Casas to William Bradford of Plymouth Plantation were awed by the ravages of epidemic disease among the native populations of America. We know that the most deadly of the early epidemics in the New World were those of the eruptive fevers—smallpox, measles, plague, typhus, and so forth. The first to arrive and the deadliest, said contemporaries, was smallpox.

At this point the reader should be forewarned against too easy credulity. Even today smallpox is occasionally misdiagnosed as influenza, pneumonia, measles, scarlet fever, syphilis, or chicken pox, for example. Four hundred years ago such mistakes were even more common, and writers of the accounts upon which we must base our exami-

---

is there such a low percentage of aborigines with B-type blood or such a high percentage—very often 100 percent—of O-type. The maps of blood-type distribution among Indians suggest that they are the product of New World endogamy. Blood-type distribution maps of the Old World are, in contrast, highly complex in almost all parts of the three continents. These maps confirm what we know to be true historically: that migration and constant mixing of genetic materials have characterized Old World history. There has also been a constant exchange of diseases and of genetically derived immunities. In the Americas, on the other hand, there must have been almost no prophylactic miscegenation of this sort. A. E. Mourant, Ada C. Kepéc, and Kazimiera Domaniewska-Sobczak, *The ABO Blood Groups. Comprehensive Tables and Maps of World Distribution* (Springfield, Ill., 1958), pp. 268–70.

nation of the early history of smallpox in America did not have any special interest in accurate diagnosis. The early historians were much more likely to cast their eyes skywards and comment on the sinfulness that had called down such obvious evidences of God's wrath as epidemics than to describe in any detail the diseases involved. It should also be noted that conditions that facilitate the spread of one disease will usually encourage the spread of others, and that "very rarely is there a pure epidemic of a single malady." Pneumonia and pleurisy, for instance, often follow after smallpox, smothering those whom it has weakened.

Furthermore, although the Spanish word *viruelas,* which appears again and again in the chronicles of the sixteenth century, is almost invariably translated as "smallpox," it specifically means not the disease, but the pimpled, pustuled appearance that is the most obvious symptom of the disease. Thus the generation of the conquistadores may have used *viruelas* to refer to measles, chicken pox, or typhus. And one must remember that people of the sixteenth century were not statistically minded, so that their estimates of the numbers killed by epidemic disease may be a more accurate measurement of their emotions than of the numbers who really died.

But let us not paralyze ourselves with doubts. When the sixteenth-century Spaniard pointed and said, *"Viruelas,"* what he meant and what he saw was usually smallpox. On occasion he was perfectly capable of distinguishing among diseases: for instance, he called the epidemic of 1531 in Central America *sarampión*—measles—and not *viruelas.* We may proceed on the assumption that smallpox was the most important disease of the first pandemic in the recorded history of the Americas.

Smallpox has been so successfully controlled by vaccination and quarantine in the industrialized nations of the twentieth century that few North Americans or Europeans have ever seen it. It is, however, an old companion of humanity, and for most of the last millennium it was among the commonest diseases in Europe. With reason it was long thought one of the most infectious of maladies. Smallpox is usually communicated through the air by means of droplets or dust particles, and its virus enters the new host through the respiratory tract. There are many cases of hospital visitors who have contracted the disease simply by breathing for a moment the air of a room in which someone lies ill with the pox.

Because it is extremely communicable, before the eighteenth century it was usually thought of as a necessary evil of childhood, such as measles today. Sometimes the only large group untouched by it was also that which had been relatively unexposed to it—the young. Yet even among Spanish children of the sixteenth century smallpox was so common that Ruy Díaz de Isla, a medical writer, felt called upon to record that he had once seen a man of twenty years sick with the disease, "and he had never had it before."

Where smallpox has been endemic, it has been a steady, dependable killer, taking every year from 3 to 10 percent of those who die. Where it has struck isolated groups, the death rate has been awesome. Analysis of figures for some twenty outbreaks shows that the case mortality among an unvaccinated population is about 30 percent. Presumably, in people who have had no contact whatever with smallpox, the disease will infect nearly every single individual it touches. When in 1707 smallpox first appeared in Iceland, it is said that in two years 18,000 out of the island's 50,000 inhabitants died of it.

The first people of the New World to meet the white and Black races and their diseases were Indians of the Taino culture who spoke the Arawak language and lived on the islands of the Greater Antilles and the Bahamas. On the very first day of landfall in 1492, Columbus noted that the Tainos "are very unskilled with arms . . ." and "could all be subjected and made to do all that one wished." These Tainos lived long enough to provide the Spaniard with his first generation of slaves in America, and Old World disease with its first beachhead in the New World.

Oviedo, one of the earliest historians of the Americas, estimated that a million Indians lived on Santo Domingo when the European arrived to plant his first permanent colony in the New World. "Of all those," Oviedo wrote, "and of all those born afterwards, there are not now believed to be at the present time in this year of 1548 five hundred persons, children and adults, who are natives and are the progeny or lineage of those first."

The destruction of the Tainos has been largely blamed on the Spanish cruelty, not only by the later Protestant historians of the "Black Legend" school, but also by such contemporary Spanish writers as Oviedo and Bartolomé de las Casas. Without doubt the early Spaniard brutally exploited the Indians. But it was obviously not in order to kill them off, for the early colonist had to deal with a chronic labor shortage and needed the Indians. Disease would seem to be a more logical explanation for the disappearance of the Tainos, because they, like other Indians, had little immunity to Old World diseases. At the same time, one may concede that the effects of Spanish exploitation undoubtedly weakened their resistance to disease.

Yet it is interesting to note that there is no record of any massive smallpox epidemic among the Indians of the Antilles for a quarter of a century after the first voyage of Columbus. Indians apparently suffered a steady decline in numbers, which was probably the result of extreme overwork, other diseases, and a general lack of will to live after their whole culture had been shattered by alien invasion. How can the evident absence of smallpox be explained, if the American Indian was so susceptible, and if ships carrying Europeans and Africans from the pestilential Old World were constantly arriving in Santo Domingo? The answer lies in the nature of the disease. It is a deadly malady, but it lasts only a brief time in each patient. After an incubation period of twelve days or so, the patient suffers from high fever and vomiting followed three or four days later by the characteristic skin eruptions. For those who do not die, these pustules dry up in a week or ten days and form scabs, which soon fall off, leaving the disfiguring pocks that give the disease its name. The whole process takes a month or less, and after that time the patient is either dead or immune, at least for a period of years. Also there is no nonhuman carrier of smallpox, such as the flea of typhus or the mosquito of malaria; it must pass from man to man. Nor are there any long-term human carriers of smallpox, as, for instance, with typhoid and syphilis. It is not an oversimplification to say that one either has smallpox and can transmit it, or one has not and cannot transmit it.

Consider that, except for children, most Europeans and their slaves had contracted smallpox and were at least partially immune, and that few but adults sailed from Europe to America in the first decades after discovery. Consider that the voyage was one of several weeks, so that, even if an immigrant or sailor contracted smallpox on the day of embarkation, he would most likely be dead or rid of its virus before he arrived in Santo Domingo. Consider that moist heat and strong sunlight, characteristic of a tropical sea voyage, are particularly deadly to the smallpox virus. The lack of any rapid means of crossing the Atlantic in the sixteenth century delayed the delivery of the Old World's worst gift to the New.

It was delayed; that was all. An especially fast passage from Spain to the New World; the presence on a vessel of several nonimmune persons who could transmit the disease from one to the other until arrival in the Indies; the presence of smallpox scabs, in which the virus can live for weeks, accidentally packed into a bale of textiles—by any of these means smallpox could have been brought to Spanish America.

In December 1518 or January 1519 a disease identified as smallpox appeared among the Indians of Santo Domingo, brought, said Las Casas, from Castile. It touched few Spaniards, and none of them died, but it devastated the Indians. The Spaniards reported that it killed one-third to one-half of the Indians. Las Casas, never one to understate the appalling, said that it left no more than one thousand alive "of that immensity of people that was on this island and which we have seen with our own eyes."

Undoubtedly one must discount these statistics, but they are not too far out of line with mortality rates in other smallpox epidemics, and with C. W. Dixon's judgment that populations untouched by smallpox for generations tend to resist the disease less successfully than those populations in at least occasional contact with it. Furthermore, Santo Domingo's epidemic was not an atypically pure epidemic. Smallpox seems to have been accompanied by respiratory ailments (*romadizo*), possibly measles, and other Indian killers. Starvation probably also took a toll, because of the lack of hands to work the fields. Although no twentieth-century epidemiologist or demographer would find these sixteenth-century statistics completely satisfactory, they probably are crudely accurate.

Thus began the first recorded pandemic in the New World, which was "in all likelihood the most severe single loss of aboriginal population that ever occurred." In a matter of days after smallpox appeared in Santo Domingo, it leaped the channel to Puerto Rico. Before long, Tainos were dying a hideous and unfamiliar death in all the islands of the Greater Antilles. Crushed by a quarter-century of exploitation, they now performed their last function on earth: to act as a reserve of pestilence in the New World from which the conquistador drew invisible biological allies for his assault on the mainland.

Smallpox seems to have traveled quickly from the Antilles to Yucatán. Bishop Diego de Landa, our chief sixteenth-century Spanish source of information on the people of Yucatán, recorded that sometime late in the second decade of that century "a pestilence seized them, characterized by great pustules, which rotted their bodies with a great stench, so that the limbs fell to pieces in four or five days." The *Book of Chilam Balam of Chumayel,* written in the Mayan language with European script after the Spanish settlement of Yucatán, also records that some time in the second decade "was when the eruption of pustules occurred. It was smallpox." It has been speculated that the malady came with Spaniards shipwrecked on the Yucatán coast in 1511 or the soldiers and sailors of Hernández de Córdoba's expedition, which coasted along Yucatán in 1517. Both these explanations seem unlikely, because smallpox had not appeared in the Greater Antilles, the likeliest source of any smallpox epidemic on the continent, until the end of 1518 or the beginning of 1519. Be that as it may, there is evidence that the Santo Domingan epidemic could have spread to the continent before Cortés's invasion of Mexico. Therefore, the epidemic raging there at that time may have come in two ways—north and west from Yucatán, and directly from Cuba to central Mexico, brought by Cortés's troops.

The melodrama of Cortés and the conquest of Mexico need no retelling. After occupying Tenochtitlán and defeating the army of his rival, Narváez, he and his troops had to fight their way out of the city to sanctuary in Tlaxcala. Even as the Spanish withdrew, an ally more formidable than Tlaxcala appeared. Years later Francisco de Aguilar, once a follower of Cortés and now a Dominican friar, recalled the terrible retreat of the Noche Triste ("Sad Night"). "When the Christians were exhausted from war," he wrote, "God saw fit to send the Indians smallpox, and there was a great pestilence in the city. . . ."

With the men of Narváez had come a Black sick with the smallpox, "and he infected the household in Cempoala where he was quartered; and it spread from one Indian to another, and they, being so numerous and eating and sleeping together, quickly infected the whole country." The Mexicans had never seen smallpox before and did not have even the European's meager knowledge of how to deal with it. The old soldier-chronicler, Bernal Díaz del Castillo, called the Black "a very black dose" for Mexico, "for it was because of him that the whole country was stricken, with a great many deaths."

Probably, several diseases were at work. Shortly after the retreat from Tenochtitlán, Bernal Díaz, immune to smallpox like most of the Spaniards, "was very sick with fever and was vomiting blood." The Aztec sources mention the racking cough of those who had smallpox, which suggests a respiratory complication such as pneumonia or a streptococcal infection, both common among smallpox victims. Great numbers of the Cakchiquel people of Guatemala were felled by a devastating epidemic in 1520 and 1521, having as its most prominent symptom fearsome nosebleeds. Whatever this disease was, it may have been present in central Mexico along with the pox.

The triumphant Aztecs had not expected the Spaniards to return after their expulsion from Tenochtitlán. The sixty days during which the epidemic lasted in the city, however, gave Cortés and his troops a desperately needed respite to reorganize and prepare a counterattack. When the epidemic subsided, the siege of the Aztec capital began. Had there been no epidemic, the Aztecs, their war-making potential unimpaired and their warriors fired with victory, could have pursued the Spaniards, and Cortés might have ended his life spread-eagled beneath the obsidian blade of a priest of Huitzilopochtli. Clearly the epidemic sapped the endurance of Tenochtitlán to survive the Spanish assault. As it was, the siege went on for seventy-five days, until the deaths within the city from combat, starvation, and disease—probably not smallpox now—numbered many thousands. When the city fell "the streets, squares, houses, and courts were filled with bodies, so that it was almost impossible to pass. Even Cortés was sick from the stench in his nostrils."

Peru and the Andean highlands were also hit by an early epidemic, and if it was smallpox it most probably had to pass through the Isthmus of Panama, as did Francisco Pizarro himself. The documentation of the history of Panama in the first years after the conquest is not as extensive as that of Mexico or the Incan areas, because the isthmus had fewer riches and no civilized indigenous population to learn European script from the friars and write its own history. We do know that in the first decades of the sixteenth century, the same appalling mortality took place among the Indians in Central America as in the Antilles and Mexico. The recorded medical history of the isthmus began in 1514 with the deaths of seven hundred Darién settlers in a month, victims of hunger and an unidentified disease. Oviedo, who was in Panama at the time of greatest mortality, judged that upwards of two million Indians died there between 1514 and 1530, and Antonio de Herrera tells us that forty thousand died of disease in Panama City and Nombre de Dios alone in a twenty-eight-year period during the century. Others wrote of the depopulation of four hundred leagues of land that had "swarmed" with people when the Spanish first arrived.

What killed the Indians? Contemporaries and many historians blame the carnage on Pedrarias Dávila, who executed Balboa and ruled Spain's first Central American settlements with such an iron hand that he was hated by all the chief chroniclers of the age. It can be effectively argued, however, that he was no more a berserk butcher of Indians than Pizarro, for the mortality among Indians of the isthmus during his years of power is parallel to the high death rates among the Indians wherever the Spaniards went. When charges against Pedrarias were investigated in 1527, his defenders maintained that the greatest Indian killer had been an epidemic of smallpox. This testimony is hard to reject, for another document of 1527 mentions the necessity of importing aboriginal slaves into Panama City, Nata, and "the port of Honduras," because smallpox had carried off all the Indians in those areas.

The Spaniards could never do much to improve the state of public health in the Audiencia of Panama. In 1660, those who governed Panama City listed as resident killers and discomforters smallpox, measles, pneumonia, suppurating abscesses, typhus, fevers, diarrhea, catarrh, boils, and hives—and blamed them all on the importation of Peruvian wine. Of all the killers operating in early Panama, however, smallpox was undoubtedly the most deadly to the Indians.

If we attempt to describe the first arrival of Old World disease to the areas south of Panama, we shall have to deal with ambiguity, equivocation, and simple guesswork, for eruptive fever, now operating from continental bases, apparently outstripped the Spaniards and sped south from the isthmus into the Incan empire before Pizarro's invasion. Long before the invasion, the Inca Huayna Capac was aware that the Spaniards—"monstrous marine animals, bearded men who moved upon the sea in large houses"—were pushing down the coast from Panama. Such is the communicability of smallpox and the other eruptive fevers that any Indian who received news of the Spaniards could also have easily received the infection of the European diseases. The biologically defenseless Indians made vastly more efficient carriers of such pestilence than the Spaniards.

Our evidence for the first post-Columbian epidemic in Incan lands is entirely hearsay, because the Incan people had no system of writing. Therefore, we must depend on secondary accounts by Spaniards and by mestizos or Indians born after the conquest, accounts based on Indian memory and written years and even decades after the epidemic of the 1520s. The few accounts we have of the great epidemic are associated with the death of Huayna Capac. He spent the last years of his life campaigning against the people of what is today northern Peru and Ecuador. There, in the province of Quito, he first received news of an epidemic raging in his empire, and there he himself was stricken. Huayna Capac and his captains died with shocking rapidity, "their faces being covered with scabs."

Of what did the Inca and his captains die? One of the most generally reliable of our sources, that of Garcilaso de la Vega, describes Huayna Capac's death as the result of "a trembling chill . . . , which

the Indians call *chucchu,* and a fever, called by the Indians *rupu.* . . ."
We dare not, four hundred years later, unequivocally state that the disease was not one native to the Americas. Most accounts call it smallpox,
or suggest that it was either smallpox or measles. Smallpox seems the
best guess because the epidemic struck in that period when the Spaniards, operating from bases where smallpox was killing multitudes, were
first coasting along the shores of Incan lands.

The impact of the smallpox pandemic on the Aztec and Incan empires is easy for us of the twentieth century to underestimate. We have
so long been hypnotized by the derring-do of the conquistador that we
have overlooked the importance of his biological allies. Because of the
achievements of medical science in our day we find it hard to accept
statements from the conquest period that the pandemic killed one-third
to one-half of the populations struck by it.

The proportion may be exaggerated, but perhaps not as much as
we might think. The Mexicans had no natural resistance to the disease
at all. Other diseases were probably operating quietly and efficiently behind the screen of smallpox. Add too the elements of food shortage and
the lack of even minimal care for the sick. Motolinía wrote: "Many others died of starvation, because as they were all taken sick at once, they
could not care for each other, nor was there anyone to give them bread
or anything else." We shall never be certain what the death rate was,
but, from all evidence, it must have been immense. Woodrow Borah and
Sherburne F. Cook estimate that, for one cause and another, the population of central Mexico dropped from about 25,000,000 on the eve of
conquest to 16,800,000 a decade later, and this estimate strengthens
confidence in Motolinía's general veracity.

South of Panama, in the empire of the Inca, our only tool for esti-
mating the mortality of the epidemic of the 1520s is the educated guess.
The population there was thick, and it provided a rich medium for the
transmission and cultivation of communicable diseases. If the malady
that struck in the 1520s was smallpox, as it seems to have been, then it
must have taken many victims, for these Indians probably had no more
knowledge of or immunity to smallpox than the Mexicans. Most of our
sources tell us only that many died. Pedro de Cieza de León gives a figure
of 200,000, and Martín de Murúa, throwing up his hands, says "infinite
thousands."

We are reduced to guesswork. Jehan Vellard, student of the effect of
disease on the American Indian, states that the epidemics in Peru and
Bolivia after the Spanish conquest killed fewer than those in Mexico and

suggests the climatic conditions of the Andean highlands as the reason. But smallpox generally thrives under dry, cool conditions. Possibly historians have omitted an account of the first and, therefore, probably the worst post-Columbian epidemic in the Incan areas because it preceded the Spanish conquest. A half century or so after the conquest, Indians in the vicinity of Lima maintained that the Spanish could not have conquered them if, a few years before Pizarro's invasion, respiratory disease (*romadizo y dolor de costado*) had not "consumed the greater part of them." Was this the great killer of the 1520s in the Incan empire? Perhaps future archaeological discoveries will give us more definite information.

The pandemic not only killed great numbers in the Indian empires, but also affected their power structures, striking down the leaders and disrupting the processes by which they were normally replaced. When Montezuma died, his nephew, Cuitláhuac, was elected lord of Mexico. It was he who directed the attacks on the Spaniards during the disastrous retreat from Tenochtitlán, attacks that nearly ended the story of Cortés and his soldiers. And then Cuitláhuac died of smallpox. Probably many others wielding decisive power in the ranks of the Aztecs and their allies died in the same period, breaking dozens of links in the chain of command. Not long afterward, Bernal Díaz tells us of an occasion when the Indians did not attack "because between the Mexicans and the Texcocans there were differences and factions" and, of equal importance, because they had been weakened by smallpox.

Outside Tenochtitlán, the deaths resulting from smallpox among the Indian ruling classes permitted Cortés to cultivate the loyalty of several men in important positions and to promote his own supporters. Cortés wrote to Charles V about the city of Cholula: "The natives had asked me to go there, since many of their chief men had died of the smallpox, which rages in these lands as it does in the islands, and they wished me with their approval and consent to appoint other rulers in their place." Similar requests, quickly complied with, came from Tlaxcala, Chalco, and other cities. "Cortés had gained so much authority," the old soldier Bernal Díaz remembered, "that Indians came before him from distant lands, especially over matters of who would be chief or lord, as at the time smallpox had come to New Spain and many chiefs died."

Similarly in Peru the epidemic of the 1520s was a stunning blow to the very nerve center of Incan society, throwing that society into a self-destructive convulsion. The government of the Incan empire was an absolute autocracy with a demigod, the Child of the Sun, as its emperor. The loss of the emperor could do enormous damage to the whole society, as Pizarro proved by his capture of Atahualpa. Presumably the damage was greater if the Inca were much esteemed, as was Huayna Capac. When he died, said Cieza de León, the mourning "was such that the lamentation and shrieks rose to the skies, causing the birds to fall to the ground. The news traveled far and wide, and nowhere did it not evoke great sorrow." Pedro Pizarro, one of the first to record what the Indians told of the last days before the conquest, judged that had "this Huayna Capac been alive when we Spaniards entered this land, it would have been impossible for us to win it, for he was much beloved by all his vassals."

Not only the Inca but many others in key positions in Incan society died in the epidemic. The general Mihcnaca Mayta and many other military leaders, the governors Apu Hilaquito and Auqui Túpac (uncle and brother to the Inca), the Inca's sister, Mama Coca, and many others of the royal family all perished of the disease. The deaths of these important persons must have robbed the empire of much resiliency. Most ominous loss of all was the Inca's son and heir Ninan Cuyoche.

In an autocracy no problem is more dangerous or more chronic than that of succession. One crude but workable solution is to have the autocrat, himself, choose his successor. The Inca named one of his sons, Ninan Cuyoche, as next wearer of "the fringe" or crown, on the condition that the *calpa,* a ceremony of divination, show this to be an auspicious choice. The first *calpa* indicated that the gods did not favor Ninan Cuyoche, the second that Huáscar was no better candidate. The high nobles returned to the Inca for another choice, and found him dead. Suddenly a terrible gap had opened in Incan society: the autocrat had died, and there was no one to take his place. One of the nobles moved to close the gap. "Take care of the body," he said, "for I go to Tumipampa to give the fringe to Ninan Cuyoche." But it was too late. When he arrived at Tumipampa, he found that Ninan Cuyoche had also succumbed to smallpox pestilence.

Among the several varying accounts of the Inca's death the one just related best fits the thesis of this paper. And while these accounts may differ on many points, they all agree that confusion over the succession followed the unexpected death of Huayna Capac. War broke out between Huáscar and Atahualpa, a war that devastated the empire and prepared the way for a quick Spanish conquest. "Had the land not been divided between Huáscar and Atahualpa," Pedro Pizarro wrote, "we would not have been able to enter or win the land unless we could gather a thousand Spaniards for the task, and at that time it was impossible to get together even five hundred Spaniards. . . ."

The psychological effect of epidemic disease is enormous, especially of an unknown disfiguring disease that strikes swiftly. Within a few days smallpox can transform a healthy man into a pustuled, oozing horror, whom his closest relatives can barely recognize. The impact can be sensed in the following terse, stoic account, drawn from Indian testimony, of Tenochtitlán during the epidemic.

> It was [the month of] Tepeilhuitl when it began, and it spread over the people as great destruction. Some it quite covered [with pustules] on all parts—their faces, their heads, their breasts, etc. There was a great havoc. Very many died of it. They could not walk; they only lay in their resting places and beds. They could not move; they could not stir; they could not change position, nor lie on one side; nor face down, nor on their backs. And if they stirred, much did they cry out. Great was its [smallpox's] destruction. Covered, mantled with pustules, very many people died of them.

In some places in Mexico the mortality was so great that, as Motolinía recorded, the Indians found it impossible to bury the great number of dead. "They pulled down the houses over them in order to check the stench that rose from the dead bodies," he wrote, "so that their homes became their tombs." In Tenochtitlán the dead were cast into the water, "and there was a great, foul odor; the smell issued forth from the dead."

For those who survived, the horror was only diminished, for smallpox is a disease that marks its victims for the rest of their lives. The Spanish recalled that the Indians who survived, having scratched themselves, "were left in such a condition that they frightened the others with the many deep pits on their faces, hands, and bodies." "And on some," an Indian said, "the pustules were widely separated; they suffered not greatly, neither did many [of them] die. Yet many people were marred by them on their faces; one's face or nose was pitted." Some lost their sight—a fairly common aftereffect of smallpox.

The contrast between the Indians' extreme susceptibility to the new disease and the Spaniards' almost universal immunity, acquired in Spain and reinforced in pestilential Cuba, must have deeply impressed the native Americans. The Indian, of course, soon realized that there was little relationship between Cortés and Quetzalcóatl, and that the Spaniards had all the vices and weaknesses of ordinary men, but he must have kept a lingering suspicion that the Spaniards were some kind of supermen. Their steel swords and arquebuses, their marvelously agile galleys, and, above all, their horses could only be the tools and servants of supermen. And their invulnerability to the pox—surely this was a shield of the gods themselves.

One can only imagine the psychological impact of smallpox on the Incan peoples. It must have been less than in Mexico, because the disease and the Spaniards did not arrive simultaneously, but epidemic disease is terrifying under any circumstances and must have shaken the confidence of the Incan people that they still enjoyed the esteem of their gods. Then came the long, ferocious civil war, confusing a people accustomed to the autocracy of the true Child of the Sun. And then the final disaster, the coming of the Spaniards.

The Mayan peoples, probably the most sensitive and brilliant of all American aborigines, expressed more poignantly than any other Indians the overwhelming effect of epidemic. Some disease struck into Guatemala in 1520 and 1521, clearing the way for the invasion shortly thereafter by Pedro de Alvarado, one of Cortés's captains. It was apparently not smallpox, for the accounts do not mention pustules, but emphasize nosebleeds, cough, and illness of the bladder as the prominent symptoms. It may have been influenza; whatever it was, the Cakchiquel Mayas, who kept a chronicle of the tragedy for their posterity, were helpless to deal with it. Their words speak for all the Indians touched by Old World disease in the sixteenth century:

> Great was the stench of the dead. After our fathers and grandfathers succumbed, half of the people fled to the fields. The dogs and vultures devoured the bodies. The mortality was terrible. Your grandfathers died, and with them died the son of the king and his brothers and kinsmen. So it was that we became orphans, oh, my sons! So we became when we were young. All of us were thus. We were born to die!

Suggested Further Reading

Borah, Woodrow W., and Sherburne F. Cook. *Essays in Population History: Mexico and the Caribbean.* 3 vols. Berkeley, 1971–79.

Cook, Noble David. *Demographic Collapse: Indian Peru, 1520–1620.* Cambridge, 1981.

Cook, Sherburne E., and Woodrow W. Borah. "The Rate of Population Change in Central Mexico, 1550–1570." *Hispanic American Historical Review* 37:4 (November 1957).

Crosby, Alfred W., Jr. *The Colombian Exchange: Biological and Cultural Consequences of 1492*. Westport, Conn., 1972.

Denevan, William M., ed. *The Native Population of the Americas in 1492*. Madison, 1976.

Friede, Juan. "Demographic Changes in the Mining Community of Muzo after the Plague of 1629." *Hispanic American Historical Review* 47:3 (August 1967).

Robinson, David J., ed. *Studies in Spanish American Population History*. Boulder, 1981.

Sánchez-Albornoz, Nicolás. *The Population of Latin America: A History*. Berkeley, 1974.

Swann, Michael M. "The Demographic Impact of Disease and Famine in Late Colonial Mexico." In *Historical Geography of Latin America: Papers in Honor of Robert C. West,* edited by William V. Davidson and James J. Parsons. Baton Rouge, 1980.

Veblen, Thomas T. "Native Population Decline in Totonicapán, Guatemala." *Annals of the Association of American Geographers* 67:4 (December 1977).

4

Encomienda and Hacienda: The Evolution of the Great Estate in the Spanish Indies

JAMES LOCKHART

What the Spanish colonial period added to pre-Columbian America can be described briefly as the contents of two complementary master institutions, the Spanish city and the great estate. Historians have now begun to penetrate deeply into these subjects, and soon it will be possible to deal with Spanish American colonial history from its vital center rather than from its surface or periphery. While the colonial city is the less well explored of the two themes, its study can proceed on a firm footing, since the continuity of location, function, and even formal organization must be evident to all. Understanding the great estate has proved more difficult, for the estate had a greater diversity of forms and changed more than the city, both in law and in substance. The most serious problem, not always recognized as such, has been the apparent lack of connection between the encomienda of the conquest period and the hacienda of the mature colony.

Earlier in this century some scholars assumed, quite logically, that the encomienda must have evolved directly into the hacienda. The restricted rights of the encomendero were thought to have become gradually confused with land possession through some process never revealed in detail. Then in a series of publications written mainly during the 1930s, Silvio Zavala and Lesley B. Simpson proved to general satisfaction that this identification was false.[1] The encomienda had no juridical

---

1 Silvio Zavala, *La encomienda indiana* (Madrid, 1935), and *De encomiendas y propiedad territorial en algunas regiones de la América española* (Mexico City, 1940); Lesley B. Simpson, *The Encomienda in New Spain: The Beginning of Spanish Mexico* (Berkeley, 1966), and *Studies in the Administration of the Indians of New Spain*, 4 vols. (Berkeley, 1934–40).

Published originally in the *Hispanic American Historical Review*, 49:3 (August 1969).

connection with land, and as time passed, it grew weaker rather than stronger, until, in Mexico at least, it was little more than an annuity.

Most historians today would no doubt agree that there is some sort of equivalence between encomienda and hacienda, as well as a certain temporal correlation in that one declined as the other emerged. But after the massive and successful drive to establish the encomienda's juridical history, scholarly opinion has tended to insist more on the separation than on the connection.

Before going on, it may be of interest to consider why scholars have so readily tolerated a gap breaking one of the major continuities of Spanish American development. A large part of the reason is that, until all too recently, the top item on the research agenda was to define the legal framework of the Spanish empire. Men concerned with the subtleties of legal concepts and procedures felt little inclination to pursue any continuity between a governmental, tribute-collecting institution, the encomienda, and a private, land-owning institution like the hacienda.

In the period since World War II, historians of Spanish America have gone beyond legalism, but rather than stepping directly onto the firm ground of social and economic reality, they have often leaped past it to statistical research and highly categorical or topical analysis. For the great estate the favorite categories have been land and labor. Unfortunately it is not much easier to see the continuity between encomienda and hacienda from the viewpoint of land and labor studies than from that of pure legalism. What could be the connection between a landless institution and one based squarely on the legal ownership of large tracts? Where was the continuity between an institution that procured shifting labor by virtue of a governmental grant and one that depended very largely, it was thought, on a permanent force of debt peons?

A final basic factor inhibiting work on the continuous history of the great estate has been lack of knowledge about the encomienda as a functioning institution, for scholarship was long forced to rely almost exclusively on legislative and other indirect sources. In recent years better sources have indeed come to light, and scholars have begun to interpret the new information. Notarial records are proving to be an excellent if incomplete means of exploring the manifold economic activities of encomenderos and their subordinates in the crucial central areas of Mexico and Peru. Much can be learned about landholding aspects of the encomienda through painstaking research with land titles in a restricted locality.

The postwar years have also brought a more complete, realistic, and articulated picture of the hacienda, yielding new points of comparability with the encomienda. François Chevalier's now classic description of the Mexican hacienda provided the first adequate social view of the institution; more recently Charles Gibson in *The Aztecs under Spanish Rule* modified the stereotype of debt peonage and showed that in the Valley of Mexico, haciendas operated even during the late colonial period with a relatively limited skeleton crew outnumbered by temporary or seasonal help coming from the Indian villages.[2]

The main purpose of the present article is to bring the separate histories of encomienda and hacienda into some connection with each other. Such an undertaking means advancing a bit beyond previous interpretations. It does not require rejection of the juridical history established by Zavala and others, however, since the continuities to be observed here are mainly social and economic in nature. Only one aspect of the legal history of the encomienda seems to call for comment. Both Zavala and Simpson recognized that in practice encomenderos could own land, but they tended to give the impression that there was literally *no* juridical link between the encomienda and land holding.

Nevertheless, aside from de facto patterns, there was a certain indirect legal connection that can be demonstrated from the encomienda titles themselves. North American scholars have generally accepted Simpson's interpretation that from the inception of the encomienda in the Antilles, it was first of all a grant of the right to collect tributes, however prominent a feature labor use may have been. Yet Zavala's more detailed treatment of the institution's development shows that the original encomienda or repartimiento of the Antilles was a grant of the right to use labor, with no initial link to royal tribute in fact or theory. It was only in the course of a long legislative and administrative campaign that the crown and its officials succeeded first in adding the tribute idea to labor use, and later in restricting the encomendero's rights to the enjoyment of tributes alone.

Actually there were two strands of institutional development, perceptibly distinct even though always intertwined. On the one hand, there was the "encomienda," created by high officials. This was a governmental office similar to the encomienda of the Spanish military orders, strictly limited in tenure, and essentially conceived as a concession of the right to collect and enjoy the king's tribute. On the other hand,

2　François Chevalier, *Land and Society in Colonial Mexico: The Great Hacienda* (Berkeley, 1963); Charles Gibson, *The Aztecs under Spanish Rule: A History of the Indians of the Valley of Mexico, 1519–1810* (Stanford, 1964).

there was the locally inspired "repartimiento," stemming from the original ad hoc division made in Hispaniola by Columbus, and spreading to other areas through a process of diffusion at the local level. This was a much more amorphous institution, without much framework of legal theory, but basically concerned with labor use.

Even in legal format, the arrangements existing in Mexico and Peru during the conquest period owed more to the repartimiento of the Antilles than to the official conception of the encomienda. The word "repartimiento" triumphed in both popular and official usage to designate the actual geographical area of the grant. The titles of encomiendas in the period before the New Laws do not emphasize tribute; in fact, they hardly ever mention that word. What was assigned, to take the documents literally, was not tribute but Indians, who were to work on the encomendero's properties, his haciendas, and *granjerías;* in Peru as in the Antilles, mines were often mentioned as well. If the titles are accepted at face value, then, the standard encomienda of the conquest period was not in itself a grant of property, nor did it provide a specific legal vehicle for property acquisition. But it was addressed to a man presumed to be a property owner, who could otherwise take little advantage of the grant in its own terms. Góngora shows that in Chile encomenderos cited their official position as justification for receiving grants of land (mercedes) within the limits of their encomiendas, and even for preventing such concessions to others in the area.

Still, legal connections between land owning and the encomienda remain tenuous. A far more significant link is to be found in the realm of actual practice, though the present state of research prevents its thorough analysis. One can say with some assurance that during the conquest period encomenderos in all the major regions of the Spanish Indies regularly owned land as private individuals and that many of their holdings were inside the limits of their own encomiendas. When the nature and extent of these holdings are understood in detail and in time depth, someone can begin to write the systematic institutional history of the Spanish American great estate. For the present, only provisional conclusions can be drawn about any actual derivation of individual haciendas from individual encomiendas.

The state of knowledge concerning land holding as a de facto aspect of the encomienda has already been very well outlined by Silvio Zavala. In his *De encomiendas y propiedad territorial* . . . , he demonstrated a drastic legal separation of encomienda and land owning. Nevertheless, the course of his argument required him to adduce several cases of land use and ownership by encomenderos. Shortly thereafter, in carrying out a study on the institutional history of Guatemala, he unearthed documents proving that the heirs of Bernal Díaz del Castillo, while encomenderos of San Juan Chaloma, had gradually built up a hacienda there through land grants and purchases from Indians. This was evidence, Zavala said, of the "sustained tendency of the encomendero's family to convert itself—by specific entitlement distinct from the encomienda title proper, that is, by land grant (merced) or purchase—into the proprietor of lands contained within the jurisdiction of the encomienda towns. Thus an hacienda would be born under the cloak of the encomienda, though independent as to juridical title." The encomendero could "create an hacienda within the encomienda."

One type of information is lacking now as in 1945, when Zavala wrote. This is the relative frequency with which this phenomenon occurred. Zavala pointed to the only conceivable method of finding out. It could be done, he said, at least for certain regions of the Indies, "on the basis of a scrupulous comparison of encomienda titles with titles supporting territorial property in the same region, inquiring at the same time into kinship between the families of the encomenderos and those of the hacendados."

In its inherent significance, Zavala's analysis of this subject is at least as weighty as his voluminous work on the legal history of the encomienda. Buried as it is in a minor publication on a different subject, however, it has been little noted, and historians have not followed his prescription for further research. Only one work of high scholarly standards attempts to trace a detailed account of land owning in a restricted area from the conquest period to independence and beyond—Jean Borde and Mario Góngora's *Evolución de la propiedad rural en el Valle del Puangue*. While estimable and indeed epoch making, this book does not represent quite the type of research that Zavala envisioned. First, though there are precious bits of information and analysis, systematic investigation of the encomienda is lacking. Moreover, its authors make no attempt to go deep into family histories and interrelationships. Such research will demand a concentrated, special effort to master an enormous amount of detail. Góngora finds that some encomiendas in the valley studied gave rise to haciendas in Zavala's sense, and others did not. Of exceeding interest for the present article, however, is the fact that the family of the valley's greatest encomendero, starting in the first generation, built up a large hacienda in the valley center, the only one in the whole region to maintain the same ownership through the entire colonial period.

Aside from this, relevant information must be sought mainly in works basically concerned with other themes. Chevalier's study is not systematic at the local level, and he is much more interested in haciendas and sugar plantations than in the encomienda. He gives some examples of encomendero families who came to own great properties near their encomiendas in central Mexico, but retreats from any pronouncement on trends, since there were many other haciendas not traceable to that origin. Gibson in his *Aztecs* demonstrates that some used the encomienda as an opportunity to acquire land and he gives the names of several encomenderos who became property owners. But he also believes that there were many other modes of land acquisition.

Elsewhere the findings are also suggestive but fragmentary. Orlando Fals Borda's local study of a highland community in Colombia, while oriented toward Indians, does show that the original encomendero of the region not only acquired a large property that became one of the area's most "aristocratic" haciendas, but even gave it the name (Aposentos) under which it continued to be known until today. For Yucatán, Arnold Strickon asserts that when encomiendas were finally abolished in the eighteenth century, the encomenderos tended to buy up the core area of their former grants, the *planta,* where the headquarters of the developing hacienda was located.

From these examples a pattern seems to emerge. In most regions there came to be considerably more haciendas than there had been encomiendas. As the Spanish sector expanded and more families grew rich and powerful, nonencomenderos managed to acquire large tracts of land in areas originally dominated by encomenderos. But in a typical case, if there be such a thing, the oldest, stablest, most prestigious, and best-located hacienda would have stemmed from the landholdings of the original encomendero and his family. Research that could establish the general validity of such a pattern, however, would require years and the effort of many scholars. And even when accomplished it would probably not reveal the heart of the matter. Unless it went far beyond land titles, it could only demonstrate a certain genealogical relationship, and we can be almost certain that even this relationship did not exist in many regions, especially in the thinly settled cattle areas where the encomienda was weak or absent.

Legal history yields few links between these two institutions, which dominated the Spanish American countryside, while any actual line of descent cannot yet be traced in detail. Accordingly, the only means available to establish the connection is a phenomenological comparison of the two. This in itself could never prove—nor is it meant to prove— that the hacienda arose out of the encomienda, but it can show that the change was far less than a transformation. The comparison, to be just and fruitful, must range broadly over associated practices and structures that, one could maintain, were not a part of the institutions proper. This procedure is necessary because the true comparability exists at the level of de facto practice, social organization, and broader functions. Neither encomienda nor hacienda ever found adequate legal expression of its full impact on society.

First of all, we may compare the two institutions as to proprietorship. It will be immediately apparent that the encomendero and the later hacendado were cut from the same cloth; they were patriarchs of a special kind who ruled both the countryside and the city. Following both custom and law, the encomendero lived and maintained a house in the city to whose jurisdiction his encomienda belonged. Similarly the hacendado, while not a full-time urban resident in most cases, kept a large town house and held citizenship in the nearest city. The urban role played by both types expressed itself in the domination of the municipal council. In the conquest period, the councils of most cities consisted exclusively of encomenderos. The later hacendados never achieved such a complete monopoly of urban office, since miners in some places and merchants in others were also council members, but nevertheless the dominance of the hacendado over municipal councils was the norm.

Each institution in its time was a family possession, the main resource of a numerous clan. Each gave rise to many entails; but, with or without legal devices of perpetuation, each had a strong tendency to remain in the family. As the effective heads of society, both encomenderos and hacendados felt themselves to be an aristocracy whatever their origins and negotiated for honors and titles from the king, particularly coats of arms and membership in Spain's military orders.

The balance between country and city shifted considerably from encomendero to hacendado. The encomendero stayed ordinarily in his city residence, as luxurious as he could afford to make it, and went to his encomienda as rarely as once a year on a trip that combined a pleasant country excursion and a tour of inspection at tribute-collecting time. He did not have a house for himself on the encomienda, though he would often build or preempt structures there to house his subordinates and to store products. In contrast, the typical hacienda had an impressive country house as one of its outstanding features. Yet though some hacienda houses were like palaces, at least as many were fortress-warehouses, massive and utilitarian compared to the hacendado's town house with its carved balconies and fountains.

The hacendado and his family could be counted on to live in town as much as possible. On occasion, for example in the depressed seventeenth century, a hacendado might not be able to afford the heavy expenses of ostentatious town living and would sit out many months of involuntary exile in the country. But when times were good, he would live mainly in the city and travel out to the hacienda for one good long vacation and inspection tour, much like the encomendero. Both types were rural-urban, with their economic base in the country and their social ties in the city. Only the balance between the two poles changed, corresponding to the slow and uneven movement of Spaniards and Spanish life out into the countryside through the course of the colonial period.

What one might call the staff of the two institutions was nearly identical. Both encomendero and hacendado had large collections of relatives, friends, and guests who partly lived on the bounty of the patron, partly worked for him. More specifically, both encomendero and hacendado had in their hire a steward called a majordomo, who took over nearly all the practical management of the estate. The man in this post would be well educated and would enjoy reasonably high standing in the Spanish world; yet he remained socially subordinate to the employer. Like his master the steward was urban-oriented; he was at home in the city markets, where he borrowed money, bought supplies, and sold the estate's produce.

On the encomienda, or at least on large encomiendas, there were beneath the majordomo a number of combined tribute-collectors, labor foremen, and stock-watchers, often called estancieros. Though their function was of considerable importance, their status was the lowest possible within the Spanish sphere. Typically they originated in the humblest strata of Spanish peninsular society or came out of marginal groups such as sailors, foreigners, or Blacks. The later hacienda had exactly the same kind of low-level supervisory personnel, sometimes still called estancieros—which significantly was the first word for cowboys on cattle haciendas. They still came from the same social strata, belonging to the Spanish world, but at the very fringes of it. By this time, mestizos were commonly found in such work, along with Blacks, mulattoes, and poor Spaniards, but their relationship to Spanish society as a whole was precisely that of the earlier estancieros. These people lived more in the country than in the city, though often against their preference. In any case, they spoke Spanish, rode horses, used Spanish weapons, implements, and techniques, and thus constituted a Spanish-urban extension into the countryside, taking their norms from the cities.

At the lowest level, raw labor in both cases was done by Indians or near-Indians, divided into two distinct worker types, as will be seen shortly. We must also take into account the ecclesiastical personnel of the great estate. Each encomienda was supposed to have its doctrinero to minister to the Indians, and this person would also serve as the encomendero's private chaplain. The priest present on the larger haciendas duplicated these functions.

In one aspect it would be natural to expect a thorough transformation—in the evolution from public to private, from a semigovernmental office to an agricultural enterprise. Here too, however, a great deal of continuity can be observed. On the governmental side, encomenderos had the nominal paternalistic duties of protecting and instructing their Indians. Although their post was not supposed to entail true jurisdiction, it is clear that they did in fact rule over these Indians during the early period, openly calling themselves their señores or lords. Hacendados, as mere property owners, lacked any legal justification whatever for such a role; yet they too achieved it in practice. As recognition of their power, the authorities would often give them positions such as captain of the militia or alcalde mayor ("district governor"), and they would exercise formal jurisdiction as well. Both encomenderos and hacendados envisioned themselves as lords with retainers and vassals.

Even on the economic side, in the evolution toward a private agricultural enterprise, there was no lack of common elements in encomienda and hacienda practice. On the encomienda, traditional, unsupervised Indian production ordinarily had primacy, but the encomendero would regularly go on to take possession of land, often on or near his encomienda. (Usually, but by no means always, he received a formal land grant from the town council or the governor.) On these holdings, most commonly called estancias, he would raise crops and livestock for his own establishment and for sale in town markets or mining camps.

Of great importance in the agricultural labor force of the estancias were Indians falling outside the legal framework of the encomienda. Almost everywhere certain Indians soon came to be attached personally to individual Spaniards, who might or might not be encomenderos; in the circum-Caribbean region, these Indians were called *naborías,* and in

Peru yanaconas. Indians of this type, plus some Black and Indian slaves, formed a permanent skeleton crew for the estancias, under the supervision of the estancieros. They were aided by a much more numerous force of encomienda Indians performing "tribute labor," particularly at times of maximum work load. In the case of Peru, we know that the yanaconas of the conquest period had the use of plots they cultivated for their own sustenance. From a very early time there were also nonencomenderos with much the same kind of estancias, though their position was rather precarious, and their possibilities were limited at first because of uncertain access to seasonal labor by encomienda Indians.

All the above characteristics persisted into the hacienda period. We should not forget that our term "hacienda" is a scholarly convention; seventeenth-century Spanish Americans used "estancia" at least as often to designate a large landed property, retaining the earlier meaning of this word. Ownership of land by Spaniards expanded greatly as the hacienda began to emerge, but the Indian villages still held much land. Even more important, the hacienda did not exploit all its vast holdings intensively; instead, certain restricted areas were cultivated under the direction of majordomos. To do this work the hacienda possessed a more substantial crew of permanent workers than the estancias of the conquest period. (The workers' names at this time were *"gañán"* in Mexico and still *"yanacona"* in Peru.) But they were still aided by a large seasonal influx of laborers from the independent Indian villages, impelled now by direct economic considerations rather than by encomienda obligation. Sometimes the villagers floated in and out according to their own and the hacienda's temporary needs, but in some places, as in Yucatán, they had a regularized obligation very reminiscent of earlier labor arrangements.

Both resident labor and nonresident labor, under both encomienda and hacienda, were still very close to pre-Columbian systems of periodic obligatory work. All types of workers performed something less than full-time duties, and obligations were usually reckoned by the household rather than by the individual. Also rooted in the pre-Columbian period were the so-called personal services that were so prominent a feature of the early encomienda. Most of these were inherited by the hacienda. This is especially clear for Peru, where in the twentieth century hacienda workers still delivered produce to town and provided rotating servants in the town house of the hacendado, as they once did for encomendero.

The renowned self-sufficiency of the hacienda was also anticipated in the conquest period. Using their rights to Indian labor and produce as a base, encomenderos created networks of enterprises in almost all branches of economic activity that were locally profitable, though livestock and agriculture always occupied a prominent place. They did their best to make coherent economic units of these varied holdings, each part supplementing and balancing the others. The whole estate was under unified management, since the majordomos were responsible both for official encomienda activities and for enterprises of a more private nature, as were the estancieros at a lower level.

The tendency to build complete, diversified estates, then, was already observable at a time when the Spanish sector of the economy was generally booming under the influence of newly opened mines and the demand of the nascent Spanish towns for all kinds of supplies. This fact throws a new light on the self-sufficiency so characteristic of the later hacienda, which has often been explained very largely as a response to depressed conditions. Much the same type of structure appeared earlier in response to social and economic forces of quite a different kind. The vision of society the Spaniards brought with them to America included a clear picture of the attributes of a great estate and its lord. Aside from his mansion and numerous servants, guests, and vassals, he must have land, cattle, and horses, and various agricultural enterprises from wheat farms to vegetable gardens. From the early conquest period, this ideal constituted a fixed pattern of ambitions for successful Spaniards. First the encomenderos and then the hacendados exerted themselves to carry it out to the last detail, even where local conditions rendered it economically irrational.

But by and large the great estate scheme was economically rational as well as socially desirable. Everything the estates produced was wanted in the cities; taken together these products helped create a Spanish as opposed to an Indian economy. The desire to assemble a complete set of varied holdings was not inconsistent with a thoroughly commercial orientation. Self-sufficiency is very hard to distinguish from the diversification or integration of a commercial enterprise, and the complete refusal to specialize, which may strike us today as amateurish, characterized not only the lords of estates, but colonial merchants as well. In an age of commercial rather than industrial capitalism, there was little thought of expansion and usually little justification for it. The constant effort of the most acute commerical minds was to monopolize, drive out competition, and sell at high prices to the severely limited market. The hacienda would carry the tendencies toward self-sufficiency and monopoly to their logical conclusion, without ever giving up a strong element of market orientation.

In fact, though inspired in part by social ambition, the hacendados' desire for lands they would not exploit fully made very good economic sense. Monopolizing the land discouraged the rise of competitors in the immediate neighborhood. If the hacendado actually developed production on the whole vast expanse, however, he would have flooded the city market, as sometimes happened in any case. It seems probable that the size of urban markets and the amount of silver available were the real factors limiting hacienda production at any given time. The most market-oriented establishments in the Spanish Indies, the sugar plantations, still did not typically become specialized, but raised much of their own maize, wheat, and cattle. A drive toward self-sufficiency, diversification, or completeness—for the three cannot be separated—was a constant in Spanish colonial estates from the early sixteenth century onward.

All in all, the replacement of the encomienda by the hacienda involved only a shift in emphasis, whatever the factual details of institutional development. A semigovernmental domain, serving as the basis of a private economic unit, gave way to a private estate with many characteristics of a government. There was also a significant movement into the countryside, but both institutions stretched from the city into the country, and indeed their main function was to connect the two worlds. The estate ruled the countryside in the city's name; it brought products to the city and the elements of Spanish culture and society to the country. After the city itself, the estate was the most powerful instrument of hispanization in Spanish American culture. During the early period, when Indian structures were relatively intact and Spanish cities relatively small, the estate could emphasize government and tribute collection over active supervision. As Indian structures deteriorated and the cities grew, supervision increased; the city came into the country.

The point of view here suggested makes it possible to treat the evolution of the great estate as one single line of development underneath the changing forms on the institutional surface. To judge from certain portions of their works, scholars like Zavala, Miranda, and Gibson have long had a good subjective understanding of this deep continuity, but they have never chosen to give it methodical expression. The standard works still tend to speak in terms of three successive systems: encomienda, repartimiento, and hacienda. The internal history of each system is worked out separate from the others; each new stage is seen as requiring a much greater transformation than was in fact the case.

But looking beneath the level of formal institutions and administrative policy, the evolution could be expressed in simplest terms as follows. At all times there were private Spanish holdings in the countryside with workers attached to them, and these holdings always drew temporary labor from the Indian villages. From the conquest period until the present century, the constant trend was for the Spanish properties and their permanent crews to grow, while the Indian villages and their lands and production shrank. It now begins to appear that Spanish agricultural enterprises, generally speaking, never achieved complete reliance on a resident working force during the colonial period. (Scholars familiar with conditions in the late nineteenth and twentieth centuries may have projected into the colonial period the solid, sedentary force of debt peons thought to characterize more recent times.) The villagers came to work on the estancias and later haciendas, first through encomienda obligations, then through the mechanism of the repartimiento, and finally through individual arrangements, but they were always the same people doing the same things. In the conquest period, the greatest landowners were the encomenderos, whose estancias formed an integral if informal part of their estates. Yet from the very beginning, there were other Spaniards with similar holdings, both small and large. Encomendero families or their legal successors seem often to have retained, consolidated, and even expanded their properties, which may have had a special aura of permanence and nobility. But the lands of the nonencomenderos increased even more, until the countryside contained several times the number of great estates present in the conquest period. This development paralleled the great expansion of the Spanish or (broadly speaking) urban sector. The organization and social composition of those who owned and managed the estate hardly changed from the age of the encomienda to the hacienda of the eighteenth century.

Giving importance to these basic social and economic continuities does not require one to believe that the encomienda as an institution involved land holding, or that it evolved directly into the hacienda. As far as agriculture and land ownership are concerned, the technical antecedent of the hacienda was the estancia rather than the encomienda. One may retain a narrowly legal definition of the encomienda as the right to enjoy labor and tribute and of the hacienda as pure land ownership (though the latter interpretation is more rarely made). At the same time, it is quite possible to appreciate that the Spaniards tried to use each legal framework in turn as the basis of the same kind of great estate. Ideally this would have combined jurisdiction over vassals with vast possessions of land and stock. In the encomienda, only the governmental aspect was formally expressed, and the rest was left to the spontaneous action of socioeconomic ambitions and opportunities. The hacienda was just the opposite, giving legal status only to land ownership and leaving the jurisdictional aspects to de facto patterns. This basic, essentially unitary social institution, the great estate, was quite fixed as to ideal attributes and social organization, and it maintained constant its function as intermediary between the growing Spanish towns and the receding Indian villages. It evolved along two simple lines—constant rise in the legal ownership of land and change in the balance of the labor force, as permanent workers increased and temporary workers decreased.

Let us view the great estate, therefore, as a basic social pattern with certain permanent attributes and a few recognized principles of evolution. By so doing, we can hope to understand the increasingly complex picture that is emerging as research proceeds to areas other than Mexico. Each region in the Spanish Indies seems to have produced a different form of the encomienda and a different timetable for its downfall. The same is true for the repartimiento or mita. Some areas suffered great population loss, while others did not; still others had little or no population to start with. Some estates arose from holdings associated with encomiendas, others from lands accumulated by administrative and judicial officials, others from humble wheat farms. From region to region, the hacienda veered toward pastoralism, cereal production, sugar growing, and other activities. But we can cope with all these variations if we understand them as retarding, hastening, or modifying an institution that was ultimately embedded in Spanish social practice and had its own coherence, its own dynamics of development.

One may conclude that the rise of the hacienda was essentially a development rather than a struggle. The evolution of the great estate responded to such realities as the size of cities and Spanish populations, the degree of acculturation among the Indians, and the nature of Spanish society in early modern times. The royal policy of discouraging an independent aristocracy and the humanitarian campaigns to protect the Indians deserve intensive study in themselves, but the struggles over these matters cannot be said to have greatly affected the evolution of the great estate. Wherever it might appear that the crown or the church became a prime mover in its development, one will find on close examination that deeper forces were at work. Crown policy has been credited with the destruction of the encomienda, but natural developments in the colonies had doomed the institution. On the one hand, the fortunes arising from commerce and mining were not directly dependent upon the encomienda; on the other hand, the sheer growth of Spanish society produced newly powerful families who began to carve out estates of their own, undermining the inflexible encomienda system.

Historians have commonly observed the general tendency of the conquest period to set basic patterns for later times. The hacienda, taking shape in the late sixteenth and seventeenth centuries, has appeared to be a major exception. But the interpretation of the great estate set forth here reintegrates the hacienda into the general picture. In the broader perspective, one may argue that the conquest period created the function and the basic social and economic modes of organization, while following years brought mainly growth or shrinkage—in other words, quantitative change. Such a view implies that perhaps scholars investigating the history of the hacienda should begin at the beginning. One of the few complaints that one might bring against the magnificent work of Chevalier is that, faced with a vast body of material on the hacienda, he accepted a conventional view of the conquest period and the encomienda, without submitting them to the same kind of analysis he applied to his more immediate subject.

In general, those who engage in future research on forms of the great estate should take into account the institution's multiple dimensions and not limit themselves to "hacienda studies," or to the study of "land and labor systems," or most especially to "rural history." In all known embodiments, the Spanish American great estate was closely related to the city, indeed almost inseparable from it. Spanish American colonial history has three principal elements: the city, the great estate, and the Indian village. Of these only the village was truly and thoroughly rural. The function of the great estate was to mediate between city and country, to carry back and forth supplies, people, and ideas that were vital to the growth of Spanish American civilization.

Suggested Further Reading

Gibson, Charles. *The Aztecs under Spanish Rule: A History of the Indians of the Valley of Mexico, 1519–1810.* Stanford, 1964. Especially chapters 4, 10, and 11.

———. *Spain in America.* New York, 1967. Especially chapter 3.

Keith, Robert G. *Conquest and Agrarian Change: The Emergence of the Hacienda System on the Peruvian Coast.* Cambridge, Mass., 1976.

————. "Encomienda, Hacienda, and Corregimiento in Spanish America: A Structural Analysis." *Hispanic American Historical Review* 51:3 (August 1971).

Konrad, Herman. *A Jesuit Hacienda in Colonial Mexico: Santa Lucía, 1567–1767.* Stanford, 1980.

Martin, Cheryl English. "Crucible of Zapatismo: Hacienda Hospital in the Seventeenth Century." *The Americas* 38:2 (July 1981).

Service, Elman R. "The *Encomienda* in Paraguay." *Hispanic American Historical Review* 31:2 (May 1951).

Simpson, Lesley B. *The Encomienda in New Spain: The Beginning of Spanish Mexico.* Rev. ed. Berkeley, 1966.

Taylor, William B. *Landlord and Peasant in Colonial Oaxaca.* Stanford, 1972.

Van Young, Eric. *Hacienda and Market in Eighteenth-Century Mexico: The Rural Economy of the Guadalajara Region, 1675–1820.* Berkeley, 1981.

Zavala, Silvio. *New Viewpoints on the Spanish Colonization of America.* Philadelphia, 1943.

5 ☀

Carting in the Hispanic World: An
Example of Divergent Development

DAVID R. RINGROSE

There is an obvious association between economic growth and the appearance of increasingly specialized transport, and much of the research into the economic history of medieval and early modern Europe has dealt with this parallel development. The medievalists have studied both water and land transport, showing that the latter was often highly specialized and able to compete successfully with water-borne carriers. Historians of the sixteenth through the eighteenth centuries, however, have tended to accept Fernand Braudel's dictum that by 1600, land transport was overshadowed by improving shipbuilding and navigational techniques. As a result, they have concentrated their energies on the latter and given little attention to land transport, except as associated with the beginnings of the Industrial Revolution in England. This tendency has obscured the fact that until the introduction of railroads, Europe went through repeated episodes of regional economic growth that depended almost entirely on overland transport consisting of professionalized carters and muleteers.

Spain and its American empire witnessed at least three such episodes: in Mexico, 1540–1600, in Castile, 1750–1800, and in Argentina, from about 1770 to the middle of the nineteenth century. The interior of the Iberian peninsula, the Mexican plateau, and the pampas of the Argentine were all large inland areas restricted to the use of land transportation. Transport in these regions developed from the technology of late medieval Spain and supported significant economic growth for considerable periods. Obviously one must avoid implicit comparisons with the headlong growth of industrialization. The episodes in question re-

Published originally in the *Hispanic American Historical Review,* 50:1 (February 1970).

semble, rather, the growth periods of agrarian Europe during the twelfth, sixteenth, and eighteenth centuries. In Castile, this development emphasized the growth of Madrid and an increase of regional specialization in manufacturing and agriculture. The Mexican case was associated with the wealth of the silver mines and the Argentine with the growth of the cattle industry.

In each of the regions being considered, demands arose for two functionally distinct types of transport service. The greater part of transport activity was involved in seasonal exchanges of wheat, wine, charcoal, and rough textiles, all essential for even a relatively self-contained community. This transport for subsistence exchanges was fundamentally unspecialized. Since the transfer of such goods was seasonal or casual, the carriers commonly used idle farm resources—their own labor, mules, and less often carts. Pack-animal carriers could normally provide only limited services beyond regional exchanges of produce for immediate consumption, because for much of the year they had to participate in farming. Often, too, the cargoes required by more complex economic activity could not be carried on pack animals.

Economic growth and development, therefore, demanded more than seasonal muleteers could provide: greater specialization, release from the requirements of the farming cycle, the ability to carry goods that could not be transported on animals alone, and reasonable unit costs for freight relative to its importance.

A part of these specialized transport services was provided by professional muleteers (*arrieros*), who appeared throughout the Spanish empire during the entire period being considered. This professionalized mule transport reached its greatest development in the region of modern Ecuador, Peru, and Bolivia. Here convoys of hundreds of animals moved toward Potosí from all directions every day. Argentina exported thousands of mules each year to Peru for transport and use in the mines. Despite the tremendous obstacle of the Andes, the Spaniards were trying to accomplish what may be called "the commercialization of primary production" with extremely primitive transport techniques. For a time this was possible because the primary products involved—silver and mercury—had high intrinsic value, but the tremendous costs go far to explain why the fabled wealth of Peru made relatively limited contribution to the Spanish royal finances. The volume of bullion that the Spaniards actually got out of Peru was no small tribute to their organizational and entrepreneurial skills. Elsewhere in Spanish America, especially in Panama and Guatemala, pack animals were used on significant land routes, but on a smaller scale or over much shorter distances.

In Spain, Mexico, and Argentina, however, more developed transportation appeared, derived from the carting techniques of medieval Castile—an important and little-known example of America's medieval European heritage. Numerous travelers reported long trains of two-wheeled carts, creaking along behind oxen or mules across the plains of Castile, the plateau of Mexico, and the pampas of Argentina. The specialized cart transport of all three areas and periods was associated with economic development. The cart transport decayed with the decline of seventeenth-century Mexico and nineteenth-century Spain, while it made possible growth in the Argentine economy before about 1810 and increased economic dominance by Buenos Aires thereafter. The technology of these three carting industries had a common source, late medieval Spain, yet three distinctive patterns appeared. Given the common culture of the Hispanic world, how similar were these three industries in their technology and organization? What passive conditions permitted their development, and what actually brought them into existence? What kinds of economic activity could they support, and how did such carting respond to differing and changing economic circumstances? This article will suggest tentative answers to these questions.

The carting industries that appeared in Mexico, Castile, and Argentina had a common origin, but developed to meet varying local conditions. In all three areas, certain basic factors were present: (1) geographical conditions that allowed the use of wheeled vehicles; (2) the carting techniques of medieval Spain; (3) some sort of subsidy or source of wealth to support economic growth despite the high costs of land transport; (4) a demand for transport services that were free of the seasonal and load limitations typical of most pack-animal transport; and (5) some suitable combination of capital, animal power, and grazing resources that would support an extensive carting industry.

The relative importance of these factors varied considerably in each of the three areas, and the overall combination appears to have been least favorable in Spain. There geography was a handicap, for the level plateau areas are less extensive than in Argentina or Mexico. Mountains or rugged highlands cut up the interior plateaus and separate them from all coasts, posing a ubiquitous barrier to wheeled transport. This ruggedness of the Spanish terrain helps to explain the type of cart commonly used.

The carting of Spain, Mexico, and Argentina all developed from the simple two-wheeled cart of medieval Castile. This cart consisted of three longitudinal timbers, the center one extending forward beyond the body of the cart as a shaft to which the draft animals were yoked. Transverse ribs held together the longitudinal beams, and the whole was covered with a flat bed of wood, woven fiber, or netting. The sides consisted of vertical stakes or boards. This medieval cart had two types of running gear. One version used relatively small wheels of heavy timber, nearly solid and rimmed with replaceable wooden strips. In this type, wheels and axle were locked together, the axle turning in mountings under the bed of the cart. The second variety was built with larger, lighter, spoked wheels, often with metal rims or cleats for traction. The wheels in this case had large hubs fitting over the axle, which was fixed to the bed of the cart with the bearing surfaces in the wheel hubs.

Although both types of cart long remained in use in Spain, the roughness of terrain caused the professional, long-haul freighters to favor the first version with small, heavy wheels—the *carreta*. These carts were typically lower and more stable than those with spoked wheels and were generally pulled by two oxen, with a third kept in reserve. They were rugged, easily reparable with a few simple woodworking tools, and capable of carrying many cargoes that pack animals could not handle. The lighter, spoked-wheel cart was used primarily for farming and short hauls. The typical Castilian freighting cart carried up to one thousand pounds (forty arrobas) of cargo at a rate of ten to twelve miles per day. The professional carters generally organized their carts into trains of twenty-five to thirty vehicles that traveled as much as a thousand miles a year, ranging from one end of Spain to the other. A few larger four-wheeled wagons appeared in the southeast, where the terrain was better, but elsewhere carters failed to use such vehicles until well into the nineteenth century.

Not only was the *carreta* suitable to terrain and existing roads; it also corresponded well to the combination of capital, animal power, and grazing resources prevailing in Spain. Few cart owners had much capital—even in the provinces where carting was best developed, they averaged little more than five carts apiece, while the national average was closer to three. The thirty-unit wagon train of Castile, therefore, represented temporary partnerships among small-scale owners who had pooled their vehicles under professional crews and managers to reduce labor costs. Spanish cart owners simply could not afford the six or more oxen or mules required for a single *carro* of the Mexican type. Anyway such a *carro* would have been impracticable for Castilian topography, and available draft animals were badly needed for Spanish agriculture, especially during the sixteenth and eighteenth centuries.

Finally, the price of draft animals and the overall cost of freighting depended heavily on the availability of grazing. Spain was an old and complex society, and every piece of grazing was either occupied or subjected to overlapping claims. The town commons were vital to local livestock as well as to carters in transit; rental pastures for the winter were coveted by sheep herders and cattle ranchers; and grazing and winter fodder were scarce in the mountain homes of the carters. Grazing land, therefore, was limited when compared with that of Mexico or Argentina, and the rising population of the later eighteenth century complicated the situation by causing pressure for enclosure.

Only strong demand for specialized transport was capable of overcoming these unfavorable conditions, and this appeared as the economy of eighteenth-century Castile evolved. Three causes produced this demand: the expansion of agrarian export activity in wool, hides, wheat, and flour; the growth of defense industries; and urbanization concentrated on Madrid. The oldest need for transport was to carry wool to the seaports, an activity going back to the Middle Ages. To this were added the requirements of defense—transport for campaigns, for the transfer of guns and ammunition, and for the movement of ship timber from interior forests to the coast. The third type of demand for specialized transport was to carry foodstuffs, building materials, and other goods to Madrid. This developed strongly in the seventeenth century and in the eighteenth it came to overshadow the others. The growth of Madrid, as the capital, was a function of governmental expansion; by 1800, the city was approaching 200,000 inhabitants. It drew commodities from almost all of Old and New Castile and had no means of supply other than carts and pack animals. By the 1780s, the needs of Madrid and the other demands mentioned had brought into existence an extensive professional carting industry.

This transport, however vital, was expensive. Through three different techniques, the royal government had to use its power and resources to support the carting on which its administration depended. The crown gave the carters an elaborate system of economic privileges, especially the use of town commons and guaranteed, low-rent winter pastures. It also established a special juridico-administrative agency to protect and enforce carting laws. By 1780, this included a central judge, dozens of local judges, and subsidized legal aid. Finally, in crisis years the crown subsidized transport outright by buying grain directly, paying for its transport at current fees, and selling the delivered grain below cost.

In general, therefore, Castilian carting, though limited to small and primitive oxcarts and hampered by scarce resources, expanded in the seventeenth and eighteenth centuries. This resulted from a rising demand for defense and especially the development of Madrid as a center for administration and consumption. The costs of this expanding transport were met by crown subsidies, direct and indirect, rather than by any great increase in the wealth of Castile.

The Mexican pattern was very different. Here the great age of carting came much earlier and in a more glamorous setting—the boom period of silver mining. The geographic problems that confronted Mexican carters were, in many ways, more favorable than in Castile, although there were some formidable obstacles. The Mexican plateau, stretching to the northwest of Mexico City, offered level terrain over long distances, except where cut by great barrancas. These ravines and the mountains in which most mines were located required expensive bridge and road construction to allow wheeled transport. Even more difficult was the route from Mexico City to Veracruz, which included a drop of several thousand feet and required really substantial outlays of capital for roads.

But the real difference between Spain and Mexico lay in the nature of Mexican demand. During the mid-1540s Mexico suddenly acquired the richest silver mines in the world. The next thirty years brought rapid economic development and expansion, as Spaniards sought out the great silver deposits of the interior against the fierce resistance of the Chichimeca Indians. Less spectacular but equally important was the development of ranching and plantation farming in some areas, producing food for the mining regions and sugar and hides for export.

These activities required transport that could easily and efficiently handle large quantities of mining and refining machinery, and heavy or bulky supplies (including salt, mercury, lead, firewood, and mine timbers) and carry as return cargoes the silver, sugar, and other products of the interior. Moreover, all cargoes needed reasonable security on a dangerous frontier. Hence the development of the large Mexican *carro*, often drawn by huge teams of mules.

Both types of Spanish cart were introduced very early into Latin America, and both were widely used in sixteenth-century Mexico, much as in Spain. During the 1550s, however, a new vehicle was introduced in Mexico—to all appearances a very large, spoked-wheel Spanish freighting *carreta*. The probable source of this innovation was one Juan Carrasco, a professional carter on the routes from Mexico City to Zacatecas and Veracruz. In a petition dated 1576, Carrasco claimed credit for inventing the large *carros* and for introducing them to the main routes. This large cart had a capacity four times that of the *carreta* and required up to sixteen mules in a team when heavily loaded. Covered with heavy planking and studded with spikes and clamps, such *carros* could serve as rolling blockhouses for protection against hostile Indians. Only these juggernauts could carry the heavy equipment required by the mines and withstand Indian attacks. Response to needs and environment also explains the frequent use of mules instead of oxen in Mexico, since mules are faster, minimizing delays and exposure to attack.

Once brought into existence, the *carros* and their mules could compete with other modes of transport to haul foodstuffs for Mexico City, and other centers, but of overriding importance was always the need to service the mines. The carting industry that resulted, like that of Castile, was independent of the agrarian cycle, but it arose in response to requirements very different from those that had prompted the development of Castilian carting.

The combination of capital, animal power, and grazing resources in Mexico also contrasted strikingly with that of Castile. Plentiful grazing meant cheap animal power. Not only was much grassland unoccupied, but the government aided the carters by introducing the system of town commons and requiring every town to provide them free grazing. Soon after their introduction, cattle and horse ranching assumed major proportions. If the price of beef in Mexico City is an indication, the animal supply had caught up with demand by the 1540s. Moreover, agriculture did not compete for draft animals as much as in Castile. The Indians did not use animals, and needs of the small Spanish population did not begin to offset the effect of the decline in the native population.

Mexican carters frequently used mules, probably because the unusually high intrinsic value of the silver cargoes made speed important enough to justify the resulting marginal increase in costs. For less urgent transport, the ox remained an important draft animal. While the ordinary Castilian cart train included carts of several small proprietors, those of Mexico seem to have been the property of single individuals with access to capital on a scale unknown in Spain. We learn of trains made up of thirty to eighty large *carros* owned and operated by individual Spaniards using Indian labor. This apparent availability of capital is clearly part of the explanation for the high level of development achieved in Mexican carting.

The wealth of the mining industry also provided capital at other key points that facilitated cart transport. The government used some of its mineral revenues to provide military protection and road construction, making possible the use of the large *carros* on a route from Veracruz to Santa Fe in New Mexico, one of the longest wagon roads of the sixteenth-century world. Along the highways to the mines were government-built forts and garrisons, while cart trains included armored wagons and military escorts. Of vital importance was the link between Mexico City and Veracruz. Constructed at great expense, this road facilitated the import of machinery, mercury, and other supplies for the mines.

The Mexican carting industry clearly benefited from favorable natural resources in comparison with Spain. The terrain on the plateau was favorable; the interior offered vast and cheap grazing lands, lands that quickly generated a plentiful supply of animal power. These, however, were passive factors, and the really dynamic sector of Mexican economic development was the silver industry. Directly, this produced an urgent, specific type of demand, while also providing capital to develop transport on a considerable scale. Indirectly, the presence of the mining towns in barren areas created markets, assuring transporters a wide range of cargoes.

Cart transport in the Argentine was generally similar to that of Mexico. It differed, however, in that geographic conditions were more favorable, while the economic conditions supporting it did not provide the volume of capital and the intense demand created by the Mexican mines. Most Argentine carting took place in a roughly triangular area extending from the Río de la Plata to Mendoza, Tucumán, and Jujuy. Within this area, the terrain is generally level, and in dry weather transport required little more than a trail to follow and regular watering places. The only notable obstacles in the region were one or two difficult river crossings, some long stretches without water, and some forested routes in the northwest. Conditions were thus suitable for any vehicle strong enough to stand up on the rutted trails and simple enough to be repaired without metal-working equipment.

The *carro* adopted in Argentina resembled that of Mexico in appearance and the *carreta* of Castile in structure. According to an unusually detailed description of 1776, the cart wheels were nearly seven feet in diameter, with hubs of solid wood one and one-half to two feet thick. Through the hubs passed an axle about twelve feet long, which supported the bed of the cart. This consisted of three longitudinal poles, the center one almost twenty-one feet long, those on the sides only twelve feet. The three poles were connected by four ribs, forming a frame slightly more than four feet wide by twelve feet long. Each side had six posts that carried bows of bent wood covered with sewn cowhides to form a roof. The sides were covered with rush mats, and the floor consisted of a heavy net or stretched, resilient hides. From ground to floor was four feet, from floor to roof, six and one-half feet. Some vehicles, called *carretones,* were built with solid plank sides.

A cart of this type was normally pulled by two pair of oxen. The nearer pair wore a yoke about seven feet long that fastened directly to the end of the central shaft. The lead oxen were similarly yoked, but attached to the shaft by a massive "quadruple" cable of solid, braided bullhide. The lead oxen, a good twenty feet from the driver, were driven with a goad on a long pole mounted on the cart's roof and so balanced that it could be managed with one hand. This left the driver's other hand free to drive the nearer oxen with a short goad.

The carts of Tucumán normally hauled 150 arrobas (3,750 pounds) of cargo, those of Mendoza, which traveled over better terrain, 178 arrobas (4,450 pounds). In addition, each carried a large jar of water, supplies of wood for cooking and cart repairs, a driver, and his belongings. The contents thus totaled 200 to 228 arrobas (5,000 to 5,750 pounds) on long trips. The carts were made entirely of wood, without a trace of hardware. Since the bearing surfaces in the wheel hubs were also wood, they had to be greased every day to prevent wear. These carts became common in the Argentine with the prosperity of the late eighteenth century, and they continued to be important for freight hauling well into the nineteenth.

Supplies of grazing and livestock were, if anything, more plentiful than in Mexico. The vast, unsettled pampas supported a cattle population whose enormous size effectively reduced the price of oxen to the export value of their hides. Relative to this, mules were a valuable commodity in Argentina, since they were in constant demand at the Peruvian mines. As a result, oxen were generally used for carting.

It appears that in Argentina, capital available to develop a carting industry was more limited than in sixteenth-century Mexico. The presence of guilds in Tucumán and Mendoza suggests that carters had to band together for political and economic leverage. Moreover, accounts of carting here explicitly describe an industry of small owners, less specialized and more seasonal than those of Castile or Mexico.

These conditions reflect the comparatively diffuse demand for transport in the Argentine, a situation that Spanish trade restrictions long encouraged. By 1800, however, this trade included (1) wine, olive oil, brandy, wheat, flour, and hides from the foothills of the Andes (Mendoza, San José, Tucumán) to supply the growing city of Buenos Aires; (2) imports from Buenos Aires for consumption in the interior or for transit to Peru or Chile; and (3) goods moving along the Andean region of Argentina between Mendoza and Tucumán. Apparently pack animals were also widely used, especially on the Buenos Aires-Potosí route, but other conditions, such as the cheapness of oxen and grazing, undoubtedly made carting a competitive mode of transport.

The scale of the demand for Argentine carting is hard to establish, but it appears to have become significant only in the last three decades of the eighteenth century. This was a period of considerable economic expansion in the region and rapid population growth in the province of Buenos Aires—from 19,200 in 1744 to 72,000 by 1797. The trend toward stock raising near the coast prevented the expansion of local produce farming around the city, since the landowners preferred to raise cattle for the export trades in hides and meat. The volume of trade into the interior of Argentina and beyond into Peru and Chile expanded rapidly after 1778, as Charles III liberalized trade within the Spanish empire. To some extent this apparent increase probably represents trade shifting from illegal to legal channels, but surely there was a net increase. Moreover, the trans-Argentina route from the Atlantic to Chile grew with Chilean demand and actually competed successfully with sea transport around Cape Horn until after the midnineteenth century.

The economic basis for the development of overland commerce was much less spectacular than the silver industry of Mexico. In part, to be sure, it was derived from the wealth of the Peruvian mines, which fed silver into Argentina in return for food, raw materials, and thousands of mules. For a long time, however, official regulations forced much of Peruvian commerce to follow the Panama route. A less glamorous commodity of some importance was the yerba maté of Paraguay, which came down river to Buenos Aires and was then carted and packed overland throughout South America as a major item of intracontinental trade.

Undeniably, however, the really dynamic part of the developing Argentine economy was the cattle industry. Argentina began exporting cowhides as early as the first decades of the seventeenth century, and even before 1750 the trade sometimes reached considerable proportions. In the last half of the eighteenth century, with the expansion first of contraband and then of legalized trade, the industry achieved consistent growth—approximately 75,000 hides a year in 1700–25 to nearly 1,500,000 a year in 1785–1800. This growth was accompanied by a parallel expansion of tallow and lard export. Toward the end of the century the government subsidized an attempt to create a meat salting industry as a complement to the tallow and hide trade, but with only moderate success. The export trade in hides, centered on Buenos Aires, was the heart of the economy, and its growth generated much of the demand for transport in the interior. As a basis for economic activity the cattle industry lacked the concentrated and spectacular wealth of the Mexican mines, but plentiful grazing, cheap animal power, and favorable terrain made possible a developed transport system with a much lower level of capital investment.

The carting enterprises of Spain, Mexico, and Argentina thus had the same cultural and technological origins, but developed three very different patterns. All retained some common characteristics, such as the use of the two-wheeled cart, with the same structure, harnessing techniques, and habits of seasonal travel. The carts of Mexico and Argentina were very similar, although in the sixteenth century the former was built with much more metal hardware. Both were much larger than their Spanish prototype, which continued to be used in central Spain. The latter had more primitive wheel mountings and only about one-fifth the carrying capacity of its Latin American counterparts. The Mexican carts were frequently pulled by mules, while those of Argentina and Castile were almost always used with oxen. In all three places the carts regularly traveled in convoys.

These differences were the results of distinctive economic contexts. In Castile, carting operated with a very low level of capital investment in a context of competing claims for grazing and rugged terrain that dictated use of small vehicles. The industry developed because of the central government, which subsidized the carters with grazing and legal protection and in crises absorbed some of the direct costs of transport. In Mexico, the physical obstacles to cart transport were sometimes great, but grazing and livestock were cheap. The obstacles were overcome by a plentiful supply of capital from the prosperous mining sector. This made possible construction of roads, use of relatively expensive mules and carts, and a relatively large scale of enterprise. The Argentine case combines characteristics of both the preceding examples. The land and animal power were very cheap, as in Mexico, but the scale of transport enterprise was smaller. The carts were large as in Mexico, but technically simpler, and the carriers relied exclusively on oxen. The commerce of the Argentine covered comparable distances, but handled more mundane commodities. This trade was generated by Buenos Aires as the center of a growing export trade in cattle products, as a source for imports, and as a market for interior produce.

These situations suggest that land transportation was not necessarily as absolute a limitation on preindustrial economic growth as is sometimes suggested. In three very different situations, specialized carting appeared and played an important role during periods of economic expansion. In agrarian, preindustrial societies, however, such episodes were inevitably limited by the structure and attitudes of society and by the limitations of technology, which created bottlenecks causing economic regression. This happened to some degree in all three of our examples, but in ways that suggest that the primitive means of transport were not always the immediate cause of stagnation.

The carting industry of Castile began to decline about 1800, contributing to the growing economic and political stagnation of the Spanish interior that marked the first half of the nineteenth century. The demand for specialized transport services steadily increased, for the population of Madrid grew by 25 percent in the last half of the eighteenth century, and the supply problem of the city was further aggravated by a rising rural population, which retained more and more agrarian produce within its subsistence economy. Also the years after 1793 saw Spain in a perennial state of full or partial mobilization for war. Further transport demands resulted from the requirements of a potentially promising import-export trade centered on Old Castile and the port of Santander and using a well-planned carting road through the coastal range.

But Spanish carting could not respond to these demands for the fundamental reason that it was competing for the same limited resources as the expanding population and export industries. More carting meant increased grazing for daily and winter pasturage, but the population increase raised grain prices and encouraged landowners to turn grazing into arable and the government to exploit wastelands. The new import-export activities, moreover, were based on wheat, flour, wool, and leather goods, all of which necessitated land for grazing or farming. As a result, the grazing available to the carters tended to diminish, and the price of carting services apparently rose much faster than the general price level.

The only factor on which the carters could rely to counteract these trends was enforcement and expansion of the privileges granted by the crown. Its authority, however, declined under inferior leadership following the death of Charles III in 1788, and the revolutionary and Napoleonic wars distracted its attention. Aristocratic and local influences took advantage of this weakness to convert the carters' grazing to more profitable uses, borrowing "liberal" assumptions about the nature of proprietary rights in land.

By the mid-1790s, therefore, the carters had lost nearly half of the guaranteed winter pastures near Madrid. In the years after 1800, they lost some of their tax exemptions, the right to graze on stubble lands, and their right to preemptive rental of private pastures. The whole mechanism of protection was badly disrupted during the Napoleonic invasion, and the restoration of 1814 was far from successful. Violations of carting privileges, establishment of illegal tolls, and deterioration of roads were all widespread. The situation worsened with the liberal revolution of 1820–23, after which government protection became even more shadowy. During the 1820s, grazing lands were enclosed rapidly with little regard for the carters' needs, and several of their other privileges were specifically revoked. Finally in 1836 the liberal regime of María Cristina abolished the protective bureaucracy of the carters. By 1840, they were reorganizing on a regional and private basis, but references to their activities imply that they were regarded as an anachronism.

Thus Castilian carting could not respond to the growing demands for specialized transport in nineteenth-century Spain. Even at the height of its development, in the 1780s, it had remained tied to the use of a primitive technology that carters could offset only in part by pooling vehicles and reducing labor costs. Unfortunately, the interior of Spain lacked any effective alternative form of transport, and the decline of carting helped to cut short such economic growth as had developed there during the eighteenth century.

The fate of the Mexican carting industry, which reached its developmental peak in the last decades of the sixteenth century, was quite different, yet some analogies can be drawn. If Castilian transport declined because the expanding economy and weakening political leadership choked off vital resources, Mexican carting declined because structural changes in the Mexican economy restricted the demand for specialized transport services. As has been suggested, the development of the Mexican economy, 1550–1600, was in large part geared to and supported by the silver industry. But at least two factors worked to distort and modify its development.

First was the growing shortage of labor in Mexico. From the time of the conquest, the huge Indian population declined steadily under the impact of European disease, forced labor exactions, and disruption of the native economic organization. After the great plagues of 1576–79 there seems to have been a chronic shortage of labor in agriculture and industry. This shortage helped to encourage latifundia farming, which used the available labor more efficiently than the Indians' own farming arrangements. During the last decades of the century, systems were developed for allocating the shrinking supplies of food and for rationing labor in order to sustain the vital parts of the economy, especially the cities and the silver mines.

Paralleling this and in part a reaction to it, patterns of social organization and landholding increasingly hampered the growth and regional specialization first created by the mines. More and more the mining entrepreneurs and other persons in government and business looked on landholding and noble rank as signs of respectability. With a lack of moderation characteristic of many nouveaux riches, these people set about acquiring large holdings at the expense of the native farmers. The result was estates of unprecedented magnitude, which frequently had the resources for a balanced, self-contained local economy.

These potentially important developments were then reinforced by the decline of mining activity after 1620. By 1640, many mines had been shut down. As the mines closed, the industry and agriculture that had developed to supply them, lacking alternative markets, went into decline also. Among these collapsing enterprises were the carters. Presumably the sources of capital available to them were shut off, and they may have sought a more "respectable" style of living in a society where aristocratic values were strong. Moreover, the decline of mining impoverished the viceregal government in Mexico City, so that it was unable to pay the rising price of labor for roadwork. As a result, it abandoned the expensive carting roads that were vital to maintaining wheeled transport over long stretches of the interior and through the mountains to Veracruz. In these circumstances, specialized cart transport came close to disappearing. Such long-distance transport as continued usually involved compact valuable goods that could be carried on mules, often owned by Indian rather than Spanish muleteers. The huge Mexican *carro* continued to be used, but primarily within the self-contained great estates.

Interestingly, the revival of silver mining and the development of textile making and agriculture in the eighteenth century do not seem to have caused a reappearance of long-haul cart transport in Mexico. As late as 1803–4, Alexander von Humboldt commented on the exclusive use of pack mules and upon the terrible condition of the roads. The route from Veracruz to Mexico City, in fact, had degenerated into a perilous mule track, and construction of a new wagon road had only just begun. The Acapulco road apparently was never open to carts for its whole length, and by the end of the eighteenth century, the only important route that remained open to wheeled traffic ran up the plateau from Mexico City to Zacatecas, Durango, and Chihuahua. Accounts from that period, moreover, emphasize the prevalence of pack-mule transport along that route. As late as the 1850s, traders might refer to large freight carts and even to a diligence service, but they continued to comment on the prevalence of pack mules in transport. Why did the economic revival fail to regenerate the long-distance cart transport present in the frontier economy of the sixteenth century? The reasons are far from clear, especially since there is evidence of large-scale pack-mule transportation. Perhaps there was a pragmatic conservatism amongst the class that provided transporters, an attitude analogous to that which Clement Motten has observed among the mine workers. Bad roads alone were enough to justify using pack mules. But the condition of the roads in turn suggests a lack of capital investment in a time of prosperity, and this also needs explanation. In fact, the whole matter of transport in eighteenth-century Mexico needs further work.

The fate of the Argentine carting industry follows yet a third pattern—one in which some of the original demands for carting services declined, but were replaced by others. In effect, the Argentine interior underwent economic changes similar in scope to those of Mexico during an earlier period, but for different reasons and with different results.

Argentine carting had come into existence to supply the city of Buenos Aires with produce from the interior provinces and to service the largely illicit commerce from the Atlantic into Peru and Chile. This commerce operated within a framework of imperial protection created by the Spanish government and maintained even after the limitations on trade within the empire were removed in 1778. This reform started the decline of some local industry, but the overall system of protection, while far from perfectly implemented, allowed handicraft manufactures and foodstuffs from the distant interior to compete with some success in the markets of Buenos Aires until after 1800.

With the Napoleonic occupation of Spain and the breakup of the empire, the merchants of Buenos Aires seized the power to shape commercial policies in the Río de la Plata area. As a result, that city obtained a near monopoly over trade into the interior and at the same time did away with protection for Argentine products in order to increase its import-export business. These changes crippled the economy of the interior, for its handicraft textiles could not compete with machine-made goods from England, nor its agricultural goods with the now unlimited produce entering from Brazil. Internal manufacturing contracted to purely local significance, as in seventeenth-century Mexico, and was then destroyed altogether. European goods, brought by ship and then carried inland by the Argentine carting industry, undercut local goods even at the places of production.

This last fact helps explain why the Argentine carting industry did not decline as did that of Mexico. The carters could shift from an agency of internal exchanges to an extension of the world trade pattern, bringing goods directly into the interior of the country. At the same time, the transit trade to Chile remained active, for as late as the 1850s, it was still cheaper to cart goods across the Argentine and pack them over the Andes than to make the long and dangerous sea trip around Cape Horn. Above all, while the interior economy regressed, the country did not lose its major source of wealth and capital, the export trade in cattle products. Thus well into the nineteenth century, this primitive form of transport remained competitive in some situations. Its ability to do so, in contrast to Spanish carting at the same time, was undoubtedly the result of the plentiful resources of a relatively open frontier society.

These three developments demonstrate the adaptability of essentially medieval transportation technology, given favorable conditions. Such adaptability kept the technology competitive in some cases well into the era of the Industrial Revolution. Given sufficient capital, such primitive technology could indeed support considerable economic growth. At a more general level these examples illustrate, in a preindustrial setting, the difficulties of achieving economic growth in old societies with complex social, economic, and cultural institutions.

To compare settled and frontier areas on the basis of three examples and a limited number of sources is a debatable enterprise. Yet the examples used have an important common denominator in their culture and technology, thus making it relatively easy to see the impact of different contexts. It would be instructive to measure the growth of these economies based on land transport against the progress of those benefiting from the assumed advantages of water transport, but otherwise similar. Land transport could and did support economic growth under certain circumstances where no other option was available. Therefore, its interactions with other economic factors must be examined carefully wherever it appears. The limitations of animal-powered land transport could and did stifle economic growth, as in Castile. Yet it did not directly contribute to the depression of seventeenth-century Mexico, and in Argentina it continued to meet the demands that developed until replaced by the distinctly superior technology of the railroad. If nothing else, this article suggests that it is risky to accept blindly the truism that water transport was always essential to economic growth in preindustrial societies.

Suggested Further Reading

Bakewell, Peter. "Technological Change in Potosí: The Silver Boom of the 1570s." *Jahrbuch für Geschichte von Staat, Wirtschaft und Gesellschaft Lateinamerikas* 14 (1977).

Barrett, Ward. *The Sugar Hacienda of the Marqueses del Valle.* Minneapolis, 1970. Especially chapter 5.

Borah, Woodrow W. *Early Colonial Trade and Navigation between Mexico and Peru.* Berkeley, 1954. Especially chapters 1, 2, and 3.

Cobb, Gwendoline B. "Supply and Transportation for the Potosí Mines, 1545–1560." *Hispanic American Historical Review* 29:1 (February 1949).

Foster, George M. *Culture and Conquest: America's Spanish Heritage.* New York, 1960.

Prabert, Alan. "Bartolomé de Medina: The Patio Process and the Sixteenth Century Silver Crisis." *Journal of the West* 8:1 (January 1969).

Radell, David R., and James J. Parsons. "Realejo: A Forgotten Colonial Port and Shipbuilding Center in Nicaragua." *Hispanic American Historical Review* 51:2 (May 1971).

Part Two ☼ Consolidation to Maturity

6 ✺

Mexico in the Seventeenth Century:
Transition of a Colonial Society

RICHARD BOYER

Mexico City in the seventeenth century was at once a distant outpost of imperial government, a metropolis, a city grounded in its region, and a compact local society focusing inward. The full range of administrative functions, commercial transactions, and social intrigue centered in the viceregal capital. The city housed styles and concerns that ranged from traditional to avant-garde, from provincial to cosmopolitan. Located on the isthmus bridge of New Spain, Mexico City was at the center of the east–west route that joined the Atlantic and the Pacific, Europe and Asia, in a world economy; it was also the axis of the north–south route that linked the capital to the mining zone. Silver produced in the northern archipelago of mines was funneled efficiently to Mexico City where it was reinvested or spent on articles of luxury and display.

As shipping between Seville and the colonies became less frequent and more erratic in the seventeenth century, Mexico City assumed a more independent metropolitan role. The viceregal capital controlled the trade of the New World with the Far East and carried burdens of administration and defense. Merchants and financiers managed an extensive commercial network that brought specie, manufactures, raw materials, and food to the city from near and far. In urban markets they controlled a wide assortment of goods, retailed or collected for trans-

Published originally in the *Hispanic American Historical Review,* 57:3 (August 1977). My thanks go to Dauril Alden, who asked me to prepare the original version of this article for a session of the American Historical Association meeting in Chicago in 1974 entitled "Reinterpretations of New Spain's Seventeenth Century." N. Amon, M. Boyer, H. M. Hamill, Edward Ingram, L. Jensen, P. Stigger, and the editors of the *Hispanic American Historical Review* all read one or another draft and offered comments and suggestions for which I am grateful. They, of course, bear no responsibility for the limitations of the final product.

shipment to Europe, Peru, the Caribbean, or northern New Spain. Silks from China; textiles, books, wine, and olive oil from Europe; cacao from Venezuela and Guayaquil; wine, silver, and mercury from Peru; grain, and other produce from the region, all entered the city from overlapping hinterlands. Artisans of every type worked within city boundaries to craft goods for local or long-distance trade. Mexico paid for its imports with exports of wheat, cochineal, sugar, pottery, textiles, furniture, and other manufactures. Exporters and importers in the capital inflated prices to increase profits, as they organized and directed the commerce, thereby accumulating capital to finance new ventures.

The merchants and artisans, the viceregal and archdiocesan courts, the royal bureaucrats and city aldermen, and the religious corporations made Mexico City the undisputed locus of wealth, power, and influence in the viceroyalty. The powerful and the rich were at home there, but all other types came too. Immigrants from Europe made Mexico City their first destination. Indians and *castas* came from the countryside and from other towns to settle in rustic faubourgs on swampy land at the fringe of the European core. Europeans became uneasy as the circle of randomly sited huts expanded and surrounded the rectilinear avenues of the city center. The influx of Indian migrants, remarkable because it occurred during the demographic collapse of native people throughout the colony, underscores the continuous destruction of Indian society as well as the attraction of Mexico City.

By the seventeenth century the capital had become so large that it was increasingly difficult to provision. The normal routines of so many people on the island site, the bustle of buying and selling, the mingling of races and cultures, the uneasy juxtaposition of rich and poor, the servility of clients to patrons, and the maneuvering for prerogative among upper orders made Mexico City a caldron that contained nearly every aspect of life and society. But social diversity and a growing population, however intriguing in themselves, point to a vitality that reflected the economic transition of New Spain. Mexico City was a barometer of the changes, but it also organized and controlled the transition in its long-standing role of metropolis of the colony. What is important about that role in the seventeenth century is not that it existed, for Mexico City has always been dominant. Rather, it is the fact that the exercise of dominance became more independent of Spain, that Mexico City more than Seville directed the colony.

This increasing latitude of New Spain to act for and by itself frequently has been neglected by students who have concentrated on the veneer of monotonously regular ceremonies staged to affirm status in local societies and loyalty to the crown. Indeed those who found the age monotonous were deceived by outward appearances. The purpose of this essay, then, is to review the historical literature of New Spain's seventeenth century and explain how recent scholarship is revising our view of the age.

The historiography of seventeenth-century New Spain may be divided into synthetic and episodic streams. Both use Lesley B. Simpson's description of "Mexico's forgotten century"[1] to justify their work, although that increasingly seems merely an excuse for assuming that the field continues to be virgin territory when it is not. Noel Stowe, for instance, described the period as the "forgotten desert stretch of Mexican history."[2] His work is an example of the episodic stream. Similar works treat cultural and intellectual themes, the Inquisition, the university, the religious orders and their work, Sor Juana Inés de la Cruz, don Carlos de Sigüenza y Góngora, the *desagüe* ("drainage system"), and the career of Bishop Palafox.

However fascinating an account of an individual, an institution, or the cultural and social life of the viceregal capital, these works are parochial—they stand alone and fail to link up with the history of the whole colony or its place in the empire. Too often they are based on the interpretation of a few key documents, works of literature, or a compact body of official papers intended to argue a cause to the king. Too rarely are they based on the random fragments of municipal council, land, encomienda, notary, and parish records from which a more representative cross section of all layers of society may be built up. Allusions to Simpson are consequently inappropriate. Instead of examining the "relatively dead stretches," scholars in the episodic stream wrote of the dramatic, the bizarre, the celebrated, the gifted, and about events already known.

Because they failed to place Mexico City in a larger economic and demographic context, no coherent vision of colonial society emerged from the episodic tradition. Simpson pointed scholars toward an alternative when he cautioned that the "dead stretch" was an illusion, that during the seventeenth century the colony's economy and social structure were transformed. Simpson realized this only when he and Sherburne Cook began to study the demography of Central Mexico. He then

1 L. B. Simpson, "Mexico's Forgotten Century," *Pacific Historical Review* 22 (February 1953), 113–21.
2 N. J. Stowe, "The Tumulto of 1624: Turmoil at Mexico City" (Ph.D. Diss., University of Southern California, 1970), p. 11.

used their demographic findings to analyze land exploitation in Central Mexico. Woodrow Borah and François Chevalier shortly afterward used demographic materials to explain an interlocking chain of economic consequences in land use, labor systems, trade and navigation, silver production, and manufactures. Their broader picture became the basis for the synthetic historiographical tradition.[3]

Borah, who presented his *New Spain's Century of Depression* as a hypothesis, immediately transformed the discussion from vignettes of descriptive social and administrative history or occasional thematic forays through the age into a seductively coherent vision of the colony from the sixteenth to the eighteenth century. Borah assumed that "economic contraction was nearly, though not quite equal, to the decline in Indians." While the Indian population declined relentlessly for more than one hundred years after the conquest, it was noticed most after the epidemics of 1546 and 1576–79. These caused a shortage of labor that in turn precipitated the economic contractions Borah termed a depression. Seventeenth-century decreases in silver and agricultural production and the reduction of trade resulted.

The Berkeley School's population estimates of both the Indian and European inhabitants of the colony uphold Borah's argument. Moreover other evidence exists. The large number of contemporary petitions from wheat farmers supports his contention that labor was scarce and indicates that agricultural repartimientos were not automatically available, especially in Central Mexico. Typically these petitions warn of lost harvests and hunger in towns and show that in the 1630s *desagüe* drafts had taken all laborers. Apparently, not only overseas trade and silver production, but also internal trade, declined.

Chevalier, like Borah, found demography crucial to his argument that the Spaniards acquired their great estates from vacant Indian lands. The Spaniards reacted to the economic contraction of the seventeenth century as Europeans earlier had reacted to stoppage of commerce following the fall of Rome. The New World seigneurs created self-sufficient rural estates. This conclusion also supports Borah's assumption. The two of them outlined the structural changes that occurred in the economy and society of New Spain in a convincing manner that integrated the main trends of the economy. Borah should feel flattered that for twenty years his essay has been treated as a synthesis, and Chevalier

3   Woodrow Borah, *New Spain's Century of Depression* (Berkeley, 1951); François Chevalier, *Land and Society in Colonial Mexico: The Great Hacienda* (Berkeley, 1963).

that his description of the great estate in northern New Spain has been assumed to apply everywhere.

Several monographs, however, have reviewed critically aspects of the synthetic tradition. Among these, the works of David Brading, Peter Bakewell, and William Taylor must be mentioned.[4] Brading, who focused on eighteenth-century Guanajuato, also contributed to greater understanding of the earlier period by emphasizing that mining production did not decline until 1632, long after the date when it should have been affected by shortage of labor. The number of miners needed was fewer than has traditionally been supposed, probably no more than 11,000. In the north, miners were usually free labor, not drafts, and therefore their availability was not directly affected by the decline in Indian population. In fact, the destruction of Indian communities could swell the mining labor pool because remnants and survivors of Indian towns and villages became vagabonds. They were absorbed culturally by the mestizo strata, and consequently became part of a mobile, wage-labor force. Shortage of mercury for the amalgamation process and new imperial credit policies explain the mid-seventeenth-century decline in production.

In the mid-1630s the crown stopped distributing mercury on credit, and many miners who had accumulated debts were ruined by rigorous demands for repayment and abandoned their mines. Consequently, by the middle of the century the industry was controlled by financiers in Mexico City. Although Bakewell describes Zacatecas after 1635 as suffering a depression, he also correctly implies that declining production was a symptom of financial reorganization. As soon as credit for mercury was controlled from Mexico City, it was more shrewdly allocated, and marginal producers were forced out of business. This was a significant development. The previous policy, although leading to impressive figures of production, hid the indebtedness of the miners and made mining seem more profitable. The reorganization withdrew the hidden subsidy of indiscriminate credit and rationalized the industry by giving priority to the most productive mines. The two attractive aspects of this new policy were that profits remained in New Spain and that Mexico City obtained greater control over the colonial economy.

To call the effects of these readjustments a depression is mislead-

4 D. A. Brading, *Miners and Merchants in Bourbon Mexico, 1763–1810* (Cambridge, 1971); P. J. Bakewell, *Silver Mining and Society in Colonial Mexico: Zacatecas, 1546–1700* (Cambridge, 1971); William B. Taylor, *Landlord and Peasant in Colonial Oaxaca* (Stanford, 1972).

ing, as modern usage implies widespread economic malaise, unemployment, and general dislocation. Unemployed miners, for example, were few in number and could carry on individually in partially abandoned sites using small smelters to refine the ore. Or, they might seek work elsewhere, for example in the Parral district north of Zacatecas, which began to boom exactly when production at Zacatecas began to decline. Agricultural labor was mainly seasonal and workers, by about 1630, were either forced to work in labor drafts or were becoming permanently attached to haciendas. Although draft labor was paid, workers' wages were spent on taxes, stark necessities, and spirits and did not create a significant consumer market. Both peonage and drafted labor were expressions of a subsistence economy; they were not affected by the depression.

Eighty percent of the people of New Spain were peasants scattered in towns and hamlets, not producing regular agricultural surpluses, consequently not consuming quantities of urban products, and not affected by fluctuations in long-distance trade in specialized commodities. Most were outside the realm's monetary economy and exchanged goods through barter rather than specie. Only when the cities were short of food and raided the nearby countryside was the depression noticed. Then shortage of labor led to reduced crop yields of urban suppliers, and the cities took surpluses from the most accessible towns and hamlets. The victims of confiscation ate less and suffered accordingly.

The case for the depression thesis, then, rests mainly on the highly visible activities of merchants engaged in long-distance trade, financiers of mines and textiles, and farmers who produced for urban rather than rural markets. Figures that show the fall in silver production and the growing capriciousness of flota arrivals from Spain point to that conclusion. It is possible, though, even to exaggerate the predicament of the market-oriented capitalists whose business methods were designed to level out cycles of glut and scarcity. Like European guildmen, such men excluded competition and monopolized narrow, limited markets. They raised prices by producing fewer goods or by withholding goods from the market. To this group of merchants, who ran the market economy, whose methods insulated them from changes in the rates of buyer demand or circulation of money, the depression thesis mainly applies. We must avoid, however, the tendency both to overstate their distress and to assume that the trouble touched all persons in the colony to the same degree.

Although fewer in number and less wealthy than its counterpart in

Seville, the economic elite of the colony was sufficiently influential to redirect capital away from the Spanish metropolis and thereby lay the basis for an independent economy. Diversification as well as autonomy was the result. New Spain benefited from the decline of trade with Seville. It is a fallacy that falling exports of silver and less trade with Seville caused an economic dark age and that society withdrew for survival into self-sufficient haciendas. Pierre Chaunu and John Lynch argue the opposite: that the decline of the export trade led to greater economic independence. By 1640, the colonies were economically dominating Spain, a trend that had begun a generation earlier.

The case for a separate economy in New Spain is supported by John Super's study of Querétaro, where "local dynamics and links to the south were the main economic underpinnings for the town's growth—with very little direct impact to be traced to the mining areas to the north." Although northern mining may have indirectly affected the prosperity of Querétaro, he implies that areas on the periphery of the export economies were relatively unaffected by the contraction of trade. If the export trade expanded and contracted without affecting or being affected by the local economies, New Spain in the seventeenth century may have been less depressed than is traditionally supposed. The different regions of the colony, each relatively self-sufficient, continued to trade with the others in particular commodities. William Taylor demonstrated this for the valley of Oaxaca. Of greater significance, he also demonstrated the increasing importance of large towns: in the seventeenth century the population of Antequera increased equally to the volume of its trade. Although Antequera remained principally a marketplace for an economically self-sufficient region, it also exported large quantities of cochineal.

Vázquez de Espinosa's picture of the region around Puebla de los Angeles early in the seventeenth century illustrates how easily the overseas and local economies could coexist. Situated between Veracruz and Acapulco, "the rich encomenderos and vecinos of the city enjoy[ed] at lower prices and more convenience the abundant merchandise which arrives at both ports." Consumption of imports by the large Spanish population was only part of the regional system, however. Puebla regularly sent a whole range of agricultural products to Veracruz to supply the fleet as well as the town itself because its population surged wildly with the maritime activity in the harbor. Puebla also provisioned Havana during its peak season and sent wheat flour to Venezuela, where there was always an eager market. Manufactures complemented agriculture.

Increasingly, pottery from Jalapa and Puebla was sought during the seventeenth century and the thirty *obrajes* ("textile-manufacturing establishment") of the region produced large amounts of woolen textiles of good quality. In a cool climate locally produced woolen blankets and clothing must have sold briskly to a variety of buyers. Stockraising supplied horses for Spanish riders and mules for the all-important freight haulage to Veracruz; from cattle came meat, hides, and tallow; sheep and cochineal gave regional *obrajes* a local source of raw materials. The network of towns exchanged agricultural produce, fresh meat, and basic supplies in local markets, and perhaps consumed a few woolens such as the coarse products of the *obraje* in San Diego de Guajosingo, also a pilgrimage town with an important regional shrine.

Relatively autonomous towns around Puebla de los Angeles might produce some commercial products such as cochineal, sheep, and fuel for the city market. Some local exchanges of textiles, pottery, and other crafts easily must have satisfied the needs of the region within a system that produced and distributed all the food that it consumed. To the degree that this economic layer remained outside the sphere of larger, more specialized enterprises and the European market economy, the small towns retained traditional social patterns and were oblivious of shifts in the European economic layer. Enterprises in that system, whether agricultural or manufacturing, looked to Mexico City, their principal market and entrepôt and the source of the greater capital they needed.

Puebla de los Angeles, however influential in its region, did not dominate the surrounding towns as completely as Mexico City. The huge emporium of the capital exerted pressure on the surrounding region to specialize production for that market. Towns bordering the lake became more oriented toward market crops such as maguey, with the consequent decline of subsistence agriculture. Within the city the division of labor reached the point where many Indians, having severed their ties to the land and become permanent town dwellers, were completely ignorant of agriculture. Inasmuch as specialization was evident in the towns around the lakes as well as in the city proper, one can speak of a metropolitan region whose "suburban" satellites were creatures of the urban core. Mexico City was different from all other towns, however, because its influence spread throughout the colony. It alone could supply capital for the reorganization of mining and farming. Its standards and styles were avidly copied. Taste, like debt, increasingly bound the provinces to the capital.

This relationship can be illustrated in the way Toluca and Querétaro were tied to the viceregal capital. Toward the end of the sixteenth
century, the encomendero class of Toluca held citizenship in Mexico
City and lived there most of the time. In food and essentials Toluca and
its region produced enough for local needs and marketed all surplus
goods in Mexico City. Querétaro in the seventeenth century was also
self-sufficient in most necessities, while its merchants generated a growing trade with the capital. For a distant mining town such as Parral,
Mexico City organized transshipments of specialized equipment, supplies, and luxury goods. This was big business for the merchants of
Mexico City given the estimate of 600,000 pesos in trade for 1673.
Parral's isolation, favorable natural conditions, and population of miners
and shopkeepers created the need for commercialized agriculture to
produce adequate regional supplies of maize, wheat, vegetables, meat,
and other necessities. Parral, because it existed solely for the mines, was
different from Toluca and Querétaro, but it was also similar in that it
maintained a regional subsistence economy and looked to Mexico City
for more specialized equipment, luxury imports, and materials needed
for mining.

Other provincial towns illustrate the importance of Mexico City for
those engaged in specialized production for sizable markets. The merchants of Guadalajara, according to Bishop Mota y Escobar's report of
1603, both lived in and ran their businesses from the capital. The same
was true of Veracruz, terminus of the flota from Spain, where commercial firms assigned factors to reside while those in higher positions established themselves more comfortably in Mexico City or Seville. A similar
pattern holds for the influential citizens of Puebla de los Angeles, Oaxaca, Toluca, Querétaro, and Zacatecas as we noted earlier. Each of
these towns was the political and economic focus of its region, but each
became individually dependent on the capital instead of interdependent
upon one another. The separate ties to the metropolis became the means
by which Mexico City could control and transform New Spain's economy. This cannot be ignored in writing the history of New Spain in the
seventeenth century. The selected fragments of city life provided by the
episodic tradition must be set against the background of the economic
and social developments charted by the synthetic, using each to enrich
the other. Both episodic and synthetic streams underestimate the importance of the capital; in fact, its history provides the link between them.

Many studies are needed to assess the influence of Mexico City
upon the society and economy of the whole colony. The tumult of 1624,

one of the most explosive outbursts of urban frustration, provides the best illustration. In the strict sense it was not a corn riot, for adequate supplies were on hand and groups did not try to raid the *alhóndiga* ("public granary") where the grain was stored. While the corn supply was adequate, however, distribution mechanisms remained faulty. Officials allowed favorites to purchase large quantities of the public supply at the official lower rate and they in turn resold the maize to the poor who had not been given sufficient quantity. Such practices surely were more infuriating than scarcity itself. Food was often short and expensive for this reason and because of poor harvests, constriction of supply routes to the island site, and the withholding of supplies by producers. City granaries such as the *pósito* and *alhóndiga,* which were designed to smooth out price fluctuations and ensure at least minimal supplies for all inhabitants, fell into disuse during years of good harvests and, as already indicated, were misused at other times.

Viceroy Gelves, who so energetically had warehoused maize since the extreme shortages of 1620, next turned his attention to the ruthless profiteer Melchor Pérez de Varáez who used his position as alcalde mayor ("district governor") of Métepec to tyrannize the people of his district. He sold the grain and other commodities he extracted there at an enormous profit in Mexico City. And while Pérez de Varáez was clearly a worthy target for Gelves's reform program, it is hard to explain why he did nothing when the capital's supplies of grain were cornered and prices were systematically raised by a single supplier. Poor people, made desperate by the squeeze, petitioned Gelves to regulate prices, the usual procedure during times of scarcity, but the viceroy refused to act on grounds that the year's harvests had been plentiful and too expensive for the government to stockpile enough maize to force prices down. This was an unpopular decision and gave Archbishop Pérez de la Serna the opportunity to intervene by excommunicating the culprit and demanding control of prices. The residents of Mexico City viewed the ensuing quarrel between the viceroy and archbishop as a struggle between the secular defender of monopolists and the priestly defender of the poor.

Gelves, to his disadvantage, had already offended important groups in the capital with his single-minded program to eradicate venality, increase efficiency, and raise tax revenues. His rigid austerity seemed repressive, astringent, and unreasonable as he broke precedent and intervened directly in the affairs of the judiciary, exchequer, and ecclesiastical spheres of authority. He dismissed local concern about chronic flooding as unfounded and peremptorily ordered work to be stopped on the drainage projects. This enabled him to reallocate *desagüe* funds, but also led to flooding in the city. His mismanagement of the issue and his arrogant style offended virtually everybody. The tumult reflected the dissatisfaction with the viceroy who had meddled unsuccessfully with issues that affected the entire community.

Mexico City was a barometer of stress because it was urbanized and depended on a sophisticated regional division of labor. Being an island sometimes made life more difficult, especially during times of flooding, when causeways were impassable and waterways crowded with debris. The aldermen and administrators in the capital struggled continuously to supply inhabitants with adequate supplies of food as its population grew. Some nearby towns that produced only one product for sale in the capital were themselves fed entirely by outside supplies. Unfortunately, the population of the countryside declined while the population of the city increased. Mexico City's white population increased nearly threefold between 1570 and 1646 (18,000 to 48,000) while in the colony as a whole, the number of Europeans doubled. The city's percentage of the colony's Europeans rose from nearly 30 to about 40 percent, and Blacks, mulattoes, and mestizos became far more numerous. Meanwhile, the Indian population for the entire Valley of Mexico had dropped from 325,000 in 1570 to 70,000 by the middle of the seventeenth century. These reductions were greater than the population losses in the plateau, coastal, or central regions of Mexico in the same period.

Either directly or indirectly, virtually all food, fuel, and fodder used in the metropolis was supplied by Indian labor. Even commercial producers of wheat and maize relied on regular agricultural repartimientos to weed and harvest crops, although increasingly repartimiento was phased out during the first half of the seventeenth century. The rapid decrease of the Indian population in the 1570s created the need for a series of measures designed to guarantee sufficient supplies. It was not coincidence that laws creating the *alhóndiga* (1578) and prohibiting price fixing and speculation (1578) were decreed, while a general sickness, *cocoliztle,* was on the rampage, killing Indians in unprecedented numbers over a five-year period.

Frequent repetition of such legislation during the following half-century indicates how difficult feeding the city had become. The regular excess of demand over supply led to a gradual but steady rise in the price of maize during the period of decreased production until 1627, when the price stabilized at nine reales per fanega (91 liters). Regular shortages and rising prices led to a new type of farming. Between 1580 and 1630 supplies of maize collected from Indian towns for tax and tribute payments became insufficient. Spaniards increasingly produced maize as a commercial crop just as they had, almost from the first, produced wheat. This was a response to the decline in rural population that before 1580 had been able to produce a surplus large enough to satisfy metropolitan needs. While Borah's assumptions do not account for the reorganization of the mining industry in the north, they may be applied to the reorganization of agriculture in the metropolitan region.

Regular difficulties of supply and instability of prices, which the new agricultural system proved unable to remedy, were exacerbated by natural disasters such as drought, frost, and floods. The legislation mentioned above was intended more to regulate the suppliers than to draw supplies from a larger region, because once production was concentrated in the hands of a few, the city became more vulnerable to a cartel of large producers.

The system of transport often proved as inadequate or as subject to disruption as the sources of supply. In 1630, when the city was flooded, the only working *calzada* ("causeway") was Tacuba. When it became a mud trap and impassable, Viceroy Cerralvo responded to the "clamour of the poor" and ordered a new loading wharf and shelter to be built, from which supplies could be ferried conveniently to the center of the city. A similar wharf on the Mexicalzingo causeway became a matter of contention when the viceroy was warned that it had been turned into a monopoly. Those who controlled it had more than tripled the price of transport to the center, an increase from six to twenty reales. Opportunism and trivial extortion were habitual. The most common and profitable device was to force Indian farmers in outlying towns or on their way to market in Mexico City to sell below the fixed market price; then, by avoiding the supervised market and *alhóndiga,* to take advantage of the scarcity to sell well above that price. Such organized plunder of Indian producers and urban consumers apparently was monopolized by gangs of Blacks and mulattoes whose "middleman" fee was an outrageous 400 percent or more. The patronage of the rich and powerful was the usual advantage to the criminal.

Mexico City created its regional system to supply the immediate needs of firewood, food, and raw products for local processing. From faraway Spain, however, came the more remote pressures of the imperial government, which seemed less important because they conflicted with local needs and priorities. The Spanish monarchy, in an effort to survive the "general crisis" of Europe and maintain its power during the Thirty Years' War, devised new sources of revenue. In practice this meant that increased taxes and stricter trade regulations were applied in New Spain. The burden was considerable. The colony's share of the Union of Arms assessment (1627) was 250,000 ducats annually for fifteen years. To raise it meant doubling the alcabala from 2 to 4 percent. In addition, in 1640 the crown levied an annual 400,000 peso tax to pay for the Barlovento fleet in the Caribbean. Those funds, however, were used instead to subsidize the protection of the Atlantic fleet, the official purpose of the Union of Arms tax. These direct subsidies to the fleet were paid out at the same time that huge sums already were committed to coastal defenses and subsidies to northern presidios or coastal towns in the Caribbean. The Philippines alone were draining away some 500,000 pesos in official subsidies by the middle of the seventeenth century, and three or four times the official amount probably crossed the Pacific in private transactions in any given year. The sums spent on defense appeared wasted in 1628 when Piet Heyn captured the entire Spanish fleet in the Cuban harbor of Matanzas. His booty from the gold, silver, indigo, sugar, and logwood was 15,000,000 guilders, which yielded shareholders of the Dutch West India Company a gratifying dividend of 50 percent. To restore some of these losses, Viceroy Cerralvo, only one year later, squeezed from colonists yet another special "contribution" of 1,100,000 pesos for the king.

These imperial demands had to be met at a time of increased colonial expenditures. The *desagüe* excavations had by 1637 drained away some 3,000,000 pesos. Meanwhile, in 1640, the Mexico City cabildo spent 35,000 pesos—far more than its annual income—to celebrate the arrival of Viceroy Montesclaros. To duplicate the extravagant welcome only two years later when Viceroy Salvatierra arrived, the city levied a special tax on renters of municipal property, asked for voluntary contributions, and borrowed 10,500 pesos from the royal treasury.

As the imperial government raised taxes, it also appealed to America for voluntary contributions no fewer than ten times between 1621 and 1665. In an effort to reassert control the metropolis suppressed New Spain's textile trade with Peru (1631), reduced the former's allotment of available mercury supplies (1630), and ended the easy credit formerly extended to miners (1634), making it necessary to reorganize some aspects of the economy. This legislation is important because it points to Seville's recognition that Mexico in essence had become the metropolis of Peru and in the process had become far too independent of peninsular regulation. The Manila commerce, controlled by Mexico and the basis for much of Mexico's influence, had long worried Spanish officials who tried repeatedly to restrict transpacific imports and their subsequent resale to Peru. The trade, though, was too lucrative and restrictions were either ignored or circumvented.

There were other aspects of Mexico's influence over Peru. Merchants in New Spain profited by undercutting the monopoly system to Peru; they transferred European imports across the isthmus from Veracruz to Acapulco and then shipped them down the coast to Callao. In addition, Mexican manufactures such as textiles, clothing, books, leather goods, and jewelry, had long been staples in the Peruvian market and were sent from Mexico to Peru in large quantities well into the seventeenth century. This must be stressed because the fact that the China trade grew so rapidly in the latter part of the sixteenth century tends to obscure the less dramatic but impressive growth of 50 to 100 percent in domestic manufactures. Peru, partly to handle this expanding trade with New Spain, doubled its merchant fleet in the period 1590 to 1690. The Mexican silk industry, in spite of the direct competition with finer and cheaper Chinese silk, continued to flourish, manufacturing large quantities of medium grade silk to 1650 and probably afterward. For its manufactures and management, Mexico received from the Viceroyalty of Peru cacao, wine, and most important, quantities of crude silver.

The imperial government's dual program to restrict Mexico's influence and extract more revenue was, of course, charged to the viceroys. They became targets of a Mexican opposition, therefore, that was most evident in the period 1612 to the 1640s. It is well known that Gelves in 1624 ran for his life when a crowd set fire to the viceregal palace and tried to kill him. Bishop Palafox removed Escalona (1640–42), in a surgically precise coup; Salvatierra (1642–48) was dismissed for his inability to control the colony. Archbishops Pérez de la Serna and Manso y Zúñiga were vocal, uncompromising opponents of viceregal actions. Able ecclesiastical leaders were natural figures to coalesce colonial opposition to unpopular crown policies for which viceroys, not the king, always were blamed. As leaders of the church they commanded resources, disbursed patronage, and embodied prestige and authority. While they affirmed loyalty to the crown, they could oppose viceroys by appealing to the interests of corporations and groups in New Spain.

Opposition also could take a more unconventional channel. Don Guillén de Lampart pronounced a spectacular plan for independence in 1642 that tried to capitalize on midcentury discontent in the colony. From the capital Lampart watched the cooling of relations between

Bishop Palafox and Viceroy Escalona when Escalona used royal and colonial funds to purchase small, unseaworthy ships for the Barlovento fleet (1641). Lampart was also in the capital in April when word arrived that Portugal and Catalonia had revolted. He saw Palafox oust Escalona in June 1642, for allegedly supporting the Portuguese. Perhaps inspired by the example of Palafox, he plotted to take over the government with forged royal cédulas. His program was designed to gather local support and included: abolition of tributes and taxes; emancipation of slaves; confiscation of enemies' estates, including the lands of the absent Marquesa del Valle; creation of a "royal" council of local elites, notably oidores and alcaldes; release of prisoners of the Inquisition; consultation with Mexico City's consulado; dispatch of envoys to Portugal, Holland, France, Venice, and Ireland, Lampart's own homeland.

The nature of Lampart's proposals show that he sensed discontent among all classes. And while he seemed to base much of his plan to seize power on obtaining the help of the lower orders, he was also shrewd enough to seek the support of existing elites through substantive and symbolic concessions. His attempt to cultivate the friendship of Spain's enemies suggests that he was willing to risk everything—he would create a new regime or be destroyed in the attempt. The domestic proposals would have created a local base of political support; the foreign policy committed supporters to a treasonable break with the metropolis, thereby strengthening Lampart's hand. He assumed, no doubt, that Spain's enemies might exchange material aid for the right to trade. The main idea, though, was that Lampart's strategy to break away from Spain was based on a shrewd assessment of grievances festering in the capital.

Opposition to viceroys, resistance to taxes, and plots for independence point to Mexico City's strong position in the first half of the seventeenth century. The colonials resented paying because they knew they were able to pay. More and more capital remained in New Spain for public works and private investment. The kingdom benefited from capital that otherwise would have gone to Europe as Spanish merchants retained it in the colony rather than risk confiscation in Spain. The colony also diversified its imports and exports thereby decolonizing its economy. The prohibition in 1631 of trade between Mexico and Peru was not a serious blow to Mexican commerce because the trade continued, frequently with the open cooperation of royal officials. That the prohibition was repeated often proves that the trade, although contraband, could not be stopped. The sugar industry, dormant since about 1570, revived in the second decade of the seventeenth century making New Spain self-sufficient in sugar. The colony's appetite for cacao grew steadily throughout the seventeenth century. For rich and poor alike, it was a dietary staple. After 1620 Venezuela became a plantation for Mexico, existing mainly to grow cacao. In the period 1620–50 more than 99 percent of Venezuelan exports went to New Spain and, although the percentage dropped to about 80 in the second half of the century, the total consumed increased nearly tenfold to 322,264 fanegas. In addition, large amounts of bitter, and therefore cheaper, cacao from Guayaquil were exported to Mexico. This was consumed by the poor and drunk with sugar, perhaps causing large amounts of sugar to be brought to Mexico City. Finally, to complete a list that is meant only to be illustrative, alcabala revenues rose until 1638 and thereafter dropped only slightly, a significant indicator of the continuing vigor of internal trade in New Spain.

Mexico City overcame the financial difficulties inherent in its colonial status. Distance, the economic vigor of New Spain, and the weakness of Spain tipped the balance. And if another factor were needed to lock Mexican attention onto its own affairs, the natural calamities that struck the capital early in the seventeenth century did precisely that. The island site was flooded no fewer than six times between 1604 and 1629, the waters of the last and worst flood taking five years to recede. These periodic disasters destroyed houses and public buildings; they were followed by famine, epidemic, and flight. The heroic but sporadic efforts to drain the lakes and the considerable repairs needed in the city required the mobilization of labor and capital on a grand scale at a time when the Indian population approached its nadir and when local and imperial taxes were rising. In any competition for funds, the immediate and local took precedence over abstract and distant imperial needs.

Attempts by viceroys to challenge these priorities became a local issue of considerable importance as several attempts to protect the city from flood waters collapsed. The cabildo, for instance, became more insistent and aggressive as the failures mounted. In 1607, when the drainage project began, city aldermen agreed to a passive role specifying that Viceroy Velasco and the audiencia should supervise it, while the cabildo, for its part, would look after street paving and drain clearing. By 1629, however, the cabildo had asserted itself. Cerralvo was not Velasco, and the cabildo was tired of entrusting the safety of the metropolis to peninsular bureaucrats ignorant of Mexico City's peculiar aquatic circumstance. Therefore, in a carefully phrased argument to the king, the cabildo proposed that the drainage project cease to be the responsibility solely of the viceroy and instead be entrusted to the city as a public work.

The merit of the city's position is best illustrated in the way Viceroy Gelves caused the needless flood of 1623. Impatient and skeptical of what he thought to be exaggerated fears, the viceroy, without consulting engineers or other experts, suspended work on the diversion channel of the Cuautitlán River that was designed to prevent water from flowing into the lakes of the basin of Mexico. The decision, one that he had no competence to make, resulted in a rise in water levels and a drop in Gelves's popularity. The cabildo protested but in vain. Gelves was decisive but wrong. His earnest successor, Cerralvo, collected opinions and commissioned additional "plans and profiles" of drainage possibilities, but was slow to act and lacked a sense of urgency. After Velasco, viceregal leadership varied in style but not in ineffectuality. The cabildo, whose importunity stemmed from the general concern that the city might founder, found Gelves and Cerralvo equally frustrating, because local experience with floods had led many to question the very survival of their city. In this, as in other matters, there was no good reason for Mexicans not to manage their own affairs.

And indeed the rich and powerful of the capital did just that. They loaned their funds to the city for public works and municipal celebrations, or invested in urban real estate and productive enterprises. They became a stylish and ostentatious society and conducted business, arranged marriages, or mingled in recreation while enjoying the awe and deference of the lower orders. Endowing a *capellanía* ("chaplaincy") or creating an entailed estate were ways to insure immortality of sorts. But before the final accounting one might settle in a lavish townhouse in Mexico City where, from close vantage, one could view, and perhaps participate in, the growing metropolitan role of the capital. The emergence of that role as Spain declined indicates that historians must view seventeenth-century New Spain not as a century of depression, but as one of transition to capitalism, economic diversification, and vigorous regional economies, both subsistence and tied to the market economy based in Mexico City. Only this approach can relate the demographic profiles of Spaniards and Indians, the decline of transatlantic trade, the trends in silver production, and self-sufficiency in defense to the structure of colonial society and to details of life in the capital and its crises.

Suggested Further Reading

Andrien, Kenneth J. "The Sale of Fiscal Offices and the Decline of Royal Authority in the Viceroyalty of Peru, 1633–1700." *Hispanic American Historical Review* 62:1 (February 1982).

———. "The Sale of Juros and the Politics of Reform in the Viceroyalty of Peru, 1608–1695." *Journal of Latin American Studies* 13:1 (May 1981).

Bakewell, P. J. *Silver Mining and Society in Colonial Mexico: Zacatecas, 1546–1700.* Cambridge, 1971.

Borah, Woodrow W. *New Spain's Century of Depression.* Berkeley and Los Angeles, 1951.

Bronner, Fred. "Elite Formation in Seventeenth-Century Peru." *Boletín de Estudios Latinoamericanos* 24 (1978).

Israel, J. I. *Race, Class and Politics in Colonial Mexico, 1610–1670.* Oxford, 1975.

TePaske, John J., and Herbert K. Klein. "The Seventeenth-Century Crisis in New Spain, Myth or Reality?" *Past and Present* 90 (February 1981).

7

Landed Society in New Spain:
A View from the South

WILLIAM B. TAYLOR

With good reason, great landed estates hold the attention of many students of modern Latin America. Landholding in wide areas of the subcontinent to the south is inseparable from latifundios. Great estates were especially conspicuous in the century after independence, often dominating local economies and political power. The size and traditional functions of these rural estates have also made them obvious targets of those who demand modernization, nationalism, and social justice in the twentieth century. Political and social reformers have naturally concentrated their attention on the land regime, not only because of its economic and political power, but also because nowhere in Latin America have landed barons given up their privileged position voluntarily. Rural estates with colonial beginnings continue to dominate regional economies and societies in Colombia, Ecuador, Peru, and Guatemala. In Mexico, where traditional latifundios have declined in the last fifty years, concentration of land in a few hands was once an even more important issue. Mexico's Revolution of 1910, and its fulfillment under Lázaro Cárdenas in the 1930s, reacted against a colonial heritage that was symbolized by haciendas and a landed aristocracy.

If large estates have a conspicuous place in the rural landscape of Indo- and Mestizo America, their functions and socioeconomic effects also have brought them under attack, as values changed in the direction of economic efficiency or social justice. Whether operated primarily for profit or prestige, the large, labor-intensive rural estates perpetuate

Published originally in the *Hispanic American Historical Review,* 54:3 (August 1974). The author is grateful to Charles Gibson and James Lockhart for their critical readings of the first draft of this essay and to Woodrow Borah for good advice at the beginning.

income inequalities and authoritarian-paternalistic rule. Even when large estates have declined, they leave behind a residue of values and attitudes that resists change. Like a gnarled old oak, the latifundio's roots reach well beyond its visible boundaries into personal and psychological relationships, such as the *patrón*-servant posture or unemployment economies that make wasteful or only partial use of the available land, capital resources, and manpower. The latifundio certainly reinforced an aristocratic view of social relations and wealth, which overvalued authority and landed property as symbols of status and tended to restrict economic growth.

Historians turning to rural Latin America have also been attracted primarily to the large estates. Magnus Mörner's historiographical essay, "The Spanish American *Hacienda:* A Survey of Recent Research and Debate," reflects this continuing interest in describing and explaining the traditional system of large estates in Latin America.[1] In fact, rural history for the colonial period in Latin America comes very close to being synonymous with that of large private and corporate estates. As Mörner's treatment implies, recent research continues to center on haciendas rather than rural society and economy as a whole, applying more sophisticated and rewarding techniques to an understanding of the internal structure of large rural estates and their impact on regional economies.

While this special attention to the heritage of landed estates is a natural partner of contemporary interest in economic development and social justice, it presents a special problem for the history of land systems during the colonial period. The importance of land reform has elevated "hacienda" and latifundio to the status of universal terms in their application to Latin America. As reformers and revolutionaries took up land systems as a key to basic changes, "hacienda" became an abstraction, tacitly taken to symbolize landed society and the colonial heritage of Spanish America. The special danger in this abstraction is that social situations are rarely equivalent in any two parts of Latin America, much less everywhere. It neglects other causes that may explain local cases of rural poverty, low literacy rates, and poor integration into national values and economy, such as the survival of semi-independent peasant communities speaking Indian languages, retaining conservative, corporate values, and that have recently experienced population growth on a fixed quantity of productive land. The hacienda as

1 Magnus Mörner, "The Spanish American *Hacienda:* A Survey of Recent Research and Debate," *Hispanic American Historical Review* 53 (May 1973).

an abstraction offers only one consistent explanation for regional variation: the presence or absence of Spaniards. Wherever Spaniards settled in large numbers the hacienda would presumably prevail; where Spaniards did not settle in number, indigenous land systems might survive, or other land tenure patterns might develop.

The hacienda as an abstraction is not necessarily incorrect or misleading. It is, however, a proposition that grows out of modern concerns with nationalism and the obstacles to economic and social development, rather than from studies of the land system done in the full context of different regional situations. That the hacienda's domination of the Mexican countryside should not be considered a closed question at any time before the Revolution may be inferred from Frank Tannenbaum's table, "Distribution of Rural Population and Land Between Free Villages and *Haciendas,*" in *The Mexican Agrarian Revolution* (p. 56). As of 1910, only in the states of northern and north-central Mexico was the percentage of the rural population in free villages less than 35 percent. In twelve states of central and southern Mexico, estates of more than 5,000 hectares accounted for less than 25 percent of all privately held lands: Oaxaca, Mexico, Hidalgo, Puebla, Veracruz, Morelos, Tlaxcala, Tabasco, Chiapas, Michoacán, and Jalisco. If the task of generalizing about the land system is undertaken at all, each proposition should be qualified by the place and period where it applies. What holds for the Valley of Oaxaca in 1750 is unlikely to hold for Colima in 1800.

This article attempts to move into the middle range between the hacienda as symbol of an inclusive colonial heritage, and particular regional land systems that have been described for the colonial period in Mexico and Guatemala. The groundwork for approaching this middle range of broad regional variations and their origins over three centuries is limited. For a very long time, land tenure research in the colonial period amounted to legal history. Colonial laws were compiled, and valuable commentary was provided by such scholars as Silvio Zavala, José M. Ots Capdequí, Helen Phipps, and Carmelo Viñas y Mey, but the operation of the land system itself received little attention. One important breakthrough was Lesley B. Simpson's 1952 study of land exploitation in central Mexico, published in the University of California's Ibero-Americana series, which analyzed sixteenth-century mercedes and supplied some idea of regional variation and time depth for ranching during the sixteenth century. However, contrary to an ideal pattern of historical synthesis where regional studies or monographs on particular facets of the subject precede and provide the foundation for a general appraisal, the synthesis preceded the monographs for colonial land systems in Mexico. François Chevalier's excellent book, *La formation des grands domaines au Mexique: Terre et société aux XVIe-XVIIe siècles,* was published in 1952 before systematic regional studies were undertaken.[2] In a sense, since the bulk of his documentation is drawn from north-central Mexico, Chevalier's work was a regional study that went on to posit a general pattern of land tenure for a much larger area.

Since 1952, several regional studies take up the land question among other topics and permit some tentative generalizations about regional variations. Wayne Osborn's careful work on Metztitlán is an interesting case study on central Mexico; Charles Gibson's richly detailed book on the Valley of Mexico includes important sections on land and labor; Charles Harris on the Sánchez-Navarro family in the late eighteenth century gives us a detailed view of southern Coahuila.[3] In approaching the middle range of emerging land systems and regional variation, I am especially interested in drawing out the implications for southern Mesoamerica of my regional study of the Valley of Oaxaca, where the landed society and colonial rule were quite different from Chevalier's findings.

Problems of Definition and the Rise of Colonial Estates

While this article offers some tentative hypotheses about colonial land systems in southern Mesoamerica from Oaxaca to Yucatán and highland Guatemala, the reader should be aware that there are many more open questions than firm points of reference in the rural history of Latin America. The thorny question of the origins of haciendas, for example, is still a much-debated central issue. Did the encomienda system generally blend into the rural estates of the seventeenth and eighteenth centuries? Were former encomenderos more likely to take up political office, while new arrivals from Spain turned to the land as prices rose and demand for foodstuffs outstripped supply? Do economic or cultural factors

2   Leslie B. Simpson, *Exploitation of Land in Central Mexico in the Sixteenth Century* (Berkeley, 1952); François Chevalier, *La formation des grandes domaines au Mexique: Terre et société aux XVIe-XVIIe siècles* (Paris, 1952) and *Land and Society in Colonial Mexico: The Great Hacienda* (Berkeley, 1963).

3   Charles Gibson, *The Aztecs under Spanish Rule: A History of the Indians of the Valley of Mexico, 1519–1810* (Stanford, 1964); Charles H. Harris III, *A Mexican Family Empire: The Latifundio of the Sánchez Navarro Family, 1765–1876* (Austin, 1975); Wayne S. Osborn, "Indian Land Retention in Colonial Metztitlán," *Hispanic American Historical Review* 53 (May 1973).

best explain the development by the late sixteenth century of semi-independent estates? These questions have yet to find satisfactory answers.

Three other open questions, and their tentative answers to date, have shaped a generalized view of landed society in New Spain and, by implication, the lower third of Mesoamerica below the Valley of Mexico. They are: the meaning of the term "hacienda"; prestige versus economic factors in the development of Spanish estates; and the extent to which Spanish estates expanded and dominated land, rural society, and regional economies.

Clear definitions for colonial estates have not yet been rendered. The term "hacienda," which gradually came into use in the late sixteenth century with special reference to certain kinds of rural estates, continues to be used in vague and sweeping ways. Most often it means little more than large estate. The definition of "hacienda" used in my study of Oaxaca—a rural estate with a mixed economy of ranching and agriculture, permanent buildings, and some resident labor—was based on colonial usage of the term in southern Mexico.[4] These three ingredients were the lowest common denominators of all Oaxaca estates that were called "haciendas." Size, employment of capital, and the extent of debt peonage varied too widely to be a definable part of how colonials used the term. This definition should be taken as a warning that "hacienda" was used in such a general way in the colonial period that the term is not very useful as an analytical tool. The tiny Hacienda de Aguayo in Oaxaca had little in common with the productive entailed estate, San José Progreso, much less with the enormous landed properties of the Sánchez-Navarros in Coahuila.

There is really very little reason to lump together all landed estates referred to as "haciendas" in colonial records. Size, the relative balance between ranching and agriculture, productivity, stability of ownership, size of mortgages, impact on local and regional economies, numbers of resident laborers, and degree of isolation are much too varied to be subsumed under a single label. Critical attention needs to be directed toward types of rural estates rather than perpetuating the vague colonial usage of "hacienda." On a scale of landed estates running from export-oriented, capitalized plantations to *labores* (small farms, generally producing for regional markets and without large capital investments) to haciendas to ranchos (livestock or pulque) to estancias, haciendas are by far the most difficult to define beyond the mixed base

4 William B. Taylor, *Landlord and Peasant in Colonial Oaxaca* (Stanford, 1972).

of ranching and agriculture. Eric Wolf and Sidney Mintz's well-known description of haciendas as "rural properties under a dominating owner, worked with dependent labor emphasizing little capital and producing for a small-scale market" is a useful model to test against specific regional examples and contrasted with plantation systems. However, since this model derives from the authors' preoccupation with modern land systems, it should not be assumed to apply to more than a narrow slice of the spectrum of colonial estates. We will need additional criteria and types to comprehend the range of colonial haciendas in various regional settings.

Prevailing views on the expansion and social character of Spanish estates have much to do with deductive interpretations of regional land systems. Chevalier has provided important benchmarks in the early evolution of landed estates in Mexico—e.g., the growing importance of land grants in the late sixteenth century, the *composiciones* of the 1640s as a Magna Carta for great estates, confirming their legal and permanent character—but the origins and eventual impact of Spanish estates are still widely debated. On the question of the forces behind the development and character of colonial estates, the literature tends to divide into two groups: one group emphasizing economic causes; the other stressing a set of noneconomic attitudes of Spaniards in America, symbolized by the hidalgo.

The noneconomic motivations of Spaniards cannot be ignored easily. For many Spaniards, America became an outlet for aristocratic ambitions. The colonization of America reaffirmed the military values of the Reconquest spirit—concern with honoring oneself as a son of God and nobleman by nature. The sense of mission and the need to prove one's nobility, rather than the ambition of settling down on a landed estate, was obvious among the early Spaniards in America. If we may believe Bernal Díaz, Cortés chided two of his soldiers who had planned to establish cacao and cotton plantations during their journey through southern Mexico by saying that to spend time planting cacao was a sign of weak character. At a time when the opportunities for validating these ideals in Spain were shrinking, America offered fresh possibilities for Spanish Christians to establish their claim to nobility. Christian Spaniards, whether noblemen or commoners, saw themselves as nobles-in-potential. What separated the noble or noble-in-potential from the commoner was not that he did what the commoner could not, but rather that he, as an Old Christian, was possessed of a better faith, a spiritual superiority. As Cortés's remark suggests, self-esteem in this society was not directly dependent on wealth. Wealth and profits themselves were not signs of grace. Wealth was desirable—it would allow the individual to live in a more noble style—but self-esteem was a product of the Spaniard's knowledge of his personal worth and dignity. According to this line of reasoning, the great rural estates of Spanish America represent the eventual solution to the Spaniard's affirmation of his values—landed estates were basically social institutions whose raison d'être was control of people in a rural setting through ownership of productive land.

Spanish historians are most likely to accept these ideological explanations in colonial history. Américo Castro's concept of the Spaniard's psychic dwelling place at the end of the Reconquista is a good example of an approach that imposes a self-willed system on Spanish history. Although Castro does not consider the hacienda system directly, he emphasizes that Spaniards came to America to act out their cultural imperatives, which included realizing their potential nobility. Chevalier, who sees economic factors accounting for the initial rise of haciendas in the late sixteenth century, nevertheless considers the mature hacienda as a self-contained society fueled by aristocratic aggrandizement rather than by market demands. He finds a neat equivalent to the hacendados of Mexico in the landlords of medieval Castile.

Economic factors make a stronger case than prestige in explaining the origins of haciendas. While the rise of mixed-base estates does not coincide neatly with a sharp decline in silver production or the dramatic onset of economic depression, the expansion of Spanish agriculture did respond to rising food prices and a growing demand for cereals at a time when the Indian population, the early source of most farm products, was drastically reduced by epidemic disease and did not successfully supply the increasing market demand generated by Spanish and mestizo populations in urban centers. The growth of Spanish agriculture and ranching in the late sixteenth century seems to be associated with a regionalization of the economy of New Spain and a drying up of external markets (e.g., for silk, dyestuffs, and cacao), if not a general decline in the level of economic activity.

Economic conditions provided the incentive for increased Spanish agriculture, but the long-range function of rural estates in colonial Mexico cannot be handled so easily with a purely economic approach. First of all, haciendas and *labores* were distinctively Spanish responses to a scarcity of foodstuffs. They did not abandon ranching—that most noble of landed activities—and more than a few *labores* failed because they tried to maintain ranching on these small parcels of fertile cropland, which should have been used exclusively for farming. Secondly, whatever their origins, landed estates of the late colony served as bulwarks of noneconomic values: *patrón* leadership and the privileges and life-styles associated with Spanish hidalguía. To be sure, recent publications have persuasively introduced economic explanations of hacienda activities. On the other hand, the tendency to treat haciendas as capitalist institutions transforms a useful method of interpretation into a frozen system. While responding to economic pressures, most Spanish estate owners could hardly be called paragons of the profit motive. Here, Max Weber's distinction between wealth and profit as signs of grace, and wealth as a vehicle rather than an end, contributes to an understanding of how Spanish estates operated. Profits were not to be loathed by colonial landlords, but it was clearly just as important how you acquired your wealth and how you spent it. The Spaniard's cultural imperative of living as a noble, rather than plowing profits back into the business, went hand in hand with shoddy or nonexistent bookkeeping practices and the voluntary encumbrance of landholdings with ecclesiastical endowments.

The history of rural estates after their beginnings in the late sixteenth century is an especially important question for colonial studies since it bears directly upon the impact of Spanish rule on the native populations and the character of rural society as a whole. For some time, the consensus has been that haciendas dominated rural Mexico through the last two centuries of Spanish rule. Scholarship on colonial latifundios continues to stress their continuous expansion, absorbing small properties, and eventually reducing peasant communities to dependent islands in a sea of rural estates. Chevalier's study conveys the impression that rural Mexico had come under the domination of the hacienda system during the seventeenth century: "[The *composición*] settlements [of the midseventeenth century] revealed the large estates' predominance all over the country." Enrique Florescano's sophisticated study of agricultural crises from 1708 to 1810 posits the eighteenth century as the period when rural estates reached their greatest extent in pre-Revolutionary Mexico: "The majority of the lands in New Spain, the best agricultural land, were in the hands of the great creole and Spanish landholders. . . . By the end of the eighteenth century, this process had produced, at its peak, a small society of landlords which dominated the countryside and the city." Charles Gibson's study of the Valley of Mexico offers convincing evidence that the Indian economy in the center of Aztec control was systematically subordinated to Spanish towns and rural estates. More recently, he has suggested that this was a fairly general pattern: "In the standard Spanish American conflict between the Indian town and the hacienda, the latter steadily gained ground." With less convincing evidence, Carmen Venegas Ramírez and Isabel González Sánchez reach the same conclusion for the jurisdiction of San Juan Teotihuacán and the province of Tlaxcala, two areas very near the Valley of Mexico. Chevalier's evidence for areas north of the Bajío and the recent work of Charles Harris on Coahuila support the consensus opinion for the arid zones of northern Mexico.

Oaxaca and Southern Mesoamerica

The emphasis on latifundios in the history of Mexican land systems has generally been based on evidence from the *mesa central* north of Mexico City. Chevalier's classic account relies heavily on documentation from the Bajío region north to Zacatecas. His section entitled "Central and Southern Mexico" is basically legal (mercedes, *composición*) and institutional (encomienda, Marquesado) and does not consider the actual development of colonial land systems in the center and south. Only in his concluding section does he briefly consider the interaction of Spanish rule with the highly developed Indian cultures south of the Chichimec frontier. Yet the densely settled zones of Indian Mexico represent an essential part of the viceroyalty, as well as of modern Mexico, and must surely be considered in a general evaluation of land and colonial society. Broad geographical and cultural differences between Mexico's north, center, and south offer at least the potential for a variety of land systems. For example, the economic bases of southern Mexico in the colonial period were primarily agriculture and the availability of skilled and unskilled Indian labor, while to the north of Mexico City mining, ranching, and maguey production were most important. Zones of export agriculture—sugar cane in Morelos and the Caribbean coast of southern Mexico, cacao in Tabasco and Guatemala—represent another general type of regional economy. With its wealth in human resources and agriculture, the Indian regions of southern Mexico (the modern states of Oaxaca, Chiapas, southern Veracruz, and Yucatán) and the adjacent highlands of Guatemala provide a good testing ground for the importance of colonial estates and the extent of Spanish domination. My earlier work on the Valley of Oaxaca is one small piece of this larger historical picture of colonial societies in southern Mesoamerica.

Landed society and economy in the central valleys of Oaxaca depart from colonial land systems dominated by latifundios in several important ways. The valleys' Indian pueblos and nobles generally controlled sizeable landholdings, certainly more than sufficient to meet basic needs and avoid dependence upon Spanish landlords. During the colonial centuries, the Oaxaca countryside did not come under the control of a few Spanish latifundistas who monopolized productive land. Non-Indians held less than half of the total area of the central valleys, most of which was grazing land. Spanish holdings were fragmented into a large number of small ranches and *labores* rather than enormous haciendas. Few landed estates were entailed, and rapid turnover, usually by sale, made for a fluid land market among non-Indians. Only Indian landholdings might be considered static in the late eighteenth century. Indian communities and individuals controlled about two-thirds of the agricultural land during the last century of Spanish rule and most communities also had several grazing sites. By and large, the Indians produced the crops of their own choice. One of the striking features of Indian agriculture is that while the land was capable of producing an abundant variety of European crops, the natives clung tenaciously to the cultivation of their traditional staples—maize, beans, and maguey— often to the exclusion of other foodstuffs. Even communities in the Etla region, whose tribute was assessed in wheat, were reported to have bought grain from sources outside the Valley, rather than turning over part of their community lands to foreign grains. José María Murguía y Galardi, speaking as a frustrated nineteenth-century hacendado and po litical leader, remarked that "the poverty of agriculture in the Valley is due to the intransigence of the Indian landholders in failing to diversify their crops."

In effect, Indian control of agricultural lands and preservation of their communities produced a colonial system that included a series of parallel structures—Indian and Spanish—that were partially independent of one another. Indian towns and their croplands coexisted, sometimes in a mutually advantageous relationship, with Spanish ranches and haciendas: large regional Indian markets operated essentially outside the Spanish economy, which was concentrated in the city of Antequera, center for political administration; secular rituals continued alongside the new traditions of the Catholic church; elements of Indian justice, administration, and hereditary classes also continued at the community level, exclusive of a Spanish ruler–Indian subject relationship. The appearance of haciendas combining agriculture with ranching after the

1580s did not pose a serious threat to local peasant economies. The early growth of Spanish estates took place on vacant lands and did not pit Indian towns against haciendas in direct conflict. While hacendados sometimes attempted to extend their boundaries by purchase and encroachment, the communities of the Valley usually proved to be an equal match. Day labor rather than resident peonage was the hacienda's principal source of labor. Consequently, few Indians were drawn onto haciendas as permanent laborers, and apparently only two communities were absorbed by private estates.

Parallel economies and societies in the Valley of Oaxaca should not, of course, be taken as absolutes. Indian life fused with the colonial system in many ways, and elements of Spanish domination also affected the affairs of most communities. Especially in politics, religion, and economic activity outside the community, the Spanish state had a potential monopoly. Spanish administration and justice had the self-proclaimed right and sometimes the will to intervene in many facets of community life, particularly in times of strife. Tribute, tithe, alcabalas, the *reparto de efectos* ("forced sale of merchandise"), and repartimiento and penal labor are specific examples of how command and coercion impinged upon peasant life in the Valley of Oaxaca and tempered the importance of parallel systems. The operation of the large urban marketplace at Antequera would seem to be a complementary rather than a dependent or coercive relationship, with Indian communities modifying their productive capacities to meet the food and specialty demands of the city. In general, Valley Indians adjusted to the material culture of the Spaniards in many ways, adopting clothing styles, livestock, Hispanic legalism, and elements of Spanish political and religious institutions and property values, but usually resisting radical changes in diet and declining to produce many European foods. The major changes in the peasant economy were in farming technology—oxen and plow replaced the digging stick—and the relatively greater importance of certain crops such as maguey and cochineal, rather than qualitative changes such as widespread acceptance of new crops or the loss of land and direct dependence upon Spanish masters for a living. A century after the demise of Spanish rule in Mexico, Emilio Rabasa found the predominance of a parallel economy little changed. Rabasa concluded that "foreign capital does not dare to engage in agriculture in Oaxaca because its lands cannot be guaranteed; even oaxaqueños prefer to invest in other endeavors." The Valley has continued to depend on agriculture at the community level.

Valley towns usually preserve strong local identities and distinctive, regional characteristics that were reinforced by the patterns of land tenure
in the colonial period.

The remainder of this article branches out from the Valley of Oaxaca example to explore three questions of colonial rural history with
special reference to southern Mesoamerica: (1) Were partial or fairly
complete parallel economic and social systems evident in other regions?
(2) How can we explain the presence of these parallel structures?
(3) How did Spanish approaches to colonial rule in these areas differ
from direct command through economic control?

To speak generally of landed society in southern Mesoamerica is
not much better than using latifundios to typify rural Mexico under
Spanish rule. In a cultural zone as vast and as diverse as Mexico and
Guatemala there is really no level higher than the regional level at which
one can come to grips with the concrete realities of the land. The Valley
of Oaxaca stands in marked contrast to a latifundio-dominated land system, but the highlands of southern Mexico and Guatemala are similar,
not identical to Oaxaca, and at this stage of our knowledge it would be
foolhardy to equate Oaxaca's landholding patterns with the southern
third of Mesoamerica. Even quite near the Valley of Oaxaca the landed
society could be very different. In the districts of Nejapa and Miahuatlán
there seem to have been rapid mestizaje and the early formation of
large private estates. On the other hand, conscious comparisons between
the Valley of Oaxaca and regions to the south will help to keep Spanish
latifundios in their proper historical perspective.

The populations and economies of southern Mexico and Guatemala
have certain characteristics in common with Oaxaca that make comparisons especially appropriate: (1) the colonial wealth of southern
Mesoamerica was its agricultural and grazing land and the labor of its
numerous Indian population. Farming, ranching, and industry primarily
supplied regional and local needs, although the tax system produced important revenues for the crown. For lack of large gold and silver deposits, mining was of little consequence in the South, and the chief exports, such as mantas and other craft goods, wax, cochineal, indigo, and
cacao were appended to local Indian economies rather than absorbing
all their energy and resources. (2) Indian societies in the South had
broad similarities: (a) the most important political and economic unit
was the individual community. Life in the highlands of Oaxaca, Chiapas,
Guatemala, and the interior of Yucatán centered upon the closed community where the core of Indian culture was contained within the physi-

cal boundaries of the town. While this village identity was present throughout the southern highlands, it tended to be more exclusive in Oaxaca, Chiapas, and Guatemala than in Yucatán, where regional identities have been fairly strong; (b) the foundation of the indigenous society was its agricultural peasantry, but a number of specialized classes and artisan groups were present—hereditary nobles, traders, *mayeques* (Indians with serflike status), slaves, artists, builders, metal and stone workers, and weavers. These skilled workers made up an important part of the regional economies of the colonial period; (c) Spanish control in the southern highlands was spread thin in the early colonial period at precisely the time when Indians began to acquire written titles to their ancestral lands.

The interior of the Yucatán peninsula provides some especially interesting comparisons to Oaxaca. The wealth of Yucatán, as with Oaxaca, was in its people. There were few mines or labor-intensive exports of lasting importance, only pockets of good farmland and elaborate Indian societies with skilled artisans and hereditary classes. In its early colonial history, Yucatán was the scene of chronic warfare and came under Spanish rule only tenuously, while Valley of Oaxaca communities generally submitted peacefully to a limited Spanish presence. In both cases, however, Spanish control in the early years was weak and ultimately depended upon alliances and boundary agreements with native nobles and individual communities. As in Oaxaca, Indian land titles to *cacicazgos* (estates belonging to caciques) and community holdings were confirmed very early in the colonial period in formal proceedings such as the surveys of Sotuta and Nachi Cocom provinces of 1545 and the Mani treaty in 1557, before resident Spaniards began to turn to land ownership as a stable source of wealth. The early colonial economy centered on use of Indian labor through encomienda, repartimiento, and taxation rather than direct Spanish control over land.

One well-documented region of Yucatán, which seems to have substantially the same land system as the Valley of Oaxaca, is the portion of the Cupul province encompassing the Spanish town of Valladolid and the Mayan pueblos of Ebtun, Cuncunul, Tekom, and Tixcacalcupul. The early preoccupation of these Mayan districts with land rights and legal documentation is impressive. Each community maintained a neatly ordered archive of land records, which served Ralph Roys well in his task of compiling *The Titles of Ebtun* (Washington, D.C., 1939). The Mayans of Cupul province established durable boundary agreements with their neighbors by 1600, agreements that were confirmed in writing by colonial authorities and apparently held good without incident until 1764. Boundary disputes between Indian communities provided the setting for these early agreements and lend further evidence of a property-conscious peasantry. As in Oaxaca, boundary disputes usually pitted one Indian community against another. Spanish estates rarely enter the land records of Ebtun, and there is little evidence of encroachment onto Mayan croplands. In the one specifically documented case, between the town of Tontzimin and don Blas de Segura Sarmiento in 1711, the Spanish judge found that Tontzimin had produced sufficient written proof of ownership and confirmed its right to the disputed land.

Very little of the land worked by Mayans in this region seems to have passed into Spanish hands during the colonial centuries. Few sales of community and private lands to outsiders are recorded, and communities quickly resorted to legal channels or force to prevent illegal encroachments. The Spanish developed their estates primarily on vacant land suited to grazing rather than taking over peasant cropland. If the Ebtun papers are representative, it was municipal lands, rather than Spanish estates, that were expanding in the eighteenth century, usually at the expense of private Indian property, but sometimes by purchase from Spanish ranchers. The apparent absence of haciendas combining agriculture with ranching in the jurisdiction of Valladolid at the end of the eighteenth century is one of the striking features of the local land system. According to the 1789–95 census for the area of Valladolid and its twenty-nine subject pueblos, there were seventy-six independent ranchos and fifty-six estancias in the area, but no haciendas, again suggesting that Spanish lands in central Yucatán were composed of vacant grazing sites. The modest *cascos* of the colonial ranches also recall the estates of the Oaxaca valley. Roys gives us the following description of the Chichén rancho that he says was the largest and most elaborate in the area:

> The standard arrangement was a one-story masonry structure with a high slightly sloping roof supported by beams, and divided into three apartments which extended north and south. The entrance is a large doorway on the east side and leads into the middle apartment, which is a loggia. Through three wide arches supported by slender stone columns it overlooks the large cattle corral on the west side of the building. Only the two end rooms are completely enclosed. At one end of the structure on a stone platform was the

noria, which drew water either from an artificial well or from a shaft piercing the roof of a cave-cenote.

The end result of this pattern of land ownership in the jurisdiction of Valladolid appears to have been two largely separate economic and social systems—Spanish ranching and Mayan farming and ranching—existing side by side with relatively little overlap. Taxation through a modified encomienda system, which lasted into the eighteenth century, and labor drafts were important outside influences on the peasant economy, but the Spanish estates themselves required little labor for their modest ranching activities. The Spanish population was concentrated at Valladolid in close proximity to the peasant communities that Roys calls "probably as nearly pure Maya as any in Yucatán." This enclavelike social pattern of a Spanish town near clusters of indigenous communities retaining much of their own culture again echoes the colonial pattern in the Valley of Oaxaca. Francisco Solano Pérez-Lila supports a similar view of landed society in highland Guatemala. Solano describes the acquisition of important land titles in the sixteenth century by the Indian aristocracy and communities' consolidation of communal properties through *composiciones;* and a pattern of small- and medium-sized Spanish holdings, except in areas where commercial crops such as sugar and indigo were produced. Solano concludes that wealthy, cohesive, landholding villages were most likely to be situated in "relative proximity" to colonial urban centers—Guatemala City, San Salvador, Quetzaltenango, Mazatenango, and Escuintla.

Some Implications of Landed Society in the South

If, as suggested here, some other parts of southern Mesoamerica had landholding systems similar to the Valley of Oaxaca, how can this persistence of Indian lands and the small size and instability of Spanish estates in these areas be explained? José Miranda has outlined five circumstances that may have aided the survival of communal lands in New Spain: (1) Indian rejection of such values as individualism and materialism, which Spaniards brought to America; (2) the physical and social distance between Spaniards and Indians produced by Indian values and Spanish segregation laws; (3) the continuation of Indian customs that were compatible with Spanish religion and laws; (4) survival of an autonomous Indian area, the municipality, that the crown recognized through the *fundo legal;* and (5) the relatively small numbers of Spaniards and geographical isolation in some regions. Miranda underlines a close connection between communal landholding and social cohesion, singling out the first circumstance as the most important ingredient. Miranda's emphasis on the staying power of a positive, if changing, indigenous culture at the community level as crucial to Indian landholding contributes to an understanding of colonial society in parts of southern Mesoamerica, the *zona indígena* of modern Mexico and Guatemala. Oaxaca, Chiapas, Yucatán, and Guatemala are all noted for less biological or cultural mestizaje and more survival of Indian ways, fusing elements of European culture to Indian life without radically changing basic attitudes and life-styles. Miranda, however, does not conceive of Indian land and culture surviving outside a communal framework. Since he associates private property with Europeans, Miranda underestimates the existence of private property in pre-Hispanic communities and the ability of individual communities to combine a larger measure of private landholding with communal patterns after Spanish penetration. For example, much private property was accumulated by individual peasants and hereditary nobles in the Valley of Oaxaca without destroying local villages or impairing their ability to retain productive land in the long run.

Perhaps peasants' attitudes toward property in the highlands of southern Mexico—in particular, their aggressive economic preoccupations, whether private or communal—would be a more inclusive explanation of their penchant for litigation and successful preservation of personal and municipal landholdings. An interesting example of an almost cash-register concern for the value of property among peasants in the Valley of Oaxaca is described by the parish priest of San Martín Tilcajete in 1777. The priest tells of an urgent summons to the sickbed of an Indian woman who appeared about to die and without confession. In a last effort to save the woman's life as well as her immortal soul, the priest ordered that a hearty broth be prepared from a chicken he found in the woman's dwelling. The priest opened the woman's mouth and administered the broth; his effort was rewarded for she recovered strength, confessed, and received the Holy Sacraments. A week later, the woman came to see the priest but not, as he expected, to thank him for saving her life. She had come to collect two reales, the value of the chicken the priest had slaughtered, and would not leave until he paid her.

As this story suggests, peasants in the Valley of Oaxaca, then as now, were notoriously conscious of property and its value, an attitude that undoubtedly promoted persistent, almost limitless defense of their lands. A concern with ownership rights, land values, and precise boundaries is echoed in each of the hundreds of colonial land suits involving peasant communities or individuals in the Valley. Peasant communities were all too ready to take up arms in defense of their lands if legal channels were not rewarding. Today, property disputes still lead to much litigation and violence, especially where the adversaries come from two or more communities. Modern Oaxacan peasants reveal a sharp sense of material value, much like our lady from Tilcajete.

Geographical isolation, a circumstance Miranda includes but ranks last, has sometimes been considered the crucial if not the only important condition for the survival of self-sustaining indigenous communities. Isolation and few Spaniards might be sufficient to explain the survival of well-landed Indian groups in the remote mountainous reaches of Oaxaca, Chiapas, or Guatemala where the mettle of local communities was not tested; but isolation alone is not very helpful in the Ebtun or Oaxaca valley examples, where strong peasant villages retaining the core of Indian life-styles existed in close proximity to such populous Spanish cities as Valladolid, with more than 6,000 inhabitants in 1792, and Antequera with about 18,000 in the same year. Miranda's attention to the positive strength of Indian cultures in their adjustment to colonial rule, facilitated by Spanish policy (legal avenues to Indian landholding from the beginning, the right of *congregados* to their ancestral land, missionaries as important agents of Spanish authority in central and southern Mexico and Guatemala in the early period, and segregation laws) is a more satisfactory explanation in these cases. Certainly the early dates and the eagerness with which communities in Oaxaca and Cupul province seized the opportunity to defend their lands and periodically stood up to the authority of local Spanish judges and priests suggests an impressive internal strength and reservoir of affirmative action.

If the strength and activity of indigenous communities themselves had much to do with their survival as social and landholding groups, what accounts for the decline of Indian society in and near the Valley of Mexico where the preconquest population was largest and the culture very elaborate? In comparison with Oaxaca and Cupul provinces, three conditions seem especially important: (1) the absence of large cities or extensive state control in the south at the time of the conquest; (2) differences in the timing of land tenure developments in the sixteenth and early seventeenth centuries; and (3) the relative size of the Spanish and culturally non-Indian populations, especially in the early colonial period.

The Spanish conquest had a more disruptive effect on the Valley of Mexico than in southern Mexico, not only because it was the center of the armed conquest, but also because there was more of a central political and economic organization to be disturbed. The lack of urban centers comparable to Tenochtitlán-Tlatelolco or a centralizing political force like the Aztecs was important to the survival of peasant society at the community level in southern Mesoamerica, since the Spaniards were especially intent upon replacing Indian officialdom above the community level. Communities within Aztec state control and the economic sphere of Tenochtitlán-Tlatelolco were especially vulnerable to the imposition of a new outside authority, for they had already lost a large measure of inner direction and local autonomy. The existence of a large urban center in the Valley of Mexico shaped and dominated the economy of the countryside much more completely than did the regional markets of southern Mexico and Guatemala, where the marketplace was more a locus of exchange than a dominant urban center. When the Spanish capital and primate city was placed directly on top of Tenochtitlán, the peasant communities that had already been drawn into the urban economy and been subordinate to the Aztecs were drawn more fully into the colonial world. By the seventeenth century, communities near the Valley of Mexico often were very specialized in their economic activities. For example, towns in the vicinity of Xochimilco, Texcoco, and Cuautitlán produced pulque for sale in Mexico City and planted nearly all their fields to maguey. This dependence upon urban demands, coupled with regular visits to the city to sell the produce, brought many basically rural communities into the web of urban life.

By contrast, in southern Mesoamerica there were no native states or cities in the post-Classic period comparable to the Aztecs and Tenochtitlán-Tlatelolco. There were small regional states or clusters of communities under one set of political leaders, but the basic unit of Indian society in the south was the local community. Regional markets were important meeting places for the exchange of goods among communities, but they did not give rise to comparable political and social ties. The strength of the local community and what seems to have been a state of chronic warfare in the post-Classic period of Indian prehistory promoted an exclusivist, suspicious posture toward the outside and coherent, cohesive attitudes within. Such a localized, enemy-oriented political and social system was both a weakness and a strength for the community. On the negative side, it prevented a united front against

Spanish penetration, promoted violent discord among communities, and enabled the Spaniards to "divide and rule"; but the same values and co-hesiveness also served the communities well in resisting outside en-croachments and in maintaining the lands that supported their local so-ciety. Spanish rule in southern Mesoamerica was always more remote and more limited than in central Mexico, not only because there were fewer Spaniards, but also because the new lords could not simply re-place an existing state with an established tradition of centralized con-trol at the local level as they could in the center of Aztec sovereignty.

Differences in timing and the relative size of populations are closely related and can be considered more easily together than separately. The Spanish population clustered earlier and in larger numbers in the Valley of Mexico than in any part of southern Mesoamerica. The large settle-ment at Mexico City from the late 1520s and the discovery of mines to the north created an early demand for foodstuffs, especially wheat, by nonagriculturalists. The natural resources of the central region near the Valley of Mexico were obviously important to this early activity. Mines and areas of cropland suited to wheat and to sugar cane, an important cash crop, gave central Mexico an initial attraction beyond the Indian presence. Combined with a declining Indian population, because of dev-astating epidemics and harsh labor practices, the result of this demand was a significant Spanish interest in the acquisition of farmland, as well as the usual attraction to ranching from about the very time the vice-regal government began to process and confirm the first large batches of Indian titles in the 1540s.

In the south, much of the Indian cropland was confirmed in formal Spanish titles even before many of the Spanish ranching grants were al-located, and certainly well before Spaniards coveted arable lands or be-gan to create estates with a mixed economic base of ranching and agri-culture. During the sixteenth century, while the non-Indian population was small, Spaniards in Oaxaca and Valladolid preferred to meet their need for foodstuffs by encouraging Indian farming, rather than taking over and operating farms. Spanish estates probably expanded onto lands vacated as the Indian population continued to decline in the early sev-enteenth century, but outright usurpation of Indian lands in the late co-lonial period was blunted by the existence of the early titles and the will-ingness of peasant communities to defend their titles by law and by force. The relatively small Spanish population in the crucial period of Indian titles was undoubtedly important to the landholding pattern, but as the non-Indian population grew after the 1560s, the land system did not change in even a roughly proportional way. By 1792, Antequera and Valladolid were both relatively large cities accounting for about 18 percent and 27 percent of the regional populations, yet the landholding pattern still preserved Indian dominance in farming, with Spanish estates being characteristically small and emphasizing ranching. Perhaps there was a threshold of Indian to non-Indian populations above which, even in the late colonial period, the indigenous communities lost most of their lands; but if so, the Ebtun and Valley of Oaxaca examples suggest that the threshold must have been well above 20 percent non-Indian.

The patterns of assimilation and displacement of sedentary Indians in central Mexico probably followed two bands of territory: (1) the lines connecting such sixteenth-century mining centers as Zacatecas, Guanajuato, Pachuca, and Sultepec with Mexico City or related trading and agricultural centers such as Querétaro or Toluca; and (2) the main lines of communication between the port of Veracruz and the urban centers of the interior. The timing of sustained, numerous colonial contacts is important to this pattern. Communities that were fairly isolated during the demographic disasters of the sixteenth century had an opportunity to make creative adjustments to colonial rule that could support them against increased political and economic pressures during the late colony without serious disruption or loss of vital property. The difference between Oaxaca and the bands of territory that were heavily colonized in the sixteenth century is not merely chronological, i.e., that areas like Oaxaca were going through the same process at a later date as Spaniards began to settle in large numbers. The rate of colonial settlement in the sixteenth century was crucial to the emerging regional societies because it was accompanied by qualitative adjustments. Where latifundios had not matured in populous Indian zones by about 1650 when the Indian communities were growing again, haciendas would not gain the upper hand in the eighteenth century, in spite of increasing colonization.

Another implication of the elements we have noted has to do with political control. Colonial government in southern Mesoamerica often operated in a manner that I would call rule by appeasement, a conscious policy no doubt hastened by the strength and cohesiveness of peasant communities, but that was also an option exercised by Spanish rule in many parts of America. Unamuno's aphorism to the effect that the Spaniard has much of the Mandarin about him but little of the *mandón* is suggestive of Spanish attitudes toward political power in colonial America.[5] The position of authority, especially in matters of justice—the highest attribute of sovereignty to the colonial Spaniard—was more important than the exercise of complete control. Within this overarching goal of maintaining its position of authority in America, the Spanish government was capable of a wide variety of techniques in dealing with political and social problems. Even runaway slaves in revolt could be threatened with extermination and simultaneously offered broad concessions including legal freedom, admission to the brotherhood of Christianity, and free land in exchange for an oath of allegiance.

No colonial power has ever ruled solely by command, but the heavy emphasis of colonial Latin American scholarship on the institutions of Spanish rule (encomiendas, viceregal government, audiencias, and great estates) and coercive labor systems (slavery, encomiendas, repartimientos, and debt peonage) gives the impression that Spaniards maintained their position of authority by direct command and economic monopolies. In fact, Spanish rule in southern Mesoamerica relied on close control and force, primarily in cases of armed uprisings, and even then, a show of force was preferable to open confrontation. The numerous political problems and community uprisings in the Valley of Oaxaca in the seventeenth and eighteenth centuries usually were resolved with litigation, concessions, or only exemplary punishments. For example, the colonial government made the concession of commoner suffrage in municipal elections only to those communities where political conflict had become a serious problem.

Another well-documented case of colonial rule by appeasement in Oaxaca is a series of events surrounding the smallpox epidemic of late 1792. Teotitlán del Valle, a peasant community in the Valley of Tlacolula especially hard hit by this epidemic, was singled out for special attention by the Board of Physicians in Antequera. At their request, the intendant ordered that the entire community be quarantined and that a makeshift infirmary be constructed on the outskirts of the town to separate the afflicted from the healthy. Residents of Teotitlán were not permitted to leave the village, even to tend to their crops, nor could families visit or send food to their isolated relatives in the infirmary huts.

To Teotitleños, this forced community isolation and separation of family members was an intolerable intervention. Their first response,

5 "In effect, the Spaniard does not like to rule. Rather, he enjoys the position of ruler—loving the glitter, the trappings, the ceremony. Whatever may be said, the Spaniard is not domineering (*mandón*) although he has much of the Mandarin about him," Miguel de Unamuno, *España y los españoles* (Madrid, 1955), p. 270.

conditioned by three centuries of colonial experience, was to hire a lawyer in Antequera, Joaquín de Villasante, to petition the viceroy to lift
the quarantine. The leisurely legal process was not, however, a satisfactory answer to this kind of real emergency. The peasants soon took the
issue into their own hands, assaulting the infirmary, retrieving sick relatives and burying the dead in the churchyard. The attack was apparently
spontaneous, beginning with a mother's attempting to recover her child
from the infirmary. The local Spanish *corregidor de indios* viewed this
turn of events with alarm, calling it a "criminal act," a "challenge to the
rule of Your Majesty," and a potentially "pernicious influence," on
other Indian villages. In an effort to "reduce them to reason," he staged
an exemplary whipping that ended with the corregidor in hasty retreat
after a knife was thrown at his feet during the proceeding.

At this impasse, the regional authorities made a brief show of force,
accompanied by an interesting plan for appeasement designed to avoid
a permanent confrontation with the communities of the Valley. The intendant first ordered the militia at Antequera to patrol the outskirts of
Teotitlán (an assignment that lasted something over two weeks), but
did not attempt a punitive expedition against the town nor dare to punish the townspeople beyond the brief imprisonment of fifteen individuals. The Spanish authorities also hit upon making a scapegoat of the
lawyer, Villasante, as a way out of direct confrontation with the peasants. In spite of the fact that the Indians had come to him for advice in
opposing the quarantine, Villasante was charged with stirring up innocent Indians and condemned to a stiff prison sentence and a heavy fine.
The Teotitleños emerged from the affair as "extremely peaceful people"
who had never been rebellious until they met Villasante—a convenient
case of Spanish amnesia, judging by the violent land disputes involving
Teotitlán with Macuilxóchitl and Tlacolula throughout the eighteenth
century.

A more grisly set of circumstances in the nearby town of Macuilxóchitl in the 1740s also brought the appeasement policy into play. Macuilxóchitl's bitter land dispute with an hacienda of the Bethlemite Order had escalated into regular raids against the estate and whippings in
retaliation by the Bethlemites' overseer. The overseer eventually blun-
dered into Macuilxóchitl to vent his anger and was immediately seized
by a large group of townspeople and taken to the *casa de comunidad* for
trial. With the entire community vociferously present, the elders pronounced the death sentence, and the unfortunate Spaniard was hurried
off to the town plaza and hanged. Several of the elders were arrested,

but in the course of gathering evidence it became clear to the audiencia that the entire community had passed judgment and carried out the sentence. Without individual culprits, the court was at a loss. It exacted a pledge of loyalty from the town and ordered a stone gallows to be erected in the plaza as a permanent symbol of the punishment the community deserved for its crime.

Although this article has centered on southern Mesoamerica as an area of Indian cultures and regional economies with important similarities to Oaxaca in the colonial period, elements of the Oaxaca pattern may apply in a more general way to landholding and colonial rule in Spanish America. In particular, rule by appeasement may well have been the basic strategy of the Spaniards in the countryside. Also, recent work on areas north of Mexico City suggests that regions dominated by stable, monolithic, financially secure Spanish estates were the exception rather than the rule. Spanish landholding frequently took the form of a collection of small properties without contiguous boundaries; the estates were heavily mortgaged, subject to sale, and had few resident laborers. In sum, the consolidation of property and emergence of mature haciendas seems to have been a halting, uneven process. Territory surrounding the intracolonial and export market systems was most likely to be dominated by Spanish estates, but these market connections alone did not always determine landholding in Indian areas, once the native peasantry began to revive in the late seventeenth century.

The tentative hypotheses offered here concerning landed society and colonial rule in southern Mesoamerica do not deny the fundamental facts that Indians were subordinated to Spaniards, that Spanish rule disrupted and changed Indian life in many important ways, and that the native superstructure was completely displaced above the community level. On the other hand, the patterns of change and control in native communities were not uniform throughout New Spain, and the south—from Oaxaca to Guatemala—has certain broad continuities that make comparison to the Oaxaca example especially promising. Certainly not in southern Mesoamerica, and perhaps in but few parts of America, did Spanish control over land and labor approach the tenure system of the Ottoman empire in the fifteenth century, with its state and lord ownership of land and the crushing burden of labor service and taxation on peasant farmers.

Suggested Further Reading

Chevalier, François. *Land and Society in Colonial Mexico: The Great Hacienda.* Berkeley, 1966.

Keith, Robert G. "Encomienda, Hacienda and Corregimiento in Spanish America: A Structural Analysis." *Hispanic American Historical Review* 51:3 (August 1971).

Osborne, Wayne S. "Indian Land Retention in Colonial Metztitlán." *Hispanic American Historical Review* 53:2 (May 1973).

Taylor, William B. *Landlord and Peasant in Colonial Oaxaca.* Stanford, 1972.

Van Young, Eric. "Conflict and Solidarity in Indian Village Life: The Guadalajara Region in the Late Colonial Period." *Hispanic American Historical Review* 64:1 (February 1984).

8

Colonial Silver Mining: Mexico and Peru

D. A. BRADING AND HARRY E. CROSS

Colonial silver mining began when European techniques of production were introduced into the New World to satisfy the sustained European demand for precious metals. At first the industry formed little more than an overseas extension of the great central European mining boom of the years 1451–1540. Certainly it was then that an association of high capital investment with a remarkable range of technical innovation succeeded in pushing German silver production to unparalleled heights. Problems of drainage were solved by cutting adits several miles long beneath the lode, or by the installation of great water wheels and whims moved by teams of up to a hundred horses. As early as 1451, the invention of lead smelting facilitated the separation of silver from the copper compounds with which it was usually found. The construction of stamp mills, impelled by either water power or horses, completed the circle of improvements. The publication of G. Agricola's *De re metallica* (1556), a lavishly illustrated work, hastened the diffusion of practical knowledge.

Despite these obvious technical debts, colonial silver mining soon acquired a structure of production radically distinct from its Old World predecessor. The difference in scale was striking. Although when at its peak in the decade 1526–35 the European industry cut 350,000 marks (of 8.5 ounces) a year, by the close of the century its output had fallen to 100,000 marks, a mere tenth of the American bullion imports then registered at Seville. Equally important, as early as the 1550s, miners in Mexico developed the amalgamation process, a cheap, simple method of refining large quantities of low-grade silver ore. In the years immediately following the discovery of Potosí in Upper Peru, Indians smelted its rich

Published originally in the *Hispanic American Historical Review,* 52:4 (November 1972). The authors wish to thank William P. McGreevey, P. J. Bakewell, and J. R. Fisher for their advice and suggestions relating to the present article.

ores in their own clay furnaces. Then again, the labor demands of the industry drove the viceregal authorities to levy work drafts from the Indian peasantry.

These differences suggest, therefore, that American silver mining offers fewer comparisons with its German antecedents than with that other great colonial industry, the manufacture of sugar. The similarities are striking. Unlike tobacco or gold, both sugar and silver required an elaborate refining process rendered possible only by considerable capital investment. In both industries labor costs dominated the primary sector of extraction or cultivation. Both devised labor systems peculiar to America, the one relying upon imported African slaves, the other—at least in the first instance—upon enforced recruitment of Indian peasants. Finally, both operated within strict geographical limits, sugar growing best in the tropical lowlands, and silver being most abundantly located in the high ranges of the inland cordilleras.

The general effects of American silver production have long been the object of academic debate. Its role in the price revolution of the sixteenth century is still in dispute. Similarly, its contribution to Europe's trade with Asia, despite contemporary concern, has yet to be justly weighed. But for Spanish America no one can doubt its importance. The mining camps and towns generated sufficient purchasing power to stimulate not merely transatlantic and transpacific commerce, but also long-distance internal trade. Potosí received cloth from Quito, mules from Buenos Aires, sugar and coca from Cuzco, and brandy from Arequipa. Merchants as well as miners built their fortunes upon the industry. It was the existence of this export sector in the colonial economies of Peru and Mexico that prevented them from becoming simple agrarian or feudal societies.

The aim of this article is to review the state of existing knowledge about colonial silver mining. We offer, however, a guide rather than a catalogue: the focus is more upon problems than bibliography. In areas where information is available but uninterpreted, we advance hypotheses.

Geologic Aspects

If the agrarian historian must take into account the effects of climate and soil formation, so too the student of mining should examine the geologic record. The location and composition of ore deposits in good measure determined the organization of the industry.

In general, nearly all American silver has been found in the great chain of mountain ranges that stretch from Canada to Chile. Geologically, the cordilleras of the western Sierra Madre of Mexico and the Peruvian Andes derive from the volcanic eruptions of the Tertiary Age. It was then, apparently, that magma intruded into the multiple faults and cavities in the earth's crust. Upon cooling, the argentiferous magma crystallized for the most part into fissure veins of varying silver concentration. These formations were as various and particular in their distribution, depth, and dip as the mountains that encased them. The bulk of these primary ores took the form of low-grade sulphide compounds, but near the surface the prolonged effects of weathering tended either to isolate the ore into particles of native silver or to oxidize it, associating in the latter case with reddish soft minerals known to colonial miners as *colorados* or *pacos*. Furthermore, the incessant percolation of rain water carried a considerable portion of these oxidized ores below the water table level, there to be reprecipitated in a process now described as secondary or supergene sulphide enrichment. An alternative mode of enrichment at this level, defined by geologists as hypogene concentration, derived from interaction of the primary ores with further interior flows. The hard, dark ores so formed, called *negrillos,* were frequently as rich if not richer than the *colorados* above them. Finally, beneath this middle enriched zone lay the great mass of low-grade primary sulphides, which slowly diminished, merging into a variety of base metal compounds.

This general pattern, needless to say, was interrupted by local idiosyncrasy. At Guanajuato, little oxidation occurred; nevertheless, its mainly sulphide ores had experienced a hypogene concentration process almost to surface levels. At Potosí, the conical shape of its isolated peak facilitated the formation of an oxidized encasement 250 yards deep, beneath which lay a zone of high-grade sulphides. Moreover, the multiple veins of its several lodes all contained a considerable scattering of native silver or argentite.

Used with caution and respect for local variation, the geologic record can provide the historian with invaluable evidence as to the physical framework governing the miners' exertions. It helps to explain the familiar cycle of bonanza, abandonment, renewed bonanza, and final depletion that characterized the history of so many American mines. For although quantities of native silver could be found near the surface, in all likelihood the most consistently rich zone of the lode lay at water table level—in Mexico at 400 to 600 feet. Few mines during the colonial period, the Valenciana and Potosí apart, pushed beneath this middle region; indeed most did not reach it until the eighteenth century.

The economic deductions that can be obtained from a comparison of the geologic formation with recorded shaft depths are extensive. Once the days of primitive surface bonanza were past, then, within the observed scale, the farther down the miner pushed the higher his likely yield. With the water table attained, both his capital and maintenance costs inevitably rose, but so too did his gross production. Naturally this presumption could always be disappointed by local variations or difficulties. Moreover, such a policy required considerable capital investment in the form of adits or shafts, frequently on a scale beyond anything available to the colonial miner. The cycle of abandonment and bonanza referred to above sprang from two combined causes: the nature of the ore deposits, and inadequate capital resources to counter their effects.

Mining Techniques

The establishment of mining as a rational industry rather than as a smash-and-grab raid upon the earth's crust primarily depended upon the construction of deep shafts and long adits. Unfortunately we know little about the development of underground excavation. True, at the end of the eighteenth century European visitors poured scorn upon colonial technology. They exclaimed over the absence of cross galleries, the tendency to cut work tunnels that corkscrewed through the lode, the lack of mules for carriage, and the reliance upon whims. Humboldt noted with surprise that Mexican miners used crowbars similar to those employed in Germany in the sixteenth century. In consequence of these criticisms the impression lingers that American technology remained both backward and immobile, isolated from later European developments. In particular, the failure to adopt the use of the steam engine has confirmed the view. Yet, in point of fact, colonial methods of excavation underwent several marked phases in the course of two and a half centuries; important differences, moreover, existed between Peru and Mexico. And for the most part these developments corresponded to local attainments and cost possibilities. If steam engines were not introduced, it was because their fuel costs were exorbitant.

To understand technical development in New Spain three main problems have to be considered: the dimensions of shafts and adits; the use of underground cartridge blasting; and the type, capacity, and number of whims. Dimensions are significant because they provide not merely a clue as to the size of a mine, but serve as an index of capital value. To construct a deep shaft costs as much as to build a factory or a church. Moreover, to know the average depth is to gain a guide as to geological possibilities and problems. The same considerations apply even more to the cutting of adits, since these horizontal tunnels rarely yielded any short-term returns to cover working costs.

In 1617 at San Luis Potosí the local magistrate helped to organize the construction of a drainage adit some 250 yards long. At Zacatecas a shaft 112 feet deep was cut during the 1640s. At Parral the deepest level was 130 yards. Nevertheless, by 1697 Gemelli Carreri inspected shafts at Real del Monte and Pachuca that had reached 200, 184, and 160 yards.

To penetrate to these levels, the Mexican miner needed two weapons: gunpowder to break the hard rock and whims to keep the shafts drained. As yet, we do not know when cartridge blasting was introduced into New Spain. Guanajuato tradition avers that it was José de Sardaneta, owner of the Rayas, who first used it during the 1720s. Certainly Zacatecas in 1732 consumed remarkably little of this commodity—a mere 1,300 pounds. The great excavations of the later eighteenth century all depended upon the intensive employment of gunpowder.

Equally obscure is the evolution of the whim from a simple hoist, worked at times by hand, to a powerful machine serviced by teams of six to eight horses or mules and capable of hauling up loads weighing 1,250 pounds. Peter Bakewell refers to their operation at Zacatecas in 1679. Gemelli Carreri found some sixteen at work at Pachuca and Real del Monte. More important, he recorded the installation of two whims in one shaft. By the close of the eighteenth century, the Valenciana employed no fewer than eight whims in one great central shaft, cut in octagonal form to facilitate their use. Elsewhere, the installation of four or five machines became common. According to an informant from Real del Monte, the haulage capacity of whims in that camp quadrupled during the course of the century.

During the Bourbon epoch, the Count of Regla drove an adit 2,881 yards long beneath the Veta Vizcaína, a project that took more than thirty years to complete. The Valenciana's great shaft, with circumference of 32 yards and a depth of more than 600 yards, cost a million pesos to construct—the equivalent of two churrigueresque churches. The new technology thus depended upon heavy capital investment.

In Peru, by contrast, deep-shaft mining remained relatively underdeveloped, and in consequence whims do not appear in common use. The reasons for this difference were simple. At Potosí and possibly at other camps, the conical peak form of the area of ore deposits made adits the more practicable form of access and extraction. Though work began near the top of the *cerro rico* where the lodes broke the surface, as early as the 1560s depths of 200 and 250 yards were reached. At this point the first adit was cut by the Florentine miner Nicolás de Benino, designed to intersect the lode at a depth of 320 yards. By 1585 Luis Capoche, a miner and chronicler of Potosí, recorded one adit, presumably Benino's, 250 yards long and referred to another five under construction. These tunnels were six feet high and eight feet wide. From these adits radiated a series of work shafts of the peak's many mines. All ore was brought out on the backs of porters clambering up rough wooden ladders. The adits at this stage were used, of course, for entry and extraction rather than for drainage.

At Potosí the system of exploitation is difficult to understand. Individual mines only measured a few yards along a particular lode, and owners of adits permitted workers from other mines to use them. Presumably the farther the shafts or work tunnels were driven into the peak's core, the greater was the need for new, longer adits to intersect the lode at lower levels. In 1640, Viceroy Chinchón related the construction of two new adits, one with a length of 400 yards. No doubt similar projects were initiated both earlier and later. During the eighteenth century, the crown sponsored the construction of a major adit with the purpose of draining the lower reaches of the peak. Work began in 1789, and by 1810 a tunnel six feet square had been driven 2,200 yards at a cost of 560,000 pesos. In its last epoch Potosí was thus still able to rival the Mexican mines in the scale of its undertakings.

Elsewhere in Peru information is lacking. At Huancavelica, the great mercury mine, it took nearly forty years, between 1605 and 1642, to construct an adit 434 yards long. Work here, however, was dangerous because of mercury fumes and at times was suspended. Once completed, the adit permitted a safer and more rapid extraction of ore. As early as 1631 gunpowder was used for underground blasting at Huancavelica. Apparently damage to the mine was so extensive as to soon stop the practice, but it was reintroduced during the 1730s.

Other Peruvian camps apparently remained technologically backward, although blasting was introduced at San Antonio del Nuevo Mundo, in the south of the Potosí district, in the 1670s. At Cerro de Pasco at least two adits were cut during the eighteenth century. But the deepest shaft did not extend beyond 100 yards and was serviced by simple hand pumps and ladders rather than by whims. Whether this state of affairs sprang from the nature of the terrain, lack of capital, or technical ignorance is still unresolved.

Refining

In contrast to the paucity of information about excavation practices, considerable knowledge exists of the two refining techniques used in colonial Spanish America, amalgamation and smelting. As early as the 1530s a group of German miners introduced into New Spain both the stamp mill and lead smelting. Within twenty years, however, high fuel costs, combined with the falling quality of ores, had rendered this method uneconomic. The situation was transformed in 1554 when at Pachuca Bartolomé de Medina, a merchant from Seville, developed the amalgamation process by use of mercury and salt. Some controversy has raged about his right to claim the invention, but without doubt it was the Spaniard who carried out the experiments that made it an industrial reality. Despite the assertion that Medina added a catalyst called *magistral* (copper or iron pyrites), it seems likely that the surface oxidized ores at Pachuca already contained sufficient *magistral*. Bishop Alonso de la Mota y Escobar, writing about Zacatecas around 1604, explicitly commented upon the recent introduction of the practice, made necessary by the increasing predominance of sulphides (*negrillos*).

The mining historian Modesto Bargalló emphasizes that the first printed reference to amalgamation in an open patio was made by Gamboa in 1761. Others describe an earlier process carried out in large vats or containers. The moment of transition remains obscure.

Other changes are equally difficult to document. A Guanajuato tradition dates the invention of the *arrastre,* a stone-drag crushing device, to the early eighteenth century. Used in conjunction with the stamp mill, the *arrastre,* rather like amalgamation itself, was extraordinarily simple, cheap, and efficient. Its reliance upon mule power reflected the lack of water in northern Mexico and the increased reliance upon the animal in New Spain.

By the close of the eighteenth century, Mexican refining was notable for the size of its establishments and the high level of technical expertise. The Count of Regla's mill at Real del Monte housed twenty-four *arrastres* and cost a half a million pesos to construct. At Sombrerete the Fagoaga mill had no less than eighty-four *arrastres* and fourteen furnaces. Similarly impressive was the diffusion of knowledge. Five books were written about refining at this time, two of them by practicing miners.

At Potosí, the story, especially in its first stage, differs remarkably from that of New Spain. There Indians dominated the refining sector of the industry from discovery of the site in 1545 until 1572. They ground the ore in their simple stone mills called *quimbaletes,* and then smelted it in small clay furnaces fired by wind-fanned dried ichu grass or llama dung. At the height of this system more than 6,000 of these *guairas* lined the hills surrounding the town. The only European element in this technology consisted in the use of lead or litharge to facilitate the separation of the silver.

By the late 1560s, however, production at Potosí fell dramatically, following the increasing depletion of high-grade ores suitable for smelting. Two attempts to introduce amalgamation failed, until finally in 1572, Pedro Fernández de Velasco, backed by Viceroy Toledo, conducted successful experiments. Immediately the structure of the industry was transformed. Spaniards took over the refining sector, constructing stamp mills, furnaces, and vats. Although some mills were powered by horses, most of these machines were driven by water wheels. To obtain a regulated flow of water, the town financed the construction of a series of dams, eventually creating about twenty artificial lakes. The total cost possibly amounted to more than two million pesos.

The process introduced by Fernández de Velasco did not vary greatly from that used in Mexico. The amalgamation took place in a stone vat or container, and was hastened by exposure to a low heat. But if production soared, so did costs. It was only toward the end of the next decade that refiners realized that the dark ores, the *negrillos* or sulphides, demanded the addition of a *magistral,* copper or iron pyrites, if an excessive consumption of mercury was to be avoided. By the end of the century they had worked out which ingredients should be added to the different types of ore. By then they found it cheaper and more efficient to conduct the process without fire. Henceforward no significant changes occurred. In Peru amalgamation was always carried out in stone or tiled containers, never in an open patio. These *cajones* held 50 *quintales* ("hundredweight") of ore, compared to the 15 to 32 *quintales* of the Mexican *montón.* The separation of silver went considerably faster than in Mexico, lasting from ten to fourteen days, whereas in New Spain it often took up to six weeks.

By the early seventeenth century, most American silver was produced by amalgamation; only high-grade ores and lead compounds were smelted. The deeper or older the mine, the greater would be the dependence on mercury. The only rival to these two methods was the *cazo* process developed by Padre Alvaro Alonso Barba, in which the ore was smelted with mercury in a copper cauldron. The great drawback here was the tendency of impurities in the copper to enter the reaction. In 1786, the Hungarian Baron de Born invented a variant of this process, using copper-lined barrels. The Spanish crown commissioned German experts to teach this method to colonial miners. In the upshot, however, the equipment proved to be expensive and complicated, and the practical results unimpressive; apparently it did not separate as much silver as amalgamation. We may note that as late as 1870, some 71 percent of all Mexican silver continued to be produced by this sixteenth-century technique.

Various problems confront the historian who attempts to come to a closer view of colonial refining. Perhaps the most important is an epistemological one. On many occasions both miners and royal officials claim that ore levels had fallen; they then provide an average figure, let us say, of one ounce of silver per hundredweight of mineral. The historian then has to decide: did these refiners know how much silver their ores *really* contained? To answer this question we must consider the basis of their knowledge. In the first place, colonial miners classed all ores according to their external characteristics, such as color, hardness, and form. But equally important, these characteristics were related to the changes experienced by the different ores when smelted or amalgamated. In each camp a local tradition or expertise soon developed and was fortified by the continuous application of generations of refiners. By the eighteenth century, a miner at Potosí or Guanajuato could probably guess the quality of ore from its external appearance. The proof, of course, was in the cooking. Here too local tradition and experience determined the right balance of ingredients. No one understood the true nature of the chemical reactions, but all could judge its state by practical tests. In the nineteenth century, the French mining authority Laur stressed that all attempts to improve the process from chemical theory invariably failed; the advice of the local *azogueros* (owners of refining mills) was always to be preferred.

To assert the skill of the cooking is not to deny its failures. Laur took tests in various Mexican camps. He found that at Zacatecas about a quarter of the silver was left behind in the residue; at Atotonilco el Chico, the proportion rose to over a third. By contrast, in Guanajuato, where the ores were noted for their tractability, the loss only amounted to 12.65 percent. He observed that the master workmen in charge of the process rarely assayed the residue, fearing their skill might be criticized. Earlier at Potosí, it was estimated that a good third of the silver was lost. Whatever the case, the historian should always guard against statements about ore general levels. By 1790, one colonial writer, Pedro Vicente Cañete y Domínguez, declared that at Potosí the average yield was three-quarter ounce of silver per hundredweight of mineral, a level considerably lower than the two-ounce average claimed for Mexico.

A similar doubt surrounds the consumption of mercury. The usual ratio was two to one, i.e., a hundredweight of mercury produced one hundred marks (50 pounds) of silver. On the other hand, most treatises on amalgamation suggested that it was possible to refine a mark with a loss of only twelve ounces of mercury. In practice, the situation varied from camp to camp according to the tractability of local ores. In New Spain the local treasuries demanded different ratios, ranging from 85 marks in Bolaños to 125 marks in Guanajuato per hundredweight of mercury distributed. For seventeenth-century Zacatecas, there were considerable variations, with 112 to 126 being the most frequent. For Potosí, Cañete estimated the ratio at 120 to 130 marks. The range, therefore, was not extensive, a conclusion that has significant consequences for estimates of silver production.

Finally, we may note that nearly all the literature concentrates upon amalgamation to the virtual exclusion of smelting. Yet the mid-seventeenth-century shortage of mercury drove the Zacatecas miners back to smelting to such a degree that in the years from 1685 to 1705, just less than half of all the camp's silver was produced by that method. At nearby Sombrerete, newly discovered, all ore was smelted.

Labor

No other internal aspect of colonial mining has attracted so much attention as its labor system. Since the denunciations of Las Casas, the royal levy of tributary service, called repartimiento in Mexico and mita in Peru, has been associated with the great question of the decline in Indian population.

To inspect New Spain first, it is obvious that the twin themes that dominate its early history, the catastrophic decline in Indian population of the center and the colonization of the north, governed the development of the Mexican mining industry. At Pachuca a weekly repartimiento of 1,108 Indians drafted from the surrounding villages in the years 1576–79 dwindled to a mere 57 men by 1661. The same process, no doubt, was at work in all the camps situated within the confines of the old Aztec empire. Even as early as 1598, volunteer wage earners outnumbered drafted workers by two to one. Moreover, in the Chichimeca north mines always relied upon free labor, supplemented by an assortment of slaves, some Indian, but mainly African, suitable for work in the refining mills. At Zacatecas most mine workers were Indian migrants from Michoacán and the central valleys. The town was soon surrounded by small villages or suburbs, inhabited by Tarascans, Mexicans, Tlaxcalans, and Texcocans. Numbers here are important. Seventeenth-century Zacatecas, which produced about a third of all Mexican silver, never required more than about 5,000 workers. Labor supply was therefore, arguably, never a problem for the Mexican mining industry, since at most it needed 15,000 men.

By the eighteenth century, mine workers constituted a labor aristocracy, characterized by lavish spending and geographical mobility. By this time the northern workers were mainly mestizo, mulatto, and acculturated Indians. Their earnings derived not so much from the basic daily wage of four reales, as from their *partidos,* a share of the ore that all pickmen received. Toward the end of the century, however, a change occurred, when in Guanajuato this practice was replaced by the payment of high daily wages of eight to ten reales. This unpopular decision probably did not extend to other camps; in part it sprang from the greater social power exercised by mine owners following the creation of the provincial militias. Whatever the system, labor still remained the chief cost in the mining sector of the industry, amounting to as much as 75 percent of total expense.

The state's direction of mining labor was more apparent in Peru than in Mexico. The Peruvian mita, as first set up in 1574, was surely one of the most remarkable economic institutions devised by the wit of man. Each year the Indians of the region stretching from Potosí to Cuzco had to send roughly a seventh of all adult males to work in the mines and refining mills of Potosí, a number estimated at about 13,500 men. It took the Cuzco contingents some two months to cover the 600-mile journey across the Andean altiplano. An identical arrangement supplied Huancavelica with 3,280 Indians recruited from the surrounding districts. Some lesser minefields were also consigned small levies.

It should be observed that the mitayos were only obliged to work one week in three, their chiefs dividing the men into three shifts upon arrival. By all accounts, most Indians hired themselves out as free laborers, *mingados,* during their two free weeks. Not merely did they then receive different wages according to their status, but also, as free pick-men, they were entitled to a small share of the ore they cut. The mita therefore supplied Potosí with an enforced labor contingent of about 4,000 men, together with the possibility of employing double that number as "free" workers.

The mita was then and later the object of fierce attack. At least three separate questions are involved. Did work at Potosí and Huan-cavelica actually kill Indians? Did the mita contribute to depopulation? Did it result in flight and social disruption?

A comparison between Mexico and Peru may throw light on this thorny subject. In New Spain a rather small number of Indians left their villages and lands in Michoacán and the central valleys to settle in the north to become professional mine workers. In the Andes, so we are told, Indians similarly abandoned their lands and villages, but in this case it was to avoid working in the mines of Potosí. The difference in be-havior is striking and inexplicable. Why should Potosí appear more hateful than Pachuca or Zacatecas? Was it so dangerous as to drive a man to desert his ayllu and abandon his lands? How does the class of permanent workers at Potosí fit into the picture? These are questions colonial historians must one day examine.

Whatever the case, the contrast between the two viceroyalties does illumine the economic significance of the mita. In fact, many Andean Indians did settle at Potosí and Huancavelica to work voluntarily in these mines. Even before Viceroy Toledo organized the mita, the chiefs of Chucuito, a province in Puno, sent 500 men to Potosí to earn suffi-cient money to pay for all the district's tributes. What the mita repre-sented was a massive input of cheap labor. The difference lay in the scale and the price, in comparison with repartimiento in Mexico. The mita helped production at Potosí alone to soar far beyond the contem-porary total for all New Spain.

Further light is thrown on this question by comparison with the eighteenth century. By then all Peruvian camps, with the exceptions of Potosí and, to a much lesser extent, Huancavelica, had followed the Mexican pattern. They all relied on free labor. By then the mita, much reduced to no more than 3,280 men, acted chiefly as a subsidy to main-tain Potosí in existence. Without this source of cheap labor the *cerro rico,* with all its rich ores long since exhausted, could not have continued to work minerals which on average yielded no more than three-quarter ounce of silver per hundredweight. Whereas it took most Mexican mines more than two hundred years to push through the enriched middle zones of their lodes, at Potosí the mita both created the first rapid boom and then subsidized continued production. The same was true at Huancavelica, where the Indians of the nearby districts, rather than working, paid a mita tax that enabled the miners to meet their labor bills.

Concentration upon the negative aspects of the mita has obscured the fact that by the eighteenth century, most Peruvian silver was produced by workers who had freely chosen to become miners. We still lack any characterization of their provenance, earnings, or social type. Yet surely Potosí's impact upon Andean culture must have been all-pervasive. Indians from a vast region were thrown together; they were put into immediate contact with Spaniards, mestizos, and Africans; they received the ministrations of a numerous clergy; they could entertain themselves in the equally numerous taverns of the town. Hitherto, emphasis upon the undoubted human suffering involved has inhibited any study of the social and cultural effects of this great annual migration.

The Crown

No consideration of colonial mining can afford to neglect the pervasive role of the Spanish crown. In addition to the issuance of a legal code to govern the physical exploitation of mines, the crown levied a heavy tax on all silver produced, monopolized the production and distribution of mercury, and greatly profited from its control of the mints. The justification for such extensive intrusion lay in the traditional legal doctrine that all natural deposits of precious metals belonged to the royal patrimony. The code drawn up by Viceroy Toledo applied in all Spanish colonies until 1783, when José de Gálvez, minister of the Indies, issued new ordinances for Mexico. The commentators all emphasized that the crown only conceded working rights to the colonial miner; failure to exploit a mine entailed the lapse of all proprietary claim. In the case of the great mercury deposits at Almadén and Huancavelica, the principle of direct royal ownership was preserved, the mines being worked by leaseholders or under contract.

The customary tax charged by the crown amounted to a fifth of production. Once his silver was cast in bar, the American miner was legally obliged to present it at the nearest treasury for stamping and payment of the quinto. Another 1.5 percent was also deducted for assay costs. In New Spain, as early as 1548, miners obtained a reduction in this tax to a tenth. This concession, at first extended only to miners, as distinct from refiners, workers, or silver merchants, later became general throughout the industry. In Zacatecas, the proportion of silver taxed at the old 20 percent rate fell slowly in an uneven curve between 1559 and 1626, from about a quarter to a seventh of the total. After the late 1620s, hardly any further quintos were collected. Evidence for other camps in New Spain is lacking until the 1660s, when Viceroy Mancera reported that the tenth was indeed the usual rate, with only insignificant quantities of silver paying the fifth. This situation was finally legalized in 1723 when it was decreed that merchants and refiners should pay the same tax as miners.

At Potosí, by contrast, the full fifth was demanded throughout the sixteenth and seventeenth centuries. Thus the *cerro rico* not merely produced more silver than all camps of New Spain combined, it also yielded the crown far more direct profit. Naturally, once the rich ores were exhausted, miners found this fiscal burden increasingly onerous, to the point where many, abetted by official laxity, smuggled their silver out through Buenos Aires. Despite various petitions and the prolonged decline in production, it was not until 1736 that the crown relented and lowered the rate to the tenth. Already several other Peruvian camps had obtained this concession. In 1621, the miners of Castrovirreyna paid only the *diezmo,* a rate that by 1640 fell to 7.5 percent. Similarly, in this latter year, 10 percent was collected at Nuevo Potosí. How far the reductions became general is difficult to know; they suggest that, as always, Potosí constituted the greater exception, and that other Peruvian camps resembled their Mexican counterparts.

After the Gálvez Visitation (1765–71), several leading Mexican miners, all engaged in risky or costly renovations of old mines, received outright exemptions from the silver tithe until their initial investment cost was reimbursed. By the close of the century, nearly all the leading enterprises at Zacatecas had secured such concessions. This policy largely applied to camps with low-grade ores; at Guanajuato and Catorce, no one was granted an exemption. Whether this liberal fiscal program was ever introduced into Peru remains to be investigated.

The second great source of royal income derived from the crown's monopoly over the production and distribution of mercury. During the colonial period, this indispensable ingredient was known in sizeable deposits in only three places: at Almadén in Spain, at Idria in modern Slovenia, and at Huancavelica in Peru. Idria, owned by the Austrian emperor, was by far the smallest, and only sporadically entered the American market. The resulting pattern was simple. Huancavelica gen-

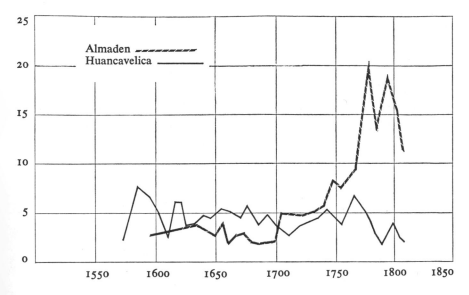

Graph I Mercury Production: Almaden and Huancavelica, 1570–1810
(annual averages in thousands of quintales)

erally supplied Peru and Almadén supplied New Spain. In both cases,
failure to produce sufficient mercury could have catastrophic effects
upon the local silver mines. At the same time, changes in mercury price
could easily alter the curve of silver production. It was this intimate
connection that bound the Mexican silver miner to Europe.

Distribution in New Spain remained a royal monopoly managed by
treasury officials and licensed magistrates. In the first years, Mexico City
auction prices ranged from 132 to 236 pesos a hundredweight. Only
slowly, in deference to local protest, did the crown lower the price from
113 pesos in 1590 to 82.5 pesos in 1627, the standard rate for the next
century and a half. Northern miners, however, had to pay freight costs
from Mexico City. During the later seventeenth century prices rose
somewhat. At Zacatecas in the period from 1680 to 1700 the average
cost varied between 90 and 100 pesos. This upward trend in price reflected prevalent scarcity. After 1640 Almadén's production plummeted
far beneath the average 4,000 to 5,000 hundredweight needed by New
Spain. During the 1670s Huancavelica sent shipments, but Peruvian mercury cost the Mexican miner 110 pesos, and at best served to supplement
rather than replace Almadén as the chief source of supply.

Although during the seventeenth century Huancavelica produced
far more mercury than Almadén, the nature of Andean topography

diminished Peru's advantage as far as prices were concerned. The cheapest route between Huancavelica and Potosí was by sea, via the ports of Chincha and Arica. The crown contracted with local miners for fixed amounts; by 1600 the usual price it paid was 64 pesos a hundredweight, from which was then deducted the royal fifth. Transport expenses were high, so that cost price at Potosí was estimated at 85 pesos. It was then sold to miners for 102.5 pesos. Supply, however, was abundant, since at the beginning of the seventeenth century Huancavelica on average produced 6,000 to 8,000 hundredweight a year, more than sufficient for the Peruvian industry.

Under the Bourbons, Almadén took the lead over its Peruvian rival, and especially after 1700 experienced an unparalleled increase, with an annual production that at times exceeded 18,000 *quintales*. More efficient management cut costs and permitted the crown to lower the sale price. In two steps, in 1767 and 1776, the Mexican price was cut by half, from 82.5 pesos to 41 pesos. The great Mexican boom in silver production in great measure depended upon this twofold achievement in more than doubling supply at half the former price.

In Peru the same success was not repeated. Huancavelica suffered a decline in the first decades of the century, which, though interrupted by a revival during the 1760s, became permanent following 1779, when Areche terminated the old contract system. Costs remained high, and the crown could reduce the sale price only to 79 pesos in 1779 and 71 pesos in 1787, a rate far above that charged in Mexico. Huancavelica's inadequate supply of 2,000 *quintales* a year had to be complemented by shipments from Almadén. After the creation of the Buenos Aires viceroyalty in 1776, Potosí received most of its mercury from Europe. During the years 1786–96, the crown obtained more than 6,000 hundredweight a year from Idria, a sign of the strain caused by Mexico's soaring production and Huancavelica's debility.

Control of the mints provided the crown with its third source of mining profit. The most obvious difference between the two viceroyalties lay in the location of their mints. Throughout the colonial period until the wars of independence, New Spain possessed only one mint, situated in Mexico City. In Peru, Viceroy Toledo established a mint at Potosí in 1572, and in consequence the office in Lima dwindled in importance until 1683, when it was refounded on a new basis. In the same year, the crown decreed that all silver, be it private or royal, must enter the mints for coinage. Until then much bullion had been exported in bar.

From their initiation until 1728, all three mints followed much the same system: they all cut 69 reales from each mark of silver and returned 65 to the miner. The official grade or quality was 11 dineros 4 granos, or 930.5 *milésimos*. Most coins of this period, especially those emanating from Potosí, were very crude, resembling stamped pieces of silver rather than true milled coins. Responsibility for this inferior performance can be attributed in part to the Hapsburg expedient of sale of office. In effect, the crown lost control of the operation; all mint officials bought their positions. Moreover, it was silver merchants rather than the mint itself who purchased silver bar and financed the coining costs.

In 1728 the Mexican mint was brought back under direct royal administration. New ordinances introduced a number of reforms. With new machinery the appearance of coins was vastly improved, even if their quality was reduced to 11 dineros or 916.6 *milésimos*. The mint continued to cut 69 reales from a mark, but now only returned 64 reales 2 maravedís to the miner. The official exchange ratio of silver to gold was pegged at 16:1, a level considerably lower than the prevailing European rate of just over 14:1. The construction of a magnificent new building and the creation of a circulating fund to purchase silver upon presentation completed this set of reforms. Henceforth the mint was to yield high profit to the crown.

In Peru these reforms were instituted somewhat later. The Lima mint was put under direct administration in 1748, and its new building completed only in 1761. Similarly, at Potosí, the veritable palace that housed the mint was constructed in the years 1753–71. Presumably it was then that the crown appointed salaried officials. However, the creation of the Banco de San Carlos, responsible for the purchase of silver, eliminated the need for a circulating capital fund. Finally, it may be noted that by the close of the century, the crown had further debased the coinage to 10 dineros 18 granos or 895.8 *milésimos*.

Capital Structure

Whereas colonial texts deal at some length with the problems of labor supply and technology, they rarely comment upon the organization of the industry or its sources of capital and credit. The problems that confront the historian relate to the size and value of the units of production in both the mining and the refining sectors, the degree of vertical integration, and the precise role of the merchant-financiers to whom occasional brief reference is made. Needless to say, in all these areas great changes occurred in the course of two and a half centuries.

Potosí especially remains an enigma. Almost nothing is known about the capital structure behind the massive exploitation of the *cerro rico*. By 1585 no fewer than 612 mines and shafts honeycombed the peak's many lodes. Capoche lists about 500 registered mine owners, at the time none of whom employed more than 50 of the 1,369 mita Indians allocated for work within the peak. This system of multiple claims and small individual shafts clearly threw the industry into the hands of *azogueros,* the owners of the refining mills. It was the guild of *azogueros* that dominated the industry and dealt in its name with the crown. Behind them stood a third group, twelve in number, the silver merchants, who bought silver bar and introduced it into the mint. Possibly, as elsewhere, they also advanced cash on credit to the refiners.

For the moment no further evidence is available concerning Potosí. Any number of questions present themselves. As the *cerro rico* declined, did the mines consolidate into large enterprises? Did the *azogueros* take over the peak and establish integrated firms? Or did the miners grow steadily more impoverished and more dependent on the refiners? By the middle of the eighteenth century, much of the peak seems to have been abandoned to Indian workers, the famous *capchas,* since by 1774, according to Viceroy Amat, they accounted for half of Potosí's production. The other important eighteenth-century development was the creation of the Banco de San Carlos in 1751. This institution bought bar for cash and hence eliminated the profits of the silver merchants; it also financed the purchase of mining supplies.

For the sixteenth century the picture in New Spain is equally dim. In Zacatecas, a process of concentration was at work. By the middle seventeenth century, the earlier multiplicity of claims was succeeded by a group of large enterprises. One miner united four shafts to form one great mine. Also of consequence was the growing reliance upon the silver merchants of Mexico City. Acting through local intermediaries, these finance houses sent cash and supplies to the northern camp in return for bar, which they had minted. During the next century both of these tendencies reached their culmination.

For the Bourbon epoch, the emphasis is on the role of mercantile capital and the tendency for single enterprises to control the exploitation of an entire lode or camp. By then there were silver banks and a handful of great mines with a capital of more than a million pesos each. The structure was complex and varied from town to town. In the smaller camps, such as Sombrerete or Bolaños, one great vertically integrated enterprise dominated the industry. In Guanajuato or Catorce, by contrast, the two sectors of the industry remained distinct. The effect of the Bourbon reforms was to drive mercantile capital into direct investment in mining ventures.

Contemporaries were aware of the great differences between the industries of Peru and New Spain. Cañete lamented that there were no miners in Peru who possessed the capital resources of their Mexican counterparts. It was for this reason that the local mines were so small; their owners did not command sufficient means to exploit even the 200 yards of lode to which they were legally entitled. Certainly, few references to a mining aristocracy such as developed in Mexico appear in the standard descriptions of Peru.

Production

There are three official sources from which the curve of American silver production can be reconstructed: the royal fifth or tenth; mintage records; and registered silver shipments to Spain.

The traditional view of colonial silver mining during the Hapsburg era has been largely determined by the impressive series of tables and graphs about transatlantic commerce compiled by Earl J. Hamilton and Pierre Chaunu. Hamilton demonstrated that the level of bullion imports registered at Seville sharply increased after the 1550s to reach an early

Graph II   Estimated Total Peruvian and Potosí Silver Production, 1560–1800 (millions of pesos)

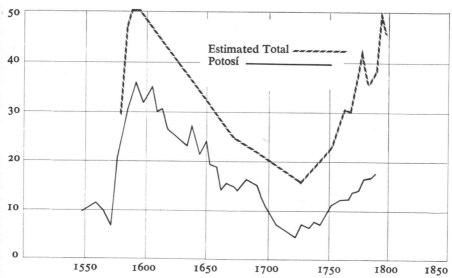

peak by the 1590s. The period of maximum production spanning the years from 1580 to 1630 was followed by a severe depression, to the point where, by the 1650s, imports fell to the level of a century before. The curve of Atlantic shipping and trade drawn by Chaunu largely coincided with this cycle of high boom and sharp depression.

Recently, however, John Lynch has criticized the entire notion of a crisis that affected the peninsula and colonies alike. He argues that "Spain's recession was America's growth." The failure in transatlantic commerce did not necessarily entail an internal depression; instead, it may well have stimulated local industry and trade between colonies. A greater proportion of royal revenue was spent in the colonies. Then again, Peter Bakewell, in his key study on Zacatecas, showed that the camp reached its peak in the 1620s. The subsequent crisis was severe—production fell by half—but in no sense was as catastrophic as Hamilton's import figures suggested.

The key to this controversy can be found in the curve of mercury supply. As we have demonstrated above, a straightforward ratio existed between mercury consumption and silver production, a ratio that on average ranged between 100 and 125 marks of silver for every *quintal* or hundredweight of mercury. Since nearly all the mercury produced by Almadén and Huancavelica went to refine silver in America, a simple calculation will yield estimates of minimum silver output. The maximum, of course, depended upon the percentage of ore that was smelted, a proportion that could vary from 13 to 30 percent. The chief value of this exercise is that it offers the one reliable check upon the veracity of the fiscal data. All the remaining figures—the quintos, the mint records, the registered shipments—were collected for taxation purposes. Mercury, by contrast, was an industrial supply. Naturally some was lost in transit; a small part was employed for other purposes; but used with caution, the statistics of mercury production and export throw new light upon an old problem.

Here then we encounter our first theme of discussion. What were the true proportions of the seventeenth-century crisis? Did Peru and Mexico vary greatly? How extensive was the first boom? What were the causes for this cycle of boom and depression? Naturally our conclusions are tentative; they are offered as hypotheses to explain the available data. Our innovation consists largely in the comparisons drawn between Peru and Mexico and the correlation of mercury consumption with silver production.

The first significant spurt in silver imports recorded by Hamilton occurred during the 1550s. It sprang from the recent discoveries of Potosí and Zacatecas and the invention in New Spain of the amalgamation process. The second jump forward took place after 1580, following the introduction into Potosí of amalgamation and the construction of refining mills. During the subsequent boom in bullion exports, Peru accounted for 65 percent of all American silver shipped to Seville. During this last quarter of the sixteenth century, the Andean industry consumed about 70 percent of all mercury produced (see graph III).

The engines of this first silver boom were the great mines of Huancavelica and Potosí, "the two poles which maintain these Kingdoms and Spain." Its author was don Francisco de Toledo. This viceroy stamped an impress upon the Andean industry that was not erased until the wars of independence. He sponsored the amalgamation experiments at Potosí. He opened up Huancavelica and set up the first contracts. He organized vast mita contingents for both these mines. He established the mint at Potosí. The results of this structural reorganization were impressive and immediate. Production at Potosí, in the doldrums in 1570, soared to unprecedented heights, and during the ensuing quarter century the *cerro rico* accounted for at least 70 percent of all Peruvian silver production, or, to put the case in wider perspective, about half of all American silver. The Toledan achievement depended upon a plentiful supply of mercury and a massive input of state-recruited labor. Its advantage—and danger—lay in the extreme physical concentration that permitted economies of scale and easy access to capital. For a brief moment Potosí acted as the magnet for the entire Atlantic economy.

The exceptional quality of the Toledan system is best assessed from the standpoint of New Spain. There, the mining industry expanded at a slower pace. It depended upon Almadén for its mercury. Its work force, by 1598 already dominated by free wage earners, was sufficient but not ample. The mines were scattered through vast distances from Pachuca to Sonora. The leading camp, Zacatecas, at most accounted for 40 percent of all production. These characteristics of geographical dispersion, free labor, and dependence upon Almadén prevented the Mexican industry from any rapid emulation of Potosí. If Zacatecas be taken as a guide, then during the 1590s New Spain's production did not exceed 4 million pesos, compared to the 10 million pesos of all Peru and the 7 million of the *cerro rico*.

However, in the three decades that followed, from 1605 to 1635, New Spain's industry experienced a steady expansion, whereas Potosí declined. A series of contrasts explain the difference. Huancavelica suf-

A. Mercury imports into New Spain

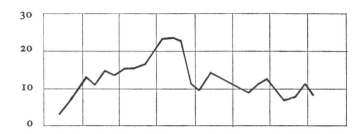

B. Peruvian Consumption

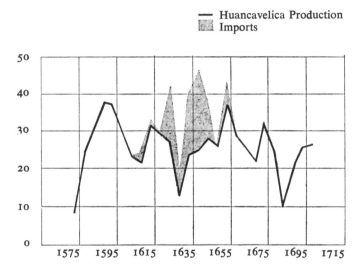

Graph III   Mercury Consumption: New Spain and Peru, 1560–1700 (five-year totals in thousands of quintales)

fered a series of technical difficulties that cut back its output, whereas Almadén, heavily assisted by Idria, shipped increasing quantities of mercury across the Atlantic. In Peru, the number of Indians recruited by the mita rapidly fell, so that by midcentury only half the original number appeared for service. In New Spain, the increase in free wage earners more than offset the disappearance of the repartimiento laborers. Finally, the very rapidity with which the *cerro rico* had been exploited soon led to the exhaustion of its high-grade ores, whereas in New Spain the rich middle zones of the lodes had barely been tapped.

All the long-term trends thus favored Mexico. Yet in the decades after 1635, it was the northern viceroyalty, and not Peru, that suffered the severest depression. The causes of this paradox were absurdly simple. In response to a passing setback at Huancavelica, the Spanish crown diverted European mercury to Peru (see graph III). After 1630, quite suddenly, mercury shipments to Mexico dropped by a half. Within five years, when all remaining stocks were exhausted, silver production followed suit. Moreover, although this preferential treatment for Peru did not extend beyond 1645, by then production at Almadén, following the termination of the Fugger lease, fell from 4,000 hundredweight to just over 2,000 hundredweight, a level insufficient to satisfy Mexican demand (see graph I). By the 1680s, the miners of Zacatecas smelted up to half their ore. Thus we can distinguish short- and long-term causes at work in the Mexican depression. The royal decision to divert mercury shipments to Peru, taken presumably since that viceroyalty paid the quinto whereas Mexico only paid the *diezmo,* provoked an immediate crisis. But it was the failure at Almadén that forbade any permanent recovery until the next century. Then in the years after 1705 both mercury and Mexican silver production slowly moved upwards.

Granted the "artificial" occasion of the Mexican crisis, there is no reason to expect a similar accident at Potosí. There, throughout the seventeenth century, the curve of total production as measured by *quinto* payments drifted slowly downward, from a yearly peak of 7.5 million in the decade 1585–95 to an average 3.2 million in the years 1670–90. Only then did production fall more rapidly, to the point where for the years 1710–30 the quintos registered little more than 1.2 million a year, a mere sixth of the former peak (see graph II). It was an almost natural process, inherent in the slow exhaustion of the ore deposits, the reduction in labor supply attendant upon the wider phenomenon of Andean population decline, and the marked fall in Huancavelica output after 1690. It represented the slow withering of the Toledan system.

The silver mining industry of both viceroyalties thus experienced a severe depression, but whereas in Mexico this crisis lasted from 1635 to 1689, in Peru its sharpest phase only began in 1680. During the desperate years of 1630–45 when the Spanish monarchy lurched from one financial expedient to another, Peru consumed more mercury than ever before. It follows therefore that Hamilton's import figures simply reflect official inefficiency and corruption; they bore little relation to the realities of silver production. Similarly, the downward curve registered by the Potosí quintos during these years was possibly false. Even as late as the decade 1671–80, the treasury at Potosí received two-thirds of all mercury distributed in the viceroyalty. It cannot be argued, therefore, that at this period the decline at the *cerro rico* was appreciably offset by discoveries elsewhere. Whatever the case, a comparison of mercury consumption with the quinto figures and Hamilton's series reveals that the major drop in Peruvian silver production probably did not begin until after 1680, and that an overall peak may well have been obtained during the years 1625–40 (see graph IV). Mexico's loss was Peru's gain.

The same blind search for revenue that had sacrificed Mexican mining drove the crown to order frequent seizures of private silver consignments, compensating the owners with rapidly depreciating copper coin and treasury notes. In consequence colonial merchants sought extralegal outlets for their silver. In Peru, contraband soon reached the epidemic proportions attested to by Acarete du Biscay in his *Voyage up the River de la Plata* (London, 1698). The seventeenth-century crisis was first and foremost a Spanish crisis. The catastrophic decline in silver imports was a Spanish rather than a European phenomenon. Throughout the seventeenth century, the mines of Mexico and Peru continued to

Graph IV   Estimated Spanish-American Bullion Minimum Production and Seville Bullion Imports, 1571–1700 (millions of posos)

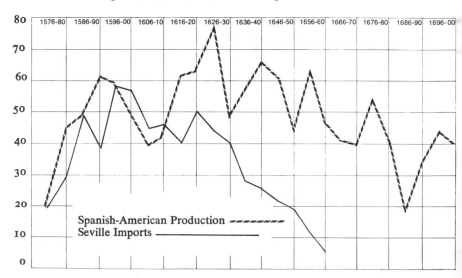

produce great quantities of silver. Possibly more stayed in the New World than before; possibly a greater amount left the hemisphere in the Manila galleon; but without doubt the overwhelming bulk of this bullion went to Europe. Combined American production reached a probable peak in the 1620s, and only slowly declined in subsequent years. The trough occurred not in the 1650s, but in the last twenty years of the century—precisely at the time when the Mexican industry had barely recovered and Peruvian output was falling fast. It was of course this *continuous* American production of silver that permitted Europe to export bullion to Asia without experiencing any marked shortage of specie. Colonial silver not only paid for Spanish American imports, it also financed Europe's trade with Asia.

During the Bourbon epoch, New Spain emerged as the favored possession of the metropolis. Mintage quadrupled from 6 million pesos in 1706 to 24 million in 1798. By then, despite the emergence of Chile and New Granada as silver producers and the revival of the Peruvian industry, Mexico accounted for 67 percent of the American total. The one camp of Guanajuato equaled the mintage of the entire Viceroyalty of Peru, or that of La Plata. This great increase, moreover, despite interruptions caused by war with Great Britain or droughts, followed a consistent upward curve throughout the century, with an especially sharp leap forward in the 1770s. This outstanding achievement rested upon the long-term, in-built tendencies of the period before 1630. In the first place, Almadén's production suddenly surged forward from its 2,000 hundredweight of the years 1680–98 to nearly 5,000 hundredweight and then after 1760 climbed to an unparalleled peak of over 20,000 hundredweight (see graph I). Without this flood of mercury the great increase in silver production would not have been possible. The second prerequisite was the formation of a permanent, probably hereditary, class of mine workers. Behind the abundant labor supply of this period lay the natural increase of the Mexican population at large, which more than doubled in number between 1740 and 1810. The third element is to be found in the continued geographical dispersion of the Mexican industry. New discoveries joined the older centers, with no camp contributing more than a quarter of all production. The tardy pace of the seventeenth-century cycle had of course left vast ore deposits untapped even in the oldest districts.

The abundant or adequate supply of mercury, labor, and ore deposits formed without doubt indispensable prerequisites of the eighteenth-century boom, but it required the union of technology, capital, and government policy with entrepreneurial talent to engineer it. The great shafts and adits of the period represented a great advance in technical expertise and sprang from extensive capital investment. Bourbon fiscal policy, more enlightened than its Hapsburg equivalent, halved the price of mercury and granted individual tax exemptions for renovations of high risk or cost. Finally, the sheer skill and enterprise of such men as José de la Borda and the Count of Regla should not be overlooked: they acted as the pacemakers of the industry. The Mexican boom, especially after 1770, sprang from as complex a group of elements as the Toledan achievement of the 1570s.

That government policy alone could not revive an industry is demonstrated by the case of Peru. Whereas by 1800 Mexico minted nearly five times as much silver as in 1632, the combined viceroyalties of Peru and Buenos Aires did not regain their 1600 level of 10 million pesos until the 1790s. This contrast began during the later seventeenth century. By the 1690s, each colony produced about 5 million pesos, but by the 1720s, Mexican mintage rose to nearly 8 million, whereas that of Peru fell still further to an average 3 million.

Peru's slow recovery took its rise from a modest revival of the Toledan system together with the development of a relatively new industry. The two old centers, Potosí and Huancavelica, after a parallel depression in the years 1680–1724, both picked up after 1730. Huancavelica augmented production from 2,500 hundredweight around 1710 to an average 6,000 during the 1760s, then collapsed after 1780, never again to yield more than 4,000 hundredweight (see graph I). Thus, the Andean viceroyalties were denied that plentiful supply of mercury that formed the natural prerequisite for any great expansion in silver production. Almadén and Idria were called upon to fill the deficit, but by this time New Spain enjoyed priority. Then again, it appears likely that the Andean population did not experience a natural increase equal to that of Mexico. Moreover, Potosí, and, to a much lesser extent, Huancavelica, still continued to rely upon the dwindling and inefficient mita for cheap labor. Other camps hired free wage earners, a class about whom, however, little information is available.

The third prerequisite, the discovery of abundant ore deposits, appears to have been satisfied. By 1774, Potosí accounted for only about 40 percent of the total production of 6.5 million. The former concentration had been replaced by a Mexican pattern of geographical dispersion. Cerro de Pasco averaged about 2 million pesos at this time. By the 1790s, the viceroyalty of Peru minted 6 million pesos compared to the

4.5 million of the region, later to be called Bolivia, which under the Hapsburgs had been the chief center of Andean mining. Of that amount Potosí accounted for 3.5 million, although about a third derived from mines situated in its district rather than from the *cerro rico* itself.

Granted the paucity of data, little can be said concerning the role of technology, capital investment, or entrepreneurial talent in eighteenth-century Peru. Cañete believed that the viceroyalty trailed behind its Mexican rival in nearly all these aspects of the industry. Royal policy

TABLE I. Estimated Minimum Spanish American Bullion Production, 1571–1700 (millions of pesos of eight reales)

Year	1 Registered bullion imports into Seville	2 Estimated minimum silver production by amalgamation	3 Adjusted total minimum bullion production
1571–75	19.7	17.3	21.6
1576–80	28.5	35.5	44.4
1581–85	48.6	39.2	49.0
1586–90	39.4	49.2	61.5
1591–95	58.2	47.4	59.3
1596–1600	57.0	41.3	51.6
1601–05	44.9	31.6	39.5
1606–10	52.0	34.5	43.1
1611–15	40.6	49.3	61.6
1616–20	49.8	50.5	63.1
1621–25	44.7	62.3	77.9
1626–30	41.3	39.1	48.9
1631–35	28.3	46.3	57.9
1636–40	27.0	51.9	64.8
1641–45	22.8	49.2	61.4
1646–50	19.5	36.8	45.0
1651–55	12.1	49.7	62.1
1656–60	5.6	37.5	46.9
1661–65		32.6	40.8
1666–70		31.9	39.9
1671–75		42.6	53.3
1676–80		33.8	42.3
1681–85		15.2	19.4
1686–90		26.5	33.1
1691–95		34.5	43.1
1696–1700		31.9	39.9

was most successfully embodied in a series of measures to cut costs: the tax reduction of the fifth to a tenth in 1736; the lowering of the mercury price to 71 pesos in 1784; the creation of the Banco de San Carlos to hasten the exchange of silver bar for specie; and finally the construction of a major adit at Potosí. Whatever the precise weight we ascribe to the various elements, it is clear that crown policy alone could not promote a major boom. Part of the problem lay in the very survival of the Toledan system, with its concentration upon Potosí and Huancavelica, and its reliance upon the mita. By then a wearisome anachronism, the mita virtually subsidized the maintenance of production at Potosí. But the chief force behind the eighteenth-century revival lay in the development of new centers staffed by free wage earners. In the long term the Mexican structure of production had proved more successful than the Toledan system, and Peru perforce followed in the wake of its northern counterpart.

Suggested Further Reading

Bakewell, Peter J. "Mining." In *The Cambridge History of Latin America*, Vol. II, edited by Leslie Bethell. Cambridge, 1984.

———. *Silver Mining and Society in Colonial Mexico: Zacatecas, 1546–1700.* Cambridge, 1971.

Brading, D. A. "Mexican Silver-Mining in the Eighteenth Century: The Revival of Zacatecas." *Hispanic American Historical Review* 50:4 (November 1970).

———. *Miners and Merchants in Bourbon Mexico, 1763–1810.* Cambridge, 1971.

Fisher, J. R. *Silver Mines and Silver Miners in Colonial Peru, 1776–1824.* Liverpool, 1977.

Garner, Richard L. "Silver Production and Entrepreneurial Structure in 18th-Century Mexico." *Jahrbuch für Geschichte von Staat, Wirtschaft und Gesellschaft Lateinamerikas* 17 (1980).

9 ☀

Social Climbers: Changing Patterns of Mobility among the Indians of Colonial Peru

KAREN SPALDING

The conquest of the Indian empires and their absorption into the Spanish colonial regime affected every aspect of the native cultures. When the Spanish incorporated Andean society into their empire, the patterns of social rank and stratification among the Indians were extensively reshuffled. Most analyses of this problem have concentrated upon the replacement of the Inca elite by the Spanish conquerors and the mechanisms governing the absorption of the native population into Spanish society. These analyses define social mobility in terms of the factors that permitted Indians to enter Spanish society or, conversely, prevented them from doing so.

Such a definition of social mobility implicitly assumes agreement by all members of colonial society that joining Spanish society meant gaining social rank and status in addition to power. This assumption can be questioned, for Indian society had its own criteria for assigning rank and status among its members, and despite the physical fact of conquest, these criteria were not immediately superseded by those of Spanish society. Throughout a large part of the colonial period, Indian society remained distinct from that of the Spaniards. An Indian ambitious for greater social position who had adopted the attitudes of Spanish society would evaluate his social rank and the avenues for raising it very differently from another Indian, equally ambitious, whose attitudes conformed to the tradition of Andean society.

For the Indian who adopted the attitudes of Spanish society, social mobility would be defined from the point of view of that society. Spanish laws defined an Indian in quasi-racial terms, as an individual born of

Published originally in the *Hispanic American Historical Review,* 50:4 (November 1970).

Indian parents. People assigned to this category made up a separate estate in colonial Peru, protected and exploited under laws and regulations different from those determining the rights and obligations of other groups.

From this point of view, the Indians ranked at the bottom of the social hierarchy in colonial Peru. Except for those Indians to whom Spanish law granted noble rank as descendants of the Indian elite, members of Indian society were burdened with a variety of restrictive regulations and heavy obligations. Legally the Indian was defined as a "miserable," which made him not only a ward of the crown, but also a minor, who could not enter into a binding legal contract without the approval of the Spanish authorities, the *corregidor de indios* or *protector de indios*. Frequently Indians were not admitted to full participation in the sacraments of the Catholic religion, and there were regulations in some cases holding that their testimony in court was worth only a portion of that offered by Spaniards. Economically they bore the major part of the labor load necessary to sustain the Spanish state and society, as well as contributing tribute payments to the crown in recognition of their vassalage. The attitudes of other members of Spanish society toward the Indians reflected their low status as the peasantry of the colonial regime, for they were generally regarded as inferior beings, fit only for the servile tasks of the society.

Despite such disabilities, Indians who entered Spanish society did not always occupy its bottom levels. Of course, those who became peons on haciendas made up the lowest stratum of viceregal society, but many Indians joined the urban population. By 1614, the Indian population of Lima, most of it residing in the native section of El Cercado outside the city walls, numbered 1,978 persons, many of whom practiced a trade or were apprenticed to someone who did. The salary received by an Indian artisan was essentially the same as that received by a Spaniard of equivalent rank, and the Indians joined together to form their own cofradías ("lay brotherhoods") and later their own guilds.

These individuals remained legally Indian, but the first available records of their attitudes and personal belongings reveal that, by the latter part of the seventeenth century at least, they had taken on many attitudes and practices of Spanish culture. They and their women wore European rather than Indian style clothing. They participated fully in the European money economy, tending to invest their earnings in urban property, stores or houses, which were then rented out for an income, rather than in cultivated land. They spent their money on expensive luxury clothing or jewelry, and even invested in the same prestige items as their Spanish contemporaries. By the eighteenth century, they drank tea from silver- and gold-inlaid matés, and a number owned Black slaves.

In sum, their personal appearance and living habits were probably quite similar to those of their Spanish counterparts of equivalent wealth and profession. By the latter part of the colonial period, many of these Indians were more than likely indistinguishable from their Spanish or mestizo associates, for the continued mixture of conqueror and conquered had made skin color and other physical features very uncertain indicators of legal race. Spanish administrators complained that if an Indian cut his hair, spoke Spanish, and donned Spanish clothing, he could not be distinguished as Indian.

A special group in preconquest Indian society were the kurakas, or ethnic chieftains, who ranged from the leaders of substantial states down to the heads of small kin groups. The social roles and status of these chieftains are still imperfectly understood, as is the structure of the Inca elite that controlled the Andean area before the arrival of the Spaniards. Recent work is only beginning to dissociate native patterns of leadership and command from the overlay of assumptions made by Spanish observers, who imposed upon the Indian ethnic leaders their own concepts of European nobility.

For the purposes of this discussion, however, these problems can be disregarded, for from the standpoint of Spanish society, the Indian nobility consisted of descendants from the Inca elite who had been granted the privileges of European nobility by Spanish law or the kurakas, whom the Spanish conquerors accepted as rulers of their people. The noble rank of these persons freed them from the disabilities of the Indian commoner and gave them legal access to the highest positions. Many among the Indian colonial nobility enjoyed an economic position far above that of many Spaniards through the wealth and lands that they claimed by virtue of their descent from the preconquest elite. There are even cases of Spaniards willing to exchange their social standing for the possessions of an Indian noble.

Despite such variations of wealth and legal rank, however, an individual who was known to be Indian was generally regarded as socially inferior to his Spanish counterpart. This discrimination increased from the seventeenth century and was applied at all levels. In the eighteenth century, Jorge Juan and Antonio de Ulloa complained that the sons of Indian nobles were treated with disdain by Spanish and even mestizo children; and the Spanish American aristocracy steadfastly refused to admit members of the Indian nobility to certain professions regarded as the perquisites of Spanish descendants. Intermarriage between Indian and Spaniard also declined throughout the colonial period. By the mid-seventeenth century it was held that "few honorable Spaniards marry Indians or Negroes."

Thus the hierarchy that emerged in colonial Peru was not a single one, with all members of Spanish society superimposed over all members of Indian society. Rather, the Indian and Spanish groups formed two parallel hierarchies. The upper ranks of the Indian hierarchy, especially below the level of the Indian nobility, were extremely thin during the early years after the conquest, but they expanded as time went on. The two hierarchies overlapped, but they did not merge. The Indian hierarchy was substantially below that of the Spaniards, and on all social levels the distinctions between Spaniard and Indian became more rigid as the colonial period advanced. Obviously, a ragged Spanish or mestizo beggar was probably considered by other members of Spanish society to have lower status than a wealthy Indian artisan or noble, no matter what the beggar himself may have felt about his social position. The judgment will be different, however, if we look at two individuals, one known to be an Indian and the other a Spaniard or mestizo, who were identical in economic position, occupation, dress, education, and other characteristics. In such a case we can say that if one was known to be an Indian, he was socially inferior to his Spanish or mestizo counterpart in the eyes of other members of Spanish society.

The social hierarchies just described, however, are not the only framework for examining the problem of social mobility among the Indians of colonial Peru. There is a different point of view, related to another definition of what makes a man an Indian—the view of the Indian himself. In other words, we can examine the problem of social stratification and mobility from the point of view of those who participated in Indian society. For an Indian, "being an Indian" meant not just the place in the colonial social hierarchy assigned to him by Spanish laws and regulations. It meant a way of living, a way of looking at the world and defining one's place in it. Included in this view was a system of social differentiation that only marginally reflected Spanish laws or attitudes.

Undoubtedly the Indian was aware of the subordinate position that he occupied in a society dominated by Spanish laws and regulations. Still, his own system of reference was not determined by the attitudes of Spanish society but by his own. From his point of view, he was not at the bottom of the social hierarchy in the Spanish world; he was outside it altogether. Discussions about the assimilation of the Indians into colonial society occasionally neglect the obvious fact that the Indians had a culture of their own. Despite the tensions and dislocations resulting from the Spanish conquest and the continuing effects of new institutions, laws, and demands created by members of Spanish society, the patterns of Indian culture continued to regulate the conduct of most Indians. The conquest did not replace traditional patterns of assigning social rank and status with Spanish patterns; instead it modified traditional reference points for assigning social position and incorporated new criteria under the impact of Spanish rule.

Analysis of these changes is complicated by our incomplete understanding of Indian social structure before the Spanish conquest. The social organization of Andean society was complex and undoubtedly not the same throughout the area. There is a temptation to regard the extensive Inca territories at the conquest as culturally uniform, a temptation made more attractive by the fact that most of our information regarding Indian society describes social and cultural patterns as practiced, understood, or imposed by the Incas. Yet they had held sway over most of their empire for less than a century before the Spaniards replaced them as overlords. While the Incas undoubtedly shared many more cultural attitudes with the groups they conquered than did the Spaniards, it is highly unlikely that all of the local groups under Inca rule had identical social organizations, or that in less than a century the Incas succeeded in making all the peoples of their empire conform to their own patterns of rank and status.

Despite these differences, however, it is possible to describe a basic pattern for the Peruvian highlands in which the major criterion for the assignment of social status was birth. Spanish society in the sixteenth century also placed much emphasis upon birth in assigning social rank. The system through which the basic resources of the society were distributed was not the same in Andean society as in that of the Europeans, however, and the Indians did not define kinship, wealth, or prestige in the same terms as did their conquerors. The terminology used to describe the social structure of western European societies, therefore, provides little insight into the patterns of internal differentiation that prevailed in Indian society.

Among the most familiar systems of social differentiation in European culture were castes, feudal estates, corporations or corporate groups, and, since the nineteenth century, social classes. Feudal estates, castes, and classes are all generally described as hierarchically arranged groups set apart from other groups in the society. The privileges and duties of estates and castes and their rank in the larger society were defined and supported by specific legal or religious rules. However, membership in one or another class conveyed no special civil or political rights. Classes were more exclusively economic groups, and while—like other forms of social organization—the system of classes tended to function so as to ensure that each individual maintained the social position into which he was born, the criterion for this position was not exclusively birth, but the economic position that was closely tied to birth. For this reason, the boundaries of the class system might be more or less fluid, depending upon the new opportunities that emerged for obtaining wealth and the degree to which the political system insured that these new opportunities were restricted to certain groups.

Provincial Indian society under the Incas consisted of peoples who did not trace their descent from Inca ancestors. These people may be divided into two hierarchically arranged groups differentiated by legal or religious rules or by their access to the goods of the society and their role in it. First, there is a clear distinction between the ethnic chieftain, the kuraka, and the Indian commoners. Second, there is a sharp difference between the members of Indian society who participated in kin groups, whether commoners or elite, and the yanakuna, or specialized retainer group, whose members were divorced from the kin group of their birth and attached to the household of a kuraka. Among a substantial number of peoples, these distinctions existed before their incorporation into the Inca empire, although the boundaries among the three groups were not always as clear and sharp as the Incas later sought to make them. The kurakas and the yanakuna were set apart from the rest of Indian society by their function in that society, to a degree by their access to its wealth, and also by distinct sets of rules and regulations governing their conduct. The Spanish conquerors immediately saw in these two groups the Indian equivalent of the European nobility and the slaves, although investigation has made it clear that while these groups may have had functional counterparts in European society, they were actually quite different.

The kurakas and the yanakuna, however, made up an extremely small proportion of Indian society. Among most members of Indian society—those who were neither kurakas nor yanakuna—there were no hierarchical groupings to which we might assign the terms estate, caste, or class without seriously distorting understanding. Rather, an individual's place in his society was defined by his position in the web of kinship relations that reached from his immediate family unit to the larger lineage group and, further, to all who regarded themselves as the descendants of a mythical ancestor-deity. The size of this larger group varied from region to region. An example is Huarochirí, an area that encompassed the three river valley systems of the Rímac, Lurín, and Mala on the western slopes of the central Andes. All people here defined themselves as the sons of Pariacaca, the local ancestor-deity. A component group within the region regarded itself as descended from one of the seven mythical children of Pariacaca, and the ayllus, the extended kin groups that survived into the colonial period, described themselves as "we who are like a single son." A Spaniard familiar with Indian society pointed out that the structure of the ayllu was not entirely unlike that of lineages in Spain and described it as "a group of people of the same origin, as we might say 'Mendozas' or 'Toledos.'" In the Andes, however, these kin ties, whether real or fictive, extended throughout the entire society, binding together all its members.

An individual claimed his position in society and his share of its goods by virtue of his place in this web of kin relations. The kin group held primary access to land, irrigation rights, and the other resources of the society, distributing these among its members. The kin group was the basis of exchange and the source of labor. An elaborate set of rights and responsibilities insured the individual access to land, goods produced in distant areas by his kin, and the aid of others to help him plant, harvest, construct houses, and perform the other necessary labors of daily existence. The ideal of Andean society was one of self-sufficiency, and insofar as possible, production and exchange were organized through kin ties. This form of organizing economic activity is very different from the market-oriented system of the European world. Similarly the social groups whose position in the society was defined by their access to its goods and resources bear only slight resemblance to the major divisions of European society, whether estates, castes, classes, or functional corporations.

Indian society was not homogeneous; there were great differences of wealth and position. The kin groups were ranked within the larger society on a recognized scale of prestige that determined the order of participation in activities such as land distribution or work parties, and ceremonial functions such as cleaning the irrigation ditches or joining in dances or worship. This scale of prestige was closely related to the amount of society's resources enjoyed by the various ayllus. Thus an ayllu of high prestige held extensive lands and herds, while one of lower rank held less. This scale was also related to the relative age of the kin group within the larger unit. In central Peru, prestige was directly related to age, as the myths of Huarochirí point out in speaking of the ayllu Checa, noting that the Checa were regarded as the youngest offspring of the deity of the province, "and for that reason they were given [by the deity] next to no land and very little clothing." Nor were the kin groups internally homogeneous; their members might range from the wealthy man who was able to provide gifts and food for many people down to the poor man, or "potato eater," who dressed in ragged clothing, sat on the outer fringes of the circle of drinkers at celebrations, and was frequently ignored in the distribution of food and drink.

Since access to goods and to the aid of others was determined by kin ties, the person with an abundance of kin had a greater number of hands available for help in the labor of amassing goods and thus greater opportunities for wealth and power. In fact, wealth in this context might be defined as effective kin ties or the ability to mobilize the assistance of one's kin. The close relationship between effective kin ties and wealth is recognized in language; the Inca word *wakhcha,* meaning "poor," is also translated in sixteenth-century dictionaries as "orphan."

The allocation of wealth, power, and prestige through kin ties suggests that social mobility was limited, since it would be regarded as degrading for a member of a wealthy family to enter into a kinship relation with a person of lower status. In fact, the myths emphasize how exclusive were the upper ranks of Indian society. In one myth the marriage of a poor man to the daughter of a wealthy and powerful individual, a union achieved with supranatural aid, aroused strong protests from the poor man's new in-laws. And the discovery by a female *wak'a,* or deity, that the unknown father of her child was a "potato eater"—also a *wak'a,* for such distinctions existed even among deities—was enough to cause her suicide.

Before the Inca conquest, it was possible for a kin group of low status to gain additional wealth by conquering new lands, which in turn would raise its rank to a position commensurate with its new wealth and power. The Incas, however, prohibited such actions within the territories they conquered, making themselves the arbiter of disputes over land. Since the capture of new lands was an important means for kin groups low in prestige and rank to improve their position, the Incas' prohibition of warfare within their domains probably also meant the elimination of earlier channels of social mobility within Indian society. But either individuals or groups might obtain new resources through the generosity of the state in return for special services such as those rendered by the Indians of the province of Huarochirí, who helped to suppress rebellion within the Incas' realms.

In the case of at least one group in Indian society, the kurakas, the Incas may have sought to intensify the distinctions of rank and status. The position of kuraka may not have become hereditary in all areas before their incorporation into the Inca empire, although in many regions the position appears to have been passed down along kinship lines, at least at the upper levels. The Incas reinforced the social position of the kuraka, while reducing his political autonomy. Although he was supervised by an Inca governor, his special rank and status within the empire were emphasized. The Incas set him apart from the rest of the community by restricting to him certain perquisites of wealth and position—luxury goods such as *qompi* cloth, feathers, gold and silver articles, special stores of prestige foodstuffs, and the services of retainers.

The Spanish conquest introduced new methods of obtaining wealth and power that substantially altered the internal structure of Indian society. The period of the conquest itself offered such opportunities through alliance with the Spaniards, and many who allied themselves early with the conquerors used that connection to improve their social position. Ethnic leaders appropriated a higher rank for themselves than they had held before the conquest or gained additional wealth by claiming title to community lands. Others who had held no positions of leadership before the Spanish conquest rose to become part of the Indian elite.

In the settled colony the social and economic system of the conquerors, together with the reorganization of the Indian community imposed by Spanish law, produced a new set of circumstances that could be used by members of Indian society to gain for themselves a greater proportion of the available goods and resources. The levies imposed by the Spaniards upon the Indians did not weigh equally upon all; some were given an advantage that could be translated into wealth and position. Furthermore, the Spaniards set up new positions of power in the Indian community that the ambitious individual could use to amass more goods than he could have obtained through traditional means. These opportunities permitted some to acquire both wealth and power, and, through the judicious use of these, the prestige commensurate with higher rank. In other words, they introduced new avenues of social mobility.

The establishment of religious and civil government in the Indian communities modeled upon that of Spain and backed by the authority of the Spaniards offered further opportunities to those who sought to increase their power and possessions. In the civil sphere, the Spanish authorities established the cabildo, and in the religious sphere they re-created the hierarchy of lay assistants to the priest that existed in Spain. The pagan religious officials were to be replaced entirely by representatives of Catholicism, just as the Christian religion was to displace the worship of native deities. The kurakas of the larger social units were assimilated into the Spanish administrative system, but their authority was limited by Spanish laws and shared by other Indian officials. The kuraka retained his traditional role as leader and spokesman of his people, but the duties and powers of the central figure in the Indian cabildo, the alcalde, overlapped those of the kuraka in some areas and replaced them in others.

The alcalde supervised the distribution of village lands and the conduct of the villagers together with the kuraka, whose function this had been before the Spanish conquest. All judicial authority over the Indians passed from the kuraka to the alcalde, and the alcalde became the representative of the village in court cases and in village dealings with the provincial authorities, particularly the *corregidor de indios*. The alcalde, together with the kuraka, was responsible for the collection of tribute and in general executed the orders of the corregidor.

The other Indian officials in the cabildo functioned largely as the administrative assistants of the alcalde. The laws provided for one to two *regidores* to aid the alcalde in his administrative duties, and an alguacil mayor, who was the village policeman. These officials, together with the alcalde, were elected yearly by the outgoing cabildo, whose members could not succeed themselves. The only permanent member of the cabildo was the *escribano,* or notary. There were also a number of officials appointed by the incoming cabildo, but these positions brought little power. For the purposes of this discussion, the significant positions are primarily those of the alcaldes and the *regidores*.

In 1575, Viceroy Francisco de Toledo ordered that there be a cabildo established in the capital town of every repartimiento, the old encomiendas converted into administrative divisions within the Indian provinces. In 1618, Philip III modified this decree, specifying that every

Indian village should have an alcalde chosen from its own population, and in villages of eighty houses or more two alcaldes and two *regidores*. In cases brought before the royal audiencia by the Indians, even small villages were usually represented by an alcalde, suggesting that many villages did conform to the rule established in 1618. Of course the most powerful posts—and, judging from tribute records, often the only positions whose occupants were relieved from tribute and labor obligations— were those in the capital village of the repartimiento.

Indian religious officialdom was not given final form until the early years of the seventeenth century. In the years after the conquest, priests gathered around them large numbers of Indian assistants charged with the care of the church and the enforcement of religious regulations and priestly dictates. In the sixteenth century one corregidor, upon assuming his position, complained that the priests of his area had appointed sixty-three alguaciles to aid them. By the early seventeenth century, however, the number of these Indian assistants to the priest was strictly limited. In each village of one hundred or more Indian parishioners, there were to be one sacristan in charge of caring for the church, two or three *cantores* to lead the choir and the responses, and a *fiscal* or alguacil to supervise attendance at mass. In addition each administrative division was to be provided with a school. This regulation was later extended by the church until each parish was required to maintain a school staffed by an Indian schoolmaster who spoke and read Spanish. It is clear that rural schools did exist in many areas, although it is not possible to judge their quality or the consistency with which they were maintained. Tribute records stipulated the exemption of specific individuals from personal service because of their position as schoolmasters, and inspections of village parishes by officials sent out from the archbishopric of Lima report the presence of schools in many parishes and prescribe fines for priests in whose parishes schools were not functioning.

Participation in this new power group offered several rewards to the Indian who chose to ally himself with the provincial representatives of Spanish authority—the priest and the *corregidor de indios*. A real but minor advantage was the compensation offered. Only the Indian schoolmaster actually received a salary, but in return for their services the others obtained exemptions from the mita or from both the labor draft and tribute payments. Far more important than the legal reward, however, was the power that derived from the position of these officials as representatives of Spanish authority. Individuals who joined this group wielded power over their fellows by virtue of the force represented by the Spanish state, a source of authority completely outside the traditional sanctions and customs that regulated power in Indian society. As long as the Spanish officials did not force their Indian representatives to observe the sanctions of Indian society, those representatives could ignore or flout traditional sanctions with impunity. Furthermore, since those sanctions also regulated access to wealth, the Indians who enjoyed a source of power outside the traditional structure of Indian society could use it to obtain a greater share of their own society's resources.

There is clear evidence, indeed, that the Indian officials did use their power to amass wealth for themselves in defiance of the rights and responsibilities by which wealth and power were customarily allocated in Indian society. In 1565, the lawyers of the Audiencia of Quito complained that the Indian *cantores* and musicians in many villages were attempting "to shake off their obedience to their leaders." Early in the seventeenth century the mestizo chronicler, Huaman Poma de Ayala, accused the Indians religious and civil officials of robbing the Indians, sending them to the high punas or the lowlands for llamas, maize, and potatoes, or requisitioning cloth for them. He also asserted that they took the young girls of the village—those who had not already been claimed by the priest—and made them their concubines.[1]

Within the structure of Indian society these activities were not mere random criminal acts. Traditionally the right to extra labor services and goods, particularly cloth, as well as the possession of more than one woman, were privileges limited to those of high status. Under the Incas, they were reserved in most cases for the elite and were distributed according to status. When Huaman Poma de Ayala accused the Indian officials of robbery, he was really saying that they were using the threat of force derived from their alliance with the conquerors to usurp for themselves goods appropriate to a status and rank far above their legitimate position in traditional Indian society. When he wailed that the world had been turned upside down, his complaint was a literal description of what he saw happening to the social hierarchy. New ways to acquire power and wealth were indeed undermining the traditional system of rank and status determined by birth.

Yet the goods obtained by the members of the new power group by virtue of their association with the Spanish authorities did not in themselves bring the prestige and rank that accompanied wealth in traditional Indian society, for such wealth had been obtained in defiance of that so-

1   Huaman Poma de Ayala, *Nueva corónica y buen gobierno* (Paris, 1936), pp. 574–75, 587, 662–63, 797–98.

ciety's patterns. Doubtless some were unconcerned by their position as usurpers of power and wealth that did not belong to them according to Indian traditions. Others, however, seem to have sought to legitimize their new positions. In addition to their roles as representatives of Spanish authority, they were active participants in and leaders of the native religious cults, maintained despite the active persecution of Spanish authorities. In 1611, a priest investigating the persistence of native religion reported that the priests of the ceremonies were frequently Indians "who know how to read and write, and have been raised among Spaniards and priests; and others are cantores of the churches and maestros de capilla. . . ." A century later, the alcalde of an Indian village confessed to serving as a priest of the native religious observances. He also implicated the *fiscal* of the church, legally entrusted with policing the parish against religious lapses. In a neighboring village, the feast of the local pagan deity was led by the *fiscal,* the sacristan, and the *cantor* of the church.

At the beginning of the seventeenth century, the Spaniards discovered the dual roles played by the Indian village officials and fought the practice without success. They found it hard to understand this behavior, for an Indian official discovered in such activities not only lost his privileged position and source of power, but was frequently penalized heavily and even exiled from his village. Yet the role of priest of the *wak'as* was one carrying prestige and power in traditional Indian society, and access to it was usually determined by birth. If we assume that the members of the Indian power group were in fact seeking higher rank and status within their own society by using the power available through alliance with the Spanish officials, their participation in the native religious ceremonies becomes perfectly comprehensible. By taking part in activities that were the mark of higher status within Indian society, they might gain the recognition and prestige commensurate with their effective wealth and power. In this way they would climb to a higher rung on the social ladder of ranked statuses within native society.

As a result of the new avenues to power and wealth opened by the economic system and by the legal regulations of the dominant Spanish group, the hierarchy of status and prestige within Indian society seems to have been reordered during the latter part of the sixteenth and early seventeenth centuries. But the social hierarchy was not overturned; there was a high degree of continuity between the old elite and the new. Many of the kurakas maintained or even increased the power, wealth, and prestige that they had enjoyed before the Spanish conquest. Furthermore, they had a unique opportunity to influence the choice of the new elite, for long-standing traditions of deference to the kuraka did not end with the Spanish conquest, and he also maintained close contacts with the local Spanish authorities. Thus while the kuraka himself was prohibited by Spanish law from taking part in Indian village government, his influence remained strong, and members of his family often joined the village officialdom. Huaman Poma cites one village in which the kuraka established his brother as mayordomo of the church. In another village the alcalde was "son and grandson of principales," and his son in turn became *cantor* of the church.

In addition to those who had traditionally held positions of high status in Indian society, however, the new Indian elite was also composed of persons who would have occupied a much lower rank in preconquest society, as well as members of entirely new privileged groups defined by their exemption from the levies imposed by the Spanish authorities. An individual who did not have to serve a turn of the mita or pay tribute levies was in a position to gain more by offering his goods and labor on the Spanish market than the Indian who had to fulfill such obligations, and this advantage could be increased by allying with the Spanish provincial authorities. Some individuals were exempt from levies on the basis of their part-Spanish parentage. The mestizo was freed of both labor levies and tribute payments, and while many of these individuals became part of Spanish society, others remained in the Indian communities. By the eighteenth century at least, the racial classifications were divided still further, and a legal status assigned the mixture of Indian and mestizo—the cholo. He was freed of the mita draft, although liable for tribute.

The law also granted special status to persons who practiced a trade. The Toledan ordinances provided exemptions from mita services for a blacksmith, shoemaker, tailor, and dyer in each Indian parish, and the decree of Charles II, incorporated in the *Recopilación,* freed all Indian artisans from labor levies. Throughout the seventeenth century, these provisions were enforced to some degree when the individual practiced his trade full-time, although most such craftsmen found better opportunities in the Spanish urban centers and migrated there. Nonetheless, individuals who practiced a trade without such legal exemptions, even if part-time and supplementary to their primary farming activities, enjoyed a potential source of additional income through their participation in the Spanish market system. Finally, the *forastero,* or migrant to the community from elsewhere, was exempted from labor services and granted reduced tribute payments. Such exemptions may well have stimulated migration despite the loss of land that accompanied emigration. However, they were not usually sufficient to permit the outsider to achieve wealth and power within his adopted community unless he also had other advantages.

When Spanish laws exempted some individuals from the levies imposed upon the rest of Indian society, these laws were not in themselves sufficient to raise these people to a higher status in that society. But they do seem to have made it easier for an ambitious individual who enjoyed such an exemption to join the new Indian power group. The proportion of these individuals among the new Indian elite is much greater than their proportion in the Indian population as a whole. Mestizos or cholos frequently appear among those holding civil or religious positions in the Indian villages, as do individuals who practiced a trade. Furthermore, members of these same groups, particularly Indian artisans, appear with relative frequency among the priests of the native religion during the seventeenth century. It appears, then, that the economic and administrative structure introduced by the Spaniards offered the Indians opportunities to obtain wealth and power outside traditional kin ties. These new opportunities, by introducing alternative means to rank and position, stimulated some realignment of the social hierarchy in the sixteenth and early seventeenth century.

These new avenues of social mobility did not remain open throughout the colonial period. From the latter part of the seventeenth century they began to be constricted, and this constriction increased throughout the remainder of the colonial period. The viceregal economy entered into a protracted decline at some time in the seventeenth century. As the stagnation of the economy increased, the Spanish population laid increasing demands upon an Indian population whose resources, in both land and labor, were declining, and the Indian power group proved unable to maintain itself. The privileged members of Indian society—both the kurakas and the members of the new power group that had emerged under colonial rule—found themselves pinched between the demands of their masters and the inability of the Indian community to meet those demands. Their positions, once means of obtaining wealth and power, were gradually converted into devices through which the Spanish authorities absorbed the wealth of the more privileged members of the Indian community. Under these pressures, many of the wealthier members of the Indian community emigrated to the urban areas, and those who were left did their best to avoid serving as village officials. The avenues of social mobility opened in the early part of the colonial period were thus closed, and as pressures upon Indian resources continued to grow, distinctions of status and position within the rural Indian communities were steadily reduced.

This summary of the impact of colonial rule upon one aspect of Indian society is clearly incomplete and tentative. Further study is needed in order to clarify the response of Indian society to the pressures of colonial rule. One major part of that study consists of archival research. Reports on local areas, land disputes, and similar documents from the years immediately following the Spanish conquest frequently contain much information on the actual function of native institutions and relationships presented in other sources only as vague, generalized abstractions.

Still, these materials fail to answer many questions about the nature of Indian society, and in order to evaluate the fragments of native culture patterns that emerge from the colonial records, comparison with the changing patterns of other societies under colonial rule can be an extremely useful technique. Inside the Spanish empire, we can compare the native societies of New Spain with those of Peru, but the Indian cultures of both areas have changed substantially in the course of the past four centuries, and the preconquest period is accessible only through written sources and archaeological evidence. We can also turn to areas where the colonial regimes were established more recently. Africa includes societies that, like those of New Spain and Peru, were complex social units organized into relatively large states. Recent investigators there have been able to question individuals who still remembered the patterns of life before European occupation. Familiarity with the process of culture change in this and similar areas can often suggest profitable lines of questioning and investigation to be applied to the Andean materials. Perhaps more important, they can provide valuable alternatives to interpretations based upon the assumptions and practices of European society.

Suggested Further Reading

Borah, Woodrow W. *Justice by Insurance: The General Indian Court of Colonial Mexico and the Legal Aides of the Half-Real.* Berkeley, 1983.

Lockhart, James, and Ida Altman, eds. *Provinces of Early Mexico: Variants of Spanish American Regional Evolution.* Los Angeles, 1976. Especially chapters 2, 3, 4, 5, and 7.

Rowe, John H. "The Incas under Spanish Colonial Institutions." *Hispanic American Historical Review* 37:2 (May 1957).

Spalding, Karen. *"Kurakas* and Commerce: A Chapter in the Evolution of Andean Society." *Hispanic American Historical Review* 53:4 (November 1973).

—————. *Huarochirí: An Andean Society under Inca and Spanish Rule.* Stanford, 1984.

10 ☼

Trade and Navigation in the
Seventeenth-Century Viceroyalty of Peru

L . A . C L A Y T O N

The movement of many vessels up and down the coasts of the Viceroyalty of Peru in the seventeenth century marked the existence of a lively commercial system within the Spanish empire. In many respects, this maritime economy evolved quite apart and under different influences from the Atlantic world. The nature and dynamics of this trade and navigation within the viceroyalty's domain in this century are the subject of this brief exploration. The primary goal is to outline the major aspects of trade and navigation and describe some meaningful trends. Secondarily, a consideration of the subject seems to reveal the existence of an economy, lively, robust, and expansive, that stands in sharp contrast to the arthritic, decaying state of Spain's general economy in the seventeenth century.

Traditionally, any description or analysis of trade and navigation in the viceroyalty has been hampered by a myopic vision that viewed the movement of treasure galleons between Peru and Panama as the principal activity of the viceroyalty's fleet. These institutional approaches were wedded to an external or imperial concept of colonial history. The flow of treasure between colony and metropolis was considered the only significant activity to study, founded partly upon the large reservoir of readily accessible material, principally royal laws and regulations, and certainly upon the impact that silver from Peru had upon the Old World. Nonetheless, it is important to recognize that Peruvian trade and navigation in the seventeenth century were to a large extent disassoci-

Reprinted by permission of Cambridge University Press and published originally in the *Journal of Latin American Studies*, 7:1 (May 1975). The author wishes to thank the University of Alabama Research Grants committee and the Alabama Consortium for the Development of Higher Education for assistance in the preparation of this article.

ated from the Atlantic connection. Indeed, the Peruvian merchant marine averaged in size about fifty vessels in the seventeenth century, and of these only four or five were employed annually in the treasure voyage from Peru to Panama. Thus, a more balanced interpretation of the viceroyalty's maritime activity in this century might be realized by considering trade and navigation in the old Mar del Sur, or South Sea as the Pacific was known to the colonists, from both the traditional or imperial and the regional or American points of view.

The Atlantic Connection

Activities associated with the cities of Potosí in Upper Peru and Portobelo in Panama have been most intensely studied by those interested in the trade of the colony. The ties that bound these cities certainly formed an integral part of the viceroyalty's maritime economy and offer a good place to begin. Potosí, of course, yielded copious amounts of silver during the colonial period, while Portobelo was the entrepôt where the silver was exchanged for the wares of Europe. Interposed was a network of sea transportation that moved the silver north and returned with the European merchandise for dispersion and sale in the viceroyalty. These ships formed a critical link in the chain of silver that bound Peru to Spain and conversely transmitted Spanish immigrants, officials, laws, and culture to the colony.

The vessels of the Real Armada del Sur were the chief carriers in the Peru-Panama traffic during the seventeenth century. The Armada itself was quite small, never numbering more than two or three galleons in the full-time service of the crown. This nucleus was most often supplemented by a like number of merchant vessels attached temporarily to the crown's service. Thus, when the Armada did sail, most contemporary observers recorded the fleet's strength at between four and six vessels, all usually quite ample and with adequate space to serve the needs of the trade.

The transportation of silver north and the return voyages from Panama were somewhat irregular activities governed by upset timetables in the Atlantic and influenced by foreign intruders, major shipwrecks, bankruptcies, or other unforeseeable circumstances in the Pacific. Once the silver yields from Potosí were ready, they were moved from the sierra to the seaport of Arica in April by mule trains. It required about ten days to embark the silver at Arica and about ten more days for the voyage to Callao, where the fleet remained for about twenty days while the merchants of Lima accomplished their business. The third leg of the trip from Callao to Panama was normally begun in late May and lasted about a month. At Panama the silver was transshipped one last time for the passage to Portobelo, where a fair was celebrated toward the end of July or the beginning of August. The merchandise acquired at the fair in exchange for silver was then brought back across the Isthmus, embarked on the waiting vessels of the Armada, and dispatched south. The return voyage was always longer because of adverse winds and currents and usually lasted about three months, with a layover at Paita in northern Peru to replenish and rest. The fleet was back in Callao by the end of November or the beginning of December, and here the bulk of the merchandise was sold and further distributed within the viceroyalty.

Credit, or *avíos,* extended in these transactions was usually covered by the silver yields of the mines during January, February, and March, usually the best months for the mines. This silver in turn made up the bulk of the treasure that was embarked on the Armada in May and the cycle commenced anew. That, at any rate, was the idealized cycle.

Of the many factors that affected the smooth operations of the cycle an important one was the self-interest of the Lima merchants. A consulado, or merchants' guild, was created in Lima in 1613 and, although these merchants were straddled between the dictates of Sevillan monopolists and crown policy and the often antipathetic desires of the viceroyalty's consumers, they managed a very prosperous existence by constantly seeking their own goals. The crown desired annual sailings of the Atlantic fleets, the famed *carrera,* to ensure a steady flow of silver from Peru to Spain. Nevertheless, the ideal was seldom realized, for between 1600 and 1650 only twenty-nine fleets came to Tierra Firme. The object of the Sevillan monopolists was to restrict the flow of goods through Panama to Peru, create an artificial scarcity within the colony, and thus keep prices at a very profitable level. The merchants of Peru subscribed to this principle, but with some modifications. They would have had the flota, or new world fleet, sail only once every two years to *ensure* scarcity and prevent the possible glut of the market that yearly sailings implied. These conditions prevailed in fact in the first half of the century and were accentuated in the second, for only nineteen fleets reached Panama in that period.

The community at large in Peru desired, as is the wont of the consumer, abundant selections at modest prices. It was much to their advantage to have frequent sailings, preferably annually, with large shipments. Whenever the extremes of the balance were reached, overabundance or extreme scarcity, acute hardships afflicted the parties: commerce would suffer and merchants go bankrupt at one end or the general public would bear the pain at the other. Not only would the commerce of Peru be adversely affected if the market was glutted, but the Spanish merchants at Portobelo, forced to sell at extremely low prices, often faced penury and bankruptcy upon returning to Spain. On the other hand, if the supply was extremely scarce, as in 1626 because of Dutch activity in the Pacific that had paralyzed commerce in the previous two years, the merchants let greed carry the day. Accusing them of virtual extortion that same year, the Lima cabildo, backed by popular indignation, jailed some merchants for not selling according to an established list price. Additionally, all parties could be upset by a natural disaster such as a shipwreck. In 1632, *Nuestra Señora del Rosario,* a large merchantman bound for Callao with goods and slaves from the Portobelo fair, foundered off Ancón, a bay some miles north of Callao. Prices skyrocketed and small merchants went bankrupt as a result of this incident.

In spite of the hazards of the trade, the merchants prospered, even though the tempo of commerce between Peru and Panama slackened in the middle and latter half of the century. The inability of the Spaniards to organize and dispatch a fleet more than once every two or three years during the century (and, as noted, this trend was accentuated in the second half) coincided with the needs of the Peruvian merchants and authorities, allowing them to prosper. Additionally, and most important, the energies of the viceroyalty's merchants were reoriented in the seventeenth century as trade and commerce with Spain fell off. Their attentions shifted from the Atlantic to the Pacific.

South Sea Trade

Of all the different voyages made by Peruvian vessels in the South Sea, perhaps none was so profitable, so long, or so demanding as the one between New Spain–Central America and South America in the seventeenth century. During this century, as in the previous one, the principal lure into the trade for Peruvians was supplied by the luxuries of the Orient, while the abundance of silver within the colony made purchases easy, for bullion was as esteemed by the East as by the West.[1] From the

1   Woodrow Borah, *Early Colonial Trade and Navigation Between Mexico and Peru* (Berkeley, 1954) remains the standard account of this trade; see also William L. Schurz, *The Manila Galleon* (New York, 1939) for the transpacific trade.

1570s onward, the Manila galleons that sailed annually across the Pacific to Acapulco brought precious goods. Chinese damasks, satins, silks, chinaware, porcelain, perfumes, and jewelry, that were transshipped in large quantities to Peru. The seemingly inexhaustible resources of the Potosí mine, which reached its peak output at the end of the sixteenth century, stimulated the trade so vigorously that the crown forbade it in the early 1590s to prevent the continued leakage of silver to the Orient.

The early development and diversification of the Mexican economy constituted another motor of the Peru-Mexico trade. Many goods manufactured in New Spain, among them textiles, clothing, furniture, jewelry, toilet and household goods, leather goods, and books, were imported by the Peruvians in the sixteenth and seventeenth centuries. Not only Peruvian silver, but wines, cacao, mercury, and other commodities flowed northward in return as Peru itself developed in the seventeenth century.

The trade between the colonies was extremely prosperous and by the early 1590s amounted perhaps to two or even three million pesos a year. A combination of circumstances, among them the crown's desire to stop the flow of silver east and the jealousy of Spanish merchants who grew increasingly irate at the erosion of their monopoly, eventually led to the official prohibition in 1593 of the reexport of Chinese goods from New Spain to Peru. Nonetheless, the trade continued to expand illegally so that by 1602, the cabildo of Mexico City estimated the value at between three and five million pesos, most of which was going to the Orient since Mexican manufactures came to no more than a tenth of the trade by value, because of the development of native Peruvian industry. The first third of the seventeenth century was marked by fruitless endeavors on the part of the crown to constrict the trade further, both from New Spain to Manila and New Spain to Peru, in continuing efforts to redirect the flow of Peruvian silver east. The number of sailings per year was reduced, the size of the vessels was limited, specie was banned from passing between Peru and New Spain, penalties were increased, and traffic between the colonies finally completely forbidden in 1634. The laws tended to stimulate the enlargement of existing channels of contraband trade and to further the creation of new ones. One indicator of the vigor of this, as well as legitimate, trade was the size and development of the Peruvian merchant marine during the seventeenth century.

Between thirty-five and forty vessels, *navíos* ("ships") and *barcos* ("barks") principally, were in service in 1590. A little more than a century later, at least seventy-two vessels were known to be in service. It is thus probable that between 1590 and 1690 the tonnage of the viceroyalty's merchant marine doubled. Furthermore, in the last decade of the century an average of at least four and possibly more vessels were built in the viceroyalty annually, a certain indicator of buoyant industry. Documentation of ship traffic passing through major ports is uneven, but it is still probable that as early as 1615 more than forty and perhaps fifty vessels were in service, as well as a like number in the early 1660s. The services rendered by this fleet to the Peruvian economy were diverse and often instrumental in the development and support of coastal commerce and key industries.

Some major crops grown in the viceroyalty in the seventeenth century were wheat, sugar, olives, grapes, and cacao. Industrially, a wide assortment of textiles were manufactured in quantity, and the arts and crafts industries of centers of population such as Lima and Quito produced a range of society's necessities and luxuries. Of all the Spanish crops introduced into Peru perhaps none was more important than wheat. Considered essential for the diet of any Spaniard, it is not surprising that the grain was brought to Peru soon after the conquest; by 1550 thousands of fanegas (about a bushel) were being harvested in Peru. The grain was initially planted all along the coast, although by the seventeenth century the major wheat-producing centers were located slightly inland or in higher zones. Grown in distant northern valleys such as the Chicama and in far southern areas in the vicinity of Arequipa, the wheat was distributed along the coasts of the viceroyalty by the merchant fleet.

Wine and olive oil formed indispensable components of the Spanish diet as well. Grapevines were introduced early into the colony and by mid-sixteenth century thousands of gallons of wine were being consumed annually in Lima alone. Spain, as might be expected, constantly opposed the manufacture of wine in Peru, and legislation to restrict it dates from as early as 1569. Philip II decreed that no new vines be planted nor those in existence replaced, while in 1602 Philip III ordered that tributary (mita) Indians not be used in the vineyards. Furthermore, as early as 1614, Peruvian wines were forbidden from entering Panama or Guatemala because of the strong competition they offered to Spanish wine. Nonetheless, the wine growers of Peru prospered, and the transportation of this valuable commodity both within the viceroyalty and northward to Central America and Mexico constituted a prime activity of the fleet. Wine formed such an important article of trade between Peru and Central America that repeated supplications to drop the prohibitions sometimes met with success, such as in 1685 when the ban on the trade was lifted for a period of three years. Even the church participated in the violation of the restrictive laws on production and distribution of wine, for the very pragmatic reason that wine was needed to celebrate masses (as well as being consumed prodigiously by the good friars) and the shipments from Spain, irregular and small, simply could not meet the demands of the church. The wines of Peru were produced in valleys to the south of Lima, Moquegua and Jayanca, and especially in the vicinity of Pisco, as well as farther inland. The province of Ayacucho, for example, produced 5,000 *arrobas* (an *arroba* was about twenty-five pounds) of grapes annually in the seventeenth century. The olive tree was introduced early after the conquest and soon thereafter restricted by the monopolists of Spain. However, the olive oil industry, like the wine and grain one, was eventually established based on the demands of a growing Spanish and mixed population whose needs could not be satisfied by the trickle through Panama.

The sugar industry also appears early in the history of the viceroyalty. Sugar plantings (canes) were most likely transported from Mexico to Peru on the heels of the conquest, for by 1549 four mills (*trapiches*) were already in operation. The sweet tooth of Limeños was such nevertheless that Peru had to depend heavily on Mexico in the sixteenth century to satisfy its craving. Restrictions soon appeared on the growth of the cane. However, it was not so much because it represented a danger to the Spanish industry as because of one of the principal by-products of the industry, alcohol. The large consumption of alcohol by the general population, but especially by the Indians, was the bane of Spanish administrators in the colonial period. They tried, quite logically, to strike at the problem at its source by limiting the growth of sugar cane, but to little avail. The valleys north of Lima, especially in and about Trujillo, became the principal producers of sugar and spirits in the seventeenth century, most of it, of course, exported by sea to other areas of the viceroyalty.

The province of Guayaquil was an especially rich source of products for the maritime trade of Peru. Cacao and a variety of tropical woods were the common exports. Cacao found its most rewarding markets from Panama northward along the Pacific coast to New Spain among a population whose favorite beverage was chocolate. Although the commerce of the bean was consistently limited and even forbidden by the crown in attempts to sever all links between the viceroyalties, contrabandists and official connivance developed this trade into one of the most lucrative in the Pacific. Tropical woods and timbers were shipped in large quantities southward to those cities located along the long and generally arid, treeless Peruvian coast. Oak, *guachapelí* ("acacialike"), yellow and black mangrove, and assorted other woods were used in the construction and decoration of public and private residences, offices, palaces, and churches, and Lima naturally enough was the prime consumer. Guayaquil also served as the major port outlet for the products of Quito, Cuenca, and the mountain area in general. Kerchiefs, hats, blankets, sandals, hams, biscuits, cheeses, pitch, and cordage were some of the exports, and attest to a most diverse economy in the interior of the Kingdom of Quito. Major imports that passed through Guayaquil were figs, wines, and raisins, the last two products associated with the grape-growing regions of Peru far to the south.

The textile industry of Peru was based on the heritage and labor of the Indians and, unlike other industries, it was rather consistently encouraged by the Spaniards. Spanish sheep were brought over in the sixteenth century and adapted well in almost all the Andean provinces, especially about Lake Titicaca, Ayacucho, Jauja, Tarma, and to the north around Cajamarca. *Obrajes,* or workshops, manned by Indian labor that was largely tributary, formed the principal producing units. The products of the *obrajes* failed to match the perfections of both their pre-Columbian predecessors and the contemporary standard of goods from Spain and Europe. Nonetheless, the industry was encouraged, for the needs of the viceroyalty's citizens outstripped the ability of Spanish merchants and shippers to supply the colony. Indeed, there was such a backlog of requests from Peru to Spain that it ordinarily required five years to fill an order. Faced with such a time lag and the possibility that the order would never reach America, how much better to encourage the native industry, using native cloths and products, and assure a steady, if not the most elegant, supply of garments for wear and trade. Limeños alone employed 323 Indian tailors, 129 cobblers, and 80 silk weavers in 1612.

Presiding over many aspects of Peruvian trade, industry, and navigation were the merchants of Lima. This group was distinguished by its wealth and commercially privileged position. In an age when a wage of 20 to 50 pesos a month was considered adequate, there existed in Lima in the early seventeenth century at least sixty merchants with capital of more than 100,000 pesos apiece and some with fortunes exceeding 500,000 and even a million pesos. They controlled the movement of goods and silver throughout the viceroyalty, acted essentially as brokers for the mine owners of the interior, were wholesalers for the host of smaller retailers in Peru, and generated much commerce for the merchant fleet.

Evidence on the national origins and social and economic status of the shipowners, masters, pilots, supercargoes, mates, and seamen is abundant but scattered. Studies of the conquest and immediate postconquest period reveal that foreigners were "the most active element in the seafaring population," and this phenomenon continued into the seventeenth century.[2] In a short but seminal article, María Encarnación Rodríguez Vicente concluded that "the numerous foreigners dedicated to the sea in Peru . . . came to constitute an essential and undeniable element in a territory particularly bound to maritime traffic." She listed Portuguese, Corsicans, Genoese, Greeks, Savoyards, Venetians, Ragusians, and even a few French as being present in varying proportions in the Peruvian seafaring population.[3] Most were employed as pilots, many were masters, some were owners or operators, while a few sailors and gunners filled out the list. Laws from as early as the 1570s forbade foreign pilots, masters, and mariners to enter the South Sea. Nevertheless, in recognition of their indispensability, exceptions were made that allowed them to live and work in the Pacific with certain reservations.

The social and economic status of mariners varied with their rank and rate. Owners occupied the top post of a vessel's hierarchy, and most shipowners, if residents of Lima at any rate, enjoyed all the privileges and rank of full membership in the prestigious consulado. While the merchants in Peru, large and small, wholesale and retail, were numbered in the thousands, only three hundred to four hundred were regularly enfranchised to elect the prior and consuls of the guild. These included those who had previously served as officers of the consulado, merchants who owned shops or were affiliated with others located on the Calle de Mercaderes (now Jirón Unión), the main entrance to the Plaza Mayor (now Plaza de Armas) or the Calle de la Cruz, and shipowners who lived in the city. The economic and political positions of owner-masters within the consulado were thus quite strong because of their enfranchisement. Many of these owners sailed on their vessels as masters and so the two occupations were most probably socially equiva-

2 James Lockhart, *Spanish Peru, 1532–1560: A Colonial Society* (Madison, 1968), pp. 114–15. Lockhart estimated the seafaring population in the following proportions: "It appears that about a fourth of all sailors were non-Iberians, a third non-Spanish, and half from regions speaking other languages than Spanish."
3 María Encarnación Rodríguez Vicente, "Los extranjeros y el mar en Perú," *Anuario de Estudios Americanos* 25 (1968), xxi.

lent. In other major maritime cities of the viceroyalty, such as Guayaquil, shipowners and masters numbered among the most prominent individuals in the community, and further testified to that occupation's
worth. Most ships carried licensed pilots in addition to masters, but in
many cases one man filled both offices. Hence, pilots also enjoyed a
modicum of similar rank within the community. The fact that a law was
decreed in 1615 that forbade the viceroy from placing his retainers
(*criados*) aboard royal treasure galleons as masters and that masters
must be "examined Pilots, and of confidence," indicates that both offices carried prestige and considerable monetary remuneration. Foreign
seafarers of the pilot or master rank must have found this employment
a convenient avenue to ship ownership, entrance into the consulado,
and, finally, into the general creole mercantile elite of the viceroyalty.

A wide chasm existed between the owner-master-pilot class and
the ordinary seaman. Historically the life of a sailor has never been
highly esteemed, and the lowest echelons of society were those usually
tapped by captains and masters in need of hands. The makeup of the
viceroyalty's ship crews appears to follow this traditional pattern. In the
sixteenth century foreigners and sailors were lumped together indiscrim-
inately and characterized as the "scum of the earth." Seventeenth-century
crews were made up, in large part, of the racial fringes of colonial society, Blacks, Indians, and mulattoes. Early eighteenth-century observers,
such as Dionisio de Alsedo y Herrera and Jorge Juan and Antonio de
Ulloa, wrote very critically of these mixed colonial crews and charged
them with lack of discipline, sloppiness, inattentiveness, and a host of
other sins. Indeed, shipwrecks were more often caused by, or at least
attributed to, negligence and bad seamanship than by the forces of natural circumstances. The blame fell ultimately on the pilots and masters,
but the hodgepodge crews they worked with certainly were a contributing factor.

The life of a sailor, if wages are used as a standard of living, was
immeasurably better than that of the average Indian attached to a hacienda or *obraje* in the viceroyalty. Whereas the wage of an *obraje*
Indian in the early seventeenth century was thirty to thirty-five pesos a
year, the average wage of a *grumete* ("striker") or *marinero* ("sailor")
fell between twenty-two and twenty-three pesos a month. Furthermore,
navigation in the South Sea was largely free of foreign threats (compared with the Caribbean in that same century) and of hurricanes, and
discipline, as noted, was rather slack aboard ship. Life as an able-bodied
seaman on any sailing ship of that period was, of course, never a lark,

but the average seventeenth-century crewman of the viceroyalty probably enjoyed a better existence than his counterpart in the Caribbean and Atlantic.

Regulation and Contraband

Sea traffic in seventeenth-century Peru was governed by a host of rules and regulations that were applied rigorously at Callao, but with a laxity that increased as one moved further away from the seat of the viceroyalty to the provincial ports. The major maritime duty charged was the *almojarifazgo*. It was first decreed for Peru in 1573, but not applied until 1591 when a 5 percent duty was levied on all commercial goods passing into the viceroyalty's ports and a 2 percent duty on goods passing out through the customs houses. The tax, figured ad valorem, fluctuated between 2.5 percent and 7.5 percent during the seventeenth century, while on occasion foodstuffs such as wheat and vegetables were exempted. Although initially handled by royal officials, by 1640 the consulado had assumed the responsibility of collecting this duty. An *asiento* or contract was signed between the consulado and the viceroy annually. This assured both parties that the price the consulado paid in return for assuming the responsibility would be in rough accord with the *almojarifazgo* taken in the previous year or two. It also provided the consulado with the opportunity to bargain with the crown for rights and privileges. The second major tax on seaborne traffic was the *averia,* a duty collected to support the Armada del Mar del Sur. It was first instituted in the early 1580s by Viceroy don Martín Enríquez after Francis Drake's raid along the Peruvian coast in 1579 and levied as .5 percent tax on all merchandise carried. The rate was elevated in 1592 to 1 percent as the Armada was augmented better to protect Peru following Thomas Cavendish's raid of 1587. In the 1630s, Viceroy Conde de Chinchón raised it to 2 percent in continuing efforts to keep the royal fleet effective. By the middle of the century the consulado had assumed the responsibility of collecting this duty as well. *Asientos* were signed for the farming out of the *averia,* and the price of the contract averaged about 100,000 pesos per year in the second half of the century. Most of this amount, however, was required by the Atlantic fleets, and the Armada del Mar del Sur received only a pittance in comparison.

Maritime laws and regulations covered more, of course, than the mere collection of duties. As noted earlier, the nationality of masters and pilots was the subject of certain regulations, although they were obeyed indifferently because of the shortage of qualified personnel. Massive amounts of litigation papers that now lie largely uncatalogued in the National Archive of Lima deal with everything from freight rates to smuggling and attest to the variety of maritime issues and disputes that were heard by the tribunal of the consulado. It was not unusual for individual cities along the coast to levy a special tax on the movement of goods through their customs houses to meet a particular local need. The cabildo of Guayaquil, for example, asked that certain duties be levied for a period of ten years to help defray the costs of constructing royal buildings (customs houses, warehouses), a cabildo, and a jail. In 1707, Trujillo petitioned for similar duties to help build a hospital, from which townspeople as well as indigent mariners would benefit. Detailed regulations existed to govern procedures after shipwrecks, with the possible recovery of goods in mind. Upon news of a shipwreck, the consulado commissioned a trusted member to travel to the site and recover what was salvageable. Those goods with recognizable ownership markings were turned over to their proprietors while the rest were sold at auction and the monies realized distributed among the owners on a prorated basis. Major shipwrecks, however, were fairly infrequent—perhaps on the average of one every five years in the seventeenth century—and passengers commonly made out well enough at least to reach land. Goods were sometimes recovered easily in shallow waters by experienced divers, and the discrepancy between the ship registers and the type and value and quantity of wreckage brought up occasionally implicated the lucky survivors—masters, owners, and the rest—in the contraband trade.

Smuggling developed largely during the seventeenth century in the Pacific. As official Spanish sources of manufactured goods diminished and the means to transport them from Spain to America shrank, the merchants of Peru turned to other European outlets for supplies, which usually reached the Mar del Sur in some sub rosa fashion. Moreover, increasing restrictions on inter-American trade by the crown were consistently evaded by determined Peruvian traders who sought natural markets for their products. Lastly, compliance with the tedious regulations that governed ship departures, sailing plans, and so forth, and the concomitant payment of heavy duties were considered onerous burdens by masters and owners who found it most convenient to avoid as many of these legal obstacles as possible.

The voyage of *Nuestra Señora del Pópulo* from Peru to New Spain and back in 1677–78 offers a classic example of the ways, profits, and risks of contraband trade in the South Sea. Although trade between Peru and New Spain was banned by royal decrees, certain exceptions were sometimes made and special licenses granted by the viceroys. *Pópulo* had sailed to New Spain in 1677 with such a license and a cargo of 3,500 *quintales* ("hundredweight") of mercury from Huancavelica destined for the silver mines of Mexico. She returned to Callao safely, but troubles commenced early on the morning of August 12, 1678. Captain Francisco Colmenares de Lara, a port inspector, approached *Pópulo* in his launch about seven that morning and noticed that *lama,* or slime, covered a yard-wide (a *vara*) band around the vessel above the waterline. He noted this in his report, along with the suspicion that *Pópulo* had returned heavily laden from Acapulco and had discharged the bulk of her cargo, contraband, before she reached Callao. She more than likely had done so at Paita in the north where she had stopped for victualing, and where royal officers were more easily bribed. Nonetheless, not all had been unloaded in the north, and Colmenares discovered enough contraband goods aboard, ninety-one *fardos,* or bundles, of pepper, fifty boxes of Chinese wax (*marquetas de cera de la tierra de China*), and so forth, to charge officers and crew with complicity to smuggle. The first to testify in his own defense was Captain Francisco de Villanueva, master and probably owner of *Pópulo*. Asked how all these contraband goods got aboard his vessel, Captain Villanueva could think of nothing more original than to claim he became ill upon arriving at Acapulco and was indisposed until his vessel left that port. Captain Antonio de Mendoza, pilot of the vessel, then gave his version. He *too* had been ill and had seen nothing; but, since his obligation was simply to navigate the ship, he certainly did not feel guilty. Others called to testify—the official scribe, gunners, and sailors—all coughed up the same, lame excuse. All had mysteriously and coincidentally been ill and now all shared in the penalties. Villanueva was sentenced to four years of exile from Callao at a distance of not fewer than fifty leagues on pain of being sent to Chile; Joseph de Solas, the scribe, received the same and others received similar penalties.

Participation in contraband trade and disregard for both the letter and spirit of the law appear to have been quite common about the middle of the century. In fact, illegal activity became so commonplace that Viceroy García Sarmiento de Sotomayor, Conde de Salvatierra, felt compelled to initiate an investigation and forcibly to remind royal officers up and down the coast of their duty. The *fiscal,* or king's attorney, in Lima, Pedro Vásquez de Velasco, was put in charge of the investigation, and his report revealed the widespread abuse of regulations in the viceroyalty. Even before ships cleared Callao they defrauded the royal treasury by not paying full duties on goods carried. Many shipped cargoes intended for contraband trade, obtained licenses to sail for legal destinations, and then deviated from their sailing plans to practice their trade. *San Francisco de Asís,* commanded and owned by Captain Pedro de Villegas, was a typical violator. She received a license to go to the valley of Trujillo and the city of Panama. From there, however, she passed on illegally to *"la otra costa,"* or Central America, to sell wines and other prohibited goods. *San Francisco de Ortega* also had been caught trafficking in a similar pattern. She had come from Pisco to Callao loaded with wine and subsequently received a license to sail for Manta. From there she passed on to Central America and probably traded at either Realejo or Sonsonate. A favorite port for contrabandists was Guayaquil, where there existed compliant officials and a good export crop, cacao. Royal officials at the port usually possessed a substantial interest in the cacao trade and, while strictly forbidden to do so, they issued licenses to clear for Central America. The cacao taken there was then transported to Mexico by land or across the Dulce Gulf to Campeche. In return, these vessels brought back with them forbidden Chinese, Mexican, and Castilian wares to be landed or transferred at ports such as Guayaquil and Paita. What particularly galled Viceroy Salvatierra and his investigators was the blatant complicity of so many royal officials in the illegal traffic. Juan de Vallarta, who investigated Guayaquil, reported that, as far as he was concerned, the culpable ones were not the masters and shipowners (although they were certainly guilty by participation), but the justices and royal officials, including the corregidor, who permitted the trade to exist. As noted above, ecclesiastics participated in contraband trade quite as eagerly as most. Viceroy Conde de la Monclova promulgated an order in 1704 that specifically forbade ecclesiastical personnel from concealing contraband material in their convents and monasteries, but it probably had little effect, since the creole clergymen tended to side with those native Peruvians who considered the entire corpus of restrictions and prohibitions "as unjust and not binding in conscience."

Even the consulado itself appears to have been indirectly implicated in the trade. On at least one occasion in 1674 royal officials discovered contraband goods on board a vessel at Callao. Subsequently she was embargoed and guards were placed on her at the cost of the owner. The consulado thereupon complained to the crown that their contract for the collection of the *almojarifazgo* had been grossly violated. The contract expressly empowered solely the consulado or its representatives to collect duties and inspect vessels at Callao, and thus the royal official, specifically *maestre de campo* don Antonio Dávila, had trespassed on his authority. The crown agreed and forbade such intrusions, thus satisfying the consulado's insistent demands for autonomy and, by implication, for freedom from strict supervision by overenthusiastic royal bureaucrats at Callao.

Various remedies attempted by the viceroys were, for the most part, ineffectual and perhaps reflected an acceptance of reality that no royal edict could change. For example, upon the conclusion of his rather extensive investigation into contraband practices and official complicity, Viceroy García Sarmiento de Sotomayor in 1650 issued a surprisingly benign set of instructions and exhortations. He called upon all royal officials stationed at port cities to be vigilant and responsible in the performance of their duties, that the royal treasury not be defrauded, that delinquents be punished, and so forth. When his instructions were more specific, the admonitions were equally flaccid. If ships were not found to possess valid licenses and registers for the ports where they were discovered, royal officials were to oblige the vessels to take their cargoes where they were meant to go. The efforts of Viceroy Monclova to combat the illegal introduction of Castilian and Chinese goods through Mexico into Peru at the end of the century had been unrewarding as well, and he attributed this failure to a lack of incentives for informers (*denunciadores*). Monclova suggested, in compliance with certain guidelines from the Council of the Indies, that informants be paid from the royal treasury if the contrabandists' goods could not be turned to cash rapidly (one-third the value of the contraband goods confiscated), that slaves be granted their liberty if they informed on their masters, and that, if slaves belonged to other masters, these be paid the worth of the slaves who would then be manumitted. Monclova's campaign against contrabandists at the turn of the eighteenth century was complicated by the appearance of the first French merchant ships in the Pacific. This group's presence off the viceroyalty's coast augured a change in the fortunes of Peru's commerce that must be treated separately. Nonetheless, their appearance helps to highlight one major geographic characteristic of the South Sea in the seventeenth century, isolation from the Atlantic, that contributed to the creation of an autochthonous shipbuilding industry.

The Ships

Most vessels, royal or private, that operated in the South Sea were built in the shipyards of Peru, while others were of Central American origin. For commercial purposes, the South Sea was a closed ocean during most of the seventeenth century. The tip of South America, guarded by bitter weather, difficult seas, and winds and frequent tempests, was an effective deterrent to all but the boldest mariners. Rarely did Spanish vessels attempt to pass from the Atlantic to the Pacific or vice versa. The futile efforts made by Sarmiento de Gamboa, one of Spain's most brilliant mariners, to plant a settlement along the Straits in the 1580s stands as tragic testimony to the difficulty of any activity, especially sailing, in these waters. Hence, a new and independent shipbuilding industry was created to meet the maritime and naval needs of the viceroyalty.

The industry came to be centered at Guayaquil, which possessed an outstanding wooded hinterland serviced by a network of streams and rivers for easy access. The small group of Spanish craftsmen in the city tapped the large native population for manpower. Black slaves and free Blacks, many of them skilled artisans themselves, were also used in the industry. They were adept and intelligent people and, indeed, by the end of the seventeenth century, played a large role in the industry as foremen and supervisors in many cases. Aside from the iron and metal fittings that were imported from Spain, almost all materials employed in the shipyards of Guayaquil were present in the Pacific. The industry at Guayaquil was thus well fitted: the knowledge came with the Europeans; the labor was plentiful; the natural resources, especially woods, in abundance. Unfortunately, no genuine pictorial record or model of one of these vessels exists, but descriptions and evaluations are available. They appear to have been rather ugly by European standards, given to straight sides and wide hulls. Nonetheless, they were good merchant ships for, if sailed properly, they could deliver a maximum amount of goods with moderate freightage fees.

The prevailing Humboldt Current and winds that pushed everything in a north-northwesterly direction along the viceroyalty's coast until turning west around the latitude of the Gulf of Guayaquil were the sources of much adversity for ships going south. The tales of exasperated travelers, who often chose to debark at Paita in northern Peru and continue their journey to Lima terrestrially, attests to the great difficulty of making this leg of the voyage, as well as to the pilots' conservative tendencies, for they commonly chose to hug the coast. Nonetheless, the best round-trip voyages from Callao south to Valparaíso or north to Guayaquil ranged from two to three months, which, if allowing for the unloading of cargo and the procurement and loading of a return shipment, is not a considerable amount of time.

Conclusion

The geographical and maritime isolation of the viceroyalty and to a lesser extent of other Spanish American colonies that bordered on the Pacific Ocean was a primary influence on the formation of trade and commerce and the development of navigation in seventeenth-century Peru. Certain indicators, such as the rapid decline of the Atlantic *carrera* system in the second half of the century compared to the rise of maritime trade in the South Sea in the same period, clearly point to the existence of different economic forces at work in the viceroyalty. Indeed, the trend toward self-sufficiency in the American portion of the Spanish empire that John Lynch described in the second volume of his *Spain under the Habsburgs* (Oxford, 1969) seems to be quite applicable to Peru in that period. Between 1701 and 1704, there were 241 ship departures from Callao, and of these only 35, or 14.5 percent, were destined for Panama, the viaduct for legitimate trade with Spain.

Furthermore, of these 241 ship departures, only 3, and they were French, were bound for Cape Horn and the Atlantic. All the rest were licensed for ports within the viceroyalty and Central America. Some preliminary and as yet largely unrefined data gathered recently from seventeenth-century sailing records in the National Archive of Peru tend to corroborate the statistics from the incipient years of the eighteenth century. Between November 1661 and November 1663, for example, seventy-five vessels with identifiable ports of origin arrived at Callao. Only fourteen of these, or 18.5 percent, had cleared from Panama. The trend, while by no means absolutely substantiated, nonetheless appears in outline. Wheat and copper from Valparaíso and Concepción; wines and olive oil from Pisco; textiles from Quito moving through Guayaquil; woods and cacao from that port; sugar from Trujillo and the northern valleys; pitch, tar, ink, and cedar from Nicaragua; and myriad other crops and products dominated the trade. Seventy-five percent of the *almojarifazgo* collected at Callao was drawn from trade and commerce directed to ports other than Panama.

The isolation of the Mar del Sur from the Atlantic axis of the empire also contributed to the growth of some distinguishing features in the realm of navigation, or broadly speaking, that subject encompassing the ships, the men, and the way they routinely dealt with the vagaries of the ocean they sailed upon. While a heavy foreign element among the class of owners, masters, and pilots appears to have prevailed, the lower mates and sailors were drawn for the most part from the racial fringes of colonial society, mulattoes, zambos, Blacks, mestizos, and Indians. Critical observers such as Juan and Ulloa wrote disparagingly in the 1730s of Peruvian crews, as noted earlier. Nonetheless, the young naval lieutenants' criticisms must be taken with certain reservations, for naval officers have historically considered all merchant sailors as little better than louts and ne'er-do-wells compared to the discipline and order they expect within their own family. The light sprinkling of shipwreck records in the archives does not appear to justify such a harsh consideration of the performance of the viceroyalty's crews.

It is clear from this short overview that trade and navigation within the viceroyalty were dynamic and vital aspects of colonial life, for the maritime services grew and prospered in proportion to the needs of a developing Spanish and mixed population. The products of native industry and the crops of the littoral were the basic commodities, both in bulk and value, carried by the merchant fleet, while silver and wares from Europe and China, legitimate or otherwise, account for the remaining percentage of the fleet's use. In many respects this reflected the growth and slow maturation of a colony that was gradually establishing an economy and identity for itself.

Suggested Further Reading

Borah, Woodrow W. *Early Colonial Trade and Navigation between Mexico and Peru.* Berkeley and Los Angeles, 1954.

Clayton, Lawrence A. *Caulkers and Carpenters in a New World: The Shipyards of Colonial Guayaquil.* Athens, Ohio, 1980.

Haring, Clarence H. *Trade and Navigation between Spain and the Indies in the Time of the Hapsburgs.* Cambridge, Mass., 1918. Reprint. Gloucester, Mass., 1964.

Parry, J. H. *The Spanish Seaborne Empire.* London, 1966. Especially chapters 6, 13, and 15.

Schurz, William L. *The Manila Galleon.* New York, 1939. Reprint. New York, 1959.

Walker, Geoffrey J. *Spanish Politics and Imperial Trade, 1700–1789.* Bloomington, Ind., 1979.

11 ☼

Magistracy and Society in Colonial Brazil

STUART B. SCHWARTZ

The government and society of the Portuguese empire formed two inter-locking systems of organization. In one of them a metropolitan-directed administration, characterized by categorical and impersonal relations, joined the individual or corporation to the political institutions that con-stituted formal government. In the other system interpersonal primary relations were based on extended families and kinship groups (*paren-telas*), shared corporate or social status and goals, and common eco-nomic interests. To understand properly the operation of government in colonial Brazil one must examine the interaction of these two systems and the relations of government employees with other socioeconomic groups. The following analysis will deal with the Portuguese professional bureaucrats, not only as performers of specific political functions, but also as dynamic participants in the complex relations that made up Brazilian colonial society.

For historical and theoretical reasons magistrates formed the core of the Portuguese imperial bureaucracy. At the center of each town in the Portuguese empire stood the *pelourinho* ("pillory"), symbol of justice and royal authority. Its location at the core of the community be-spoke the Portuguese medieval concept of kingship which stressed the role of the monarch as dispenser of justice and protector of the poor and weak. This close identification of king and justice led quite naturally to the embodiment of royal authority in the judicial-administrative offi-cers of the realm. This group, the magisterial bureaucrats, rose to power with the dynastic revolution of 1383 that brought the House of Aviz to the Portuguese throne. Thereafter, the demands of royal centralization and the development of a conciliar structure of government depended

Published originally in the *Hispanic American Historical Review*, 50:4 (Novem-ber 1970).

increasingly on the magisterial bureaucrats. What resulted was a kind of symbiotic relationship, since the importance of the magistrates as a class proceeded directly from royal authority, while the king relied on the performance and loyalty of the magistrates to achieve and maintain this authority.

The rise of the magisterial bureaucracy did not go unnoticed or unchallenged. Other groups in Portugal, the landed and military nobility and the metropolitan municipal councils, opposed the social ascendancy of the bureaucrats and the concomitant political dominance of the crown. This opposition was often expressed as antilegal sentiments, criticism of lawyers and scribes who seemed to inherit without effort the privileges of the nobility in Portugal and the conquests of the soldiers beyond the Algarve. By the mid-seventeenth century the parties to the conflict were ardently debating the relative value of arms or letters to the empire. Magnates in Portugal, soldiers in India, and sugar planters in Brazil all complained about lawyers and the legal class. Their protestations were in vain, for although the military nobility continued in high positions in the colonies and councils, much of the business of empire and the structure of government had come irretrievably into the hands of the professional bureaucrats.

In theory, the Portuguese monarch made all political decisions. In practice, however, the complexities of government forced him to lean heavily on various administrative and advisory councils, especially for those matters requiring specific knowledge or technical competence. In the daily process of decision making, the king's signature often became a rubber stamp for conciliar suggestions. Two secretaries of state at court acted as intermediaries between king and councils, but they did not assume any significance until the union of Spain and Portugal in 1580. Rarely did they influence policy, and in colonial affairs it was only after 1750 and the rise of the Marquis of Pombal that colonial secretaries replaced the Overseas Council as creators of policy.

Unlike the Spanish government, that of Portugal never fully divided its conciliar system by geographical areas or between metropolis and colonies. Thus, between 1550 and 1808 there were three specifically colonial councils: the Treasury Council (Conselho da Fazenda, 1594–1641), the India Council (Conselho da India, 1604–14), and the Overseas Council (Conselho Ultramarino, 1642–1808). None of these ever controlled all aspects of imperial government, and other bodies continued to play a part in colonial affairs. The Board of Conscience (Mesa da Consciência e Ordens) resolved moral and theological problems in both metropolis and colonies, handling matters as diverse as student riots at Coimbra and ecclesiastical benefices in Brazil. More central to this study, a Board of Justice (Desembargo do Paço) exercised in its sphere appointive, regulatory, and policy formation functions throughout the empire.

Designed as the apex of the judicial system, the Board of Justice had responsibility for the recruitment, promotion, procedures, and standards of the magisterial bureaucrats. Despite considerable jurisdictional conflict with the specifically colonial councils, the Board of Justice never relinquished its control over the judicial-administrative aspects of government. In effect, the goals and standards of the magisterial bureaucrats were established and maintained by professionals who had risen to the Board of Justice. As a result, the bureaucracy enjoyed a degree of autonomy, professionalism, and relatively high standards.

In the New World, the magisterial bureaucrats shared authority with other branches of government in a complex arrangement of checks and balances. After 1621 Portuguese America was divided into two large administrative units, the States of Maranhão and Brazil. Each was ruled by a governor-general and subdivided into a number of captaincies administered by governors who also bore the title of captain. These officers, usually military men of aristocratic background, formed an executive group as direct representatives of the crown. Although the captaincies were theoretically centralized symmetrically under the governor-general, centralization and symmetry were never achieved. Governors-general in Bahia often found it impossible to control subordinate governors in Rio de Janiero and Pernambuco. Moreover, all officials and in fact "even the meanest vassal" were encouraged to communicate directly with the king, thus providing him with multiple sources of information while allowing subordinate and coordinate officials a certain degree of autonomy.

Within the formal table of organization, the magistrates constituted a second level of administration, balancing the authority of the governors and checking the independence of the municipal councils (câmaras), which characteristically represented dominant local interest groups. The first royal magistrate (ouvidor geral) arrived in Brazil in 1549 to perform his traditional functions as judge and defender of royal prerogatives. Relatively inefficient successors followed, and not until 1609 was a larger group of magistrates sent to Brazil. In that year, as the result of judicial reform instigated by Spain in Portgual, a high court or Relação staffed by ten magistrates (*desembargadores*) and a number of minor officials arrived in Brazil. The Relação became the core of the magisterial bureaucracy in Brazil. Eventually provincial magistrates (ouvidores) in the captaincies and after 1696 royal municipal magistrates (juizes de fora) also served, but they remained professionally and jurisdictionally below the high court.

A myriad of lesser officials at the captaincy and municipal levels characterized the lower echelons of government. As early as 1552, the perceptive Jesuit, Manuel da Nóbrega, pleaded for more colonists and fewer government employees who wanted "nothing more than to do their time and collect their pay . . . , and as this is their principal goal they do not love the land and all their affection is for Portugal." By the seventeenth century Brazilians held many of these offices, but the effect of the change was not wholly invigorating. Colonials were anxious to become a "child of the paymaster" (filho da folha), and the tendency was for these offices to multiply without improving in performance.

Offices in the lower echelons of government were often rife with venality and incompetence. These posts were traditionally granted as rewards or favors; the usual response of the crown to a legitimate petition was to promise "some office of justice or the treasury." Under both the Hapsburgs and the Braganças there was considerable purchase of office, often with hereditary control. Pluralism (holding more than one office) was condoned and the use of deputies (serventia) a common practice. Instances of municipal councillors and elected judges who were functional illiterates and of notaries who could scarcely sign their own name occurred from time to time.

Such incompetence was unknown, however, within the ranks of magisterial bureaucrats, whose central role in the formal structure of government and royally sanctioned position as guardians of that structure rested on their competence and professionalization. A short discussion of the professional and private lives of these men, therefore, may illumine our analysis.

The Board of Justice administered a personal and professional examination to all those seeking entry into the ranks of the royal bureaucracy. The applicant was expected to be a graduate in civil or canon law from the University of Coimbra with at least two years of practice as a lawyer. Socially he was expected to be the legitimate son of honorable and orthodox parents. More precisely, anyone who had artisan or shopkeeper forebears or whose family was tainted with the blood of "New Christian, Moor, Mulatto, or other infected race" was theoretically prohibited from royal service. The extent to which a friend at court or family connections influenced career patterns is obscure, but it seems unlikely that positions of magisterial rank were bought outright. Some nepotism was institutionalized, since the sons of magistrates were given preferential treatment. Clandestine purchase and nepotism, however, did not imply a complete breakdown of performance or standards, since the required competence examination by the Board of Justice insured at least minimal qualifications of all appointees. Still, personal influence vied with seniority as the principal requisite for promotion. Performance was evaluated by successful completion of the incumbency examination (residência), and thus a premium was placed on adherence to norms rather than on innovation or outstanding achievement.

The magistrates who served in Brazil between 1609 and 1759 came from social groups of middle rank. In a statistical sample of one hundred high court magistrates, the sons of merchants, soldiers, and artisans were more numerous than those who claimed noble (fidalgo) origins. Far more significant, 13 percent were the sons of minor and municipal officials and 22 percent of university-trained lawyers and bureaucrats. In fact, a legist class is represented in these figures. Sons followed fathers into the university and then into royal service. These men often married the daughters of other bureaucrats so that endogamy and class perpetuation became identifiable characteristics of the group. *Filho da pez sabe nadar* (the fish's son knows how to swim), the Portuguese equivalent of "the apple doesn't fall far from the tree" was often true. A good illustration was António Rodrigues Banha, who entered the high court of Bahia in 1729 and whose father and maternal grandfather had both preceded him in that tribunal. Such a case was not uncommon in Portuguese bureaucracy.

The typical high court magistrate in Brazil entered royal service at age twenty-six. First he served a three-year term in Portugal as a royal municipal judge. Then he was moved to another town and reappointed at the same level or promoted as provincial magistrate (ouvidor) for a similar term. After about fifteen years of service on the average, the magistrate expected promotion to a high court, and it was precisely at this juncture that, prior to 1680, most of the magistrates came to Brazil. Before that date many tried to avoid Brazilian service, but by the end of the century a post in the Bahian high court was ardently sought as an important step up the promotional ladder, and the excess of deserving magistrates forced the crown to make supernumerary appointments. After six to eight years of service in Brazil the bureaucrat could expect to return to a position in the Oporto Relação and the Supreme Court of Appeals (Casa da Suplicação) in Lisbon.

This career pattern meant that the age of the average high court magistrate on arrival in Brazil was forty-two and that he had been seasoned by fifteen years of professional experience. These men, therefore, were senior magistrates of proven competence and loyalty. In the last years of the sixteenth century, direct promotion from subordinate colonial positions to posts in the Relação became common. After 1682, 42 percent of those who served in the Bahian tribunal had previous colonial experience and 70 percent of these in Brazil. Thus only at the end of the century did a colonial subsystem begin to form, and even then prior or subsequent service in the metropolis was never excluded to colonial magistrates.

Only in rare and exceptional cases did magistrates who had served earlier in Portuguese India discharge professional duties in Brazil. However, those who served in the West African colonies—Angola, Cabo Verde, São Tomé, and Guiné—were often promoted to the Bahian high court. There were, in effect, two colonial channels of promotion, which we can call the Indian Ocean and the Atlantic Ocean branches. Both were integrated into the metropolitan system, but they remained distinct from each other. Only 15 percent of the magistrates who saw service in Brazil rose to conciliar positions in Portugal. This fact indicates that the highest levels of government were filled by officials who had risen by direct metropolitan appointment or through the Indian Ocean branch. If the magistrates in Brazil perceived this inequality, they may have been more willing to exploit their immediate position for personal gain since adherence to bureaucratic norms did not insure the achievement of their highest professional aspirations.

Although the ecclesiastical bureaucracy lies beyond the scope of this discussion, the function of the church as an administrative arm should as least be noted. The king exercised control of the church in matters temporal, and churchmen, both regular and secular, performed tasks of direct benefit to royal government. The influence of the church pervaded society, and for many Brazilians the parish stood as the most immediate and recognizable institution of organization. Moreover, despite much jurisdictional conflict between civil and ecclesiastical officials in the colony, church doctrine generally supported the crown and the dominant theory of government.

Control over the official hierarchy, over colonial officials, and colonial affairs depended on regulation, jurisdictional overlap, multiple lines of communication, and shared, if not conflicting, powers. Blurred and disputed lines of authority meant constant reference to Portugal and arbitration by metropolitan councils. Statutes and royal commands combined with periodic and extraordinary investigations (*devassas*) to stop abuses, insure honesty, and assure compliance with expected behavior. Each official from viceroy to doorkeeper of the customshouse lived under the shadow of a terminal examination (residência) that would come at the end of his incumbency, and this too was expected to check misbehavior in office.

In this system of countervailing powers and institutionalized mechanisms of metropolitan control, the Relação and the subordinate royal magistrates were the principal cogs. Considered by the crown as the most loyal and efficient body of officials, they were charged with preventing the dominance of any political and economic force in the colony, while maintaining the prerogatives and standards of the crown. It was the magisterial bureaucrats who conducted the various investigations and the judicial review and who staffed special advisory councils and administrative boards. To control the magistrates, the crown depended on certain regulatory powers of the governor-general within the system of checks and balances and on the multiple lines of communication. Probably to an even greater degree, the crown looked on the professional standards and goals of the magistrates, on mechanisms such as rotation in office, and on their collective ties to royal power as means of keeping them subservient to royal desires.

These men of nonnoble gentry and professional backgrounds hoped to find in the promotional channels of the bureaucracy a means for status gratification and social ascendancy. Upper magistrates considered themselves the social equals of the titled and landed nobility in Portugal. By the eighteenth century, jurists argued that the study of law literally ennobled an individual. Also by the accretion of rewards and titles the professional bureaucracy began to identify with the attitudes and aspirations of their former class and political rivals. A certain amount of group consciousness, however, kept the magisterial bureaucrats from becoming simply integrated into the nobility. The means by which they sought to fulfill their particular status and financial desires within their professional position form the links between formal and informal government in Brazil.

The crown was not unaware of these personal and class aspirations and realized that the role of the magistrates in the formal structure of government would be compromised by extraprofessional contacts. Thus the crown tried to isolate the bureaucrats from the pressures of individual, familial, or class interests. Statutes sought to separate the judges from Brazilian society by limiting their residence, social relations, dress, and habits. No magistrate, for example, was to marry in the area of his jurisdiction or to enter into business there. To lift the magistrates above society the crown invested them with great authority, paid them substantial salaries, and granted them membership in the honorific military orders.

These measures, designed to reinforce the authority and effectiveness of the magistrates in a society deeply respectful of ascriptive status, had two unforeseen consequences. First, the bureaucrats, with their shared university background, esprit de corps, and group consciousness, could articulate policies or desires independent of the crown's goals. This, however, they rarely did. More commonly the magistrates used their authority and prestige for personal or familial aggrandizement. Though salaries were high, graft and malfeasance, for example, did not disappear. Instead the access to more capital increased the opportunities for magistrates to invest in prohibited business ventures. Seen from another angle, the dignity, authority, and wealth of the magistrates did not isolate them at all from an awed society. Quite to the contrary, their prestige made them seem more attractive allies to important socioeconomic groups, especially the dominant planter oligarchy. The role—or more exactly roles—of the magistrates presented a paradox. On the one hand, disinterested magisterial bureaucrats formed the keystone of the formal governmental structure erected by the crown. On the other, though, they pursued individual and collective goals and entered into a variety of personal relations that openly conflicted with their expected professional behavior.

Brazil contained various means for creating an extensive "social genealogy"—the web of both kin and other primary relations. Curiously, just as church doctrine and officials had bolstered the formal political structure, so church-sponsored marriage, godparentage, and religious brotherhoods supplied vital integration to the informal structure. Although expressly forbidden by law, high court and lesser magisterial bureaucrats in Brazil did marry Brazilians. Twenty-six magistrates of the Bahian high court (15 percent) married in Brazil, and although the social origins of all the brides have not been ascertained, it is clear that many were daughters of the planter oligarchy or of other government officials. A second institution for creating social linkage was that of ritual godparentage (compadrio), which created close ties and placed mutual obligations on all parties concerned. Magistrates, their retainers, relatives, and friends also entered into these ritual relationships, thereby extending their obligations and influence. It should be made clear, however, that the nature of Brazilian society and the social aspirations of the magistrates limited most of these personal relations to the highest strata of colonial society. Chances are slim indeed that the marginal mulatto, the enslaved Black, or even the Portuguese cobbler ever became the compadre or the brother-in-law of a magistrate.

In their search for financial gain and status positions concomitant with their rank, the magisterial bureaucrats in Brazil also created a secondary layer of nonritualized relationships. High court magistrates often served on the board of directors in the honorific Holy Brotherhood of Mercy (Misericôrdia) and sometimes controlled its senior position of *provedor*. The Misericôrdia counted among its brothers the wealthiest and socially most prominent members of Bahian society, and thus the opportunity for friendship and personal interaction between the magistrates and certain groups was increased. Moreover, ritualized and non-ritualized primary relations tended to become concentrated in the same individuals and reinforce each other. Of the six magistrates who served as *provedor* of the Misericôrdia of Salvador, five were married to Brazilian women and the sixth was Brazilian-born. Either these men had used family connections to obtain the position, or their family connections made others in the society more ready to accept them.

Many magistrates also engaged in business activities—whale fishing, slave trading, commerce, and plantations—entering into contracts and partnerships. Some, like Pedro de Cascais and Caetano de Brito de Figuereido, went deeply into debt, while others, like the Bahian-born Cristóvão de Burgos, became fabulously wealthy. In our discussion their success or failure is a secondary concern. What is important is the existence of these extraprofessional activities and the accompanying network of personal relations that they imply.

Blood and ritual ties, business enterprise, favoritism, and venality could all be viewed strictly as violations of expected behavior that hampered the normal operations of government. At the same time these mechanisms permitted primary relations to penetrate into a highly rationalized system of categorical and impersonal ones. Despite royal attempts to eliminate these "deviancies," these primary relations, which constituted and constitute so much of Portuguese and Brazilian life, continued to prevail. Indeed, they gave an unintended flexibility to government and facilitated the resolution of problems on the local level when official channels were too slow or obstructed.

The colonial bureaucrats, seen from the standpoint of a virtuous governor, metropolitan councillors, or even those colonials who had no personal ties with them, often appeared to violate the required standards of their vocation. To be sure, they were never totally absorbed and always capable of pursuing independent or royal interests. Still, the dominant socioeconomic groups in the colony never found the royal bureaucrats beyond the reach of colonial pressures or ignorant of colonial desires. Local interests could be expressed and implemented through the web of primary relations, so that policy making was never simply a matter of royal fiat and bureaucratic compliance.

In effect, the existing social and political organization could accommodate modifications in the structure of colonial society such as the economic ascendency of an urban mercantile class after 1730. Through the formation of social alliances with the bureaucracy, groups and individuals could acquire social legitimacy and the security of powerful friends and relatives. Thus within the formal table of government—a static pattern of organization—new interests could be articulated by the creation of new groupings. These changing social patterns provided, therefore, a dynamic element in the relationship of society to bureaucracy.

This is not to ignore the difficulties created by individual and collective abuses. Tax evasion, graft, defaulting on debt payments, and especially misuse of authority were charges often brought against magisterial bureaucrats in Brazil. Occasionally a magistrate could be fairly described as was one royal municipal judge in Pará—"the most evil and perverse man by nature, habit, and design that has until now been honored with the authority of an official." Generally, however, the system of checks and balances kept magisterial activities within bounds, while their professional goals, their loyalty to the crown, and their personal interests prevented them from becoming the tools of any one colonial group or faction.

Although statutes prohibited Brazilians from serving in the Bahian Relação or in subordinate royal positions in Brazil, the law was bent to meet colonial demands. Between 1653 and 1753, ten Brazilian-born magistrates served in the Relação and others held positions as provincial judges. This practice did not stop even after an attempt in 1663 to eliminate such violations of the law. In fact, when a second Relação was established at Rio de Janeiro in 1752, the man selected for its senior position (*chanceler*) was the Bahian, João Pacheco Pereira, former provincial magistrate of Ouro Preto. Moreover, the crown took special pains to inform Brazilians that they were not excluded from royal employ in other colonies or in the metropolis, a fact in which the colonials took considerable pride.

Ten Brazilian-born magistrates in the high court, twenty-six married to Brazilian women, thirty-five who had served previously in Brazil, others related to former governors of Minas Gerais and Pernambuco, and still others who had fathered illegitimate children in the colony—the network of these personal relations was wide indeed. Offended parties in Brazil might censure individual magistrates, but the royal bureaucracy never seemed a distant and oppressive imperial tool to the Brazilian oligarchy. Instead, Brazilians themselves hoped to matriculate their sons in Coimbra and find a career for them in the bureaucracy. These opportunities may at times have been more apparent than real, but there seems little doubt that the theoretically open nature of the professional bureaucracy muted the distinctions between colonials and peninsulars. While the formal structure of administration placed Brazil in a classic colonial position, the informal structure allowed colonial interest groups to treat the magistrates as simply another source of power subject to alliance and cooptation.

After 1750, the administration under the Marquis of Pombal changed much of the formal governmental structure, and his policies resulted in the creation of new interest groups and the restructuring of old alliances. In essence, however, most of the informal structure remained unchanged. Royal government in colonial Brazil was never efficient but it never totally collapsed. Magisterial bureaucrats played the crucial though often unintended role of balancing colonial and metropolitan interests.

Suggested Further Reading

Boxer, C. R. *Portuguese Society in the Tropics: The Municipal Councils of Goa, Macao, Bahia, and Luanda, 1510–1800.* Madison, 1965.

Haring, Clarence H. *The Spanish Empire in America.* New York, 1947.

Parry, John H. *The Audiencia of New Galicia in the Sixteenth Century: A Study in Spanish Colonial Government.* Cambridge, 1948.

Phelan, John Leddy. "Authority and Flexibility in the Spanish Imperial Bureaucracy." *Administrative Science Quarterly* 5:1 (June 1960).

————. *The Kingdom of Quito in the Seventeenth Century: Bureaucratic Politics in the Spanish Empire.* Madison, 1967.

Russell-Wood, A. J. R. *Fidalgos and Philanthropists: The Santa Casa da Misericórdia of Bahia, 1550–1755.* Berkeley, 1968.

Schwartz, Stuart B. *Sovereignty and Society in Colonial Brazil: The High Court of Bahia and Its Judges, 1609–1751.* Berkeley, 1973.

12 ☀

Women and Society in Colonial Brazil

A. J. R. RUSSELL-WOOD

Introduction

No aspect of Brazilian history has received so stereotyped a treatment as the position of the female and her contribution to the society and economy of the colony. The white *donzela* ("young lady") and the lady of the "big house" have been depicted as leading a secluded existence, be it in the innermost recesses of their homes or in conventual cells, immune to harsh realities and safe from brash overtures by pretenders. Of the white woman, it was said, during her lifetime she left her home on only three occasions: to be baptized, to be married, and to be buried. The role of the white woman was seen as essentially passive, victim of the demands of an overbearing and frequently unfaithful older husband to whom she would bear children, or of a martinet of a father. As for the Amerindian woman, whose beauty led the discoverers to initial raptures of platonic appreciation and then sexual overindulgence, she has rarely been depicted in any role other than that of concubine or lover. The Black and mulatto woman, slave or free, became a symbol of sensual arousal and sexual fulfillment. Her power over the white male settler was lauded in popular mythology, verse, and prose. Her domestic duties were irrevocably tied to her sexual role as the plaything of adolescent sons, the butt for the cruelty and sadism of jealous white wives, or the object of the affections of the master of the house.

That there is some truth in each of these stereotypes is undeniable, but uncritical acceptance and repetition by scholars have ignored the basic fact that the female formed part of a larger society. Her role and her contribution were determined, in part, by factors totally unrelated to the nature of her sex, but which formed guidelines for society as a

Reprinted by permission of Cambridge University Press and published originally in the *Journal of Latin American Studies,* 9:1 (May 1977).

whole in the colony. The position of the woman was established by a code of ethics, by theological and legal decrees, and by social and religious attitudes that had comprised the cultural heritage of the Christian countries of Western Europe, and had been transferred to the New World, there to be preserved, strengthened, or modified to meet the needs of colonizing societies. Social mores and the economic situation in this tropical environment were to affect the female no less than the male colonist. In short, it would be as impossible as it would be unrealistic to dissociate the position of the woman from the general economic and social developments in Brazilian history. No less than the male, she was to experience the stresses and strains within society, and those regional variations and economic imbalances that characterized Portuguese America. This article will argue that the female played a significantly more important role in the social, economic, and ideological development of the colony than has been appreciated. Although, in the case of the white woman, the demands of society required that she be out of sight, this should not be interpreted as suggesting that she was out of mind. The roles of Amerindian and Black women have received extensive treatment elsewhere. Thus my discussion will deal with the white female, digressing to describe the position of the Black or mulatto woman only when this would establish a point of comparison, heighten the contrasting role between females of different colors in the colony, or serve to reinforce the argument.

Two caveats must be entered at the outset. Evidence on the role of the white woman in colonial Brazil is not readily available. Memoirs, diaries, or chronicles written by females in Portuguese America have not survived the ravages of time, if they existed at all. Registers of royal orders, gubernatorial correspondence, and legislation are rarely informative in this regard. Thus I have relied on sources in private and public archives such as wills, inventories, municipal licensing ledgers, brotherhood and conventual records, and fiscal registers. Such evidence was gleaned from Rio de Janeiro, São Paulo, Salvador, and Minas Gerais. But it is well to bear in mind that such was the human and ecological heterogeneity of Portuguese America that regional variations may well be found to differ from the picture here depicted. The second caveat is prompted by the latter-day adulation of Clio. The welter of recent publications on family history, especially those based on a quantitative approach, has yet to embrace colonial Brazil. Whereas selected cities and regions of Spanish America have provided case studies for scholars, only in São Paulo and Salvador have steps been taken for the collection of demographic data for the colonial period. At the present stage, it would be misleading to adduce conclusions based on partial evidence and tentative findings. Something so basic to our understanding as a documented estimate as to the numbers of migrants to Brazil from Portugal and the Atlantic Islands before 1822 has yet to be made. A historian of the role of women must contend with the dearth of data on such fundamentals as the number of female migrants to the colony, or what proportion of the overall population was composed of females. Inadequate conventual, baptismal, and marriage registers make impossible any determination of percentages of women marrying, entering convents, or remaining unmarried. I hope that the evidence here presented will throw new light on attitudes toward women and inspire a reassessment of their contribution to the building of Portuguese society in the tropics.

Ideologies, Values, Attitudes, and the Legal Position of Women

The attitudes of male colonists in Brazil toward women did not differ markedly from their counterparts in Portugal. Male-oriented, male-dominated, patriarchal, and patrilineal societies, the role ascribed to the female was marginal, isolating her from the mainstream of developments in the colony. At first sight, such attitudes might appear negative, humiliating the female by relegating her to an inferior position. In fact, closer scrutiny shows that the converse was the case, and the female was held in high regard. Ideals and precepts that in our age would be regarded as restrictive and male chauvinist were regarded as the normal outcome of theological teaching and unreservedly accepted as such by Catholics of colonial Brazil. In a profoundly religious society, even the most foul-mouthed and domineering slave owner was deeply conscious of right and wrong and faced death with fear and trepidation. In practice his attitudes toward women depended on their social position and color. He did not look on a white woman with those same eyes with which he looked on Black or Amerindian women. However, rather than a double standard of values, there was a double standard of expectations and of enforcement. Expectation of deviation from behavioral ideals demanded of the white woman increased in inverse proportion to the decreasing degree of whiteness and financial means of the woman. While it was accepted that the white woman was sexually unassailable and sexual promiscuity on her part could result in death at the hand of her husband or father, for the colored woman it was conceded that she was in no position to repel sexual advances by her master and that she might resort to prostitution to buy her freedom. Such was the sexual mystique enshrouding the colored woman that infidelity and promiscuity on her part were regarded as almost inevitable.

European travelers to colonial Brazil commented on the seclusion of the white woman, be she daughter or wife. This was the ideal state for womanhood in the eyes of the colonists, not from any desire to attribute an inferior position to the woman, but rather to isolate her from the realities of everyday life. Possibly this attitude was mingled with yet another cultural legacy from the Old World to the New: Marianism. The large number of brotherhoods dedicated to the Virgin was evidence enough of the veneration in which she was held by the colonists. Some of this veneration may have been transferred into everyday attitudes toward laywomen. In colonial Brazil the female was a possession to be cherished and protected against coarseness, sexual advances, or any act that might tarnish her purity. This explains in part why colonial fathers were so willing for their daughters to enter convents. If the girl were to choose marriage, no effort was spared to ensure that the transition to her new role should be as painless and effortless as possible. Rare was the girl who came to the altar without being endowed within the financial means of her parents who tried to ensure that the groom should be his bride's social equal. Against this ideological context, the closing of certain avenues to the white woman in Brazil—be they sexual, social, or economic—may be viewed as a positive aspect of colonial society in Portuguese America.

The most explicit contemporaneous commentary on the position of the white female in colonial Brazil and her relations to her family is contained in a tract written by Nuno Marques Pereira and entitled *A Narrative Compendium of the Pilgrim in America* (Lisbon, 1728). A journey to Minas Gerais provided the pretext for a moralistic tract on the evils of the colony. At each stop on his journey, the "pilgrim" took the opportunity to moralize and to gloss that commandment most relevant to his host's situation. His observations doubtless reflected the attitudes of Pereira's contemporaries and merit close attention.

The "pilgrim" advocated that, ideally, marriages should be between partners of similar social and economic standing and of about the same age. Once married, the wife was to shun the company of ecclesiastics and women of questionable repute because of their propensity for sexual alliances and malicious gossip. The ideal wife should dress modestly, should not covet anything beyond her financial means or social station, and on no occasion speak disparagingly of her husband. In short: "And thus married women must be strong, discreet, and prudent. Within their homes, they should be diligent. Outside their homes they should be retiring. And at all times they should be exemplary in their conduct and mien and be reputed as long suffering rather than spendthrifts." Pereira noted that women in Portugal were less tolerant toward their colored domestics than were their Brazilian counterparts, who would go so far as to condone misbehavior or conceal criminal offenses committed by a slave girl.

The "pilgrim," while describing the obligations of a wife to her husband, emphasized the responsibilities of a husband toward his wife. Pereira noted that many wives were *mal cazadas* ("badly married") and had wearied of the married state because of their husband's inconsiderate behavior. In such cases it was the Christian duty of the husband to mend his ways and accord to his wife the attention and respect she deserved. He was not to take concubines, whom the "pilgrim" compared to turtles who emerged from the water, deposited their eggs on the beach, and then returned to immerse themselves in an ocean of sin. Nor was the husband to place temptation in the way of his wife. He should not take young men to his home, nor exhibit his wife to male friends as he would a sample of cloth. He was to be vigilant over the company she kept, forbidding her from visiting female friends whose composure or conversation might be injurious. In sexual matters he was to be moderate and not overly demanding.

As paterfamilias, the father was responsible for the physical, spiritual, and economic well-being of his household, which embraced wife, children, and servants. By his example and by maintaining constant vigilance over his children, whom he should not hesitate to chastise, the father should always be conscious of his duties. This vigilance was especially applicable to daughters. The "pilgrim" counseled:

> Know, Sir, I said to him, there is no force on this earth against which a battle must be so relentlessly waged as woman. The first duty of a father is to bring up his daughters in the faith of the Lord and ensure that they are married at the appropriate time. When the vine matures it must be given shelter and special care. Likewise, a girl on reaching womanhood needs protection, a home, and a husband.

A girl's innocence could only be guaranteed if the father "were to be as vigilant as Argus by day and by night." On no occasion should the father allow a daughter from his sight. She should not keep the company of slave girls of dubious morals. Her teachers should be rigorously screened. Pereira quoted the dictum of one mother that she preferred her daughters to be less knowledgeable and more secluded. The conscientious father would "count and measure," be it the regularity of music or the spacing of a daughter's words or footsteps whenever she was out of his sight. Selection and final approval of a marriage partner were the final responsibilities of a father to his daughter. Pereira cited the adage that "a father need not lose a moment's rest in marrying off ten sons, but the marriage of a virtuous daughter is the labor of a decade," and gave a final warning against fathers who married off daughters against their will.

The dearth of documentary evidence on female reaction toward such attitudes and the manner in which the white female perceived her own role in colonial society makes assessment difficult. From testaments made by females and occasional letters it appears that white females did not challenge the position ascribed to them by society. In fact, even if a girl or woman had wished to protest it would have been difficult for her to find adequate channels for self-expression. Wills made by females comprise only a small number of those dating from the colonial period and that are extant in private archives; nevertheless, these are sufficient to illustrate attitudes of white women on certain issues. Five such themes, basic to an understanding of colonial society, may be singled out for further study: attitude to manual labor, treatment of slaves, religiosity, marriage, and vanity.

The dependence of the white female on slaves for the running of her household was unquestioned. That delegation of responsibility to female slaves was allied to scorn for manual labor by white females was documented only when they faced the possibility of being deprived of slave labor. Two examples, both taken from institutions, will illustrate this. The Retirement House of the Most Holy Name of Jesus in Salvador (opened 1716) provided a haven for girls of middle-class families who were of marriageable age and whose honor was endangered by the loss of one or both parents. When the issue of menial labor was first raised, Dom Pedro II had ordered that the inmates should care for themselves and cited the precedent set by convents in Lisbon where even noble recluses had no servants. In 1721 the inmates revolted, alleging that the female warden "treated them as if they were slaves . . . ordering them to wash crockery and scale fishes and dealing with them harshly despite the fact that they were white women and wards [of the Misericôrdia]." The inmates presented their case to the all-male governing body. The warden was dismissed and the number of slaves increased to such excess as to be the subject of a royal inquiry in 1754. Slaves were also employed for general duties in the Convent of the Poor Clares in Salvador (founded 1677). Nuns were also permitted to have personal servants, but only after petitioning for an apostolic brief. The petition had to be supported by a document signed in secret by the members of the conventual community favoring such an addition and by a letter from the family saying it would meet the additional costs. This directly contravened the papal brief of Clement IX (May 13, 1669), which had authorized fifteen servants for general duties, but had expressly stated that no nun should have a slave for her particular needs. Many nuns came to have not only one, but two servants. Some petitions were made less from necessity than from social considerations. In 1701 the two daughters of Manuel Alvares Pereira urged their father to meet a man who had two Black female slaves to sell at the bargain price of 150$000 reis for the two. The daughters recognized that not only would the slaves satisfy their domestic needs, but their possession would enhance their standing in the conventual community. In 1883 the archbishop of Salvador ordered the abbess to reduce the number of servants. At that time thirty-seven servants were serving thirteen nuns and ten resident laywomen.

In the attitudes by white females toward slave girls, distinctions of class, color, and civil standing precluded any feeling of common cause. In the early nineteenth century Henry Koster was to write that "It is said that women are usually less lenient to their slaves than men." This echoed the advice of the Count of Assumar to an overzealous official in Minas Gerais about to prosecute the slave of a captain-major. The governor advised restraint "because these Americans venerate their Black slaves as they would demigods." In their treatment of female slaves, white women ran the gamut from Christian charity to sadistic cruelty. Many left legacies of dowries for slave girls to be married, together with household linen and even furniture. Such legacies often included a clause granting a slave girl her freedom. At the other extreme were white women who prostituted their slave girls for their own gain or were spurred by jealousy to acts of cruelty.[1]

1   Henry Koster, *Travels in Brazil* (London, 1816), p. 388.

In their attitudes toward marriage, white women followed the precepts of colonial society. White female testators recognized their responsibility to assist unmarried nieces, more distant relations, or the daughters of friends, to make a suitable marriage. Clauses in wills specifically allocated substantial sums of money for dowries. Many followed the example of Joana Fernandes and Maria de Leão, Bahian ladies of the seventeenth century, who provided the capital for trust funds to be established to provide orphan girls of the city and the Recôncavo with dowries to enable them to marry. By such generosity the white female not only recognized her obligations to society, but was also moved by a profound feeling of Christian charity.

Works of social philanthropy were but one aspect of religious conviction. Equally indicative of colonial attitudes were testamentary provisions for funerals and the saying of masses. In this respect the wills of female testators differ only in minor points from those of their male counterparts. Pomp and piety melded to ensure that the funeral would be worthy of the social standing of the deceased and that her soul would be provided for by the saying of masses. Catharina da Silva, twice widowed, who died in São Paulo in 1694, ordered that her body should be buried in the church of St. Francis. Her cortege was to be accompanied by the brothers of the Misericôrdia and by representatives of other brotherhoods. Masses were to be said for her soul. In Salvador in the early seventeenth century, Maria Salgada left a two-storied house to the Misericôrdia with the obligation of saying masses in the brotherhood's chapel for her soul.

In such provisions there was not a little of that vanity and nobilomania that pervaded colonial society. Easily documented for males in their petitions to the crown for the concession of knighthoods in the military-religious orders, evidence of similar aspirations on the part of the white female is more difficult to document. Colonelcies in militia regiments were highly coveted. In 1725 Dom João V warned the governor of Minas Gerais to scrutinize the social background and capabilities of candidates because it had come to the royal notice that unsuitable people were obtaining such posts, "dazzled by the honor which such positions bestow on the incumbent, to which their wives are no less susceptible."

The legal position of the female in the colony depended largely on color and social standing. Because political activity, even at the local level, was regarded as an exclusively male preserve, females were excluded from the lists of the "good folk of the Republic" permitted to vote in municipal elections. In other respects the white female enjoyed due process of law and, if this failed, she could appeal directly to the crown. She could serve as an executrix of a will, inherit and possess land and properties, and could and did frequently hold the legal position of head of household. She could conduct trade and commerce in her own name and could bring legal charges against others. It was not unknown for a daughter to prosecute her father, if he were reticent in furthering her hopes of marriage, and demand payment of her dowry. However, whereas proven adultery was sufficient cause for a man to divorce his wife, for her part the wife was often required to prove a second cause such as cruelty, desertion, or forced prostitution to obtain a divorce. In such cases a lien was placed on all possessions of the defendant, who was responsible for making financial arrangements for the upkeep of the estranged wife and children. During the period of legal separation the estranged wife was placed in the home of a respectable citizen on the order of the vicar-general. After six months she could file for divorce and final judgment would be made by the vicar-general. In some cases the ecclesiastical authorities were overzealous. In the 1750s one such divorced woman, Thereza de Jesus Maria, alleged that she was being held against her will in the Retirement House of the Misericôrdia in Salvador on the personal orders of the archbishop while her good-for-nothing bookkeeper husband fled to Portugal with her wealth. The crown judge in Salvador, influenced by archiepiscopal pressure, refused to accept her appeals and order her release. Courts looked leniently on crimes of passion where a husband had beaten or killed an adulterous wife, or a wife merely suspected of infidelity.

The colored woman possessed certain legal rights, but these were less likely to be respected, and courts were reluctant to hand down a judgment in her favor if the defendant were a white person. Slave girls appealed to local authorities and even to the crown, alleging physical cruelty by masters. Where a master refused all reasonable offers by a slave girl to buy her "certificate of freedom," she could prosecute and force him to accept a sum arbitrated by an independent third party. Few slave girls followed this course, either because they were unable to meet the costs of a protracted legal suit or because of fear of reprisal by former masters. Appeals to the crown were usually successful, although governors warned that charges often lacked substance and that slave girls accumulated money for manumission by resorting to prostitution with the full knowledge of their masters. Only in 1871, as the result of the Rio Branco law, were the offspring of slave mothers born free. Previously such children merely became welcome additions to the slave holdings of a master. Marriage to a slave girl by a free colored reduced him likewise to bondage, and marriage by a male slave to a free Black woman did not absolve him from bondage.

Although Amerindians were protected by law from enslavement, bureaucratic negligence in registering royal decrees, pressures by colonists, and their own inability to appeal made Amerindian women susceptible to many of those abuses experienced by Black slave women. In 1719, the Count of Assumar told the king about Amerindian girls being sold publicly, left in legacies, given as dowries, and set to work without pay. Such women petitioned district judges and governors for their freedom. Maria Moreira and her three children gained their freedom in 1765 by gubernatorial decree. A Carijó, she had resorted to direct appeal because defective baptismal records made it impossible to obtain documentary evidence and she was too poor to prove her origins through the judicial process. As in other cases concerning Amerindians, she was subjected to "visual inspection," and perception played a large part in determining the outcome of such appeals.

Not all Amerindian women were victims of ill-treatment. Catharina Florença, a native of the island of Itamaracá, had been sold in Rio de Janeiro and brought to Minas Gerais with her children. When granted her freedom, she waived charges against her master because he had clothed, housed, and fed her and her family. When Amerindian women were married to Black slaves, they were especially susceptible to enslavement, if they were to accompany their husbands. However, their offspring remained free. Although Blacks and mulattoes were regarded with suspicion, the crown saw Amerindians as possible means of increasing the population of the colony and as stabilizing factors. A decree of 1755 encouraged Amerindian-white marriages and ordered that the use of such injurious epithets as *caboclo* ("breed") or *negro* ("nigger") to describe the Amerindians should cease. In the 1740s, the crown approved suggestions by town councils in Minas Gerais that as many as 200 Amerindian couples be moved from São Paulo to Minas Gerais at royal expense.

Social Role of the White Woman

The Single Girl

The role accorded to the single white girl was no other than that of preparing herself to *tomar estado* ("to take state"), which meant either entering a convent or marriage. In either case, until the final documents had been signed, the parents lived on tenterhooks of doubts and fears to the point of obsession. The girl's childhood and adolescence were passed in seclusion to remove any possibility of doubt as to her virtue. In some instances family pressures were exerted on the girl either to marry or to enter a convent, but for the most part the concern of the parents was no more than that the girl should "take state." Testators left legacies to daughters, nieces, and the female offspring of friends for this, without specifying marriage or convent. Although in 1732 Dom Lourenço de Almeida was to comment caustically that "it was very fitting for people of low birth to have their daughters take the veil," there is nothing to suggest that this practice was more prevalent in any one class of colonial society. Even if the final outcome were in defiance of the parents' wishes, a rare event, nevertheless there was a feeling of relief once the decision on the girl's future had been taken.

Should the girl choose to enter a convent, the question arose as to whether this should be in Portugal or Brazil. The outcome was decided by three factors: the proximity of a convent, the color of the intending nuns, and the financial resources of the parents. By 1750 most cities in Portuguese America counted at least one convent. Such foundations were the fruits of public and civic pressures, but could not meet the demand for places. Colored girls were not admitted to convents in Brazil and were compelled to go to Portugal or the Atlantic Islands where they were accepted. Finally, the cost of sending a girl to Portugal, paying the fees for her to enter a convent, and the costs of her upkeep were substantial. Such considerations led the "native citizens and good men" of the city of São Paulo to remind the crown in 1736 of a royal favor permitting the Retirement House of Santa Thereza de Jesus to become a convent under the initial supervision of an abbess and nuns from Portugal. The petition informed the king that thirteen potential nuns from that city alone had raised 56,000 *cruzados* for such a foundation. A further fourteen people from Minas Gerais had expressed interest. The thirty-three signatories included the wife of the Paulista pioneer, Pedro Taques de Almeida Paes.

Judging by the number of petitions to the king asking for permission to send or accompany girls to Portugal to enter convents, there was no shortage of fathers willing to meet such costs. Some fathers were prominent figures in the colony. In 1725 the agent in Lisbon of Manuel Nunes Viana gained royal approval for the infamous *poderoso do sertão* ("a man influential in the backlands") to come to Portugal "to make nuns of his daughters." In 1726 he placed his six daughters in the convent of São Domingos das Donas in Santarém and returned to Bahia. Nunes Viana deposited 16,000 *cruzados* with the friars of São Vicente de Fora in Lisbon, the annual interest to meet the costs of upkeep and maintenance of his daughters. In the 1750s the nuns brought legal action against their brother, Dr. Miguel Nunes Viana, charging him with fraud and embezzlement of this capital. This was the subject of a royal inquiry, culminating in a ruling upholding the nuns' claim. Other fathers had aspirations beyond their financial means. In 1729 the viceroy supported the appeal to the king by the secretary of state Domingos Luís Moreira, asking Dom João V to intervene on behalf of three daughters whom he wished to place in the Convent of the Poor Clares in Oporto. After twenty years of loyal service, Moreira was too poor to pay the entry fees of his daughters to the convent, but had embarked the girls, trusting in the royal favor.

Many colonists were unable or unwilling to meet such financial costs. In Salvador they could choose between the Convent of the Poor Clares or the Lapa Convent. The demand for places in the former was such as to lead the city council in 1717 to petition the king for an increase in the number of places to one hundred from the original fifty authorized in 1665. Some fathers entered their daughters as "pupils" (*educandas*) in the hope that as such they would be favored when a vacancy occurred among the stipulated quota of nuns. Other hopeful but frustrated fathers followed the examples of Manuel de Almeida Mar who asked the king to intervene so that his niece could be admitted to the convent, or of another prominent Bahian, Domingos Pires de Carvalho, who made a similar appeal on behalf of his daughters. In fact, the granting of such favors fell outside the royal jurisdiction, and places were not reserved for royal nominees. Those who were successful in gaining admission often placed all their daughters in the convent. The secretary to the city council, João de Couros Carneiro, gained the abbess's permission for entry of his three daughters in 1686. The guarantee of protection and seclusion was not cheaply bought. In 1684 master of the field, Pedro Gomes, paid 600$000 reis and fees for each of his two daughters to be admitted as novices. Such "dowries" were not refundable should the girls not take their final vows. In 1751 the "dowry" for a girl wishing to take her vows as a nun was 160$000 reis. Nevertheless, for their own peace of mind the citizens of Bahia did not balk at such expenditures.

Marriage was the more commonly chosen option open to the single girl. At no time in her life was the female the object of so much attention. The choice of groom was made from a small circle of possible pretenders, selected and approved by the girl's parents. For the rural aristocracy of Pernambuco and Bahia, marriage served the double purpose of strengthening family ties among this elitist group and improving their economic position and land holdings. As plantation families fell on hard times, potential suitors from the rising and prosperous urban merchant class were courted to bolster the family position by the infusion of new capital.

The female was aided in her quest for marriage by the institution of the dowry. So important was the dowry that it served as a microcosm for attitudes and ideals and illustrated the interplay of social and economic pressures in colonial Brazil. A dowry was both a symbol of social status and a palliative. On the one hand, the social and economic standing of a doting father could only be enhanced if it were to become common knowledge that his daughter had a large dowry. On the other hand, a substantial dowry could offset lack of charm or beauty on the part of the girl. Such an institution was open to abuse. Many a man married a dowry rather than a bride. So prevalent was this mercenary practice that one petitioner for a royal favor cited in support of his appeal that he had married his wife for love and not for her dowry. Some women fell victims to the wiles of unworthy opportunists. The example of the bookkeeper of low birth who married a rich Bahian widow, Thereza de Jesus Maria, and then absconded to Portugal with her wealth was by no means unique. Whatever the evils of the tradition, for the daughter of a wealthy family it was never doubted but that she would be endowed. For the daughter of a middle-class or poorer family, a dowry was no less a prerequisite for marriage. For the daughter of poor parents or an orphan, a dowry could mean the difference between an honorable marriage and prostitution.

Dowries made by fathers and mothers to their daughters frequently took the form of possessions, rather than outright cash payments. Several factors may have contributed to this practice: first, the shortage of currency in some regions at different periods; second, the desire to preserve the overall estate intact albeit under different ownership; and third, the fact that in certain areas an economy prevailed that was based on barter rather than coin. The variety of such possessions is well illustrated by the following case taken from São Paulo in the seventeenth century. Messia Rodrigues, the widow of João Pires to whom she had borne nine daughters and one son, endowed her youngest daughter,

Margarida, especially generously. Her husband, Captain António do Canto, received 268$000 reis in cash and possessions valued at 450$000 reis. The breakdown of these was as follows (values in brackets): reinforced mud houses (100$000 reis); house with a tiled roof (20$000 reis); eight dining-room chairs and a sideboard (18$000 reis); clothes (44$000 reis); one bed, covered with a cotton panoply and bed linen (16$000 reis); six silver spoons, table pieces, and cotton towels (8$000 reis); one hundred cows (200$000 reis); forty calves (16$000 reis); eight mares and one colt (17$000 reis); six sheep and one lamb (7$000 reis); tools and equipment (4$000 reis). The dowries of the other daughters included Amerindians, pigs, roofing tiles, and bales of cotton. The practice of giving Amerindians as dowries was especially prevalent in São Paulo, where enslavement persisted despite royal decrees forbidding this practice.

The preservation, or if possible, enhancement of social standing by marriage was never far from the minds of the prestige-conscious colonists. Legacies of dowries to daughters and relatives reveal the strength of this preoccupation. The last instructions of the Paulista Pedro Vaz de Barros to his widow were that she should marry off their two daughters "as quickly as possible with worthy men who have the ability to follow an honorable career." Jorge Ferreira, a wealthy property owner who died in Salvador in 1641, bequeathed the fruits of his labors to his niece, Jerónima Ferreira, as a dowry "so that the husband whom she marries may be the more ennobled thereby." Similar sentiments filled Francisco Zorilla and Affonso do Pôrto Poderoso. The former had seen military service and held minor posts including that of procurator of the Indians (*procurador dos índios*). In 1620 he exacted from the king the royal favor (*mercé*) that this post should be granted to his widow in trust for the man who married their only daughter. In 1673 Pôrto Poderoso was granted royal permission to retire from his post as clerk to the High Court of Bahia, which he had held for some thirty years. This post, at his discretion, was to pass to his oldest son or to the man who took his daughter in marriage.

Other dowries were given in recognition of the fact that without them daughters or female relatives would stand little chance of getting married. This was recognized by Marcelino Vieira Machado, captain of Monserrate fortress in the Bay of All Saints. In 1809 he petitioned the crown for promotion to the rank of sergeant-major, citing thirty-eight years in the royal service. He had been moved to make this request because on an annual salary of 10$000 reis it was impossible for him to endow his three daughters. The requested promotion would almost double his salary and permit him to provide dowries for his girls, thereby enabling them to find suitable husbands. That it was essential to bring a dowry to marriage was recognized not only by anxious fathers who made special bequests to daughters. Colonists, many of whom had no children of their own, made testamentary provisions for dowries to be given to nieces, godchildren, the daughters of their executors, or simply to the unmarried female offspring of friends. In an age when personal legacies were comparatively few, and testators preferred to leave their fortunes for the saying of masses or charity, legacies for dowries afforded a notable exception.

Orphan girls were perhaps the most in need of dowries. Loss of a father or of both parents placed the girl's virtue and future in jeopardy. Concern for a girl's moral well-being provoked a response on the part of colonists that was nothing short of magnificent. Foundlings left on doorsteps were adopted and provided with dowries. This generosity extended to dowries for slave girls and even for their female offspring. Many testators preferred that the Misericórdia should administer such dowries for orphan girls. These fell into two categories. Specific sums were left to the Misericórdia for immediate allocation to deserving cases, or legacies were made to the Misericórdia for the capital to be placed on loan and a number of dowries financed each year from the interest.

The Married Woman

To separate the position of the white woman in colonial Brazil from her role in marriage would be to ignore the social, ideological, and religious context of an age and country. It was unquestioned that her raison d'être was to be virtuous as a girl, honorable as a bride, loyal as a wife, and loving toward her children. It was in marriage, with its multiplicity of demands and responsibilities, that the white woman made her major contribution to society. Moreover, only through marriage would a girl become a woman in her own right and in the eyes of others. Attitudes toward the institution of marriage have already been discussed, and we may now turn to the more physical aspects of the life of the married woman. The demographic history of colonial Brazil is fraught with difficulties, but certain sources have not been fully exploited in providing data on marriage patterns. One such source comprises testaments dating from the colonial period. In no way can these conclusions be considered definitive, but it is hoped that they may stimulate further detailed research on the part of scholars.

The age at which a girl was regarded as being "marriageable" depended in part on her parents' financial position and social background. Some girls may have married at only twelve years of age, but such early marriages were the exception rather than the rule. Fourteen was a generally accepted age for a first marriage, and daughters were encouraged by parents to marry early. The relief expressed by Catharina de Araújo "who rejoices greatly at seeing her daughter protected and made mistress of her own household as she desires," on the occasion of the marriage of her fourteen-year-old daughter, Bernarda, to a Bahian goldsmith, was symptomatic of the reaction of many parents. To judge by conditions imposed by the Misericôrdia for the granting of dowries, the age span for first marriages was considered to be between fourteen and thirty years of age. That girls matured earlier than boys was recognized by the census of 1776. Males from seven to fifteen years were classified as boys (*rapazes*), whereas the upper age for girls (*raparigas*) was fourteen. Furthermore, whereas for a woman old age was considered to start at forty, the male only qualified for such a classification on reaching his sixtieth year.

Possibly marriages were contracted against the girl's will, but less frequently than popular mythology and "cord" literature would suggest. The custom existed of orphan girls in convents and retirement houses being provided for by wealthy benefactors until they came of an age when their elderly protectors would claim them in marriage. This practice met with the consent and approval of the authorities. That young girls should marry much older men was commonplace. Parents viewed with approval the suit of a man old enough to be the girl's father or even grandfather, because of the financial security and social position such a marriage would provide. Some child-wives may have accepted such a fate with resignation, but horrifying pictures have been painted of young girls being forced into marriages with tuberculous septuagenarians.

The question of fertility of white women in the tropics is controversial. At the present state of research conclusions must be tentative. There is evidence to support the hypothesis that many white women in colonial Brazil did not bear children. Whether this was because of physiological, psychological, or environmental factors is unclear. The answer may well lie in a combination of all three influences. Repeatedly the testaments of white property owners in the colony asserted the absence of offspring and, in default of these, bequests were made to the church or to religious orders.

There is no reason to believe that such a situation was restricted to testators whose wills have survived or who were careful enough to make a will, not a widely practiced custom in the colony. However, this is not the whole story, and the figures presented (Figure 1) may give a more representative picture of family composition in Portuguese America. This chart was prepared from data obtained from a sample of 142 married couples in São Paulo in the seventeenth century. Much information is lacking, but membership of the Misericôrdia or Third Orders suggests that such couples were white and of middle- or upper-class background. Children registered are the offspring of first marriages only. All told, there were 731 legitimate children, which, divided among the 142 families, gives an arithmetic mean of 5.14 children per family. But to assert that the average household (*fogo*) was composed of parents and five children is misleading, because of the asymmetrical distribution of the data. Some families counted as many as sixteen children, but the most frequent value, or mode, is one to two children.

The white woman of colonial Brazil has been depicted as a matronly figure at twenty, worn out by successive pregnancies and lack of exercise. Evidence on frequency of childbirth is scanty. Testators often

FIGURE 1. Chart Showing the Frequency of Children of First Marriages

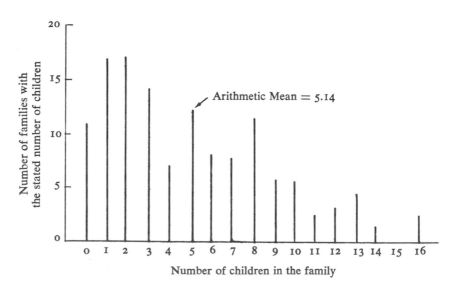

Arithmetic Mean = 5.14

Number of families with the stated number of children

Number of children in the family

failed to mention the ages of deceased children or of married offspring no longer living under the parental roof. Some few examples tend to bear out the view of repeated pregnancies. Isabel Gomes, who died in 1628 in São Paulo, bore her husband ten children of the following ages: twenty-three, twenty, eighteen, twelve, ten, eight, six, three, and one year and one not listed. The offspring of another Paulista mother were aged nineteen, seventeen, fifteen, twelve, ten, nine, four, and two years. Although one married child of Ignez da Costa was not listed by age, the recorded ages of the remainder of the family were twenty, nineteen, eighteen, sixteen, fifteen, ten, eight, seven, and two years. Infant mortality among whites was high, but not as high as among offspring of Black families. The belief that higher colored infant mortality was offset by larger numbers of offspring was challenged in 1821 by the German mining engineer, von Eschwege. Based on observations made in Minas Gerais, his conclusion was that white women were more fertile than mulatto women, and that the fertility of a Black woman depended on whether she were free or slave. A survey for the Passo parish of Salvador in 1799 suggests a mortality coefficient of 172.4/1000 for "innocents" of white parentage. Although wills rarely specified the age of a child at death, there is no doubt that, be it as a result of infant mortality or later sickness, many white children failed to survive their parents. Such productivity was not without its risk to the health of the mother. Several wills mention that the wife was pregnant at the time of making her last dispositions, "sick in bed and in fear of death." The inference is irresistible that her death resulted from complications during pregnancy, or in childbirth.

Of greater interest to students of family history are data concerning generational differences within a family. The age span between eldest and youngest was sometimes as much as twenty years. Of the seven children of the Paulista Agostinha Rodrigues, her eldest son was thirty, whereas her youngest was only five. The sixteen children of another Paulista family ranged from thirty-four to eight, spanning twenty-six years. Such large families provided a form of security, especially in agricultural areas, against the death of a breadwinner. Then, as now in Brazil, children joined the labor force at a tender age, and many a dying father could take solace in the fact that his widow would be helped by their already adult offspring.

A survey of 165 testaments made in São Paulo in the seventeenth century provides information on first and multiple marriages (Table I). Conclusions based on such partial evidence must be treated with caution,

TABLE I. Incidence of Marriage and Remarriage

Number of Marriages	Male	Female
0	2 (2%)	— —
1	99 (87%)	43 (84%)
2	12 (10%)	7 (14%)
3	1 (1%)	1 (2%)
	114	51

but are not necessarily unrepresentative of marriage patterns in the colony. It was unlikely that a white woman of marriageable age would remain single in the colony. Those alternatives open to her male counterpart—cohabitation or promiscuity—were barred to her. It also appears that the white woman was more likely to contract a second, or even third, marriage than her male counterpart. The shortage of white women in the colony placed a premium on the eligible widow. Furthermore, the custom of early first marriages by females often resulted in widowhood at a comparatively young age. Finally, the woman's own search for the financial security and social position guaranteed by marriage may have contributed to the greater incidence of remarriage among white females than white males.

The Woman as Head of Household: Social Aspects

The white woman in colonial Brazil frequently occupied the position of head of household. As such she made her most important contribution to the life and economy of the colony. Circumstances contributing to her assuming such a position were divorce, desertion, and widowhood. Judging by the paucity of references, rarely did estranged couples go to the lengths of formally filing for divorce. In those few recorded cases, the property of the couple was divided by the legal authorities and the female received half of the value at which the property and possessions had been assessed. Custody of children was invariably granted to the mother. In such cases the father was liable for maintenance of the mother and children. The only exception to this rule was when the wife was found to be the guilty party. In 1782, Manuel Nicolau, a native of Crete living in Salvador, was granted permission to return to Portugal with his three young daughters. Custody of the children had been granted to him after his wife had been found guilty of adultery and had been jailed together with her lover.

Far more frequently, the wife was thrown into the position of effective head of household as the result of desertion. Sometimes, she was the victim of circumstances; on other occasions such desertion was intentional. In a highly mobile and essentially opportunist society, the woman not only exerted a stabilizing influence on the family, but also had to shoulder the responsibility of bringing up children during their father's absence.

Conditions in the colony were not conducive to a secure family life. Heads of household, with their wives' consent, left families in Portugal or in a Brazilian coastal city rather than endanger their lives in the interior. Few followed the example of one doughty character who traveled from the hinterland of Pernambuco to Minas Gerais in the 1730s, accompanied by his wife and eight children. Wives and families were often the victims of vengeance born of jealousies and rivalries. In Pitangui in the early eighteenth century, the four young daughters of a prominent Bahian, Manuel de Figueiredo Mascarenhas, were orphaned. Domingos Rodrigues do Prado, "a rabble rouser, criminal and well known instinctive killer" had killed their father, the *juiz ordinário* ("magistrate"), because he suspected Mascarenhas of informing the governor of Prado's criminal deeds. On another occasion in Minas Gerais, when Martinho Affonso de Mello threw his support behind the local crown judge in attempts to establish a village in Papagaio, his life was threatened by the furious local populace, his house and property fired, and his wife compelled to leave the area. Threats of attack by Amerindians or groups of runaway slaves were constant. White settlers were the frequent victims of rape, pillage, mutilation, and murder. To such hazards could be added unsanitary living conditions and the usual gamut of tropical diseases and inadequate medical attention.

Against such a background, breadwinners could scarcely be criticized for not wishing to expose families to such hazards. Many a father left wife and family in Portugal with promises to return. Some died in the colony. Others committed bigamy or took a concubine. Others simply lost contact with relatives. Soldiers in the dragoons often served terms of ten years in Minas Gerais before petitioning the crown for leave of absence of one year to return to their families in Portugal. Royal approval for such leaves and increased family allowances failed to prevent the disintegration of family ties. Petitions by widows for the discharge of soldier sons were invariably granted. Appeals by deserted widows and offspring to the crown and to the Misericórdia, seeking assistance in tracing husbands and fathers, were commonplace. In 1747, Dom João V asked Gomes Freire de Andrada to verify the whereabouts of one João Pereira Borges. Some twenty years previously he had gone to Minas Gerais, leaving wife and child in Lisbon. His wife complained that seventeen years had passed without news of her husband. Thanks to the charity of neighbors and to her skill with her needle, she was supporting herself and their twenty-two-year-old daughter. But such was their indigence that she could not "give state" to her daughter. The husband was traced to Brumado in Catas Altas where he had a smithy. The king ordered his return to Portugal to support his family.

Cases of desertion were not limited to wives and family in Portugal. In Brazil, men left home for long periods while on expeditions to the *sertão* ("backlands"). In default of any news of their whereabouts, they were presumed dead. Soldiers who had married in the colony, and whose tour of duty was over, preferred to desert their wives rather than return with them to Portugal. Colored wives were frequent victims of such neglect.

The emphasis placed by colonial mores on single girls and marriage tended to conceal the inescapable fact that the majority of marriages would end in widowhood. It was more usual for the white female to outlive her spouse than vice versa. For the woman who chose not to remarry, the alternative was a struggle not only for her own survival, but also as guardian of her children and frequently as owner of property. In such a role the widow was a true head of household with extensive responsibilities. Although relatives and older married children rallied round at times of need, success or failure for the widow and her family lay in her hands. The difficult role into which the widow was cast was acknowledged by husbands who made special clauses in their wills to support their widows.

The first hurdle to be faced by the widow was bureaucratic. This was especially the case if the husband had died intestate, or if the offspring were younger than twenty-five years of age. The local *"provedor* of the dead and absent" not only made an inventory of the possessions of the deceased, but also placed a lien on them and all currency holdings. Given the mobility of colonial society, it was not unusual for a person's possessions to be distributed throughout Brazil. Delays were inevitable, severely prejudicing heirs because of devaluation of plantations and death of cattle as the result of neglect. Heirs in Brazil often lost their inheritances because of the ruling that no *provedor* should release the possessions of the deceased without written authorization obtainable only in Lisbon. This absurd ruling was relaxed in 1719, but three years later the town council of Vila Rica informed the king that because of restrictions placed by *provedores* many rich men were buried as paupers and many a young widow was made destitute. Despite reforms and crown intervention in specific cases, delays and abuses were endemic. Heirs in Portugal making claims in Brazil were passed over by local *provedores*. Delays of twenty to thirty years were not infrequent. Euzebia Maria da Assumpção, widow of the businessman, Alexandre Manzoni, who had died in Salvador in 1773, asked the crown for assistance in settling her husband's estate. From Lisbon it was impossible for the widow to enforce payment of debts due to her husband in Bahia, Minas Gerais, and Goiás. In 1788 the queen ordered a judge of the High Court in Salvador to be appointed to oversee the collection of these debts. In 1813, the populace of Xique Xique asked for the status of township (*vila*) to be conceded to their village. This appeal was based on the grounds that only thus could a remedy be found to the present situation whereby widows and orphans were left destitute, lost properties, and were unable to collect debts because their nearest legal recourse was fifty leagues distant.

Arrangements made by the deceased for his widow and family varied. The simplest arrangement derived from the time of marriage when a "division of properties" was made, enabling the wife to maintain legal possession of her half. Where this was not stated in so many words, the customary practice was for an inventory to be made of the possessions of the deceased. The wife received half of the proceeds derived from the sale of such possessions. Debts and legacies were made from the husband's portion and the residue subdivided. In some cases the deceased had set aside one-third of his portion for the saying of masses for his soul. In other instances this was left to a favorite niece or daughter, or even to his wife. The remaining two-thirds were usually divided among his sons and heirs. Matters could become complicated when, for example, a testator ordered that his "third" (*terça*) should be divided equally between legitimate and illegitimate children, and then that the respective halves should be further subdivided so that each child would be a beneficiary.

In some instances the legacies made to the widow were substantial enough to guarantee her security and enable her to bring up children without undue financial strain. But all too many testators left their survivors with no more than their blessing, "heirs to the poverty I possess."

Sometimes the sum realized by the sale of the deceased's properties and possessions was insufficient even to meet the liabilities and debts he had incurred during his life. Rather than being the beneficiaries of his will, the heirs and widow had to realize their own capital investments to pay these debts. Such straits led the archbishop of Bahia to grant licenses to widows and *donzelas* to ask for alms in public.

The widow was often the executrix of the terms of her husband's will. In this she was usually assisted by a male relative or friend of the deceased. Should the widow die soon after her husband, such a relative became the guardian of the orphaned children. Certain testators placed limitations on the role of the mother as guardian, should she remarry. One Paulista in the seventeenth century made his wife the guardian (*curadora*) of their children only for as long as she did not remarry. Francisco Pedroso Xavier left his widow Maria Cardoso his "third" in addition to the half of his property she had received as his widow. But this supplementary legacy was conditional "only for as long as she does not remarry because I trust that she will behave honorably towards our children and when and if she should remarry then my 'third' is to be divided among my sons and daughters."

The widow was helped in her task by two factors: first, those benefits derived from larger families; and second, specific funeral bequests made to her by the deceased for this purpose. Older offspring were exhorted by a dying father to help their widowed mother. One Paulista, Manuel da Cunha Gago, went so far as specially to ask the second son of his first marriage to be generous to his stepmother, Maria Rodríguez, the widow of his father's second marriage. Bequests to provide the widow with the means of fulfilling such responsibilities included the placing of sums of money in trust for dowries to female offspring, supplementary legacies to the widow, and a home or a small-holding to provide a source of income and sustenance.

This assistance could not detract from the awesome responsibility to be shouldered by the widow. Many widows faced the task of bringing up younger children and then providing boys with basic skills or ensuring that girls were suitably married. Maria Rodríguez, the widow of Manuel da Cunha Gago to whom she had borne twelve children and by whom she was pregnant at the time of his death, confronted a household of children aged from twenty to one. The duties of the widowed mother were not merely directed to supporting herself and her family. Her prime obligation was toward the physical and spiritual welfare of her children. To her fell those tasks as guardian and protector that the "pilgrim" had seen as the necessary duties of the pater familias. Hers was the responsibility of teaching the children Christian doctrine and "ensuring that they are taught good habits and behavior, the girls to sew and perform domestic tasks and the boys to read, write and count."

For boys several options were open to the widowed mother. A son could take over the estate or small-holding when he came of age. Other male offspring were induced to sign up for military service or were apprenticed to a trade. Few widows were able to meet the costs of a university education, but some still entertained the hope of most parents in the colony that at least one of their sons might enter the church. It was not uncommon for fathers or relatives to make legacies specifically for boys wishing to follow such a vocation. The expenditure was substantial, involving travel to Europe and study there over a period of years. Thus the dedication and sacrifices demanded of one Paulista widow, Euphemia da Costa, cannot be underestimated. Four of her sons took holy orders. For daughters the hopes of the widow were centered on marriage, and fathers made bequests for the realization of such hopes.

The responsibilities of the widow were not limited to her immediate family and offspring. The taking of concubines and extramarital relationships were prominent features of colonial life. If a mistress were to be discarded or die, it was customary for the man to bring the children home to his legitimate wife to be cared for, reared, and educated alongside their legitimate children. Foreign travelers to Brazil never ceased to comment on the presence of such children, often of darker hues than the legitimate offspring, at the family table and treated on a basis of equality with children born within wedlock. The attitudes by fathers to such illegitimate offspring were ambivalent. Many simply deserted mother and child, and there may have been grounds for the crown's insistence on a correlation between concubinage and the number of foundling children whose upkeep was a financial drain on town councils in Brazil.

But this was only one side of the story. Other fathers acted most responsibly toward offspring born on the wrong side of the sheet. For the most part the fathers followed the example of Aleixo Leme de Alvarenga who, while acknowledging paternity of children by slave girls, refused to allow bastards to be his heirs. But he made allowances for such children. Aleixo Leme left to his illegitimate daughter, Paula, her mother, who was still in bondage, and two more slaves. Should Paula die, then the mother would become the property of the other illegitimate children she had borne Aleixo. Diogo de Cubas, a Madrileño living in

São Paulo, exhorted his wife and daughter to look after his illegitimate daughter by a slave. Not only were they to care for her well-being, but were to "indoctrinate her, teach her good customs and make her pray." This generosity extended in most cases to the mother of the child if she were known. Slave girls not only received their freedom but also household linen, domestic utensils, and even, on some occasions, a dowry.

The Woman as Head of Household: Economic Aspects

The vital contribution made by the white woman to the formation of Brazilian society could not be matched by her role in the country's economy. Social mores and the institution of slavery stifled any initiative that the white woman might have been spurred to make. Even at the domestic level slaves were charged with the day-to-day provisioning and maintaining of the household. Those few "cottage industries" that there may have been were performed by Blacks or Amerindians. The contribution the white female made to the colonial economy was less by dint of her own efforts than as the result of circumstances she could not avoid. As the widow was forced to assume the position of head of household, so too was death to be instrumental in placing the white woman in positions where she was compelled to take decisions on financial matters and the management of estates. In this regard she belied her traditional image of being divorced from the commercial life of the colony.

Some white women dodged this responsibility and were content to delegate the administration of estates or inherited properties to sons or more distant relatives. Not infrequently such trust was abused, bringing financial downfall to the woman. Luzia Freire, a widow living in Bahia, refused to make any legacy to her sons-in-law in her will of 1685. Both had cheated her in the management of a sugar plantation and cattle corrals, had misappropriated animals, and had stolen her slaves. Other widows followed the example of Magdalena da Silva, the widow of Manuel Thomé da Cunha and a native of Mathoím in Bahia. On her husband's death, she rented out her cane plantation for a guaranteed yearly income of 25$000 reis. Other widows or daughters who had inherited estates assumed full responsibility for their management. Catharina Paes, after the death of her husband André Lopes, continued to manage their estate, divided between two major areas in São Paulo. Total holdings comprised 224 cows, 4 oxen, 31 heifers, and 97 bullocks. That such examples were not merely a few entrepreneurial merry widows was shown by a seventeenth-century description of Pernambuco and Alagoas that listed 24 women as cane growers. They comprised 17 percent of the total number of sharecroppers in that area.

On rare occasions the white woman did take the initiative. In 1726 one league of land near the "new road" was granted to Izabel de Sousa at her request. Recently widowed and with children, her financial resources were slight and she intended to establish herself and support her family by raising cattle. Others maintained small-holdings, small stores, and may even have engaged in black market activities. In the 1760s dona Ana Maria Barboza de Penha de França, a widow in Minas Gerais, revealed in a petition to the governor a thorough understanding of the economics of operating a gold-mining *lavra,* employing some seventy slaves. She asked that restraints be placed on trespassers cutting wood in her lands on the banks of the Rio das Velhas. She needed wood for boxes, wheels, and axles as well as for working the placer mines in the river and for reconstruction of aqueducts bringing water from as far as four leagues away.

Economic interests and landholdings involved their female owners in such topical issues as land grants, division of judicial districts, and taxation. During the 1730s, there was hostility throughout Minas Gerais at the collection of the royal "fifths" (quintos) by means of a capitation tax. In Papagaio, in the hinterland of the Rio das Velhas, this culminated in a revolt and attack on the local judge. The evidence indicated that the revolt was the outcome of a conspiracy by powerful landowners and leading Paulista families with business interests in that area, rather than a truly popular uprising. Cited as conspirators in the official inquiry were dona Maria da Cruz and her son Pedro Cardozo, the nephew of Domingos do Prado. In 1737 she and her son were arrested by the intendant of the royal treasury in Sabará, Dr. Manuel Dias Tôrres, who had journeyed into the *sertão,* accompanied by thirty dragoons. Family connections involved the leading families of Vila Rica and São Paulo, and one conspirator fled to the ranch in Jacobina of dona Joanna Cavalcante, member of a prominent family, and who was sympathetic to the cause.

This role of the white woman in the colonial economy contrasted markedly with that of the Black woman, both slave and free. Subsistence crops, their marketing, and sale on the streets was largely controlled by such women. The repetitive nature of local legislation, forbidding sales of drinks and foodstuffs in mining areas, is testimony enough to the extent of such activities. Free and slave colored women, either on their own behalf or working for a master or mistress, successfully dominated the Black market in foodstuffs, produce, fruits, and fowls. As owners of shops, taverns, and slaughter houses, they played a vital role in community life. Although few, if any, practiced artisan trades, such paramedical professions as midwives and foundling mothers were the virtual prerogative of Black females. In this respect there was little occupational distinction between slaves and free coloreds.

The White Woman and Brazilian Colonial Society

In the absence of literary sources, diaries, chronicles, or personal correspondence, it is difficult to assess the value systems of a society. Colonial Brazil is no exception to this rule and has been categorized as male-dominated and patrilineal. New evidence suggests that in this mobile and precarious society, the woman was regarded as a stabilizing element and as the guardian of values that had originated in Europe, but had undergone modification in the tropics.

In their wills, male testators gave prominence to female survivors, be they widows, daughters, or nieces. Many such testators were not legally married or, if so, had no offspring. Frequently they had lost contact with wives and children, to say nothing of more distant relatives. When the time came to make their wills, "in fear of death," they were acutely conscious of two factors: the possibility of scurrilous claims being made against their wills; and an abhorrence of the possibility (very real in a multiracial society) that a son or heir might have bastard children by a slave woman and that these would inherit. In preambles and dispositions of their wills, many testators responded first to ideological precepts derived from Europe concerning "purity of blood," and, second, to a realistic assessment of the prevalent social mores in the colony. Even where there was a legitimate son to inherit, a testator would insist that inheritance of his possessions be restricted to female descendants only. This favoring of the distaff side of a family casts the role of the woman in colonial Brazilian society in a wholly new dimension, as will be seen from the following examples. Diogo Fernandes, who died in 1621, a tertiary of Saint Francis and brother of the Misericôrdia of Salvador, insisted in his will that only descendants on the distaff side should inherit his wealth or possessions. Another Bahian of the early seventeenth century, the bachelor Francisco Dias Baião, also disqualified the sons of his descendants from benefiting from his will and stipulated that only the daughters of such descendants could inherit. Another Bahian bachelor, also of the seventeenth century, António Dias de Ottões, allocated his considerable wealth for a variety of charitable purposes and for the saying of masses. While making legacies of 200$000 reis to each of his three sisters, and allocating 200$000 reis for his nieces if they were legitimate and alive, he specifically ruled that no legacy should be made to his nephews. Felippe Correia, owner of a sugar plantation in Pituba, ruled in his will of 1650 that a trust be established so that dowries of 400$000 reis be available for the female offspring of his sisters. Beneficiaries were limited to female offspring of the distaff side only. Fear that a male descendant might dishonor the family was well expressed in the will of Jerónimo de Burgos and his wife, who instituted a charitable trust in 1664. Any sums left from such a trust were to go to their son, the crown judge, Cristóvão de Burgos, and his descendants on the male side and, failing such, the female side. However, this legacy was made on the express condition that they "not marry anybody tainted by the blood of the prohibited races." Such clauses suggest that the female was seen as the guardian, not only of the social prestige of the family, but also as the preserver of ideals of purity of blood deeply rooted in white colonial society.

Such considerations may in large part explain the enthusiasm shown by white colonists for the building of convents and retirement houses. That such convents housed sanctity, piety, and devotion is indubitable, but the justification for such expenditures and the impetus leading to their construction were wholly secular. In a petition requesting royal approval for the foundation of the Convent of the Poor Clares, the "councillors, nobility and people" of Salvador emphasized how fitting would be such consent as a reward for the many services rendered by the citizens to the crown in the building of the capital of Brazil and the opening up of the hinterland. The townfolk of São Paulo followed a similar tack in their request of 1736 that the Retirement House of Santa Thereza de Jesus be given conventual standing. In 1738, the governor and city council of Rio de Janeiro emphasized how important it was that the city should have a convent. Completion of the Convent of Nossa Senhora da Ajuda had been delayed because the royal consent had contained a clause ruling that intending nuns would have to secure the approval of the Overseas Council in Lisbon. The local worthies had seen this as an insuperable barrier to gaining admittance for their daughters, and enthusiasm had waned. In 1736, two Capuchin friars had asked the king to allow them to occupy the empty and uncompleted shell. This spurred the city council to ask Dom João V to reject this request and throw his royal support behind the early completion of the building and its occupancy by Capuchin nuns. On his visit to Minas Gerais in 1743, the bishop of Rio de Janeiro collected alms for this purpose.

Equal enthusiasm was shown in the founding of retirement houses. Although wholly secular, such foundations were motivated by Christian sentiments and an awareness of the need for social charity. Best known was the Retirement House of the Most Holy Name of Jesus, opened in Salvador in 1716 under the auspices of the Misericôrdia, and made possible by an endowment of 80,000 *cruzados* by the local philanthropist, João de Mattos de Aguiar, in 1700. This was exceptional, and most retirement houses were more modest. After the death of her husband, Sebastiana Pereira da Conceição lived with her sister and two nieces in cloistral seclusion in a house in the parish of Sto. António Além do Carmo in Salvador. Encouraged by promises, she petitioned the king for permission to establish a retirement house with fifteen girls. In 1757, the viceroy dampened such hopes in a report to the effect that the promised financial aid would never be forthcoming. He asked the king to refuse permission "especially because this city already has a great abundance of convents and retirement houses." Finance was not the problem of the Italian Jesuit, Gabriel de Malagrida, who founded a retirement house for poor women, prostitutes, and girls whose honor was endangered, next to the Soledade church in Salvador. With entry fees ranging up to 3,000 *cruzados,* by 1739 the financial resources of the enterprise topped 90,000 *cruzados.* Granted conventual status, this institution was thereafter known as the Convent of the Ursulines. Wealthy colonists endowed such foundations. In 1787, the queen accepted a proposal by the miner, António de Abreu Guimarães, to set up a trust fund in the district of Sabará: this was destined for the building of three charitable institutions—a leprosarium, a seminary to bring up poor children, and a retirement house for needy girls.

Both convents and retirement houses admitted paying residents for varying periods of time under the names of *educandas, recolhidas,* and *porcionistas.* Young girls of good parentage were placed in convents until they married or decided to take the vows. Retirement houses catered more to orphan girls of middle-class parentage whose honor might otherwise be jeopardized. Husbands also placed their wives in retirement houses while journeying to Portugal or on an expedition to the interior. Finally, many widows or divorced women adopted such institutions as more or less permanent homes. Abuse could lead to royal intervention. Laymen were forbidden to meddle in the administration of convents. Nevertheless, such intervention was almost inevitable, given the importance of convents to urban society. The "rigging" of elections of abbesses by outsiders was not unknown, and convents did not escape charges of harboring amorous intrigues. Benefactors of retirement houses invariably ruled that the occupants should be "white, honorable, poor, and Old Christians." This also applied to convents. This makes all the more significant the request to Queen Maria by Anna Joaquina do Coração de Jesus, a mulatto (*parda*) native of Bahia, asking for royal approval to establish a Convent of the Immaculate Conception of the Mother of Christ for colored girls. The queen ordered an inquiry in 1797, but there are no records to indicate the outcome of this petition.

Convents and retirement houses afford an instance of collective female behavior, both in domestic affairs and in business management. For their patrimony such institutions depended largely on legacies or fees paid by the incoming incumbents. This capital enabled them to engage in business operations. No banks existed in the colony. It was to such convents that businessmen would come, cap in hand, to request loans to finance their commercial ventures. One such was José Ricardo Gomes, a Bahian businessman, who secured a loan of 7,000 *cruzados* from the Convent of the Poor Clares in 1793. By making such capital available, the convents played a vital role in the economy of the colony. Some convents traded in tobacco, sugar, and other commodities. Frequently these were the produce of plantations acquired as legacies or as the result of foreclosure for debts due to the conventual community. Retirement houses did not usually have so secure a financial base, but the Retirement House of Our Lady of the Conception of Macaúbas near Sabará had cultivated so diligently a land grant on the banks of the Rio das Velhas, granted by Governor dom Bras Balthazar da Silveira, that by 1725 the twenty recluses asked for a further six leagues of land so that they could expand their cattle ranching interests.

The lay brotherhoods afforded another example of collective female action. Although women were not permitted to join such brotherhoods, governing bodies looked more favorably on applications by males when they were married. Barred from holding office, wives performed charitable works and helped in the decoration of the brotherhood's church on the occasion of major festivals. Some brotherhoods followed the example of Nossa Senhora da Boa Morte in Salvador and reserved the title of "judge" (juiza) for female benefactors or ladies of noble birth. In all cases brotherhoods assisted, to the best of their financial ability, the widow and offspring of a brother. A wife or widow was also entitled to the privilege of a funeral accompanied by the members of the brotherhood and the saying of masses for her soul in the brotherhood's church.

It may well have been that it was in such convents that the white women of the colony received an education and cultural upbringing otherwise denied to them. Opportunities in the colony to gain an education were minimal even for the male, let alone the female. The female offspring of the wealthier families received private tuition in music and learned to read and write. But even at the highest levels of white society, illiteracy among white women was not unusual. Henry Koster, who visited Brazil in the early nineteenth century, attributed this situation to the

> ignorant state in which they are brought up; they scarcely receive any education, and have not the advantages of obtaining instruction from communication with persons who are unconnected with their own way of life, of imbibing new ideas from general conversation. . . . Bring these women forwards, educate them, treat them as rational, as equal beings; and they will be in no aspect inferior to their countrymen; the fault is not with the sex, but in the state of the human being.[2]

The stifling of intellectual curiosity and lack of interest in cultural matters was matched by a similar indifference to personal appearance on the part of the white woman. From Johan Maurits onward, European visitors commented unfavorably on the sedentary life of the white woman in Brazil. On those rare occasions when she did leave her home, she was carried by slaves in an enclosed *palanquim* ("palanquin"). Nor did the average white woman show any flair for fashion or in dressing herself. Social and financial standing could lead to reservations concerning this generalization, as, too, could the standpoint of an individual. But no researcher can fail to be impressed by the small amount of personal clothing recorded in inventories of deceased females of good birth and of financial means. Apart from everyday wear of an embroidered chemise or smock, items listed in inventories might include a taffeta cloak, a burlap skirt, a loose or a sleeveless jacket, and cheap silk and satin petticoats. Any judgment must take into account two factors. The first was climate. Tropical heat, humidity, and the fact that the white woman was usually secluded in her home were inducements enough to wear the minimum of formal clothing. Furthermore, limitations were imposed by sumptuary laws (1749) intended to reduce expenditure on luxury items and to protect the Portuguese textile industry.

2   Koster, *Travels,* p. 388.

Conclusions

The role of the white woman in colonial Brazil and her contribution to the life of the colony were circumscribed, and to some extent preordained, by tradition, law, and religious beliefs, but at no time was she divorced from the mainflow of colonial existence and reduced to mere marginality. Every aspect of colonial life was pervaded by a consciousness of her presence. Secluded she may have been in physical terms, and unable to realize her potential in the intellectual or political life of the colony, but she contributed to the building of Portuguese America despite such limitations.

The king, ecclesiastical authorities, viceroys, governors, town councillors, and colonists were perpetually concerned for the well-being of the white female. To each she held a particular importance. The crown saw her presence as a stabilizing factor, the preserver of Lusitanian traditions and language, and a catalyst to curb the wanderings of restless and opportunistic males. Moreover, the white woman was seen as the instrument for populating the vast expanses of Portuguese America, offsetting to some extent countless numbers of slaves and free Blacks. For the colonist, the white woman was wife and mother of his children, guaranteeing him a certain respectability within colonial society by the mere fact of being married. Moreover, marriage made him eligible for certain official positions denied to bachelors. To every Portuguese, be he king or colonist, the white woman was an object to be cherished and protected.

The idealism surrounding the white woman did not render her impotent and incapable of action on her own accord. As head of household, she took up the reins of authority, raising and educating children, and finally ensuring that they had a trade, vocation, or respectable position when the time came for them to leave the homestead. Women managed estates and properties, involving themselves in the day-to-day workings of gold mines, cattle ranches, and sugar plantations. Thus did the white woman make significant contributions to the society and economy of the colony.

The position of the white woman in Portuguese America differed from that of her counterparts in Spanish and English America. This was partly the result of different patterns of migration. Although there was a numerical predominance of males migrating from Spain to the New World, even during the first decade of the sixteenth century, some 10 percent of all licenses granted were to women and wives accompanying their husbands.[3] Although extensive miscegenation did occur, Spanish America possessed a larger proportion of white women than did Portuguese America for much of the colonial period. In the case of the English colonies in North America, and once allowances have been made for differing migration patterns between New England and Virginia or the Carolinas, the customary form of colonization was the family unit. It would appear that in Spanish and English America, the larger number of white women guaranteed a cultural continuity absent in Portuguese America. Spanish and English were more widely spoken in the home and the custom of handing over a child to a Black nanny for rearing was less prevalent than in Brazil. It is also possible that, because of a less absolute degree of dependence on slave labor, the Spanish- or English-born wife was more likely to champion the continuation of European customs, albeit in a New World environment. Finally, it would appear that there was a lesser tendency by English and Spanish to "go native," or to permit the fusion of their cultural and linguistic heritage with African and Amerindian lifestyles and languages. In short, as the pattern of colonization and the development of Portuguese America were to differ from other European colonies in the Americas, so, too, was the role and contribution of the white woman in Portuguese America to be unique and distinctive. The embodiment of much of the tradition and ideology of the Old World, she showed a remarkable capacity for adaptation to meet the challenge of the New World.

Suggested Further Reading

Boxer, C. R. *Women in Iberian Expansion Overseas, 1415–1815: Some Facts, Fancies and Personalities.* New York, 1975.

Lavrin, Asunción, and Edith Couturier. "Dowries and Wills: A View of Women's Socioeconomic Role in Colonial Guadalajara and Puebla, 1640–1790." *Hispanic American Historical Review* 59:2 (May 1979).

————, ed. *Latin American Women: Historical Perspectives.* Westport, Conn., 1978.

Lockhart, James. *Spanish Peru, 1532–1560: A Colonial Society.* Madison, 1968. Especially chapter 9.

Martín, Luis. *Daughters of the Conquistadores: Women of the Viceroyalty of Peru.* Albuquerque, 1983.

3   Magnus Mörner, *Race Mixture in the History of Latin America* (Boston, 1967), pp. 15–16; James Lockhart, *Spanish Peru, 1532–1560: A Colonial Society* (Madison, 1968), pp. 163ff.

Pescatello, Ann M., ed. *Female and Male in Latin America: Essays.* Pittsburgh, 1973.

————. *Power and Pawn: The Female in Iberian Families, Societies, and Cultures.* Westport, Conn., 1976.

Ramos, Donald. "Marriage and the Family in Colonial Vila Rica." *Hispanic American Historical Review* 55:2 (May 1975).

Russell-Wood, A. J. R. "The Black Family in the Americas." *Jahrbuch für Geschichte von Staat, Wirtschaft und Gesellschaft Lateinamerikas* 16 (1979).

Soeiro, Susan A. "The Social and Economic Role of the Convent: Women and Nuns in Colonial Bahia, 1677–1800." *Hispanic American Historical Review* 54:2 (May 1974).

Part Three ❖ Eighteenth-Century Society

13 ☀

Government and Elite in Late Colonial Mexico

D. A. BRADING

Colonial Mexico was a society of orders or estates. According to Roland
Mousnier, stratification and status in such a society are determined by
the privileges, functions, and comparative esteem of the various estates
rather than by the hierarchy of economic class or relation to the marketplace. New Spain presents a complicated variant of this type of society
in that the functional distinctions of Europe were replaced by an ethnic
stratification based upon the five estates of Spaniards, mestizos, mulattoes, Indians, and Blacks. These categories indicated only the approxi-
mate genetic character of an individual and are best regarded as definitions of civic and fiscal status. As descendants of the conquering nation,
Spaniards constituted the noble estate within this colonial scale, exercising a virtual monopoly of all appointments in church and state. By
the close of the eighteenth century, however, through natural increase,
intermarriage, and the silent intrusion of mestizos and mulattoes, this
stratum had come to make up about 18 percent of the Mexican population. Defined by occupation, at least three-quarters of all American-born
Spaniards belonged to the upper ranks of the populace rather than to any
elite. One consequence of the expansion, not to say dilution of the Spanish group, was that only the peninsulares, immigrants from the metropolis, and a reduced number of creole families possessed the quintessential
nobility of their estate.

At the forefront of the Spanish estate stood the *gente decente,* the
respectable, the quality. No single criterion such as ownership of land

Published originally in the *Hispanic American Historical Review,* 53:3 (August
1973). This article is a revised version of a paper presented by the author at the
December 1972 meetings of the American Historical Association. Some of the
themes it explores are already familiar to readers of his *Miners and Merchants
in Bourbon Mexico, 1763–1810* (Cambridge, 1971).

or common legal privilege governed entrance into this heterogeneous colonial elite, which numbered less than 5 percent of the Mexican population. Instead, it comprised most European Spaniards, all clergymen, qualified doctors, lawyers and notaries, the royal bureaucracy, merchants, hacendados, and successful silver miners. As such, its membership derived from the operation of the three distinct principles of ethnic nobility, legal privilege, and wealth. The metropolitan origin of the peninsulares, be they officials or merchants, conferred an assured elite status that led them to dismiss any creole claims to superiority. Then again, the clergy, by reason of the fuero that exempted them from all civil jurisdiction, and their education, possessed a social position second to none. Similarly the merchants, organized into a guild with its court and fuero, enjoyed an acceptance more reminiscent of Boston than of Madrid. By contrast, the place of the landowners within the elite was ambiguous and difficult to define. Ownership of a great estate brought more prestige than legal status. In general, the Mexican hacendado lacked the privileges, the fiscal exemptions, and the command of political office that was associated with gentry status in Europe. There was no fuero, no specific quality or title of nobility that went with ownership of an hacienda. In effect, New Spain was dominated by the network of towns rather than by an aristocracy of the countryside, and town councils, the chief institution of local society, were rarely headed by landowners. As far as can be ascertained, hacendados consorted on relatively equal terms with the local clergy, royal officials, and prosperous merchants.

In this article, I propose (1) to analyze the composition of the Mexican elite during the eighteenth century and to trace the different patterns of social mobility exhibited by its creole and peninsular members; (2) to examine creole participation in the bureaucracy; (3) to discuss the allocation of political benefits to the different sections of the Mexican elite; and (4) to scan the changes wrought by the attainment of independence. A major theme throughout is the economic and political debility of the Mexican hacendado. To illumine the drift of the argument, I find it instructive to begin with an English comparison.

I

Some years ago Lawrence Stone presented a brilliant visual image of Tudor England. He compared English society of the 1540s to the United Nations Building at New York. The overwhelming majority of the population—up to 95 percent—inhabited the podium. Its great lateral extension, with many corridors and several floors, offered a considerable range of horizontal movement, between both districts and occupations, and included a limited chance of upward social ascent. Towering above the masses were several status groups that occupied the skyscraper, defined for the most part by the amount of land they owned. Inside the tower an infrequent elevator connected the levels, carrying, however, more passengers on the downward journey than in the reverse direction. Outside the skyscraper, exposed to the winds, ran four ramps, labeled Law, Office, Church, and Commerce, up which individuals climbed to the height permitted by their talents and fortune, whereupon they entered the skyscraper through the purchase of land. Stone concluded with a contrast to the England of 1700, which he claimed could be best illustrated by San Gimignano, a town standing on a hill with a series of vertical towers rising above the cluster of houses beneath. By then, each economic and status group had its own elevator and hierarchy, running independently of the central tower of landownership.

Bourbon Mexico more closely resembled Tudor than Hanoverian England. At least 95 percent of its population lived at the base of the social scale, denied much opportunity of upward social mobility beyond the prescribed limits open to *la plebe* ("the common people"). Within this range, however, there existed distinct economic strata. A silver miner earning 350 pesos a year or a *ranchero* with land and livestock worth 500 pesos differed markedly from a hacienda peon paid a maize ration and an annual wage of 47 pesos, and still more from a vagrant hired hand gaining 2 reales a day where and when employment could be found. These variations at times bisected the hierarchy of ethnic estates; but they form a subject in themselves and here is not the occasion to explore them.

Lifting our view to the inhabitants of the social skyscraper, we find that in Mexico as in Tudor England fortunes created in commerce, mining, and public office were generally invested in the purchase of landed estates. Unfortunately as yet we lack an adequate characterization of the Mexican hacendado of the eighteenth century. By 1810, with 4,945 listed haciendas and estancias, there were probably little more than 4,000 families who belonged to the landlord class. Within this limited number we must distinguish a mere hacendado, holding a single estate worth about 20-50,000 pesos, from a great magnate, owner of a chain of haciendas collectively valued at anywhere between 300,000 and a million pesos. At both levels this class experienced financial difficulties of such proportions as to constitute a downwardly mobile sector in society. The Marquises of San Miguel de Aguayo, with entails covering half of Coahuila, barely supported their inherited debts of nearly half a million pesos. Smaller fry were soon sold up. In his study of the Valley of Oaxaca, William Taylor has found that those haciendas for which he possessed complete records, on average changed hands five times during the eighteenth century. In León my own research yields a somewhat lower value; there, a sample of twenty-five haciendas averaged four sales over the period from 1700 to 1860. The causes of this turnover in ownership, precipitous by European standards, have yet to be fully defined; tentatively, we may advance three factors: (1) The testamentary system. Entails were uncommon and primogeniture forbidden by law. Since the physical partition of haciendas was normally impractical or forbidden by mortgage contracts, the equal division of a fortune among all heirs frequently required the sale of an estate. (2) Ecclesiastical mortgages and annuities. Over the years many haciendas had been so burdened that all their income went for the payment of interest. In a sample of twenty-seven haciendas, Taylor calculated the sum of clerical charges at 67 percent of their total capital value. (3) The relatively low and uncertain rate of agricultural profit. With exports denied by reason of transport costs, the great estates derived their income from sales to the fairly limited urban markets. Enrique Florescano has argued that competition from small producers—*rancheros* and Indian villages—forced the haciendas to rely for profit upon the intermittent years of scarce harvests when they could release their stored grain at high prices. Whatever the cause, and no doubt each region followed a different pattern, the colonial hacienda did not constitute a firm foundation for the establishment of a stable American nobility or gentry.

The chief vehicles of upward economic mobility were commerce and mining. Apart from the windfall of marriage to an heiress, the commonest way of making a fortune was to open a shop. Reliable figures as to the number of merchants, as distinct from mere dealers, cannot be readily obtained. In 1791 the census listed 1,384 *comerciantes* in Mexico City, a term that probably included the *cajeros* or apprentices; only 85 men, however, chose to vote in the consulado elections of 1787. In much the same year, Guanajuato, the leading silver-mining town, housed no more than 162 merchants and 149 *cajeros,* while the entire intendancy supported about a thousand persons described as *comerciantes.* In all, I should be surprised if more than 10,000 merchants and *cajeros* were to be found in New Spain at this time. Needless to say, great differences existed in the scale of enterprise. Many traders finished an arduous life worth only a few hundred pesos; the most successful usually built upon family relations and business connections that provided early access to credit and capital. With few exceptions, once accumulated, mercantile capital was invested in the purchase of landed estates.

One remarkable feature of colonial commerce requires emphasis. All available evidence suggests that the wealthiest merchants in both the capital and the chief provincial towns were immigrants from the peninsula. An inspection of the 1791–92 census shows that in the Bajío about half of all *comerciantes* and *cajeros* were European Spaniards. In all, the immigrant community of these years, excluding members of the religious orders, did not number more than 9,250 persons, of whom a mere 400 were women. About a quarter of this number (and more than half the females) resided in Mexico City. The remainder clustered in the major urban centers—314 persons in Guanajuato, 249 in Oaxaca, 190 in Querétaro, 113 in Orizaba, 93 in Jalapa, 51 in Toluca, 40 in San Miguel el Grande, and 19 in San Juan del Río. A scattered sample of jurisdictions, mainly located in the Bajío, but including Toluca, Orizaba, and Jalapa, reveals that less than a fifth of these men lived in the countryside. At least 55 percent of all immigrants, and probably more, entered trade. European settlement in New Spain thus could be graphically represented as a network of urban knots connected by the fine lines of commercial credit and family relation. In the last resort, it was probably more in his person than by reason of his occupation that the gachupín merchant enjoyed social acceptance.

Silver mining can be compared to a primitive open hoist moving at dizzying speed, onto which men jumped at their peril. Most novices crashed to their ruin; the few survivors, however, often rose to the highest levels of colonial society. The extreme volatility of this profession prevents any easy calculation of number, all the more since the 1792–93 census does not distinguish between the great mine owners and mere technicians or prospectors. Wages at all levels were high, with skilled pick- and blastmen forming a labor aristocracy. In all, I doubt whether the industry, in both its refining and mining sectors, employed more than a thousand persons with the pretension or possibility of elite status.

Viewed as an economic system our model offers few surprises. The significance of the export sector lay in its profitability, rather than in the total value of its product. Only through mining and the importation of luxury goods (all European cloth can be reckoned a luxury) could great fortunes be readily assembled. But mining was a peculiarly speculative business and trade a decidedly tedious one, and in each occupation success depended upon personal flair not easily transmitted to children who were educated to consider themselves gentlemen. In the absence of banks, joint-stock companies, and national debt bonds, the only sure investments were in land, urban property, and the church. In general, therefore, a continuous process was in motion whereby surplus capital accumulated in the export sector was sunk in the purchase of landed estates, there to be slowly dissipated through conspicuous consumption, testamentary partition, clerical bequests, and seasonal losses.

Regarded as a social system, the model contains some unusual features. In Western Europe also, wealthy urban merchants, themselves often the sons of impecunious gentry or prosperous peasants, frequently bought the estates of impoverished noblemen. The rise and fall of such families was a commonplace in the literature of this period. In New Spain, however, this circular movement, so often a journey spread over three generations from the countryside to the town and back again, was interrupted. The peninsular immigrants who dominated commerce ascended the social scale, the creole landowners descended it. Silver mining attracted both groups and injected a feverish quality into the scene, with a few miners, creoles among them, becoming millionaires and the majority ending their days without reward. Needless to say, the downward progress of the creole upper class often stretched across more than the proverbial three generations, and no doubt in some cases skillful management averted total ruin. The general trend, however, remains unmistakable.

Equally startling to a European observer is the rapidity with which families moved up and down the social scale. To take the aristocracy as a yardstick, we find that of the forty-nine new titles of nobility granted in Mexico over the years from 1700 to 1810 no fewer than twenty-six went to miners and merchants and twenty-one to immigrants, excluding officials from the latter calculation. Yet despite initial fortunes often worth more than half a million pesos, several newly ennobled families did not weather the passage of time. In 1775 an official inquiry into the tax debts of the aristocracy found that some titles had been renounced because the current descendants were poverty-stricken.

The downward social mobility of so many elite families obviously exacerbated the tension that characterized the relations of the peninsulares and the creoles. By the close of the seventeenth century, both travelers and viceroys commented upon their mutual antipathy. Apparently the two branches of the Spanish nation resident in Mexico had developed distinct social identities. The stereotypes of their respective characters bear a remarkable similarity to the social psychology of colonial Europeans defined by O. Mannoni in his classic study of twentieth-century Madagascar. The European Spaniard had to prove his elite status by achievement; his arrogance sprang from the conviction of his superiority to the colored masses about him, an attitude that was confirmed by his command of the chief avenues leading to financial success. By contrast, the upper-class American Spaniard was born a gentleman and demonstrated his superior status by conspicuous consumption. The peculiar bitterness of the situation came from the creole knowing that he was trapped on a downwardly moving economic escalator, his descendants doomed to lose their rank in society.

An acute sense of displacement, or best to say, disinheritance, lay deep within the Mexican mind, with its collective roots reaching back to the late sixteenth century when encomendero families found their social position challenged and in many cases overshadowed by new waves of immigrants enriched through mining, trade, or public office. As early as 1599, Gonzalo Gómez de Cervantes exclaimed: "those who but yesterday served in shops, taverns and other low jobs now today possess the best and most honorable positions in the country, whereas gentlemen and descendants of the men who conquered and settled it are poor, humiliated, disfavored and cast down." Over the years the initial hostility toward newcomers was to deepen into set patterns of prejudice invoked even by the children of later settlers against all immigrants to New Spain. It is noticeable that the chief exponents of creole patriotism were all sons of peninsulares.

If creole resentment rarely exploded into overt political action, it was presumably because in each generation the most gifted Mexicans of the upper classes entered the priesthood, and there, in the multiple functions of the ministry, in preaching, lecturing and writing, in the administration of the sacraments and the direction of conscience, and in the management of the financial resources of the church, found an ample field for the exercise of their talents. In effect, the American clergy acted as the moral and intellectual leaders of colonial society. The gachupín merchant, disdainful of creole business ability, accepted their spiritual guidance with the greatest complacency and encouraged his children to enter the church. By 1810 the clergy included 4,229 secular priests and 3,112 friars. Actual parish benefices numbered 1,073, besides another 107 cathedral prebendaries. Viewed as a source of employment, the church overshadowed all other professions. In 1804 the audiencia counted a mere 386 registered lawyers in Mexico, of whom only 210 were in practice. Similarly notaries and qualified physicians, as distinct from *escribientes* ("clerks") and *cirujanos* ("barber-surgeons"), each numbered about 150 persons for the entire country.

Judged in secular light as a career or livelihood, the church served as a haven for the impecunious creole without the financial means to support his social pretensions; and for the most talented it offered a path of promotion. Income derived from the ecclesiastical tithe, from parish fees, and from the 5 percent interest paid on the multitude of *capellanías* ("chaplaincies") and other endowments charged on haciendas and urban property. A considerable part of church capital came from landowners and merchants who established *capellanías* as perpetual annuities for those of their descendants who entered the priesthood. In this fashion, many a hacienda yielded an income to families who years before had relinquished ownership of the estate. At one level, a major cause of the economic debility of the landowning class, at another level, the church employed much of its income to support the children of the same class who chose to become priests or nuns. Full comprehension of this intimate symbiosis, as much as the effect of clerical celibacy upon the composition of the colonial elite, awaits further research. An instructive exercise would be to calculate how much accumulated capital went into the construction of the churches, convents, and altars that are still the architectural glory of Mexico.

II

As yet our description lacks a political dimension. What were the relations of the royal bureaucracy and the colonial elite? First let us clarify our terms. S. N. Eisenstadt has defined the polity of the Spanish empire as a historical bureaucracy, a system of government associated in continental Europe with dynastic absolutism and that succeeded the patrimonial and feudal regimes of the Middle Ages. In his study of the Audiencia of Quito, John L. Phelan has demonstrated the utility of this Weberian category. No longer mere household servants of the crown, the bureaucracy acted as a semiautonomous body jealous of its professional prerogatives, and as such can be viewed as an interest group comparable to the territorial aristocracy, the church, or the urban elites. Within most polities of this type crown officials had the tendency to assimilate to the condition of the aristocracy.

Here we must guard against the habit of applying grand abstractions to small groups of people. Until the Bourbon reforms of the late eighteenth century, the Spanish crown depended upon a mere handful of officials to govern its American empire. In New Spain the entire judicial bureaucracy, i.e., the salaried members of the Audiencias of Mexico and Guadalajara, numbered about 20 persons. The fiscal bureaucracy was equally exiguous. The court of audit and the treasuries did not employ more than 60 men above the level of mere clerks. Save for the frontier patrols and the port guards, there were no armed forces worthy of mention. The district magistrates, the alcaldes mayores and corregidors, did not fulfill any known criterion of bureaucracy. With the accession of the Bourbon dynasty all pretense at paying what was already deemed a derisory salary was abandoned, so that these magistrates, 150 in number, had to subsist upon the meager fruits of justice or else engage in illegal trade. Appointed for periods of three to five years, without professional qualification or tradition, these officials viewed their positions as mere prebends, as an opportunity for personal enrichment.

Interest in colonial government has largely centered about the question of creole exclusion from public office. The traditional notion, still enshrined in most textbooks, stemmed from the debates at the Cortes of Cádiz in 1811, when the American deputies compiled lists to demonstrate the derisory number of native-born viceroys and archbishops. Although even then their evidence was challenged by Juan López de Cancelada, their contentions were eagerly embraced by propagandists for independence. Later publication of colonial documents confirmed the current orthodoxy. As early as 1604 a Mexican viceroy commented: "It is common opinion that of necessity only descendants of the Conquerors should serve as corregidores. . . ." At the start of the eighteenth century, Dr. Juan Antonio de Ahumada addressed an outspoken memorial to Philip V, demanding that all crown appointments in America should be reserved for the natives of that hemisphere, to the heirs, so he argued, of the men who had conquered it. Without the hope of public office, young creoles lacked incentive to study and sank back into idleness and vice, becoming mere "pilgrims in their homeland." In 1771, the ayuntamiento of Mexico City reiterated his arguments with equal vehemence. They frankly dismissed European Spaniards as foreigners in Mexico, and hence sought a creole monopoly in the royal bureaucracy.

The traditional view, however, has been challenged and in part refuted. In a series of four articles, all published in 1972, Leon Campbell, Mark Burkholder, Jacques Barbier, and D. S. Chandler demonstrated that during the eighteenth century, creole membership in the

American audiencias was common and at times predominant. My own inspection of the Mexican court pointed in the same direction. It has been conclusively proved that during the 1760s the majority of oidores in the Audiencias of Lima, Santiago de Chile, and Mexico were creoles. This preponderance was of relatively recent origin. It derived from the extraordinary decision of the first Bourbons to sell audiencia judgeships to qualified bidders. Between 1701 and 1750, a quarter of all new appointments were sold, with a heavy concentration of such transactions occurring in the 1740s. During this period Americans received two-fifths of all places, the majority—less than two-thirds—obtaining their office through purchase. In Lima and Santiago de Chile, most creole oidores were intimately linked by descent, marriage, or financial interest to the landowning elite of these capitals. Here, as with cabildo membership, sale of office ironically opened the way to a form of representative government. By 1770 most American audiencias represented the rich and powerful families of their respective provinces.

The Audiencia of Mexico displayed the same characteristics as its counterparts in Lima and Chile. In 1767, of the eleven men with ascertained backgrounds (there were twelve places) eight were creoles and three peninsulares, although at least three of these creoles had European fathers, with the parent of another coming from the Canary Islands. Although only half of the American oidores were born in the provinces subject to the Mexican court, another two came from Jalisco, and a third, a native of Guatemala, was educated in Mexico City. No fewer than five oidores, including two peninsulares, were directly connected through marriage or by descent to the titled nobility. Equally important, at least five judges were the children of government officials, two being the sons of oidores. Evidence as to their individual wealth is not available; education and talent, however, constituted an important role in their advancement. At least four were educated at the famous Jesuit College of San Ildefonso in Mexico City. Two creoles, Francisco Javier de Gamboa and Joaquín de Rivadeneyra, had spent considerable time in Spain, where both made their reputation upon the publication of substantial books. The Mexican oidores thus formed a tightly knit elite group, with similar social backgrounds and education; one or two were distantly related by marriage.

With the paucity of prosopographical studies, it is still premature to generalize from the one instance of the audiencias. The success of American Spaniards in buying their way onto the bench implies a lack of competition from wealthy lawyers in Madrid. By contrast, the high profits expected from the alcaldías mayores, in particular those that produced cochineal, probably awakened peninsular avarice. In this case, sale of office may well have worked against creole participation. In point of fact, we know remarkably little about the social background of these magistrates. Similarly, the sources of recruitment into the fiscal bureaucracy are equally obscure. Only future research will settle such questions.

No discussion of colonial government can afford to ignore the role of the church. Dependent upon the crown for beneficed appointment and promotion, the clergy formed a parallel administrative bureaucracy that, judged as a system of social control, operated far more effectively than the secular magistracy. The church dominated the intellectual and spiritual life of the country and in addition provided that range of welfare services—schools, colleges, hospitals, asylums, and orphanages—that is now supported by the state. It collected its own tax—the tithe—and ran its own courts. Ecclesiastical judges did not confine their attention to cases of clerical discipline or spiritual transgression; in instances of default in payment of either tithes or interest upon church mortgages they could also order the embargo and auction of private property. More generally, it was to the 1,073 parish priests rather than to the 150 alcaldes mayores that the populace looked for guidance and leadership. In the same fashion, it was to the clergy that both crown and the upper classes appealed when the masses went out on riot. The mission role of the Jesuits and Franciscans in frontier pacification requires no comment. Despite their importance, we know virtually nothing about the social composition of the Mexican clergy save that at some ill-defined moment in the seventeenth century secular benefices below the rank of bishop became a creole monopoly. For what it is worth, we may note that during the 1790s at least four sons of audiencia judges were members of the cathedral chapter of Mexico.

To convert the American empire into a more profitable possession, Charles III and his ministers relied upon the classic instruments of absolutist monarchy: the soldier and the tax collector. A small regular army of about 10,000 men was organized for permanent duty in New Spain, the rank and file mainly recruited from the districts in which they were stationed. The fiscal bureaucracy experienced an unprecedented expansion with the augmentation of old institutions, such as the treasuries and the court of audit, and the creation of new departments, such as the tobacco monopoly, the excise service, and the intendancies. The 1791–92 census listed 311 persons in Mexico City as *empleados de real hacienda* (employees of the royal treasury) and another 105 in the Guanajuato intendancy, figures superior to the combined total of lawyers, physicians, and notaries in each district. I estimate that as a consequence of the Bourbon reforms the number of well-paid permanent places in the colonial bureaucracy quadrupled. The emphasis remained upon revenue collection. Apart from the installation of 12 intendants as provincial governors, local government was neglected, being farmed out to subdelegates, the new version of the alcaldes mayores, who were expected to subsist upon a 5 percent commission of tribute collected from their Indian and mulatto subjects.

The research mentioned above has confirmed that Charles III and José de Gálvez as minister of the Indies actively sought to reduce creole participation in both church and state. High officials in the tobacco monopoly and the excise service were brought directly from the peninsula. Through a variety of devices the creole share of audiencia places was cut to about a third or quarter of the total membership. Similarly, about a third of the prebendaries of the archiepiscopal chapter were eventually occupied by Europeans. Once again, caution is advisable when interpreting incomplete evidence. The increase in government activity undoubtedly gave employment to many creoles who at an earlier period would have petitioned in vain for some kind of office. Then again, creole exclusion mainly operated at the highest level. Nearly all the parochial clergy continued to be locally recruited. A case in point was the colonial army. An inspection of the officer record sheets for the years from 1798 to 1800 reveals that the six regiments and one battalion of the central force (we exclude from our calculations the scattered companies of the north) were led by 268 officers with ranks of ensign to captain. Of these men 112 were peninsulares, 28 Americans from other colonies, and the remaining 128 natives of Mexico. As might be expected, however, all save one of the colonels were Europeans. It was against this discrimination that the Mexico City ayuntamiento complained in 1771, and again in 1776. In effect, when the American deputies at the Cortes of Cádiz protested against creole exclusion from public office, they denounced the policy of the past generation rather than the practice of the entire colonial period.

In the case of the upper bureaucracy, tantalizing hints of a more subtle kind of change can be found. Many of the chief ministers of Charles III—Campomanes, Floridablanca, Roda, and Gálvez—were manteístas; that is to say, at university by reason of their inferior social rank, they were denied entrance into the prestigious colegios mayores ("university colleges") administered by the Jesuits, whose pupils traditionally secured the lion's share of government appointments. Now for seventeenth-century Spain, Richard Kagan has demonstrated the existence of a *letrado* ("university graduate") nobility, a hereditary bureaucratic elite, recruited from families of noble status, which despite possession of landed entails, drew their chief sustenance, generation by generation, from their virtual monopoly of high public office. Were the senior officials in New Spain recruited from a colonial extension of this *noblesse de robe?* Here it is relevant to recall that no fewer than five of the Mexican oidores in 1767 were sons of royal officials. The current dean of the audiencia, Domingo Valcárcel, a peninsular who served in New Spain from 1721 until his death in 1783, clearly sprang from this class. His brother, his father, and both his grandfathers were members of the Council of Castile. Then again, the fact that most colonial judges and leading churchmen had been trained by the Jesuits no doubt increased their dislike of the new regime. These class antagonisms and family connections often stretched across the Atlantic into the ministries at Madrid and bisected the usual distinctions of creole and peninsular.

Equally important, Charles III and his ministers relied upon a different kind of trained intelligence to administer the projected expansion in government activity. The Hapsburgs had recruited the bureaucracy from the law faculties of the leading universities. In important matters of state they took counsel with theologians and used the arguments of scholastic philosophers. In the first decades of the eighteenth century, the Mexican audiencia still formed the only pool of reliable public servants available to administer the complex operations of the mint and the mercury monopoly. After the Gálvez visitation, however, a new breed of official appeared on the scene, by origin army officers and accountants, men without a university or legal education, yet with a formation and discipline more than adequate for the efficient conduct of state business. The key institution here is presumably the army and the training received by its officers. The military background of the last viceroys and most intendants demonstrates the significance of this transition. Needless to say, since Gálvez doubted creole capacity as much as he suspected their loyalty, he recruited the majority of this new type of bureaucrat, especially the revenue officials, from the peninsula.

III

In addition to decisions about the occupancy of public office, a political system also deals with the allocation of scarce economic resources. The historical bureaucratic polities all had to come to terms with the powerful vested interests of the traditional elite groups. In Eastern Europe, for example, the absolute monarchies of this period based their new found authority upon a close alliance with the territorial aristocracy and gentry. Landowners enrolled in the army and the civil service and in many instances acted as provincial governors. In exchange for their support, the monarchy confirmed and extended their feudal jurisdiction over the peasantry. So too, many noble families in England owed their rise in fortune to attendance at the Tudor and Stuart court, which served as a veritable fount of favor, privilege, and office. Given the lavish expenditure expected from the aristocracy, it can be argued that in premodern economies the maintenance of great landed fortunes required the exercise of political power or material assistance from the state.

In sixteenth-century Mexico, the Spanish grandees who became viceroys maintained an open court and acted as the leaders of encomendero society. Within their hand lay the reversion of vacant encomiendas, the right to grant title for vast tracts of land, and the duty of appointing most alcaldes mayores. It is noticeable that at this time many royal officials became wealthy men. In the last resort, however, the viceregal court was but a pale simulacrum of its Madrid original. Once the period of initial settlement was past, it no longer acted as a dynamic center of autonomous political action. Save at is periphery, the empire faced remarkably few external or internal challenges; piracy never threatened mainland possession. In consequence the crown relied upon the audiencias and the church to maintain law and order; there was no attempt to mobilize the landowning class for military or administrative service; the function of the colonies within the imperial system was to provide revenue and to serve as a market for Spanish goods.

The predicament of the creole elite now becomes apparent. The persistent clamor for public office—expressed with an emotional intensity quite at variance with the limited range of places available—sprang not so much from a craving for bureaucratic employment as from a desire for political power and its perquisites. The creole sense of grievance stemmed from the historic failure of the first conquerors and encomenderos to establish a seigneurial society in New Spain. The Spanish crown's refusal to grant perpetual encomiendas and its insistence upon cash remuneration for repartimiento workers denied the Mexican landowner a supply of free or even cheap labor. The precipitous fall in silver production in the years after 1630, when coupled with the long demographic decline of the central region, produced a widespread economic crisis, which far from creating a feudal society simply bankrupted many landowners, forcing them either to abandon or to sell their estates. The comparison with Russia is instructive. There too the nobility and gentry faced financial ruin at the beginning of the seventeenth century. The tsars, though, intervened to rescue them by reducing the peasantry to the condition of serfs with the obligation to work for their masters without recompense. In later years it established a state bank to grant loans to the nobility at low rates of interest. For similar assistance the creole landowner pined in vain.

But what of debt peonage, that much advertised Mexican equivalent of serfdom? For the hacendado in need of cheap labor it was a remarkably poor substitute. More of an inducement than a bond, it required the outlay of a considerable sum in cash or in goods to a group of laborers who might well abscond without repayment of the loan. In any case, these peons still had to be fed a weekly maize ration and to be paid a monthly wage at the going rate. It was for this reason that many landlords preferred to rent much of their land and to hire workers at harvest time upon a daily basis. Apart from the frontier exigencies of the far north, Mexican landowners rarely exercised political or judicial authority over their workers. Most Indians, for example, continued to reside in villages governed by their own elected leaders and magistrates. In consequence, unlike the feudal manor or the serf-estate of Eastern Europe, the Mexican hacienda had to survive upon its economic merits as a unit of production, unassisted either by seigneurial rights or the free labor of resident serfs. By 1700 it was not uncommon to find landlords in debt to their workers. Small wonder that the turnover in ownership was so rapid; it was the price paid for political impotence.

The class that benefited most from the policies of the Spanish monarchy was the colonial merchants. Already by the 1670s their advance in social prestige was the subject of viceregal comment. The ensuing century (until 1778) formed their heyday. The consulado, the merchant guild, now farmed the collection of the alcabalas for a contracted sum. At much the same time the great silver merchants took over the management of the mint, and from this vantage point dominated the credit structure of the silver-mining industry. Then again, in 1678, the power to appoint alcaldes mayores was taken from the viceroy so that these offices could be auctioned to the highest bidder in Madrid. As late as 1754 the Cádiz firm of Pardo and Freire bought the rights to no fewer than three magistracies: Querétaro, Guanajuato, and Tehuacán. With the Bourbon refusal to pay salaries to alcaldes mayores, these officials were driven to become traders, issuing goods and cash on credit to their unfortunate subjects, who stood menaced with imprisonment and flogging for any failure to meet their obligations. To finance these *repartimientos de comercio,* most magistrates relied upon merchant backers, resident in Mexico or the provincial towns. It was in this enforced distribution of merchandise rather than in debt peonage that the political authority of the crown was most obviously utilized, not to say prostituted, for the financial profit of a particular economic class. It was precisely the same practice that most provoked popular unrest, leading in some cases to open rebellion. Thus the immigrant *almaceneros* (merchants, usually owners of import houses), the very embodiment of commercial capitalism, emerged as the dominant figures within the colonial economy, enjoying a social status equal to that of the upper bureaucracy and the territorial magnates.

An essential part of the Bourbon revolution in government launched under Charles III was the destruction of the commercial monopoly exercised by great import houses of the capital. The promulgation of *comercio libre* ("free trade") in 1778 opened the way for a free flow of trade between the chief ports of the peninsula and the American possessions. In Mexico new consulados were set up in Guadalajara and Veracruz. At the same time the regime attempted to free the productive sectors from the former reliance upon merchant credit. *Repartimientos de comercio* were prohibited, and a finance bank was established to aid the mining industry. In all this, there was little to assist the landowning class. Instead, the favored child of the government was the silver miner, whose endeavors were now encouraged by a positive battery of inducements, both financial and institutional. A private jurisdiction, a central court, a technical college, a new code of law, numerous individual tax rebates, titles of nobility—all these fell into the lap of the fortunate miner. By contrast, apart from the removal of a few export duties, nothing was directly undertaken to assist agriculture or the landowning class. Indeed the inflexible enforcement of ecclesiastical amortization after 1804 led to the embargo and auction of many haciendas. The later Bourbons strove to release the productive capacity of the colony from the restrictions imposed during the Hapsburg era, but it was still the export sector, silver mining, and not agriculture, that benefited the most from the new order.

One great exception can be advanced to this proposition. Through the recruitment of militia forces the crown sought to mobilize the political loyalty of the wealthy classes. A commission in the militia conferred an extensive fuero; it brought both social distinction and some quasi-political influence. A full colonelcy—which could be purchased for about 40,000 pesos together with an unspecified gratuity for the viceroy—carried the address of *vuestra señoría* ("Your Lordship"), the same as that enjoyed by an oidor. In return, some great landowners, especially in the north, obtained command and military jurisdiction over a force often in part recruited from their own estates. Here as elsewhere sale of office opened the door to extensive creole promotion. The sixteen regiments and three battalions of the militia were led by 496 officers of the ranks ensign to captain, of whom 209 were peninsulares and 287 creoles, a ratio of about forty to sixty. More important, no fewer than 13 creoles (compared to 20 peninsulares) held the rank of colonel or lieutenant colonel. As yet we lack material for any analysis of the social background of these officers. Among the 15 full colonels were four noblemen and another two who later received titles. Two men had made their fortunes in trade, and another three were mining millionaires. Both colonels of the San Luis Potosí brigade, the Count of Peñasco and Manuel Rincón Gallardo (later Marquis of Guadalupe), were creole landowners with vast estates in that zone. At the same time, the great number of peninsulares at all levels of the militia reinforces our notion of their standing in colonial society.

IV

The manner in which each country in Spanish America attained independence affected its history for a generation to come. In South America, patriot armies disbanded after defeating the royalist forces in open battle, and their place was taken by district militia subject to local landowners. Officers who chose a professional military career rarely gained access to high public office. Instead, both Argentina and Venezuela were governed by caudillos, the political agents of the landowning class. The gaucho regiments that swept Rosas to power in Buenos Aires were recruited from the workers resident on his family estates.

In Mexico the lower clergy called out the masses behind the banner of Our Lady of Guadalupe in a movement that at times resembled a peasant jacquerie. It was the peninsulares, however, the ethnic nobility within New Spain's spectrum of estates, and not the rich who were the chief target of popular hatred. Nevertheless, their material interests threatened, the great hacendados rallied to the crown to suppress the priest-led rebellion. In the absence of European troops (the first expeditionary forces arrived in 1812) the viceroy had to depend upon young upper-class creoles to officer the rapidly expanded colonial army, men who over the years came to adopt the ethos and career of the professional soldier. It was these royalist officers who first supported Iturbide's declaration of independence, and then, with the tumultuous decade of the 1820s once past, effectively ruled Mexico until the Reform. Presidents Bustamante, Barragán, Herrera, Paredes, and López de Santa Anna all passed their early manhood in combat against the insurgency. Their equivalents in South America were not caudillos like Rosas or Páez, but rather the military presidents of Peru and Bolivia—Gamarra, Santa Cruz, Ballivián, and Castilla—all one-time officers in the royalist forces of Goyeneche. After independence, with expenditures that frequently absorbed up to four-fifths of the national budget, the Mexican army constituted a virtually autonomous power structure, unrepresentative of any one economic class, which not merely paralleled, but in many instances dominated the civil authority of the state.

Military predominance only partially accounts for the evident debility of the political system. As much as Argentina, Mexico experienced the struggle between the towns and the wilderness so eloquently described by Domingo Faustino Sarmiento. Old insurgents like Juan Alvarez in Guerrero still haunted the back country and the mountainous periphery. At the same time, however, the network of provincial capitals housed ambitious politicians, backed by considerable state revenue and urban militia, eager to preserve their local autonomy. Neither group of leaders possessed the resources or power to break the hegemony of the regular army. Then again, the church, with prestige undermined by its activity during the civil wars, asserted its independence from the state, despite the constitutional endorsement of Catholicism as the established religion. In effect, the Bourbon Republic or Regency, as some choose to name this period, lacked that intangible but quite necessary quality of legitimacy. The old habits of civil obedience and social deference had been lost; new bonds of loyalty and interest were slow to emerge. The result was bitter stasis, a political system of institutionalized disorder with an empty throne at its center. The monarchy had been destroyed, but the republic had yet to find its soul, or best to say, its constitutive principle.

With political malaise went chronic economic depression and social dissolution. The old stratification according to ethnic estates was slowly transformed into a hierarchy of economic class. At the level of the elite, however, Mexico remained a society of orders. The clergy and the army preserved their fueros, their exemption from the common jurisdiction of the republic. When Dr. José María Luis Mora interpreted the course of politics as a conflict of the church and army against the states, he wished to emphasize the persistence of the ancien régime. At the same time, the influence of the productive classes, of landowners, miners, merchants, and industrialists, was counterbalanced by the rise of lawyers and intellectuals, scions of the professional class, who sought political office both to advance their principles and to assure themselves a livelihood, if not a fortune. Save perhaps during the last decades of the Porfiriato, Mexico was never to be governed by the simple alliance of the economic classes. Upon the urban intellectual proletariat—to use a favorite term of Francisco Bulnes—fell the mantle of the historical bureaucracy; whether they ever cared to convert it into a cover for what Max Weber called legal domination is a matter for debate.

The disruptive effect of the economic depression cannot be overestimated; it brought widespread unemployment for the masses and thrust many of the upper class into debt. Agriculture emerged from the insurgency with many of the great estates in ruin, their livestock slaughtered, and their barns and dams destroyed. Land values, already depressed by the amortization decree of 1804, declined still further, with the consequence that the burden of ecclesiastical mortgages relative to capital assessment became all the more oppressive. In the Bajío and adjacent areas, a perceptible trend toward the subdivision of haciendas has been noted. Given their bankrupt condition, it can come as no surprise to learn that as a class landowners exercised relatively little political influence. A sympathetic commentator, Carlos María de Bustamante, lamented their absence from Congress and deplored their public incapacity. The great conservative of the epoch, Lucas Alamán, sought in vain their effective, united support. Instead, his reactionary coalition was built upon an alliance of the church, the army, and the industrial interest.

The traditional vehicles of social advancement—silver mining and commerce—also experienced a profound change. Many of the great enterprises that had dominated the mining industry were wrecked by the insurgency. Gross national production fell to less than half the 1805 peak, a level not to be permanently surpassed until the 1870s. Extensive investment of British capital restored many mines to working order, although a substantial recovery in output did not begin before the late 1840s. It seems safe to assume that few Mexican fortunes were created in silver mining before that decade. At the same time the expulsion of the last remaining Spanish merchants in 1827 and 1829 permitted a fresh wave of immigrants to seize control of the import trade. But these British, French, and German merchants differed from their gachupín predecessors in that they rarely established families that entered the social elite of Mexico. The French came closest to this pattern, but even during their Porfirian heyday they never rivaled the previous peninsular command of the main avenues of upward social mobility.

All available evidence thus suggests that the process of elite recruitment and social change that we deem characteristic of New Spain cannot be readily applied to the Mexico of Santa Anna. True, the great estate continued to absorb as much credit as it could obtain. The difference lay in the debility of the export sector and the intrusion of foreign investment. Capital accumulated in mining and trade no longer flowed so abundantly into domestic agriculture. The chief contrast, however, centered upon the more active role of the state. Monies that previously would have been shipped abroad to finance the military ventures of the Spanish monarchy now stayed at home to fructify in native pockets. Whether mere occupancy of public office enriched many politicians is doubtful. On the other hand, speculation in national debt operations brought great wealth to an entire group of merchant–financiers, the infamous *agiotistas*. Then again, the men who established the new mechanized textile industry depended upon government credit and tariff protection to assure the success of their venture. At last, therefore, political power was deployed to advance the economic interests of at least one section of the Mexican elite.

Suggested Further Reading

Barbier, Jacques A. "Elite and Cadres in Bourbon Chile." *Hispanic American Historical Review* 52:3 (August 1972).

Brading, D. A. *Miners and Merchants in Bourbon Mexico, 1763–1810.* Cambridge, 1971.

Burkholder, Mark A., and D. S. Chandler. *From Impotence to Authority: The Spanish Crown and the American Audiencias, 1687–1808.* Columbia, Mo., 1977.

Kicza, John E. *Colonial Entrepreneurs: Families and Business in Bourbon Mexico City.* Albuquerque, 1983.

Ladd, Doris M. *The Mexican Nobility at Independence, 1780–1826.* Austin, 1976.

Socolow, Susan M. *The Merchants of Buenos Aires, 1778–1810: Family and Commerce.* Cambridge, 1978.

14 ☼

Haciendas and Villages in Late Colonial Morelos
CHERYL ENGLISH MARTIN

Ever since Moctezuma I established a lush retreat for the Aztec emperors at Oaxtepec, the unique climate and fertility of what is now the Mexican state of Morelos have caught the attention of conquerors, travelers, and scholars alike. "This well-ordered, magnificently varied garden" so enchanted Fernando Cortés that he appropriated much of the area into his personal domain. In the nineteenth century Emperor Maximilian often sought repose in Cuernavaca, today's capital, and Fanny Calderón de la Barca marveled at the prodigality of nature with an enthusiasm today echoed in promotional literature distributed by Morelos's many spas and resorts. In a more analytical vein, modern geographer Ward Barrett has noted advantages of water, climate, soil, and proximity to urban markets that make Morelos unique in Mexico and that have given the state a distinct agricultural and social history. The complementarity of Morelos's diverse agricultural production with that of the higher and cooler Valley of Mexico has endured from pre-Hispanic times to the present. The area's suitability for sugarcane cultivation encouraged sixteenth-century Spaniards, beginning with Cortés himself, to establish haciendas and to import African slaves to work them. Because it remained an important center of indigenous population despite the encroachments of haciendas and the ravages of sixteenth-century epidemics, Morelos differed from other sugar colonies in the Western Hemisphere in that its plantations coexisted with indigenous communities whose claims to land and water were buttressed by pre-Hispanic custom and colonial law.

Published originally in the *Hispanic American Historical Review,* 62:3 (August 1982). Initial research for this article was undertaken during a seminar on Agriculture and Rural Society in Western Europe and the Americas, sponsored by the National Endowment for the Humanities and conducted by Professor Richard Herr at the University of California, Berkeley, during the summer of 1979.

This distinct agricultural and social history prompted one recent author, John Tutino, to omit Morelos from a well-documented and otherwise thorough study of elites and hacienda-village relations in central Mexico during the late colonial period. Although Tutino quite rightly suggested that the specialized techniques of sugar production required that the region be studied separately, many of the phenomena that affected hacienda-village relations elsewhere in late colonial New Spain also occurred in Morelos. The area's hacendados wholeheartedly shared the goals and values of the elites described by Tutino; indeed, such prominent sugar planters as Gabriel de Yermo, Martín Angel Michaus, and Angel Puyade held extensive investments in agricultural and commercial pursuits outside Morelos. Like their counterparts elsewhere, Morelos hacendados infused large amounts of fresh capital into their estates and increased production to meet growing urban demands for foodstuffs. They sought to enhance their own interests by experimenting with crop diversification, exploiting ambiguities in governmental policy, and attempting to turn agricultural crises to their own advantage. Meanwhile, the Indian villages of Morelos experienced much the same population pressure and resultant social tensions felt in pueblos throughout central Mexico during the late colonial period. When the ascendant sugar planters made new encroachments on land and water claimed by the pueblos, the villagers of Morelos added their lawsuits to the hundreds of *pleitos* addressed to judicial tribunals on behalf of indigenous pueblos.

The present study seeks to demonstrate the degree to which the unique agricultural and social history of Morelos conditioned the region's responses to these common phenomena during the years from 1780 to 1810. Because Morelos's propitious climate and its proximity to Mexico City favored the production of a wide variety of crops in addition to sugarcane, hacienda owners found attractive opportunities to increase their profits through agricultural diversification. At the same time, growing numbers of Indians, and especially *gente de razón* (non-Indians), raised fruits, vegetables, and indigo, and therefore competed with hacendados for access to land, water, and markets. When these *gente de razón* rented land from the Indian villages, they acquired a concrete interest in those communities' retention of the privileges accorded by colonial law to incorporated indigenous pueblos. The villagers' ability to persist in their demands owed much to the benign climate, which spared the low-lying tierra caliente of Morelos from the severe agricultural crisis that spread hunger and devastation to most parts of New Spain in 1785–86. Claims advanced by these stubbornly resilient campesinos understandably alarmed the hacendados, who had invested so much in the mills and irrigation works necessary for sugar cultivation. Meanwhile, the haciendas' sizeable resident populations, descended in part from slaves imported by planters during the sixteenth and seventeenth centuries, tempted hacendados to project a future in which they might no longer need to recruit seasonal labor from corporate villages. Anticipating the goals of their successors a century later, late colonial planters heralded the coming of a social order in which corporate villages had no place.

Without question the most visible feature of Morelos's late colonial agricultural history was the sugar industry's remarkable recovery from serious reverses suffered during the late seventeenth and early eighteenth centuries, when low sugar prices, the decline of the slave labor force, poor management, and the prohibition of aguardiente production forced some mills to cease operations and many others to succumb to bankruptcy proceedings. After midcentury, a newly invigorated hacendado class, drawing on extensive ties to mercantile and bureaucratic elites in Mexico City, rehabilitated old sugar mills and constructed new ones. Favored by a monarchy eager to promote agricultural production, these ambitious planters augmented the acreage devoted to sugarcane while refining techniques to increase the yield of land and labor. Consequently the hacendados achieved impressive production increases by the end of the eighteenth century. Tithe records indicate that sugar output in the Archdiocese of Mexico (virtually all of which came from Morelos) expanded from 4,857 tons during the period 1785–90 to 7,952 tons between 1800 and 1804. Moreover, the destruction of sugar plantations in Haiti after 1791 afforded the Morelos planters a brief but exhilarating entrance into export markets, while the legalization of aguardiente production after 1796 presented additional prospects for gain.

The late colonial planters' success was not based on sugar alone, however. It is clear that a diversity of agricultural endeavors added to their profits and served political and social purposes important to the hacendados. As did their counterparts in such predominantly grain-producing regions as the Bajío, landowners in Morelos leased small parcels of land to persons known locally as *terrazgueros* or *peujaleros,* who produced maize and other crops. Rent, usually paid in kind, furnished hacendados with grain for their workers and livestock, and perhaps a small surplus for market. In addition, many hacendados and would-be hacendados engaged directly in the production of such commodities as maize, indigo, and vegetables.

Such diversification appealed to hacendados participating fully in the sugar boom, to those lacking sufficient capital or water to expand sugar production, and to individuals accumulating capital to invest in sugar mills. A thriving hacendado such as Antonio Velasco de la Torre, who purchased the region's fifth most productive hacienda (Cocoyoq) in 1786, rented lands to tenants who cultivated frijoles and garbanzos. The Cortés family mill, whose estimated production was slightly larger than Cocoyoq's, began coffee cultivation in 1805. Inventories taken in 1796 at two moderately sized *ingenios,* Pantitlán and Oacalco, revealed the presence of indigo mills on both haciendas. The owner of San Carlos Borromeo was an enterprising curate who supplemented his profits by cultivating indigo on lands belonging to an allegedly defunct cofradía in Yautepec, as well as by charging his parishioners excessive fees for his priestly services. The Urueta family, owners of two mills located downstream from such heavy water consumers as Pantitlán and Cocoyoq, rented a total of almost seventy-three *fanegas de sembradura* (about 642 acres) in 1789 to tenants who produced maize. At seven to eight *cargas* (or fourteen to sixteen fanegas), in rent per *fanega de sembradura,* the Uruetas received over a thousand fanegas of maize annually. They further diversified their enterprises by producing indigo.

Lands at a site known as Olintepec further illustrate the economic role of leasing to small producers. During the 1780s the Brothers of San Hipólito rented this land to José Nicolás Abad, who in turn sublet it in plots varying in size from one-half to two *fanegas de sembradura,* at five *cargas* per *fanega de sembradura* and, after the agricultural crisis of 1785, eight. Meanwhile, Mexico City merchant José Martín de Chávez, having recently acquired the sugar hacienda Tenextepango, adjacent to Olintepec, was making generous loans to the chronically bankrupt Brothers of San Hipólito, who used the funds to operate their insane asylum in the capital. Finally, in 1790 Chávez agreed to accept the Olintepec lands and an adjoining property in lieu of repayment. He continued to lease Olintepec to *peujaleros,* and thus garnered increased profits for his ascendant hacienda.

Production of maize, both on their own demesne and on lands leased to *peujaleros,* offered hacendados additional rewards less tangible, but perhaps more significant, than the grain they fed their livestock and workers. Because Morelos and other tierras calientes escaped the devastating frost that ruined crops throughout central Mexico in 1785, civic and ecclesiastical leaders explored the possibility of promoting grain production in these areas. The committee of leading citizens who met in the fall of 1785 to discuss solutions for the present crisis and means of averting future famines endorsed an emergency measure proposed by José Antonio Alzate y Ramírez, foremost scientist of the realm. Alzate suggested that sugar planters be urged immediately to plant winter (irrigated) maize, which could then be harvested in the spring of 1786. Since the planters normally left one-fourth of their sugar lands fallow each year, they could easily plant winter maize on the fallow fields. The committee also recommended that hacendados of Morelos and other tierras calientes be encouraged to increase their own and their tenants' output of *maíz de temporal* (maize grown without irrigation), planted in the spring and harvested in the fall.

Prompted by substantial bounties, the hacendados of Morelos responded eagerly to the committee's requests, and winter maize from this tierra caliente appeared in Mexico City during the difficult summer of 1786. In return, landowners received heartfelt acclaim from the highest political officials, as well as a new rationale to use in advancing their own interests. For example, in April 1786, José Vicente de Urueta rebuffed a request of downstream landowners for a general inspection and adjustment of aqueducts by all who drew water from the Yautepec River. Urueta persuaded Viceroy Bernardo de Gálvez that the overhaul must await the harvest of his and others' crops of irrigated maize. In 1790, José Nicolás Abad similarly touted his patriotic response to the famine when explaining why the Brothers of San Hipólito should compensate him for improvements made on lands he leased from them. As a conscientious citizen, Abad said that he had spent a considerable sum clearing portions of the land for cultivation by *peujaleros*. Production of irrigated maize and leasing to *peujaleros* thus served important political ends for the hacendados of late colonial Morelos.

Both the hacendados' expansion of sugar production and their attempts to diversify their activities posed formidable threats to peasant agriculture. During the first half of the eighteenth century, residents of villages in the tierra caliente had taken advantage of hacienda reverses to expand their own production of fruits, vegetables, and other commodities that they sold locally and in the viceregal capital. Antonio Villaseñor y Sánchez reported that in the 1740s many towns specialized in one or more products, including melons, garbanzos, maguey, a wide variety of *"frutos regionales y de Castilla,"* timber, charcoal, fish, and even sugarcane. Moreover, the Indians of the tierra caliente had long been famous for their winter crops of irrigated maize, frijoles, and squash, which they planted in the fall and sold in Mexico City during the winter and spring, as exhaustion of the previous year's harvests drove prices up. As sugar estates revived after 1750, hacendados diverted water from small producers in order to irrigate their increased acreage of sugar and other crops, and to operate their large and more numerous water-powered mills. Yet another factor adding to the pressure on the water supply was the tendency of eighteenth-century hacendados to concentrate milling operations in the dry season, when their own *terrazgueros* as well as Indian villagers were more readily available for seasonal labor. Alterations in existing patterns of water usage created the illusion and frequently the fact of scarcity, even though the region's population in 1791 reportedly reached less than 10 percent of its preconquest or present-day levels.

The history of Oaxtepec and its relations with the nearby Hacienda Pantitlán clearly illustrates the competition between peasant cash crops and ascendant sugar plantations. Because Pantitlán's mill had been idled for at least two (and perhaps as many as four) decades during the first half of the eighteenth century, the villagers of Oaxtepec had enjoyed exclusive use of water from a spring behind their parish church, a source previously shared with the hacienda. This water enabled them to expand their production of bananas and sugarcane until Pedro Valiente acquired the decrepit hacienda and began its renovation in 1752. The installation of his new wheel, powered by water taken from Oaxtepec's spring, inaugurated a half century of litigation, occasionally punctuated by threats of violence.

The villagers and Valiente struck a compromise; in return for his promise to leave them enough water for their fields, the Indians rented him a piece of land adjoining the hacienda. By 1776, however, this settlement proved no longer workable. Valiente's successor claimed that the villagers had taken more than their fair share from the spring, idling his mill at the height of the processing season. Protracted litigation and several attempted out-of-court settlements over the next two decades failed to produce lasting accord between the village and the hacienda. Finally in 1797 a militant faction of villagers went to court seeking exclusive control of the water for the town. The local alcalde mayor rejected Oaxtepec's claim, but was able to enforce his decision only after local hacendados mustered a force of sixty armed men to fend off the defiant villagers, who had vowed to die rather than yield. While rumors

circulated that with their priest's help they were plotting a general uprising along with other pueblos in the area, town officers appealed the
verdict to the audiencia. Before the high court ruled, however, the village and the hacienda reached yet another compromise, which constituted an essential victory for Oaxtepec. The hacienda's owner agreed to
build a new aqueduct to draw his water from the Yautepec River instead of from the disputed spring. The villagers' only concession was to
allow a portion of the conduit to cross their land. Significantly, the villagers' case against Pantitlán, as well as an equally protracted and bitter
dispute with Cocoyoc, received enthusiastic support from non-Indians
who rented village lands, and from the town's curate and surgeon, both
of whom cultivated substantial numbers of banana plants.

Many other complaints voiced by corporate villages centered on
the hacendados' diversion of water, without which the villagers' intensively cultivated orchards and gardens died. Villagers boldly damaged
aqueducts in order to redivert water to their own crops, often halting the
ingenios ("mills") at critical times. Indeed, Antonio Velasco de la
Torre of Cocoyoc insisted that the villagers of Oaxtepec maliciously
tapped his water whenever they learned he was about to begin milling.
In 1793 the owner of Hacienda Miacatlán charged that residents of the
village of the same name had made more than twenty apertures in his
principal conduit, causing his mill to stop. The villagers, both Indians
and *gente de razón,* retorted that the hacienda had appropriated the water they had always used to irrigate their fruits and vegetables. In November 1807, a similar dispute between the village of Atlacholoaya and
burgeoning hacendado Vicente Eguía sparked a confrontation that resulted in injury to one of Eguía's employees. Three years later Eguía
and Atlacholoaya reached a compromise reminiscent of the Oaxtepec-
Pantitlán accords. Eguía agreed to sacrifice a small amount of canefield
in order to build an aqueduct to serve the villagers' needs, with the understanding that they were to pay him fifteen pesos per year for this
concession.

Population pressure prompted villages to challenge the haciendas'
appropriation of land as well as of water. Village leaders demanded that
haciendas respect their rights to the six hundred varas of land in all directions guaranteed by colonial law to Indian villages, as well as to additional lands for which they held viceregal mercedes or other titles.
Because village claims might include the very ground on which the hacendados' costly capital installations stood, hacendados viewed these
demands with considerable apprehension. Even more disturbing to many

hacendados were the attempts by unincorporated communities to settle and form duly constituted pueblos on hacienda lands. One such community was Zahuatlán, whose aspirations to achieve pueblo status on lands claimed by the Dominican plantation Cuahuixtla served to deepen the paranoia shared by other Morelos landowners during the closing years of colonial rule.

Once an outlying *sujeto* ("subject town") of Yecapixtla, Zahuatlán was incorporated into that town as the barrio of "Zahuatlán el Nuevo" in the governmentally ordered resettlement (*congregación*) of 1603. Some time during the late seventeenth century, barrio residents began cultivating lands at the abandoned pueblo, within sight of the vestiges of their old church and homes. Finally, in the 1730s an Indian named don Gregorio took his large family to live permanently at Zahuatlán el Viejo, which lay well within Cuahuixtla's bounds, according to the Dominicans. Although the Dominicans repeatedly attempted to eject them, don Gregorio and his numerous descendants and associates remained at the spot for more than half a century, numbering 48.5 tributaries in the count of 1788. The Dominicans' legal maneuvers yielded favorable rulings from the audiencia, but failed to dislodge the community from its isolated redoubt, surrounded by steep barrancas and inaccessible to civil or ecclesiastical authorities. The residents doggedly ignored all court subpoenas and were said to "fear no one." Finally, in 1793, when faced with the prospect of a full-scale *tumulto,* or riot, by the residents of Zahuatlán, local authorities yielded to the Dominicans' pressure to have the settlement burned to the ground.

A similar challenge posed by a barrio of Cuautla, called Ahuehuepa, nearly evoked an equally violent response from the proprietors of Hacienda Hospital. Though declared a barrio in 1603, Ahuehuepa had won permission to remain on its original site one league from Cuautla. By the late eighteenth century, Ahuehuepa's residents supported themselves by cultivating a few lands of their own and by pasturing livestock on lands made available to them by Hospital and other haciendas, presumably in exchange for labor, rent, or at least "good behavior." Beginning in 1790, a faction of residents began pressing for title to the six hundred varas. Brother Antonio Rodríguez, administrator of Hospital, reacted with alarm, allegedly threatening to obliterate the community.

Documents airing the views of Fray Antonio and other late colonial hacendados reveal a genuine sense of being under siege. With remarkable candor, the hacendados acknowledged the vulnerability of their waterworks and other capital installations. In 1788, for example, the Dominicans charged that the government's unwarranted solicitude for such upstart communities as Zahuatlán could easily result in tyranny over the hapless owner (*"pobre dueño"*) whose hacienda might be dismantled in order to honor villages' claims. Hacendados' petitions readily invoked Enlightenment doctrines of efficient government and material progress in order to impress upon those in authority the substantial contributions made by hacendados to the well-being of the realm. These self-justifications repeatedly cited the tax and tithe revenues the haciendas generated, their role in providing essential foodstuffs for the growing population of New Spain, and the employment they offered to persons who might otherwise have no livelihood.

Hacendados' manifestos also uniformly maligned those peasant communities that challenged their claims to land and water. In virtually every lawsuit pitting villages against hacendados, the latter recited a familiar litany, belittling whenever possible a community's claim to pueblo status and charging that those who initiated village demands were "outside agitators" and racial mongrels who had fled tribute payments, punishment for crimes, and the customary restraints of civilized society in their native communities. Often with considerable validity, the hacendados touted the obsolescence of the colonial social order, predicated on governmental solicitude for Indian communities supposedly insulated from Spanish society except for the presence of civil and church officials. The Dominicans, for example, asserted that Cuautla no longer merited special treatment as an "Indian" town, because the house sites, gardens, and orchards of *gente de razón* occupied most of the space between the center of town and the canefields of neighboring haciendas.

Documentary evidence supports the hacendados' contention that in many of Morelos's supposedly "Indian" communities, the *gente de razón* substantially outnumbered Indians by the end of the eighteenth century. According to an ecclesiastical census of Cuautla in 1797, Indians made up only 16.6 percent of the town's communicants. Tribute records of 1796 reveal that only 128 of Cuautla's 253 Indian tributaries lived in the town and its three outlying barrios; the rest had taken up residence on nearby haciendas. The late colonial census published by Manuel Mazari shows many other communities where Indians constituted a minority of the population (see table I). Nevertheless, because many of these communities lay in the tierra caliente, adjacent to expanding sugar plantations, their leaders continued to demand the special protection theo-

TABLE I. Non-Indian Residents of Selected Towns, circa 1795

Town	Total population	Number of non-Indians	Percentage of total population
Jantetelco	890	666	74.8
Cuernavaca	2,722	1,985	72.9
Tlaltizapán	591	404	68.4
Oaxtepec	323	213	65.9
Miacatlán	267	172	64.4
Yautepec	1,570	908	57.8
Jonacatepec	1,850	956	51.7
Yecapixtla	1,717	740	43.1
Tepoztlán	2,851	223	7.8

retically accorded to "Indian" communities with even greater vigor than their counterparts in more isolated and therefore more predominantly Indian villages.

In place of the allegedly outmoded system of insulated corporate villages, the hacendados proposed a new social order based on permanent hacienda residence for Indians and other lower-class people. In 1796, Angel Puyade, owner of Hacienda Santa Ana Cuauchichinola, concisely articulated the hacendados' vision of the new order. Denouncing the scandalous conduct of residents in a nearby settlement, also called Cuauchichinola, Puyade denied its assertion of pueblo status. He suggested instead that its land should be declared property of the Marquesado del Valle and therefore available for perpetual lease by some hacendado (namely, Puyade himself) who could ensure that the people behaved themselves and paid their tributes. In other words, Puyade was arguing that an hacendado could effectively fulfill the disciplinary and fiscal functions assigned to civil and ecclesiastical officials under the old order. A lawyer reviewing the proposal on the Marquesado's behalf admitted that the plan offered a more reliable guarantee of peace and stability than acknowledgement of the settlement's bid for pueblo status. Puyade's scheme, in the lawyer's opinion, promised "all that we could desire," especially since it would be impossible to force the community's ten Indian and eight non-Indian families to return to their places of origin. In arguments rebutting Cuautla's petition for six hundred varas, the Dominicans echoed Puyade's proclamation of a new social order, claiming that the Indians who had abandoned Cuautla to live at Cuahuixtla and other haciendas found far greater comfort than they had enjoyed in the town.

Persons who chose hacienda residence, either as *terrazgueros* or as full-time hacienda employees, presumably had fewer reasons to challenge hacienda claims to land and water than persons who remained in corporate villages. In fact, tenants favored and perhaps incited haciendas' usurpations of Indian lands. In the case of Zahuatlán, for example, the Dominicans wished to rent to others a portion of the lands cultivated by that community. It was the pretentions of these Indian and pseudo-Indian communities to time-honored prerogatives that late colonial hacendados found so distasteful, not the presence of the people themselves. Indeed, on one occasion the Dominicans modified their usually inflexible attitude toward the people of Zahuatlán, offering to allow them to remain on their lands provided they did so as tenants of the hacienda and abandoned their corporate identity as an "Indian" village.

What the hacendados proposed, and to a certain extent achieved, was the de facto creation of the social order given juridical sanction by the Liberal Reform over half a century later. By encouraging Indians and others to settle on hacienda lands, hacendados attempted to hasten the coming of that new order. A *peujalero* or full-time hacienda employee faced the hacendado as an individual, stripped of the legal protection accorded to members of indigenous communities. His relationship with his landlord or employer was a tenuous, one-to-one affair, subject to alteration or termination at the hacendado's whim. The new order also provided hacendados with a source of labor to replace their dwindling slave forces. Because *terrazgueros* produced only temporal (rainy-season and therefore nonirrigated) crops unless their landlords disposed otherwise, they were presumably available to help with harvesting and processing cane in winter months.

Against a social order based on hacienda residence, the villages offered the profoundly conservative model of the Indian pueblo supported by all of the guarantees enshrined in royal legislation of an earlier era. The actions of such communities as Zahuatlán and Ahuehuepa represented conscious efforts to reverse two centuries of colonial rule in order to return to the status quo that predated the *congregaciones* of 1603. Land petitions of pueblos and of communities aspiring to pueblo status usually reflected an accurate understanding of the history of rural society in Morelos, with references to the epidemics that had substantially reduced the indigenous population, the subsequent *congregaciones,* and the incursions into erstwhile Indian lands by sugar estates.

In this conflict between two antithetical social orders, the hacendados clearly held impressive advantages. Local officials, many of whom apparently aspired to hacienda ownership themselves, usually supported hacendados over villagers. Like the hacendados, they feared the threat to the peace posed by such communities as Zahuatlán. Though officials in Spain and Mexico City continued to pay lip service to the guarantees accorded to Indian communities, the Bourbons' sustained emphasis on the production of tropical staples precluded any meaningful application of those guarantees. Such royal gestures as a cédula issued in 1785 upholding village claims to the six hundred varas undoubtedly prompted the villages of Jantetelco to shout the praises of their sovereign as they marked off the lands usurped from them by hacendado Nicolás de Icazbalceta. Local officials, however, quickly overruled the villagers' action, and indeed the king himself had more to gain from Icazbalceta than from Jantetelco.

Cleavages within peasant communities often facilitated the hacendados' attack upon village prerogatives. While carrying on their campaigns against surrounding haciendas, both Ahuehuepa and Cuautla were torn by bitter factional disputes. Whenever possible, hacendados exploited such divisions and attempted to manipulate village politics in order to secure continuity in office for those leaders most amenable to hacienda interests. Moreover, the unequal allocation of land by village leaders, apparently a common characteristic throughout central Mexico in the late colonial period, forced many persons to leave their villages in favor of permanent hacienda residence.

Yet despite formidable factors favoring the haciendas, the villages showed remarkable resilience, tacitly acknowledged by hacendados in such compromises as the Oaxtepec-Pantitlán agreement. Persons who remained in the villages, either as "Indians" (regardless of their actual ethnic origins) or as tenants of community lands, benefited from the exodus of surplus population to the haciendas. As long as they retained access to water and land, village dwellers profited from cash-crop production and persisted in their demands for traditional village prerogatives even though their communities no longer resembled the pueblos envisioned in colonial law. Indeed, the very pursuit of such demands may have served to reinforce community cohesion by directing villagers' discontent toward abuses committed by haciendas and other outsiders rather than toward the self-serving conduct of community leaders. Conflict with outsiders thus preserved village solidarity despite the presence of such potentially divisive factors as economic and ethnic differentiation within the communities.

The benign climate of Morelos further bolstered the resilience of the area's corporate villages in the late colonial period. In 1749, and again in 1785, Morelos escaped the inopportune frosts that destroyed crops elsewhere in New Spain. Most illustrative is the case of the agricultural crisis of 1785–86, which Charles Gibson has called "the most disastrous single event in the whole history of colonial maize agriculture." Though insufficient rainfall reduced Morelos's 1785 maize harvest somewhat, the people did not suffer the terrible mortality that afflicted inhabitants elsewhere. Parish registers from Yautepec, for example, show that burials there were actually fewer in 1786 than they were in 1785. Marriages also rose in Yautepec in 1786, and baptisms showed only a slight drop. Morelos obviously did not escape all causes of widespread mortality in the late eighteenth century. For example, it suffered the effects of the smallpox epidemic of 1779–80, whose casualties were meticulously recorded by the same priest who presided over parish functions throughout the ensuing decade. The agricultural disaster of 1785–86, however, is not reflected in the parish register figures for Yautepec.

Peasant agriculture therefore continued to demonstrate a vitality similar to that described a half-century ago by the Russian economist A. V. Chayanov in his theory of peasant economy. According to Chayanov, the peasant family's economic decisions are governed by the desire to strike an acceptable balance between consumption and drudgery, rather than by considerations of profit. Because peasant families can compensate for low agricultural prices by increasing labor intensity, they are able to continue production in market situations untenable for the large farmer dependent on wage labor.[1] In eighteenth-century Mexico, however, periodic agricultural crises interfered with the operation of this "Chayanov principle" and tipped the balance decisively in favor of the hacendados, who found a most effective means of weathering years of abundant harvests and low prices. They simply withheld their produce from the market, stored it in their ample granaries, and waited until a bad harvest brought opportunities for exceptional profits. Peasants, on the other hand, had no reserve to tide them over a crop failure. Many of them sold tools and livestock in order to purchase food, thus jeopardizing their ability to produce in future years. They could not

1 A. V. Chayanov, *The Theory of Peasant Economy* (Homewood, Ill., 1966), pp. xv–xviii, 81, 88–89, 239.

look to hacienda jobs for relief. Hacendados, whose current production and need for labor were adversely affected by the famine, preferred to dismiss workers rather than pay the customary rations in maize.

In Morelos, however, villagers had grain available for their own consumption during the late fall and early winter of 1785–86. Those with access to water for irrigation could produce winter crops and join the hacendados in reaping windfall profits in 1786. Meanwhile, hacendados searched in vain for additional workers to help harvest the irrigated maize. They pleaded with the authorities to enact coercive measures to force villagers to work for them. Hacienda profits during the crisis would definitely have been higher had it not been for the villagers' ability to sustain themselves without recourse to hacienda labor. The fundamental tension between hacienda production and peasant agriculture identified by Chayanov thus remained operative in Morelos during the worst agricultural crisis of colonial Mexico.

The inability of hacendados to depend on villages for seasonal labor produced a greater degree of hacienda-village antagonism in Morelos than in other parts of central Mexico during the closing decades of colonial rule. John Tutino has described in detail the unequal, but nonetheless symbiotic, relationship in which hacendados grudgingly tolerated the existence of Indian villages as convenient reservoirs of seasonal labor, and villagers looked to part-time hacienda work to obtain needed cash. The available evidence suggests the considerable attenuation of this relationship in Morelos. Those who remained in villages were often able to support themselves satisfactorily without recourse to unpleasant and arduous work on the sugar plantations. Not without a touch of envy did the Dominicans of Cuahuixtla note the relative ease with which at least the more fortunate of Cuautla's villagers supported themselves.

Fortunately for the hacendados, an alternative labor source came close to meeting their needs for sugar production, if not the irrigated crops they produced in the winter of 1786. Generations of intermixture among slaves, free Blacks, mulattoes, and Indians had produced a large resident *pardo* population on most Morelos haciendas by the late colonial era. Invariably designated as *trabajadores del campo* ("field workers") in the census of 1791, these *pardos* and their less numerous "Spanish," *castizo,* and mestizo counterparts nearly met the hacendados' needs for the field labor required for sugar production. Hacienda Hospital, for example, had 137 male residents described as *trabajadores del campo*. Ward Barrett has estimated Hospital's productive capacity at

175 tons, which required field labor equivalent to that of 134 full-time laborers, working 315 days per year. Cuahuixtla, with an estimated capacity similar to Hospital's, had 156 *trabajadores del campo*. Since the census of 1791 omitted Indians, these figures probably understate the numbers of field workers resident on these haciendas. On the other hand, the ecclesiastical census of 1797 includes Indians, but does not indicate the occupations of individuals listed. Table II shows the numbers of adult male hacienda residents of all ethnic groups, excluding those who used the title "don" and were presumably indisposed to perform labor other than supervision. Since some of the residents were undoubtedly mill workers, the figures in column iv include both field and mill workers necessary to produce at the mills' capacities. It is clear that on haciendas such as Tenextepango, Cuahuixtla, Hospital, Casasano, and Guadalupe the resident males were at least theoretically sufficient in number to maintain sugar production at the capacity levels estimated by Barrett. It is also quite possible that at least some of the female hacienda residents performed field labor. Because sugar cultivation required large numbers of workers at peak periods, however, it is impossible to determine with certainty how close the resident workers actually came to supplying the hacendados' labor needs for sugar production. Nevertheless, the owners of most Morelos haciendas could reasonably envisage a day when they might recruit all of their workers from within the haciendas' bounds, even if, for the present, some remained partially dependent on the villages for labor.

The vulnerability of the hacendados' waterworks gave them still

TABLE II. Resident Male Population on Haciendas, All Ethnic Groups, 1797

Hacienda	Non-Indians	Indians	Total	Estimated field and mill workers required
Buenavista	72	13	85	111
Guadalupe	83	43	126	111
Santa Inés	88	21	109	156
Calderón	88	25	113	156
Hospital	116	21	137	156
Casasano	145	9	154	156
Tenextepango	186	71	257	156
Cuahuixtla	166	11	177	156

more reason to view the villages more as obstacles to their progress than as handy pools of seasonal labor. Because the villagers' continued ability to benefit from agricultural crises and to support themselves without recourse to hacienda employment depended so crucially on access to water for their irrigated crops, their hostility toward the haciendas frequently focused on the costly aqueducts that conveyed water to the canefields and *ingenios*. These imposing structures not only appropriated water that might otherwise have irrigated the villagers' croplands; at times they also inflicted both injury and property damage on the communities through which they passed. In 1801, for example, Hacienda Buenavista's new aqueduct overflowed, inundating a barrio of Cuautla. On another occasion, a pregnant woman was killed and several persons injured when a portion of the same conduit collapsed.

William B. Taylor's study has shown that although late colonial villagers in central and southern Mexico frequently resorted to violence to eliminate perceived threats to traditional sources of community well-being, they lacked both the weaponry and the sense of identification with other villages necessary to achieve any revolutionary change in the social or political order. Instead, these good rebels but poor revolutionaries focused their protests on specific individuals or objects identified with particular abuses.[2] The Morelenses clearly conformed to Taylor's model, but, unlike villagers elsewhere in New Spain, they found in the haciendas' aqueducts a set of targets ideally suited to their limited revolutionary potential. Angry villagers could easily imperil a recalcitrant hacendado's profits by damaging his waterworks, even though they were incapable of mounting a sustained and coordinated assault on the hacienda system.

The distinctive features of Morelos's agricultural and social history thus combined to make conflict rather than symbiosis the essential feature of hacienda-village relations during the late colonial period. The planters therefore proceeded to attack the villages with a vehemence usually attributed only to their descendants a hundred years later. In fact, the late colonial hacendados clearly anticipated the outlook and achievements of their successors. If the ruins of Cuauchichinola and Ahuehuepa "rotted into the earth" in Porfirian times, the process of decay was well advanced by the end of the colonial era. When Porfirian hacendados expressed their wish to see cane growing in the village plazas, they merely echoed the sentiments of their ancestors a century before. Meanwhile, villages that resisted absorption by the Porfirian haciendas owed their

2 William B. Taylor, *Drinking, Homicide and Rebellion in Colonial Mexican Villages* (Stanford, 1979), pp. 115–28, 145.

survival to the same generosity of nature and prospects for cash-crop production that sustained the late colonial pueblos. When a national revolutionary movement created a propitious climate for revolt, the villagers of Morelos, even less purely Indian than their late colonial forebears, voiced a familiar refrain in demanding restitution of land and water once guaranteed by ancient custom and viceregal merced to indigenous communities.

Suggested Further Reading

Altman, Ida, and James Lockhart, eds. *Provinces of Early Mexico: Variants of Spanish American Regional Evolution.* Los Angeles, 1976.

Brading, D. A. *Haciendas and Ranchos in the Mexican Bajío: León, 1700–1860.* Cambridge, 1978.

Stern, Steve J. *Peru's Indian Peoples and the Challenge of Spanish Conquest: Huamanga to 1640.* Madison, 1982.

Taylor, William B. *Drinking, Homicide, and Rebellion in Colonial Mexican Villages.* Stanford, 1979.

Tutino, John M. "Hacienda Social Relations in Mexico: The Chalco Region in the Era of Independence." *Hispanic American Historical Review* 55:3 (August 1975).

Van Young, Eric. *Hacienda and Market in Eighteenth-Century Mexico: The Rural Economy of the Guadalajara Region, 1675–1820.* Berkeley, 1981.

15 ☀

Women and Crime: Buenos Aires, 1757–97

SUSAN MIGDEN SOCOLOW

Crime reflects social values, for it indicates what is viewed as abnormal or deviant behavior (and conversely what is acceptable behavior) and the degree to which that behavior is abhorrent to society in general. In addition to reflecting general values, crime as it involves one racial, sexual, or social group can shed light on the attitude of the ruling elite toward a specific group and the social position of that group within a larger context. Last, crime reflects class and power relations by allowing us to study the relationship of the criminal to the victim and their relationship to the legal mechanism. The study of crime as a valid field for historical research has been well explored by European historians, but, within the field of Latin American history, it is relatively new. It is, nevertheless, an area deserving of study in our attempt to understand more fully colonial Spanish society.

The few studies in Latin American history that have to date touched on the problem of crime and punishment have generally looked at illegal behavior as it affected non-Spanish groups. This study is concerned with criminal behavior and crime as it affected women, both Spanish and non-Spanish, in late eighteenth-century Buenos Aires. A study of women and crime allows us to view the role of women in colonial society, as well as to test colonial society's perceptions of sex roles and the way men and women actually behaved. Moreover, cases concerning criminal law demonstrate how markedly practices could differ

Reprinted by permission of Cambridge University Press and published originally in the *Journal of Latin American Studies,* 12:1 (May 1980). The author wishes to thank the National Endowment for the Humanities whose support made this research possible. An earlier version of this article was presented at the Conference on Women and Power, University of Maryland, November 1977. The author also thanks Herbert Klein for his most helpful criticism.

from written statutes, and how class, sex, and race served to modify the law as it applied to different individuals.

To study the patterns of crime in which women were either victims or perpetrators, criminal cases brought before courts of the first instance for the area under the jurisdiction of the city of Buenos Aires have been reviewed. The cases under study cover a forty-year period in colonial Argentine history, a period in which Buenos Aires and the surrounding countryside underwent dynamic economic and population growth, as the city became a center of commercial and administrative activity. This study purposely stops short of the years of the English invasions when political chaos and military conditions created a somewhat abnormal social environment. It should be pointed out that the civil and criminal jurisdiction of the city of Buenos Aires covered large rural areas, and that many of the crimes reviewed occurred in a rural or semi-rural setting.

For the lower classes, colonial Buenos Aires was a violent society, a society based on hierarchy and full of conflict situations. The subordination of women was a given of the social order, but there was also subordination of the lower classes and the poor. Although justice was available to all in theory, the records show that, especially in the rural outskirts of the city, justice was often inaccessible, and much crime did not come to the attention of the legal authorities.

Feminine behavior differed greatly from one social group to another and from one racial group to another. The ideal was no doubt that of the Spanish (or white) upper-class female, who led a gracious, albeit sheltered life. Life for these women was often a choice between marriage partners, one mortal, the other divine, although a few upper- and middle-class women remained single. Early marriage was followed by strict rules of decorum and, for those who had chosen an earthly partner, by a rapid succession of offspring. Well-bred women were kept in a state of semi-isolation; their major diversion consisted of church-going.

In theory women of the better classes did not work, but often Spanish single women and widows were forced into some type of economic activity to maintain themselves. The preferred means of earning a livelihood was twofold: renting rooms in one's house, while sending out some of one's slaves to work for day wages. Both of these economic activities avoided direct entry into the larger masculine world and were, therefore, acceptable for the finer class of women. But less passive female economic activity did exist and became more frequent as one went down the social scale. In the urban areas, middle- and lower-class women were found working as teachers, midwives, launderesses, and ironing women. Rural women shared the chores of farms and ranches with men. At the bottom of the social scale were the female Black slaves, who were as active as their male counterparts in the labor market, although they tended to be employed inside the house.

For this study information has been gathered from a total of seventy criminal cases that were prosecuted in one of the two municipal courts of the city, the *juzgado del alcalde de primer voto* and the *juzgado del alcalde de segundo voto*. All cases involving women, approximately 20 percent of the total of 355 cases brought before these judges, were included in the group. This relatively low percentage tends to reinforce the view of colonial women as sheltered individuals who passed their lives outside the public domain. But this group of cases does not, unfortunately, contain records from the ecclesiastical courts or the Inquisition, where it is suspected that a large number of cases involving women as plaintiffs or defendants were presented. In the case of Buenos Aires none of these records has survived.

Those records that did survive reflect a growing participation of women in crime, either as plaintiff or defendant, after the founding of the viceroyalty in 1777. The total number of cases involving women found for the twenty-year period before 1777 is sixteen; by contrast, fifty-four cases have been found for the twenty-year period after that date. This reflects both an increase in the population of the area, and the tightening up of legal practices and institutions after the founding of the viceroyalty. Approximately half of those cases studied occurred within the city of Buenos Aires; the other half were crimes committed in an area extending 145 miles from the city and included in the city's legal jurisdiction.

Because of suspected underreporting of crimes involving women, known omissions in the case material reviewed, and haphazard records, this study does not attempt to specify absolute rates or numbers of certain crimes. It is impossible to know how many crimes involving women never came to public attention. Nevertheless, existing criminal records provide a picture of the variety of crime and allow the historian to examine underlying social ideals and realities.

Crime is often divided into three general categories: economic crimes, or those against property such as robbery, larceny, and theft; interpersonal crimes, or crimes resulting from conflicts between individuals, including homicide, rape, slander, stabbing, and bigamy; and political crimes, or conflicts between individuals and the state, such as treason and lese majesty. Although the records of the city magistrate courts include multiple examples of so-called economic crimes, almost all crimes involving women fall into the second category, interpersonal crimes. In addition, almost all of the crimes that involved women were of a sexual nature.

This lack of female involvement in cases of economic crime does not prove that colonial porteña women never stole or committed larceny. In any society that employs a large number of household servants, some petty thievery, for example, will always occur. What is obvious is that if these crimes were committed by or against women, they were never reported, indicating that they were either not considered serious enough to appeal to royal justice for legal redress, or that the thief was punished privately. In addition, the lack of female involvement in economic crimes suggests that women were not forced to be economically independent to the same degree as men. Women who found themselves in need of economic support would enter into illicit sexual relationships, rather than steal. In some cases men would steal to provide for women, but the women themselves were usually dependent on either husbands or lovers to furnish them with worldly goods.

Not only were women always involved in interpersonal, rather than economic or political crimes, but women tended to be either the victim or accomplice, rather than the perpetrator of a crime. This again reflects the generally passive role of the female. In only six of the cases studied (less than 9 percent) were women accused of committing a violent crime, and in two of these cases the women accused were cited as accomplices rather than perpetrators. It was rather as victims of violent interpersonal crime such as wife beating, rape, and kidnapping that women most frequently entered the legal records. More than half of the cases reviewed fall into these categories. By far the most common crimes against women were physical abuse and wife beating, followed in frequency by rape and kidnapping. These crimes were usually committed against lower-class women, both in the city and in rural areas.

The crimes reported to the alcaldes ("magistrates") tended to involve artisan and lower classes, and the racial heterogeneity of the city was reflected in the cases. Indians, Blacks, mestizos, mulattoes, and poor whites appear as victims, assailants, defendants, and witnesses. In general the victim was of the same or less socially prestigious racial group than the assailant, but there were exceptions to this pattern. A few cases of rape and seduction involved white men and Black women (one Portu-

guese was accused of having an uncontrollable passion for Black women),
and a mulatto man was also accused of attacking a white woman. Although the very fact that charges were brought by Black women or their
husbands against white men points to some degree of legal recourse for
all classes and races, the crimes also reflected the city's racial hierarchy,
only occasionally violated by "audacious" and "insolent" crimes.

Central to an understanding of women's role in power relationships
is the question of the relationship between criminal and victim. Who
committed crimes against whom? In the case of crime involving women
in colonial Buenos Aires, crime was usually committed by family, friends,
acquaintances, or neighbors. Rarely was crime of any nature against
women committed by a stranger. The localized nature of crime reflected
the familiar perimeters of the feminine world. In addition, most crime
against women was committed in the home, again suggesting a limited
social milieu for women. Most reported crimes were committed by people of social background similar to the victim's, a reflection of the lack
of social mobility and of the class boundaries found in colonial society.

In general, crimes against women fall into two categories: domestic
disturbances and sexual offenses. The first category, which included
beating, stabbing, and attempted homicide, was almost by definition
composed of crime that occurred within the family. In these crimes, the
wife was usually a victim of her husband's anger, although women were
also abused by kinsmen. Male anger could be fired by unseemly conduct
on the part of the woman, her failure to conform to the norms of expected female behavior, especially sexual conduct. But several cases reflect male violence in protecting his rights over the female members of
his family when there was no indication of misconduct.

Much family crime also reflects the high level of personal violence
and frustration that was a normal part of lower-class male life. Men of
the marginal urban and rural sectors, subsistence farmers, unskilled laborers, peones, and ranch laborers, lived in a world which they could
little control. Armed with knives, they turned their frustrations with their
economic and social roles to the nearest available victim, their wives,
who were in a socially sanctioned subordinate position.

Domestic crime was usually reported to the local magistrates by the
female victims themselves. Women, especially married women, who had
been repeatedly abused by their male kin, eventually sought protection
from the local justices. Frequently their charges carried the complaint
that they were being abused by the very men whose duty it was to defend

them. Here they expressed the idealized societal norm that a man's duty was to protect his female kin.

Occasionally physical abuse of a married woman was reported by a male relative such as her brother or father. Obviously, many women, no matter how badly treated, were afraid to seek legal redress against their husbands, for they feared that the physical abuse to which they were being subjected would be exacerbated. Testimony in these cases suggests the high degree of physical abuse that was tolerated by some women, often over long periods of time.

At times, unrelated outsiders, often neighbors, would intervene to report the crime even when the victim herself chose not to press charges. This was especially likely in cases where the physical abuse of a woman reached the bounds of attempted homicide. Neighbors generally ignored wife beating, considering it to be within a man's prerogatives to control and punish his wife, but when the physical abuse of a woman became so blatant and extreme as to threaten her life, custom and public morality forced neighbors to step into domestic disturbances to protect the endangered woman.

Although physical abuse was reported, judges tended to be lenient when dealing with these cases. Much of their questioning was concerned with the character of the woman involved, for if there was any stain on her reputation, her husband's conduct, no matter how inhumane, was absolved. The right of a husband to discipline a wife suspected of unseemly conduct (*mala conducta*) applied to all men regardless of race or legal condition; a slave could beat his wife although she belonged to another master. The court's insistence on the need to document a female victim's good conduct, and the corollary that any treatment was justified to correct an evil woman, was also applied to cases involving wife-murder. A wife's misconduct was the universal defense, although when murder was involved, witnesses were questioned closely, and this defense could occasionally backfire.

The second major group of offenses that victimized women, sexual offense, including rape, kidnap, and hair cutting, also tended to be committed by men from within the same social world as the victim. Sexual offenses were almost uniformly committed by men known to their victims, by neighbors, acquaintances, or kin, fictive and real. Although lust was frequently the motivating force, these crimes were not random crimes of passion, but rather crimes in which the victim was well chosen by the assailant. When the victim of violent sexual crime was a married woman, the violence directed against her was at times just one step in a personal dispute between the assailant and the woman's husband. Arguments between men that had started over land, personal insults (*palabras injuriosas*), and affronts to a man's honor escalated to involve the married woman. For example, after Bartolomé Bordela intervened in a fight involving Alexo Machado and ordered him out of his house, Machado, swearing that Bordela would be made to pay, returned and attempted to rape Bordela's wife. A married woman was the perfect victim in these disputes, for she was the means by which an enemy could assail her husband's manliness. A husband's responsibility was to protect and care for his wife, for through the sacrament of marriage she had become part of his own flesh. A husband who was too weak to defend his wife, and his family's honor, was unworthy and despicable, the very antithesis of the macho ideal. These crimes suggest that, at times, the married woman was assaulted as much because she was an object of desire, as because she was the means by which to attack her husband and his honor.

When married women were the victims of violent sexual crimes, the legal complaints were always initiated by their husbands. This reflected both the legal position of the married woman (unless she were the plaintiff and her husband were the assailant, she could not appear in court without his permission) and the belief that as head of his household, any attack against a man's wife was inevitably an attack against him. It was the man whose honor had been jeopardized, and it was the man who sought legal redress. But, even in the very act of reporting the crime to a local magistrate, the man publicly admitted his vulnerability, and the fact that he was too weak to seek his own retribution. This is, perhaps, the reason that so many of the sexual offenses reported to local magistrates were charges of "attempted rape," rather than rape. Successful rape and kidnapping were seldom reported to the authorities as such because of the attendant shame involved. But cases of attempted rape often included testimony on previously committed rape and kidnapping that had gone unreported.

In cases of sexual assault of unmarried women, it is more difficult to decide whether the woman was victimized because of her relationship to one of two feuding males, or because of uncontrolled sexual passion. Again, as in crime against married women, the assailant was always an acquaintance of the woman involved, someone she had known, even fleetingly, before the crime was committed. Those single women with male protectors—a father, brother or brother-in-law—turned to these men to report the crime and press charges. In the case of single women with male protectors, some were victimized to destroy a male kinsman's honor. But the victims of violent sexual crimes were most often single unprotected women. Underlying this pattern of violence was the reality of a strongly male-dominated society that viewed unprotected females as fair game for sexual advances. Women, even temporarily without husband, fathers, or brothers, were viewed as unprotected property, waiting to be claimed through male sexual prowess. For example, María Lino Cufré and María de la Concepción Masias, two women living alone in the city, were raped by two men who broke into their home at eleven o'clock one evening.

In the countryside, women alone were even more frequent victims of rape and violence than in the city. Here both married and single women, alone in their ranchos while their male kinsman worked on the range, were attacked by men described as *guapos* or *gauderios,* men without obligations, precursors of the nineteenth-century gauchos. Once a woman was sexually attacked, her violator often felt free to return and reclaim her whenever he pleased.

Testimony from many of the cases suggests that among the more marginal social sectors, especially those living in the rural jurisdiction of the city, kidnapping and rape of unmarried girls was part of the local courtship pattern. After meeting an eligible young woman, a man would steal her from her home, usually at night or when the girl's male relatives were absent. At some distance from the "bride's" family, the girl was deflowered and the marriage thereby consummated without benefit of clergy. The couple then set up household, publicly living as man and wife. Only when the girl's family disapproved of her suitor, or when her new husband continued to "court" other women in the same way as he had wooed her, was any formal complaint lodged.

In the absence of a male relative, single women brought rape and kidnapping charges against their assailants, either by themselves or through a female relative who acted in their behalf. Single women had almost the same access to the legal system as did men, but they always underwent harsh grilling before their testimony was accepted by the magistrates. Even when charges were substantiated, the rape or kidnapping of a single, unprotected woman was often unpunished. Only the rape of a married woman was treated by the judges as a serious crime, for these crimes entailed damage to a husband's honor. In all cases involving single women, the burden of proof was placed on the victim, and punishment was rarely meted out to the offender. Punishment was more likely to be exacted in those cases where a woman had a male guardian, husband, brother, or father helping her in court. Again, criminals were punished more to assuage the masculine sense of honor and shame than to repay a woman for harm done her.

Even when sexual offenders were successfully prosecuted and punished, punishment tended to be lenient. The most frequent sentence for rape or forcible kidnapping was temporary exile to one of the towns on the other side of the La Plata estuary. Occasionally a criminal was sentenced to a longer period (one to ten years) of exile in Colonia, Montevideo, or Santo Domingo Soriano, but there is little suggestion that life was harder in these towns than in the rural district of Buenos Aires. Exiled criminals were not closely guarded, and convicts frequently returned to Buenos Aires, only to be later accused of another crime. Corporal punishment, consisting of twenty to two hundred lashes, was rare and was usually reserved for men who had raped young girls, or for slaves.

The same attitude toward sexual attack on single, unprotected women, was present when female slaves were the victims of sexual assault, but here the crime was complicated by the fact that female slaves were also property. The slaves were, by their very condition, open to sexual abuse but, surprisingly, some of them did initiate legal action on their own behalf, even at times against the wishes of their owners. In addition, female owners sometimes joined with their female slaves to complain of rape or sexual abuse of the latter.

The only cases of rape that greatly upset the local magistrates were those of child-rape, cases in which the victim was younger than fifteen years old. But even here, as in all cases of rape of an unmarried woman, the burden of proof was on the female, and complete physical entry had to be proved before the charges were felt to merit serious punishment. Even when child-rape was proved, the local judges tended to be more lenient than the law permitted. Leniency was also shown in a case involving a man guilty of "the most enormous and atrocious crime," having sexual relations with his wife's two adolescent daughters. The criminal was sentenced to 150 lashes, a milder punishment than the death penalty the court pronounced for a young man accused of raping a male victim. This punishment is the harshest sentence recorded for any sexual offense. Sodomy, unlike the rape of female children or women, was abhorrent, unnatural, contrary to God's law, and, therefore, warranted the most severe punishment.

Hair cutting, although of lesser violence than rape or kidnapping, also had sexual significance. Cutting a woman's hair was tantamount to publicly branding a woman as morally loose. Jealousy or rejection was often the motive behind this crime, but again women were also slandered in this way in order to attack the honor of their male kinsmen. Antonio Pando went to court to bring charges against a neighbor who had cut his daughter's hair, for as a father, he was "more interested than anyone in the honor of my family."

In almost all cases of crime against single women, the female victim was presumed both by the court and society to have deserved the injury. If a woman invited a man into her house, even in broad daylight, rape was justified. Rape was justified if a woman failed to lock her door at night or if she had shown any form of friendship to her assailant. Women alone, whether for short or long periods of time, were also presumed to be inviting sexual abuse. The same presumption that women deserved what befell them is also found in cases of physical abuse.

Because the courts, society, and their husbands, could and did see the woman as deserving of the crime, some women, especially those of higher social standing, brought slander charges against neighbors and kinsmen who even suggested that their conduct was in any way less than proper. The social code called for women to be pure, protected, and beyond reproach, and any indication that a woman failed to fulfill these norms presented great danger to her honor, that of her husband, and that of her family.

Although the social ideal was the pure woman, almost half the cases reviewed involved women as accomplices in sexual misconduct— adultery and licentiousness. If the woman involved in the action were married, which she frequently was, her husband viewed himself as the public victim of her bad conduct. Charges were filed by the woman's offended husband, a local priest, or a morally indignant neighbor. Although the Laws of Toro required that both adulterers be charged and punished, usually only the man was formally accused. In those cases where the woman was formally charged with adultery, she was neither imprisoned during the trial, placed in *depósito* ("on bond"), nor sentenced after the verdict had been reached. Instead she was returned to the care of her husband. Implicit in this attitude and in much of the testimony was the belief that women were, by their very nature, disorderly, prone to sexual excesses, and irrational in their sexual behavior. Regardless of the woman's cooperation in forming the adulterous union, the tempestuous female was not as guilty as her lover; rather the crime of adultery was perceived by society as being committed by one man against another man's wife.

There is no way to know how many women involved in adulterous unions were passive victims (single women or widows forced by economic pressures into sexual relationships with married men), but some of the testimony suggests that there were women who took active roles in forming and perpetuating "illicit friendships," renewing them even after legal sanctions had been taken against the offending male, fleeing from their husbands to be with their lovers. María Pallero, wife of Matías Benites, fled twice—once from the home of a local priest where her husband had placed her for safekeeping—to join her lover. María Antonia Florencia, wife of Juan José Fredes, "known in all of the district where she lives and even farther away as a strumpet because of her impudence and fickleness," deserted her husband at least three times to live with three different men. Such testimony suggests that women were involved in sexual relations of their own volition and reflects a degree of sexual freedom for the women of lower social groups within colonial society.

Court records also show that among the urban and rural poor, adultery was widely tolerated for long periods of time. Several cases contain testimony on adulterous unions that had been going on for as long as twenty years and were public knowledge. Adultery was also tolerated by husbands who, although aware that they were being cuckolded, were either ashamed or afraid to file charges with the local judge. High incidence of illegitimate births attests to the widespread acceptance of illicit unions of both casual and long-lasting natures. Adultery was not only generally ignored, but, much to the despair of civil and church authorities, couples often ignored repeated warnings to stop. Even imprisonment, which rarely lasted more than three months, did little to deter determined couples.

Buenos Aires justice, and by extension Buenos Aires society, might have been lax in reprimanding adultery among the poor, but those groups with pretensions to higher social status were most vigilant in preventing their women from involvement in such sinful liaisons. Adulterous relationships involving *gente decente* ("decent people") are totally absent from the municipal court records, for in colonial porteño society, there was a fundamental conflict between honor and legality. For a man of the upper or middle class to appeal to municipal authorities to redress the wrong done to his honor by an adulterous wife was to demonstrate his vulnerability and to place his honor in even greater jeopardy. This did not mean that the guilty wife got off scot-free; instead adultery among the upper and middle class was viewed as a personal matter, and the sinning wife was packed off to either the local House of Religious

Retreat or the Girls' Orphanage until she mended her ways. All testimony points to the ease with which upper- and middle-class men could use extralegal mechanisms to send their wayward wives or daughters to these houses of correction or place them under the care of outstanding churchmen. This form of punishment maintained adultery as a private crime; only rarely did adultery among the *gente decente* become public knowledge through legal suits or divorce proceedings.

According to Spanish law, a man was within his rights in murdering a wayward wife and her lover, but among the more respectable classes of society this was never done. Again, such an action would have endangered a husband's honor by publicly manifesting his wife's betrayal. But adultery did at times lead to homicide among the lower classes, and a husband's right to punish the offenders was always a successful defense. Occasionally it was the husband who was the homicide victim, and here the law showed no mercy to the defendants.

In addition to complaints involving adulterous unions, charges were frequently brought against single men for waywardness and evil lifestyle (*mala vida*). Included in these general charges were complaints of rowdiness, concubinage, lawlessness, and repeated instances of attempted kidnapping and rape. The plaintiff was usually not any specific victim, man or woman, but rather a group of neighbors who feared that they would be victimized next. In many cases, this group action protected a man's honor by providing a degree of anonymity. When the legitimate victim, because of fear, helplessness, poverty, or social sanctions, failed to press charges, neighbors would join with him to file legal complaints if the criminal's actions were viewed as sufficiently threatening to the community at large. Colonial justice, while tolerating a high degree of personal violence, was, nevertheless, on guard against the type of lawlessness that threatened to terrorize whole districts of the city or countryside.

Criminal court proceedings provide a glimpse of women as actors and objects, involved in the social and, to a lesser degree, the economic life of the city. Only upper-class women were able to conform to the societal norm of living sheltered, protected lives. Most colonial women, slave and free, Black, Indian, mulata, morena ("swarthy"), and even poor white, were forced by economic necessity to work in both urban and rural settings. These women were to be found on the ranchos of the countryside, in the rooms and *casitas* of the city, and in the homes of prominent local citizens. As *dependientes* ("dependents"), slaves, *agregadas* ("resident laborers"), day laborers, as single, married, or widowed women, they occupied a socially tenuous position, for the economic factors that forced them to work also exposed them to male violence, visited upon them by men of the same social class. In colonial society, women who were forced to defy the female norm of the protected, cloistered woman left themselves vulnerable to male abuse.

Frequent reference in criminal proceedings to unreported crime reflects one of the major problems of the colonial system of justice—its inaccessibility to large segments of the population. Especially in rural areas, generally isolated from even the officers of the Santa Hermandad, victims of crime had little recourse to justice. Reporting a crime entailed travel, time, money, and great determination. Once a crime was reported, the criminal had to be apprehended (not always an easy matter), witnesses found, and a judge and notary present to continue legal proceedings. Often defendants, victims, and witnesses were forced to travel to Buenos Aires for the trial.

Testimony from criminal trials reflects only a small percentage of actual crime, but it does present a picture of the types of crimes that women participated in or were victimized by, as well as reflecting the male dominant culture of colonial Hispanic society. There were definite inconsistencies in that culture's view of women. Women were expected to be pure, docile, obedient, church-going. But, beneath the surface, women were believed to be sensual, lascivious creatures, in constant need of protection, guidance, discipline, and punishment. A husband's legal duty was to provide sustenance and shelter for his wife. She in return was bound to obey him, show him respect, protect his honor, and submit to his discipline. A man publicly stating that "he felt like fighting and punishing a woman" was hardly viewed as unusual. Especially among the lower classes, women were viewed as natural outlets for male aggression.

Colonial society displayed a high level of personal violence, especially among the lower classes and more rural elements. Frequently crime against women, especially violent sexual crime, served as a surrogate, an effective way of impugning a man's honor by damaging his property and emphasizing his inability to defend his woman in a "manly" manner. The weak in this society were triply victimized—by those who attacked their honor, by the frustrations involved in appealing to local justice, and by the general lack of retribution that this justice, once activated, provided.

Suggested Further Reading

di Tella, Torcuato S. "The Dangerous Classes in Early Nineteenth-Century Mexico." *Journal of Latin American Studies* 5:1 (May 1973).

Kagan, Richard L. *Lawsuits and Litigants in Castile, 1500–1700.* Chapel Hill, 1981.

MacLachlan, Colin M. *Criminal Justice in Eighteenth-Century Mexico: A Study of the Tribunal of the Acordada.* Berkeley, 1974.

Pike, Ruth. "Penal Servitude in the Spanish Empire: Presidio Labor in the Eighteenth Century." *Hispanic American Historical Review* 58:1 (February 1978).

Civil Disorders and Popular Protests in
Late Colonial New Granada

ANTHONY F. MCFARLANE

Historians of colonial Spanish America have long recognized that Bourbon policies designed to rebuild and intensify Spain's political and economic control over its colonies generated tensions at many levels in colonial society. At times these tensions were openly and violently revealed in large-scale insurrections that merged the agitations of disparate groups into direct conflict with the royal authorities. The most striking instances of such mass rebellion occurred toward the end of the eighteenth and the beginning of the nineteenth centuries, and have often been regarded as precursors of the movements for independence. These were the Comuneros' rebellion of New Granada in 1781, the rebellion of Túpac Amaru, which convulsed Peru and Upper Peru in 1780–82, and the Hidalgo revolt, which initiated the Mexican insurgency in 1810–11. It is becoming increasingly apparent, however, that these extraordinary moments of mass mobilization formed part of a broader pattern of riot and rebellion in late colonial Spanish America. Recent studies have suggested that, among the Indian peasant communities of central Mexico and the central and southern Andes, rebellion was an endemic and recurrent feature of social life, and was probably increasing in frequency during the latter half of the eighteenth century.

The phenomenon of rebellion in late colonial Spanish America is of interest for many reasons, not least of which is that it offers a means of investigating the behavior, ideas, and attitudes of those groups in colonial society that stood outside the small and exclusive circles of the

Published originally in the *Hispanic American Historical Review*, 64:1 (February 1984). The author would like to thank the British Academy for financial assistance that enabled him to undertake research in Colombia, and Professor John Lynch for his reading of an earlier draft.

economic and bureaucratic elites. For, as historians of early modern Europe have shown, the analysis of collective popular action in civil disorders offers a useful approach to the socially subterranean world of the poor and inarticulate, throwing light not only on their material lives, but also on the values and beliefs that formed essential elements of their intellectual world. Taking up this approach, this article will focus on civil disturbances that occurred in the Viceroyalty of New Granada during the eighteenth century, in order to examine aspects of the political behavior of the subordinate classes in a colonial society, and to explore the values and conventions that framed popular attitudes toward colonial government and its agents.

Interest in popular protest in late colonial New Granada has focused almost exclusively on the Comuneros' rebellion of 1781. At its height, this great insurrection mobilized a force alleged to have been more than 20,000 strong, and plunged the viceregal authorities into a crisis of unprecedented gravity. It was not only without parallel in the history of colonial New Granada, but also comparable to the few great regional uprisings that occurred in Spanish America during the late colonial period. The sheer scale and duration of the rebellion have assured it a prominent place in the historiography of the period, and have encouraged historians to regard it as an event of special significance, symptomatic of deepening tensions within colonial social and political life. For historians bent on unearthing the roots of Colombian emancipation, the Comuneros' movement appears as the first great expression of colonial opposition to Spanish rule, the precursor of the revolution of independence initiated in 1810. Another approach has linked the rebellion to the discontents of the lower classes, portraying it as a frustrated social revolution in which the poor and dispossessed attacked the bastions of wealth and authority, only to be betrayed by creole leaders in pursuit of more limited political goals. In his study of the Comuneros, John L. Phelan argues that both approaches are oversimplified. Phelan demonstrates that at no stage did independence from Spain enter into the aims and plans of the Comuneros and their leaders, nor did they seek to overturn the existing social order. While accepting that the economic conditions and social structure of the Socorro region provided fertile ground for rebellion, he suggests that "the crisis of 1781 was essentially political and constitutional in nature. . . . The central issue was . . . who had the authority to levy new fiscal exactions." The aims of the Comuneros were largely defensive; they rejected the innovations of the visitor-general who sought to overhaul colonial government and fought to preserve existing administrative and fiscal arrangements. Not only the aims of the rebellion were fundamentally conservative; its ideology was deeply traditional. Phelan argues that the actions of the rebels were informed by long-established and generally accepted ideas about the common good of the community, its rights to express its interests by representation to and negotiation with the colonial bureaucracy, and to defend those rights, by force if necessary. In Comunero rhetoric and in the slogans of the rebels, Phelan detects echoes of the political ideas and conventions of the Spanish Golden Age; conventions that, he suggests, had been transmitted through the practices of Hapsburg government. The Comunero movement was, then, a reaction to the violation of these customary arrangements and practices, animated by a shared belief in "a *corpus mysticum politicum,* with its own traditions and procedures designed to achieve the common good of the whole community."

The Comuneros' rebellion undoubtedly constituted an uprising of singular importance. It was distinguished not only by the scale of popular mobilization, but also by its character as a coalition of forces that temporarily transcended class and ethnic lines and, under creole leadership, united behind a coherent political program. Local protests were thereby fused into a broader, regional movement of insurrection capable of presenting colonial government with a threat of uncommon proportions. And yet, the defiance of authority that underpinned the Comuneros' movement was neither a novel nor an uncharacteristic feature of colonial social and political life in New Granada. There were many other incidents of civil disorder in eighteenth-century New Granada, which, although they did not achieve the same proportions or generate such wide repercussions, show that the Comuneros' movement was neither the first nor the last manifestation of popular opposition to colonial government.

These incidents have rarely been studied or even recorded by historians, and their significance for understanding both popular action in the Comuneros' revolt and in the later movement for independence has been overlooked. They are recorded in the reports, investigations, and legal proceedings of various officials with judicial responsibilities, of which the *sala del crimen* of the audiencia was the most prominent. Variously labeled "tumultos," "levantamientos," "sublevaciones," "motines," and "rebeliones," they encompass many distinctive moments of civil disturbance and disorder. They took place in both rural and urban settings, and involved Indians, mestizos, mulattoes, and whites in combinations that varied according to the ethnic composition of the local community. They covered a wide range of conflicts, including the clashes of unconquered or semipacified Indians with settlers in frontier regions, the protests of hispanicized Indians in the areas of established Spanish settlement, riots and attacks on officials in mestizo and white communities, and conflicts that took place in Black slave communities or that involved slaves.

This article will consider neither the first nor the last of these types. Indian frontier uprisings and Black slave rebellions are, in some senses, special cases that merit detailed discussion in themselves. It will focus instead on incidents of civil disorder that affected the white, mestizo, and hispanicized Indian sectors in both rural and urban areas of New Granada. As a preliminary account of the phenomenon of civil disorder in New Granada, it does not pretend to offer a social geography of rebellion, or seek to establish any systematic correlation between the timing of popular protests and changes in material conditions in the colony as a whole. The principal aim is rather to investigate the actions and, through these actions, the political attitudes and values of sectors of the population normally excluded from the formal, institutional apparatus of government. Attention will, therefore, focus on two main themes: first, the occasions of civil disorder and the issues behind those disturbances that were prosecuted as unlawful breaches of public order; second, the character and forms of behavior, the extent of participation, and the organizational bases of these disturbances. The main objective is to show that although such incidents took place in unique local settings, they have a significance that goes beyond the local level. For, insofar as they manifest common practices and purposes, they may be regarded as elements in a tradition of popular protest that is characterized by discriminating and structured forms of behavior, informed by a conception of community interest, and underpinned by a sense that forceful, illegal action was permissible under certain conditions.

Although the Comuneros' rebellion is clearly distinguished by the scale of popular mobilization that it entailed, and the coherence of the political program that it engendered, many of the issues and grievances that it raised were to be found in other, lesser civil disorders that occurred in New Granada during the eighteenth century. At the heart of the rebellion was lower-class antagonism toward the new fiscal regulations imposed by the Bourbon visitor-general. The rebellion began with a cluster of riots protesting the introduction of new controls over the production and sales of tobacco and aguardiente, and the revision of the sales tax. After several weeks of sporadic rioting, a creole leadership emerged in Socorro and popular protest entered into a more organized phase. Coordinated by a supreme council, rebel forces marched on the viceregal capital and forced the colonial government to negotiate a settlement. By this time, the range of issues raised by the rebels had broadened, and the program of "capitulations" drawn up by the Comunero leadership incorporated a spectrum of grievances that went beyond simple opposition to new taxation. It included demands for protection against arbitrary imprisonment of the poor; preference for local men in the disposition of government offices; controls over the abuse of power by clergy and officials, particularly in their treatment of Indians; and freedom for Indians to retain their *resguardo* lands as individual proprietors.

The formation of such a broad-ranging program of demands and its presentation to the colonial authorities was without precedent in the history of New Granada. The grievances and antagonisms encapsulated in the demands of the Comunero movement, however, were all expressed in other incidents of civil disorder that occurred in New Granada during the eighteenth century. Moreover, in the behavior and aims of its participants we may also detect features of action and purpose that appear, in muted but unmistakable form, in other, lesser disturbances. Indeed, the Comuneros' rebellion may be regarded as simply the outstanding episode in a pattern of popular action that manifested itself at other times and in other places in eighteenth-century New Granada, and that embodied actions and attitudes similar to those that launched the uprising of 1781.

The grievances about taxation that lay at the center of the Comuneros' uprising were certainly not a novel source of popular disaffection. There was, indeed, a recent precedent for the Comuneros' attacks on the *estancos de aguardiente*. In the mid-1760s, government efforts to exercise closer control over the distillation and distribution of aguardiente had provoked a rash of civil disorders in the southern regions of the viceroyalty, in the province of Popayán, the neighboring mining provinces of Raposo and the Chocó, and in the Audiencia of Quito.

In the years between 1764 and 1766, the viceregal government implemented royal instructions to extend the state monopoly over the sale of aguardiente to previously unaffected areas, and to improve the efficiency of its administration in areas where it already operated. Until then, the regulation of aguardiente distillation and sale in New Granada had been exercised with due regard for local interests. From the late seventeenth century, attempts were made to control the manufacture and consumption of the liquor in New Granada, but it took many years for royal directives to have any effect. It was not until 1736, after several abortive attempts to establish a monopoly, that the crown ordered the foundation of an *estanco de aguardiente*. Even then, private interests in the colony were taken into account, with the privilege of distilling and selling the liquor being farmed out, allowing private contractors a share in the profits generated by the monopoly. The small returns to the exchequer suggest that enforcement of the regulations was lax. This probably explains why fiercer opposition to the monopoly did not develop in the early stages of its life.

Around midcentury, the colonial authorities embarked on a more perilous course. Faced with the rising costs of administration and defense, the viceroys of New Granada became increasingly interested in bringing this potentially rich source of revenue under firmer state control. At first, tentative moves in this direction proved difficult to implement. In 1744, Viceroy Sebastián de Eslava recommended that the management of the *estanco* in the town of Honda be transferred from the cabildo and its contractors to direct government control; but this plan was frustrated by opposition in the audiencia in Bogotá. Widespread and open resistance to governmental interference in the fiscalization of aguardiente appeared during the 1760s, however, when the authorities sought to extend direct administration of the monopoly to areas where it had previously been farmed out to local contractors.

The most striking outburst of popular protest against this policy was in Quito, where city people mounted a resistance that lasted for several months, brought royal government to a standstill, and virtually constructed an autonomous government of their own. The Quito uprising began with the implementation of a royal order establishing an aguardiente monopoly and introducing reforms in the administration of sales taxes within the city. Opposition to these reforms moved through various stages and drew on representatives of all the main sectors of the city's white, mestizo, and Indian populace. Launched by a *cabildo abierto* in which the urban patriciate, clergy, and commercial interests expressed their dissent to the viceroy of New Granada, it moved into popular riot in May 1765. For the next six months, the city was to experience a period of disorder and insurrection that was unprecedented in its history, with few parallels in the history of Spanish American urban life, and of a scale and duration comparable to the Comuneros' rebellion that was to take place, for similar reasons, some sixteen years later.

On May 22, 1765, pasquinades appeared in the city warning of an imminent uprising in the barrios against the new measures introduced by the director of the aguardiente monopoly. The Audiencia of Quito responded by increasing the guard on the buildings of the royal treasury, but the small force used did not discourage opponents. At seven or eight that night, amidst the clamoring of parish church bells, the beating of drums, and the discharging of fireworks, the vecinos of the two main barrios of the city—San Roque and San Sebastián—joined together in an attack on the *estanco* and customs building, stoning its windows, hurling down the doors, destroying the contents of the building (including its tax records) and sending a stream of aguardiente pouring into the streets. Only when friars and Jesuit priests interceded did the crowds, an impressive multitude of men, women, and children variously estimated at between four and ten thousand people, become pacific. They agreed to disperse when promised by the audiencia that the alcabala would be reestablished on its old footing, that the *estanco de aguardiente* be abolished, and that a general pardon be granted to those who had participated in the riot. The people of the barrios, however, were intensely suspicious of the government's intentions and remained on the alert in the weeks that followed. Any threat of reprisal against the rioters met with an immediate response, and the atmosphere in the city continued to be very tense. When the corregidor of Quito sought to reaffirm royal authority in the barrios, this tension was released in another, more violent riot that became a full-scale urban insurrection. After attempts to make arrests in the barrios, their inhabitants erupted into violent action once more. On the night of St. John's Day, June 24, a major battle broke out between government supporters and large crowds that massed in the barrios to attack government buildings in the center of the city. A battle for control of the *plaza mayor* and the audiencia palace then ensued, with many fatalities, mostly on the rebel side. The houses of peninsular Spaniards identified with opposition to the rioters were attacked, until finally, faced with overwhelming odds, the ministers of the audiencia retreated, together with peninsular Spaniards and their families, to the sanctuary of monastic houses, leaving the city in the hands of the victorious crowds. On June 28, the audiencia formally capitulated to the rebels' main demands. They agreed to the surrender of royal arms and to the expulsion of peninsular Spaniards from the city within a week, and promised to intercede with the viceroy in Bogotá for another general pardon. In the months that followed, control of the city passed from the audiencia into the hands of deputies from the barrios and the creole alcaldes of the city's cabildo. An uneasy calm returned to the city, but it was not until the following year that the audiencia felt confident that tension and agitations were dissolving. Even then, the viceroy was warned that another uprising might take place on the anniversary of the June riots, when celebrations for the marriages of the Spanish prince and princess would allow people to mass in the streets, to move about freely in the city, and to disguise themselves with the masks customarily used in such festivities. The viceroy was advised that the city remained in a state of great agitation, that efforts were being made to subvert the people by spreading the rumors that reprisals were to be taken against them, and that consequently there was the risk of a "fatal catastrophe," which would begin with a pogrom against the peninsulars. There was no repetition of the great riots of 1765, but it was only with the arrival of troops from Guayaquil in July 1766 that the crown felt confident of a complete restoration of its authority in the city.

The Quito rebellion was, like the later rebellion of the Comuneros, a spectacular demonstration of the force of opposition that could be mounted against royal efforts at fiscal reform. And, again like that of the Comuneros, resistance in Quito moved from the level of lower-class rioting to become an organized, large-scale, and lasting rebellion that brought different social and corporate groups into temporary alliance, and drew other issues into the conflict precipitated by fiscal innovation. Thus, while popular protest initially focused on rejecting reorganization of the *estanco* and alcabala, the riots against these targets also released antagonisms against peninsular Spaniards. The riots had also shown that the crown could not rely on the creole patriciate to control the lower orders. Indeed, there were strong suspicions of creole collusion, if not active involvement, in the rejection of royal policy and the organization of the rebellion. In his assessment of the event, Viceroy Manuel de Amat of Peru was in no doubt that there was a "hidden hand" behind the riots, revealed in the failure of the Quiteño nobility to contain or re-press the "disorderly common people." Nor were the clergy exempt from suspicion. Like the urban patriciate, the interests of important sections of the regular clergy were adversely affected by the introduction of the *estanco* and, although they sought to appear as mediators, there is little doubt that the rioters regarded them as sympathetic to their cause. This does not mean that the Quiteño rioters were simply the manipulable instrument of a clique of disaffected urban patricians and clergy, seeking to use a disorderly rabble for their own ends. Behind the riots in Quito, as in the lesser disturbances provoked by encroachments of royal tax-gatherers in Vélez and Ocaña (see below), was an interaction of aggrieved groups, in which the opposition of prominent members of the community to government policy gave a focus, direction, and sense of legitimacy to the lower-class rioters who acted as the main force of resistance.

Opposition to the introduction of the monopoly administration was also found in other areas of the viceroyalty in the mid-1760s, though in a more attenuated form. The city of Popayán was one such area. At the end of 1764, even before the riots in Quito, fears for public order were already being expressed in the city. The peninsular merchant who operated the city's mint reported that his house had been stoned, his family threatened, and pasquinades against the projected *estanco* affixed to the doors of the *casa de moneda*. He also reported that a "tumult" had taken place in one of the city's barrios, but gave no details on this event. After the May riots in Quito, the *estanco* administrator in Popayán became exceedingly nervous, and informed the viceroy that some of the principal citizens of the city were seeking to raise the plebe against him. The governor of Popayán took care to avoid any provocative measures, however, and the monopoly regulations were not rigorously enforced; the city remained quiet with only some minor breaches of the peace.

This was not the case in the neighboring town of Cali, an urban center of size comparable to that of Popayán. In mid-December 1765, Cali experienced a series of minor riots in which pickets of men roamed the streets at night, shouting such slogans as "Long live the King, down with aguardiente, and down with the *estanquero.*" On December 14, the cabildo reported that the plebe was about to rebel, and that meetings were being held between the plebeians of Cali and those of the surrounding rural area, allegedly for the purpose of planning a general uprising. In this instance, however, violence remained purely verbal, for the cabildo of Cali convoked a special meeting and, deciding that the fifty Spaniards in the town could not provide an adequate defense against the much more numerous common people, agreed to suspend the *estanco* regulations.

In the adjacent mining provinces—in several small settlements in the province of Raposo and in the two main urban centers of the Chocó—there was more direct action. On April 10, 1766, it was reported that, in the settlements of Sombrerillo, Las Juntas, and Calima, gangs of porters who carried provisions to the mining areas had attacked the local *estanquillos,* and had poured away or drunk the aguardiente that they had found. They had directed their action only against the *estancos,* which they refused to allow to operate. In Quibdó, capital of

Chocó Province, Governor Nicolás Díaz de Perea reported in April 1766 that many mulattoes had come into the town for Holy Week and had there conspired with some whites to attack government offices. On Good Friday, the governor forestalled the uprising, by calling in all the arms in the town, enlisting the aid of trustworthy vecinos, and confronting the mulattoes with orders to disperse. Later that year, he reported that he was unable to dispense appropriate punishments, as "these malcontents were helped and protected by all the common people," and any attempt at reprisal might lead to further disturbances. From Nóvita, another mining and administrative center in these frontier provinces, there were also reports of trouble. The aguardiente *estanquillo* in the pueblo of San Agustín was sacked in April 1766 by some mulattoes and free Blacks, "with a view to destroying the *estanco* in these provinces," and there were reports that "a large number of mulatto plebeians and free Blacks" were planning to attack the treasury in Nóvita itself. Despite some fears of a general uprising in the Pacific lowland mining regions, nothing more came of these protests. The social composition of the region's population probably played a part in inhibiting the formation of any organized opposition to the *estanco,* for these were areas in which slaves formed a substantial, at times dominant, sector of the local population, and where white settlers were extremely sensitive to any threat of disruption. The difficulty of enforcing any government regulation in such distant outposts of colonial society may have also blunted protest, once ways to evade the new restrictions had been devised.

Defiance of the government's efforts to extract higher yields from taxation underpinned many other incidents of civil disorder that occurred in late colonial New Granada. Although these incidents often originated in differences and disputes among local factions, popular protest was commonly precipitated by the behavior of local officials who contravened local conventions and practices concerning the collection of taxes. Some examples will indicate the occasions for such protest, and the aims and actions of those involved.

An early instance of urban protest precipitated by opposition to the intrusion of tax collectors occurred in the town of Vélez in 1740. In April of that year, the corregidor of the province of Tunja arrived in Vélez to carry out a visitation of the town and its jurisdiction, and to raise a loan required by the viceroy to help meet the extraordinary expenditures needed to strengthen colonial defenses at a time of Anglo-Spanish war. The first signs of resistance to these plans appeared when a meeting of the principal vecinos of the town, convoked to apportion the loan, had to be postponed because of the refusal of the *alférez real* don Alvaro Chacón to take part in it. Resistance assumed a more serious form on the same day of the abortive meeting. At about seven on the night of April 9, a major riot, allegedly involving between 2,000 and 2,500 armed men, took place in the main square of the town. With shouts of "Death to the thieving dog" and "Long live don Alvaro Chacón, King of Vélez," the crowd attacked the house where the corregidor was lodging, forcing him to take refuge in a convent while the rioters manhandled his servants and a priest who sought to calm their exalted spirits. In a further effort to restore order, the Holy Sacrament was publicly paraded among the gathered people. Even this failed to restrain them, however, and it was only when priests addressed the people from the pulpit that some modicum of calm was restored. The disturbances were not, however, over. Late in the afternoon of the following day—Palm Sunday—there was a recrudescence of disorder. This time the crowd was in a more festive mood, ignoring the corregidor and marching around the plaza, shouting acclaim for the *alférez real,* and celebrating into the night. The beleaguered corregidor seized this opportunity to escape, and made his way under cover of darkness from the town, to journey on to Bogotá where he denounced the municipal leaders as the instigators of the rebellion. When the audiencia learned of the riot, it sent a judge to investigate the event and to prosecute the *alférez real.* This provoked further resistance, with threats against the lives of the newly elected alcaldes and another riot in which an unspecified number of townspeople protested against attempts to arrest Chacón. The investigation dragged on into 1742, but did not result in any attempt to prosecute the offenders, except Chacón, whose prosecution was cut short by his death in prison.

Resistance to the fiscal demands of the state and to the actions of officials discharging the orders of viceregal government also played a central part in provoking disturbances that occurred in the town of Ocaña in 1755, 1756, and 1760. The first reports of trouble in this small, predominantly white and mestizo settlement were made by the corregidor in March 1755, shortly before Easter. He accused members of the cabildo of promoting disturbances in the town, but did not specify the nature of these disturbances. Further reports made by the corregidor, however, in May and June of that year concerning conflicts between his civil authority and that of local ecclesiastics, combined with reports from the officer who managed the recently established branch of the royal treasury in Ocaña, suggest that these disturbances were rooted in a quarrel over the collection of taxes. The corregidor informed the viceroy of the difficulties that he was having with the local clergy, arising from the action brought by Francisco Segura—a peninsular Spaniard who had married into a distinguished local family—against both the *alférez real* and a local priest. When Segura took his case against the priest before an ecclesiastical tribunal in the town, both he and his case, together with the royal official who accompanied him, were ignominiously thrown out. Segura then carried his complaint to the corregidor, bringing the latter into conflict with the local clergy. Both Segura and the corregidor were now threatened with excommunication, and the town was kept in a state of agitation by the constant and clamorous tolling of church bells. According to the corregidor, these efforts to dishonor and intimidate Segura arose because he had tried to prevent the disturbances and riots that had taken place, and because he consistently refused to concur in all the "infamies" of those who now sought to discredit him. A further request from the corregidor in 1756 for military assistance to deal with disorders, and a report on the breaking of a prohibition on bearing arms indicates that these conflicts within the community persisted into the following year.

Although the corregidor was vague about the reasons for these disturbances, reports from another source suggest that they arose from opposition to the activities of the recently installed *oficial real*. For, at the end of May 1755, that officer, one Sánchez Barriga, reported to the viceroy that to counteract the fall in tithe revenues, he had taken their administration under his direct control, and was considering action against the alcaldes and their property for the failure to administer the tax properly. The presence in Ocaña of that official, his efforts to exert his authority and to reorganize the collection of taxes created conflicts both within the town and in its hinterland. In 1760, the vecinos of Playablanca, part of the small mestizo and mulatto farming community of the village of Simaña, protested his plans to impose new taxes on the storage and transportation of goods in their area, coupled with the collection of the alcabala on products that had not previously been encumbered with the sales tax. Not only did they appeal against his "tyrannical procedures" in dealing with them, but they referred to the "well-known misfortunes which the city of Ocaña is suffering due to his harsh measures," and to the fact that "not even the Church of God has been exempt from his outrages." Assuring the viceroy of their loyalty and obedience, they did not repudiate the taxes, but argued that they should be allowed a special exemption, as they were too poor to pay. A report from the cabildo of nearby Tamalameque supported the Playablanca petition, and refuted Sánchez Barriga's pretensions on several grounds. One of these was the argument that it had been customary to take the poverty of small producers into account by charging them at lower rates for the receipts that recorded their tax payments.

The problems in Ocaña to which the Playablanca petitioners referred issued in open conflict in 1760. On December 11, a riot took place in the town, in which a mob of between 300 and 500 "personas inferiores" attacked the local magistrates and repudiated their authority. The riot started when the alcaldes were called to deal with a disturbance in the house of some local priests, among whom were clerics who had played a leading part in the disturbances of 1755. The alcaldes had broken down the door of the priests' house in order to force an entry, prompting one of its occupants to call into the street for help. With his shouts of "Rally to the church," "Sound the alarm," the priest summoned aid from the townspeople. The alcaldes took up the rival cry of "Rally to the King," but this brought them no support. A rioting crowd gathered in the main square, wielding sticks and swords, and forced the alcaldes to retreat, pursued by shouts of "Long live the church" and "Death to these pícaros" from the rioters. Another mob, mainly of women, gathered at the priests' house and refused orders from the *oficial real* to disperse. Unable to deal with these mobs, the alcaldes decided to hide, and took refuge with the *oficial real,* Sánchez Barriga, in his house. When, at two in the morning, they attempted to return to their own homes, the crowd was still in position and in an aggressive mood. On the approach of the alcaldes and their guards, the crowd menaced them with shouts of refusal to recognize the alcaldes as magistrates, and an attack in which one of the magistrates received a light stab wound in his arm. At this point, the alcaldes' party fired some shots and retired from the fray, calling on the *oficial real* to spend the rest of the night with them to provide him protection. On the following day, this same official, Sánchez Barriga, sent his officers to arrest some of the rioters, only to find that these men—who included "citizens who were both white and of inferior quality"—had taken refuge in the church, together with several priests.

The affair ended inconclusively, apparently without arrests and without dispelling the animosities that inspired the riot. The violent events of December 11 were succeeded by a long postscript of mutual recriminations in the decade that followed, with claims and counterclaims from the factions involved, with investigations into the behavior of Sánchez Barriga, and a struggle for control of the town's cabildo. The riot of 1760 was, then, the prominent incident in a longer struggle in which leading members of the town's community resisted the authority and activities of the *oficial real*. Indeed, the alcaldes who were the targets of the crowd's actions during the riot argued that there was a long-standing conspiracy among local clerics and their relatives to oppose the *oficial real*, whose policies were not to their taste, and that these unruly priests abused their spiritual authority in inciting the riot. Nevertheless, although these clerics clearly played a leading role, the enthusiastic popular response to their calls for support indicates that they enjoyed considerable local sympathy in their opposition to the *oficial real* and his allies. While the clerics provided leadership, there were concrete grievances at the heart of the riot, grievances that arose from the high-handed actions of an official who refused to countenance local procedures in fiscal matters and who sought to impress his authority on a community accustomed to a more relaxed form of government. Thus the alcaldes' attempt to quell the disturbance at the priests' house on December 11 provided the populace with an opportunity to express their resentment in direct action, legitimized as a defense of the church.

The riots that occurred in Vélez and Ocaña should not necessarily be regarded as typical of civil disorders in eighteenth-century New Granada. They do present some features, however, that, as we shall see, were present in other disturbances. First, they indicate the dangers facing royal officials who sought to introduce innovations, especially in the sensitive matter of taxation. Second, they convey a sense of local distaste for interference by outsiders and suggest the presence of expectations that royal officials should govern by collusion, rather than seek to impose their authority without regard for local interests and sensibilities. Third, they suggest that when prominent citizens—in these cases, municipal officers and local clerics—resisted the exercise of authority by officers of the crown, this generated or aggravated factionalism within the community. This, in turn, both undermined respect for authority and provided a source of leadership and legitimacy for direct action by a broader section of the community, opening opportunities for the release of latent hostilities, of the poor toward the wealthy, the humble toward the powerful, and of taxpayers toward tax collectors.

Many of the disturbances reported to the judicial authorities in eighteenth-century New Granada were also inspired by resentment at changes in taxation, or were ultimately rooted in competition over local economic resources. Like the riots in Vélez and Ocaña, they were invariably defensive actions, in which members of mainly rural communities resisted new demands on their resources, usually from venal officials. They occurred in both mestizo and hispanicized Indian communities, and generally stemmed from the imposition of new or changed taxes, unaccustomed demands for labor services, or conflicts over land.

Cases marked by civil disorder in Indian communities indicate some of the occasions on which Indian peasants made forceful collective protests to defend themselves against the economic incursions of officials and other outsiders. For the Indians of Turmequé in the province of Tunja, an occasion for violent protest arose on December 14, 1705, when the corregidor of Turmequé, accompanied by the commissioner of the Tribunal de la Santa Cruzada, arrested their cacique, Marcos Gordo. This precipitated a riot in which some 800 Indian men and women attacked these officials and the vecinos who came to their aid, and threatened to burn down the village if Gordo were removed from it. Some creole or mestizo vecinos were disarmed by the mob of Indians, others were pursued by stone-throwing crowds and forced into hiding, while the priests who tried to pacify the rioters were insulted and manhandled. For two days and nights, the Indians were congregated outside the jail, "talking in their own tongue and demonstrating their anger." It was only with the arrival of a small force from the provincial capital of Tunja, a week later, that order was fully restored and steps taken to arrest and punish some of the rioters. Although it was triggered by the arrest of the cacique, this protest arose from more deep-seated local grievances. It later transpired that the Indians were aggrieved by the actions of their local priest, who, along with his henchmen, was said to abuse and terrorize the community and to force the Indians to provide him labor for his private use under the pretext that it was for work on the church. Gordo's arrest followed his return from Bogotá where, with other local Indian leaders, he had registered complaints on behalf of the community, and had defied the authority of the commissioner of the Tribunal de la Santa Cruzada. Thus, behind the immediately visible reason for the riot lay a struggle against the extortions of a local priest, and, the attacks on local vecinos suggest, other outsiders engaged in exploiting Indian land and labor.

Resistance to the depredations of local officials also lay behind Indian defiance of the corregidor of Coyaima, near Ibagué, in 1731. The corregidor, who congratulated himself on his zealous service to the royal treasury, reported that his attempts to draw up a census of the Indian villages of Coyaima and Natagaima had been opposed, and he blamed the Indian *teniente* for leading opposition to royal taxes. The Indians, on the other hand, protested that their only aim was to free themselves from exploitation by the corregidor, who tried to force wines, aguardiente, and imported textiles on them at inflated prices. In the Indian community of Guamo, also in the jurisdiction of Ibagué, official interference in village economic life led to a riot by its inhabitants in 1756. When the administrator of the aguardiente monopoly for the Ibagué region went out to Guamo to break up the illegal stills operated by the villagers, the infuriated peasants rioted against him, stealing his sword, shotgun, and other belongings, and forcing him to leave the village. In the village of Soatá, in the corregimiento of Duitama, the activities of local tax collectors provoked several tumults over a period of years before 1752, involving attacks on the agent of the aguardiente *estanco* and the collector of the alcabalas.

In a place like Soatá, where mestizos and whites illegally occupied Indian community lands, opportunities for confrontation and breaches of the peace were increased by the presence of such intruders. As non-Indian vecinos took advantage of Indian exemption from the obligation to pay alcabalas to evade sales taxes on their products, this no doubt increased the harassment of Indians by tax collectors. These fraudulent practices were one reason given by the corregidor of Sogamoso and Duitama in 1765 when he recommended that the Indians be segregated from the vecinos. He pointed out that bad relations between the Indians and vecinos was a cause of frequent riots in which Indian peasants threatened their non-Indian neighbors, an allegation that was borne out by the investigation that followed a riot of the Indians of Sogamoso in July 1772. In this incident, some 400 Indian peasants, accompanied by "drum and trumpet," attacked the house and mill of a local vecino, stripped his wife of her clothing, and expelled her from the *resguardo*. This attack, it was said, was one of many tumults that had taken place in Sogamoso during the previous twenty years.

These instance of collective protest by Indian peasant communities did not, of course, present any serious threat to colonial government and rarely led to more than summary investigation and mild punishment. If competition over Indian lands was a constant source of friction in areas where dwindling Indian communities were pressured by land-hungry white and mestizo farmers, the Indian peasantry was too divided and demoralized to stage any major rebellion. Indeed, by the mid-eighteenth century, the Indian communities of the most densely populated regions of New Granada—the provinces of Santa Fe de Bogotá and Tunja—had virtually succumbed to the encroaching influences of Hispanic society. To evade the demands of church and state, Indians had moved away from their communities to merge into the surrounding mestizo parishes and villages, accelerating the decline of indigenous societies already undermined by demographic losses. While Indian petitions and protests continued to reach the authorities in Bogotá until the end of the colonial period, the hemorrhage of Indian communities through the processes of migration and miscegenation weakened their capacity for resistance. For this reason, peasant rebellion is less visible and no doubt less common in New Granada than in those areas of Spanish America where an indigenous peasantry still constituted a numerous and vigorous element of the population.

It was only in areas where Indians formed the major element of regional population and retained strong economic and cultural identity that large-scale Indian uprisings took place. In the Audiencia of Quito, within the jurisdiction of the viceroyalty but outside New Granada proper, the Indian communities that formed the basis of rural society staged several major rebellions over the course of the eighteenth century. In New Granada itself—roughly the territory of modern Colombia—the Indian population was much smaller and the threat of large-scale Indian insurrection was correspondingly weaker. Only two areas posed such threats from time to time: the first was in the eastern frontier province of the Llanos de Casanare, where white and mestizo colonization was relatively recent, and where the population remained overwhelmingly Indian in origin. Here a major Indian insurrection took place in 1781, at the time of the Comuneros' revolt. While Indian peasants in the central provinces of New Granada were drawn into the Comuneros' movement, it was in a weak and subordinate role; only in the Llanos did Indian peasants' participation provide the main force for regional insurrection and give this episode in the Comuneros' rebellion a distinctive character and trajectory. The second area was in the southernmost reaches of Colombia, merging into northern Ecuador. In the region around the town of Pasto and in the corregimiento of Los Pastos, rural society retained a predominantly Indian character and its Indian peasantry showed signs of that capacity for resistance often found among its counterparts in the central and southern Andes. When Indian peasants murdered the corregidor of Los Pastos and his brother in Túquerres, in 1800, the authorities immediately feared that insurrection would spread rapidly through the region, and they took swift steps to prevent this. They sent in detachments of troops under the command of the governor of Popayán both to punish the rebels and to maintain peace in the area. Here, then, was an Indian peasantry that was regarded as a potentially explosive force, whose control was a military, rather than a simple policing, matter.

Elsewhere, the decay of Indian society in the main centers of Spanish settlement, and its replacement by a predominantly mestizo population, does much to explain the infrequency of large-scale peasant insurrections in eighteenth-century New Granada. The mestizo population was not subject to the burdens of tribute, labor levies, and forced supply of goods that so often weighed on indigenous communities and created latent conflict between Indian peasants and those who wielded authority over them. Nevertheless, although the mestizo peasantry was less vulnerable to economic pressure from the agents of church and state, it was not entirely free of such exploitation. Apart from the taxes levied by the crown, the local authorities in Spanish urban and village communities might call on local resources of money and labor to maintain public buildings, especially churches, and to provide for the upkeep of roads and trails within its jurisdiction. At times, the enforcement of such regulations by unscrupulous or unpopular officials could provoke strong, organized, and sometimes violent collective resistance.

An instance of such resistance occurred in the small mining town of Zaragoza, in the province of Antioquia, in 1793. In that year, the alcalde of Zaragoza reported that, on November 21, a mob that included the local priest and leading citizens had risen in mutiny against the *capitán a guerra,* had threatened his life, and had forced him into hiding. In the event, no violence was committed against the offending official and, the alcalde reported, the crowd responded to his persuasion to disperse peacefully. The copious documentation that accompanied this report revealed that this minor riot was the culmination of a longer, legal campaign of community complaint against the *capitán a guerra.* In the previous year, the principal vecinos of Zaragoza had twice petitioned the viceroy for his replacement. In August 1792, they had complained that this official, like all his predecessors in recent years, was a constant burden to the town. They asserted that these officials not only lacked experience of the country and its people, but, being poor, were also prone to using their authority to enrich themselves. At the end of the year, the vecinos reiterated their complaint: their representative informed the authorities that the town was in a state of great agitation because of the activities of the *capitán a guerra* and his main allies, the alcalde and *procurador general* of the town council. After a quarrel between these officials and the local priest, local society had broken into factions, with the *capitán a guerra* systematically persecuting his opponents among the leading citizens of the town, and heaping even greater misfortunes on the poor, who were less able to defend themselves. A new tax had been imposed on measures of maize, and both money and labor services extorted to build a new jail. It was also said that this official was offending and corrupting public morals: on his nightly patrols, he used his authority to visit not only the houses of the town but also its matrimonial beds. Thus, the riot a year later was not simply a spontaneous outburst of violent anger; it was part of a longer campaign, carried out by legal means, to remove an unpopular official. When negotiation with the authorities had been slow to yield results, members of the community expressed their anger and frustration by other, more direct means, with their action sanctioned and led by leading citizens.

This blend of direct protest and legal action also characterized the defiance shown by the villagers of the settlement of Chinú, in the province of Cartagena, toward local officials. In June 1798, the villagers were summoned together by Agustín Núñez, a delegate of the alcalde, and ordered to open a trail. They refused, reiterated their refusal when the order was repeated by the alcalde and the *capitán a guerra,* and resisted attempts to arrest their leaders. Then, to the beating of a drum, they marched on the house of Núñez, and sought to expel him from the settlement. Later, when a picket of troops was sent to arrest the leaders of this resistance, local people again rioted in order to secure the release of those arrested.

The villagers had refused to open the trail on the grounds that it was not a camino real, and that such orders were not customary. Their subsequent petitions to the governor of Cartagena, however, transmitted through a lawyer hired for this purpose, reveal that other issues were involved. It transpired that Núñez was not merely a vecino and ranch owner in Chinú, he was also a regidor and *alcalde provincial* in the neighboring town of San Benito Abad, and the collector of tithes in its jurisdiction. His use of his power and influence in the region was the real source of resistance in Chinú. The vecinos complained that the trail was for personal rather than public use, as it passed through Núñez's cattle ranch. They also alleged that he employed violent and oppressive methods to collect tithes; that he used public messengers, paid at low rates, for private business; that he exploited dayworkers by forcing them to accept low wages or payments in kind made at inflated prices; that he forced people to accept goods that they did not want; threw people off their lands and took them over, killed their animals when they strayed on to his property, and expelled anyone who resisted. Clearly, then, the tumults in Chinú were more than simply spontaneous outbursts of aggression toward an official discharging his duties. They were incidents in a campaign, led by prominent local men, financed by the community, and represented by a lawyer in Cartagena, to defend local interests against the depredations of a powerful individual.

Although the incidents described above took place in varied environments and covered a range of issues, they all show that neither the viceregal government nor local officials could make economic demands on the colonial populace with complete impunity. If there was a general acceptance of the crown's right to tax its subjects, efforts to extend or to improve the range of fiscalization could provoke strong reactions. Equally, if it was accepted that local officials would manipulate their authority for personal gain, there was a point at which grudging acceptance of this practice gave way to angry defiance. No doubt this point varied among communities, and the occurrence of disturbances in some places rather than others must be related to specifically local circumstances. Nonetheless, the incidents examined suggest that defiance displaced deference when innovation was attempted, or when official malpractice coincided with intracommunity disputes involving both conflicts of political authority and competition over local economic resources.

As protests against official incursions into local economic life, these disturbances reflect unstated assumptions about the legitimate claims of government and its agents. These assumptions were basically conservative: they did not challenge the right of government to levy taxation or to organize the administration of the colony, but protested against specific taxes and the behavior of particular officials. Indeed, in several of the cases examined, tumults were only part of more prolonged actions, in which members of communities expressed their ultimate confidence in government by carrying their protest beyond the local level by appeals to higher authorities. In this sense, these protests were ultimately respectful of royal authority: they were directed against changes in taxation, not taxation itself; against the representatives of government, not government itself. While respect for governmental authority was encouraged by habits and traditions of deference, combined with the threat of punishment, it also depended on official observance of existing customs and practices. If these were ignored or broken by fiscal innovations or new economic incursions by local officials, defiance of authority could be regarded as a justifiable means of defending local interests. Implicitly, then, these disturbances carried a claim to "rights," if only in the vague sense that they embodied a readiness to defend the status quo against the fiscal and economic pressures of government and its agents.

Such implicit claims to unspecified "rights" were also reflected in disturbances that arose from conflicts over office-holding and the administration of the law. In both these matters, respect for authority was neither automatic nor uncritical. By taking direct action to hinder the holding of office by unpopular individuals, and to pressure local magistrates to enforce the law in particular ways, members of communities in New Granada again showed pretensions to rights of intervention and participation to which the Bourbon state allowed them no explicit or formal claim.

One manifestation of such pretensions is found in disturbances that produced demonstrations of hostility toward local officials, aimed at preventing them from taking office or at expelling them from office. The choice of a local official appears to have been a matter in which members of communities felt that they should have some say. This attitude is reflected in disturbances that occurred when an official was not to local taste. On Sunday, January 9, 1724, a large crowd of citizens of the small mestizo town of Monguí near Tunja turned out to express a vocal vote against the newly appointed *juez ordinario* by giving him a tumultuous reception when he arrived to take up residence. On arriving in Monguí, the magistrate found a mob of about a hundred men, armed with swords, waiting in the town square to greet him with threatening gestures and shouts of "We will not receive don Juan de Vargas," "We don't want him," "Any other alcalde is better." The crowd then pursued him, forcing him to retire to his house outside the town. A similar incident occurred in the hamlet of El Plato, near Mompós, in 1803. When don Joseph Vicente Gómez, a relatively wealthy man from the nearby town of Tenerife and the collector of tithes in El Plato, was designated interim magistrate by the cabildo of Tenerife, the vecinos of El Plato banded together "in tumultuous uproar" to reject him. Even when he was replaced, collective action against him did not cease. On two occasions in July 1803, crowds gathered to demand his expulsion from the village on the grounds that he had insulted the local people by calling them thieves, and refused to contribute to community works. When an alcalde of Tenerife was sent to investigate, and refused to expel Gómez, the locals rioted against the alcalde, filling his courtroom with dirt, posting a crude and insulting pasquinade, and abusing him with threats and insults until he retreated to Tenerife.

In other incidents, also reported as "tumultos" or "motines," intimidation of unpopular officials was staged by small groups operating in a semiclandestine manner, rather than crowds engaged in public demonstrations. These incidents usually arose from rivalries within small communities, in which groups of vecinos related by ties of kinship or friendship attacked officials of whom for some reason they disapproved. While the motives behind such attacks are often obscure, the manner in which they were carried out shows that they were more than merely criminal assaults by lawless thugs. Thus, when don Joachim de Lis, *alcalde provincial* of the town of Purificación, was attacked on the night of December 31, 1776, his assailants were not simply indulging in a spree of mindless violence, but were making a calculated show of force for political ends. The gang of eight men and two women, "all armed and disguised in different costumes," who burst into Lis's house and manhandled him did so in order to force him to sign a document formally renouncing his post as *alcalde provincial*. As the men were all members of the town council, and their attack took place on New Year's Eve—the day before the new alcaldes were chosen—the timing and nature of the assault were clearly related to political goals. Similar tactics of intimidation were employed in Moniquirá, a mestizo parish in the province of Tunja, on December 28, 1802. In this incident, a group of about a dozen people, including some women disguised as men, made a nocturnal attack on don Rafael Conde, who was about to become the alcalde in the coming year. They assaulted Conde, warned him that "many alcaldes in the world had been killed," and told him that he would suffer the same fate if he took up his post. Insulting pasquinades were also pinned up in the parish, making the same kinds of threats. Again, the timing and character of the assault show its political intentions. Indeed, these were not denied by the defense counsel for the accused. He did not dispute involvement but simply argued for leniency on several grounds. First, he argued that the attack did not constitute an act of rebellion, but was merely the misguided mischief of illiterate and invincibly ignorant rustics who had aimed not to kill Conde, but to intimidate him, as they feared that he would prove to be an excessively severe magistrate. Second, he suggested that other people were involved, and that prominent vecinos had instigated the assault, thereby implying that there was considerable community opposition to Conde.

An interesting aspect of these incidents (and one to which further reference will be made later), is the element of ritual apparent in the behavior of the assailants. In both cases, reference is made to the use of costumes or disguise, although these did nothing to camouflage the identities of their wearers. This feature is more clearly described in an incident of assault on an official that occurred in Cheva, Tunja Province, in 1809. On the night of November 13 of that year, the corregidor of Gameza was attacked in his home in Cheva by a group of some twenty-five people who, he alleged, were led by the local parish priest. He reported that this group, "their hands and faces stained in black, dressed in petticoats worn back to front, and headscarves . . . and armed with daggers and cudgels, led by the said priest, in similar disguise" had broken into his house, yelling curses and insults. They had dragged the corregidor, still dressed in his underclothes, from his bed and, showering him with blows to his buttocks, mounted him on a mule and galloped him violently around. They then brought out his wife in a similar manner, tied them together on the same steed, and rode them far from the village before abandoning them, with a warning never to return to Cheva, on pain of death. The subsequent investigation into this affair shows that it arose from a clash between the corregidor and prominent vecinos of Cheva, including the *juez pedáneo* and the collector of tithes, over access to Indian labor.

These affrays involving local factions are another indication of a popular readiness to participate and intervene in colonial political life. Although they were the work of small groups behaving in a more or less covert manner, they were not simply the violent acts of criminal gangs in pursuit of personal vendettas. They were rather an aspect of local politics in which, by engaging in disputes over office or bringing pressure to bear on officials to conform to private needs, the participants displayed an underlying assumption that authority should be exercised in collusion with local interests. Because they were marked by attacks on officers of government, these affrays were treated as acts of rebellion. But if they were illegal, they were not anti-institutional. They did not attack the machinery of the state, but sought to control and manipulate its agents.

The employment of force by groups seeking to exert pressure on officials is also found in incidents of riot that occurred in the city of Tunja in 1727, and in the town of Cali in 1743. Treated as acts of rebellion, these riots were subsequently investigated by specially appointed judges who made lengthy reports. The documents are worth close consideration not only because they convey a sense of how popular disturbances might develop, but also because they throw some light on both popular attitudes toward the law and on the social tensions and antagonisms present in colonial communities.

The Tunja riot of January 23, 1727, took place when a crowd

sought to pressure magistrates to enforce the law in an equitable manner, following a street brawl in which a peninsular Spaniard had wounded a mestizo shepherd. Both men were apprehended by prominent local citizens who were in the vicinity at the time of the fight, and a curious crowd soon gathered. The alcalde ordinario, don José Calvo, quickly made his way to the scene, having been informed that a crowd had gathered in the main square and that the city would be lost if he failed to arrest the Spaniard, Pedro Sertuche. Calvo was persuaded, however, that the two men should be held separately. He ordered that Sertuche be placed under house arrest, in a house that was the home and property of a fellow peninsular. On the other hand, the injured mestizo, Vicente Barbosa, was sent to the city jail.

This unequal treatment provoked a strong reaction from local peasants and small tradesmen. A vociferous crowd of some twenty-five men and women, including relatives of Barbosa, gathered outside the house where Sertuche was held and staged a threatening demonstration. Members of the crowd complained loudly that there was no justice in the city, and that it was becoming like the Sierra Morena. This disparaging reference to Spain was accompanied by shouts of "Death to Sertuche and all Spaniards," and "From here to the Sierra Morena, death to all Spaniards." It was also said that people had shouted acclaim for the *maestre de campo* as their king, referring to a prominent creole, don Martín Camacho, present at the time. This crowd became so aggressive that it was decided that Sertuche should be imprisoned in the city jail, if only for his own safety. In the meantime, his erstwhile opponent, Barbosa, had been released from the jail by another crowd before Sertuche was placed there, bound with manacles at the behest of the mob. Later that night, there was another disturbance caused by people trying to break into the jail to attack Sertuche.

The immediate causes of this riot are plain enough. After a violent brawl between a Spaniard and a mestizo, in which the Spaniard used a firearm to wound his opponent, the local magistrate's unequal treatment of the two offenders stirred angry feelings among local people. More interesting is the manner in which the action developed and the attitudes that it reveals. It is clear that this was far from the frenzied outburst of a mob hungry for revenge; on the contrary, it was a structured show of force carried out by a threatening, but basically orderly, crowd. Although some witnesses drew attention to the fact that members of the crowd carried swords, stones, and cudgels, there were no attacks on either persons or property. Indeed, most witnesses stressed that the crowd behaved in a restrained and respectful manner. It is also apparent that an element of class antagonism was present and contributed to the development of events. The incident brought a confrontation between individuals who came from distinct social groups. On one side stood the friends and partisans of the peninsular Spaniard, all of them prominent citizens and office-holders in the city. On the other were the relatives and allies of Barbosa, the active nucleus of the protesting crowd, including peasants, artisans, and small traders. Thus the incident was colored by the opposition of rich and poor, of powerful and humble. The antagonism of plebians to patricians, however, was not indiscriminate. The threatening shouts against Spaniards were accompanied by cries of acclaim for a prominent local creole, don Martín Camacho, whom members of the crowd evidently regarded as a possible champion for their cause. In the subsequent investigation, there was never any direct accusation that Camacho had instigated or played a leading role in the riot. But he took part in a subsequent incident showing that tensions between Spaniards and colonials were aroused. He admitted that the day after the riot he had posted a handbill in the town square, challenging those Spaniards who had been heard to make insulting remarks about himself and fellow creoles during the events of the preceding day. His prompt and public reaction to this alleged slander suggests that antagonism between colonials and Spaniards was not far below the surface of social life in the city, and that it affected both rich and poor.

The disturbance in Tunja, then, is of interest for several reasons. First, it suggests the existence of a popular sense of justice, by showing that the poorer members of the community could be moved to concerted action when they felt that basic norms of justice were being flouted. Second, it indicates that although the crowd was ready to use threatening behavior to force municipal officials to meet its demands, it nevertheless recognized the authority implicit in their offices. Third, it reveals an animosity toward peninsular immigrants, a sensitivity toward their arrogant behavior, and a vague sense that local men were the rightful leaders of the community.

In the Tunja incident, popular action was directed toward forcing a magistrate to discharge his duties in an equitable manner. In a riot that occurred in Cali in 1743, a crowd took direct action to prevent a magistrate from perpetrating a perceived violation of the rights of a citizen. The riot took place on February 20, 1743, when a large crowd made a nocturnal attack on the town jail to release a prisoner, and destroyed a gibbet that had recently been erected in the main square. This incident, however, also involved enmities between colonials and Spaniards, reflected in an assault on the house of one of the alcaldes of Cali, who was a peninsular merchant.

Underlying this event was a long history of factional strife in eighteenth-century Cali, stemming from a struggle for control of the cabildo between newly arrived peninsular merchants and members of the established creole families. In the disturbances of 1743, the clergy appear to have played a leading part in both instigating and leading the riot, and the evidence collected suggests that it was part of a campaign of resistance against the incumbent alcaldes. The riot of February 20, however, was more than simply a clash of patrician factions. It involved the mobilization of a crowd for the purpose of forestalling a threatened violation of the normal methods of the law. Rumors had circulated in the city to the effect that a prisoner was about to be tortured—to extract information about a pasquinade—and subsequently hanged. To prevent this, the jail was attacked, and a large crowd mustered in the main square where, despite the parade of the Holy Sacrament by priests seeking to restore calm and despite being fired upon by an embattled alcalde, it refused to disperse until the gibbet had been cut to pieces. Although some witnesses state that most of the rioting crowd was drunk, this was evidently not simply a disorderly melee, but the work of a crowd acting with a definite purpose and a degree of discipline.

Although the direction of a riot undoubtedly owed something to organization by leaders of a faction active in town politics, the rioting crowd should not necessarily be regarded as the blind and unwitting instrument of elite groups competing for control of urban government. The prior circulation of rumors about the alleged mistreatment of a prisoner suggests that the populace had to have some justification for action. In spreading the word that the alcaldes were abusing their power, the populace made an appeal to principles of justice both to promote and to legitimize crowd action of an unlawful kind. By attacking the jail, however, and destroying the gibbet, the crowd did not aim to overthrow the law; it sought rather to prevent a perceived abuse of the law by local magistrates by briefly taking the law into its own hands. Thus, beneath the surface of this rowdy incident in urban politics, we once again may dimly discern a popular conception of justice and of the law that did not tolerate the unrestrained exercise of power by representatives of the state.

The various incidents of civil disorder that have been described do not fit any single mold. They arose in distinctive environments throughout the Viceroyalty of New Granada, sprang from a range of issues, and displayed degrees of participation that ranged from open collective protest by large crowds to semicovert actions by small groups. To seek any general hypothesis that might explain the causes, frequency, and distribution of these disparate events would be premature. In many cases, the information provided by contemporary sources is very limited, and the uneven and inconsistent quality of the primary data makes it difficult fully to investigate and compare reported cases of civil disorder. The problems posed by the primary sources are compounded by the paucity of local and regional histories of New Granada. Until studies of the social, economic, and political life of the communities in which these disturbances occurred become available, it is impossible to comment with confidence on how common such disturbances were, or on their relationship to social and economic conditions. Nevertheless, the disturbances described should not be dismissed as simply spontaneous, unrelated, and insignificant outbreaks of disorder. Beyond the obvious differences in the local milieus in which they occurred, we may detect some characteristic forms of behavior and intention that in turn throw light on popular social values and attitudes toward government.

At a general level, these incidents indicate that, while the inarticulate mass of the colonial populace had no opportunity to participate in the formal organizations and institutions of government, they were able to express their grievances and voice their beliefs by informal means. Although of sporadic timing and scattered incidence, the events described strengthen the impression given by some contemporary observers that the mass of the colonial population could be a restive and potentially turbulent force. For the emissaries of the Bourbon state in New Granada, this was a measure of the lamentable lawlessness of the lower orders, who were insufficiently exposed to the disciplinary guidance of church and state. In a vivid formulation of this view, Archbishop-Viceroy Caballero y Góngora condemned the insubordination of the lower classes in unequivocal terms. The mestizos, he stated, were without "the two principal sentiments which Nature inspires in rational man—belief in one God, whom he should love, and in one king, whom it is just to obey." As for Indians and Blacks, according to the archbishop, they were governed by even baser feelings. In all, the common people formed an "indomitable monster," whose criminal proclivities were at the root of the colony's ills.

Made soon after the Comunero revolt, Caballero y Góngora's remarks reflect the instinctive horror of popular rebellion natural to a high official of church and state; hence, they may exaggerate the extent of popular insubordination. Nevertheless, the archbishop-viceroy's comments reflected a basic reality of colonial life. Governmental control over the extensive territory and diverse society of New Granada was undoubtedly weak and uneven. The largely mestizo population, most of which was thinly spread over large rural areas, was accustomed to little direct interference from government; indeed, in some areas in late eighteenth-century New Granada, Bourbon officials were still trying to build a basic infrastructure of royal administration. Furthermore, though the population was divided by considerable inequalities of wealth and social status, lower-class habits of deference do not seem to have been as well developed as those of their counterparts in Europe: the uncouth and insolent manners of the lower orders occasionally drew scandalized comments from peninsular observers during the eighteenth century, while the familiarity of the lower classes with their social superiors was to be a source of surprise for foreign visitors during the early years of independence. When colonial government sought to impose its will without regard for these conditions and the conventions they had fostered, it risked defiance, sometimes on a widespread scale. This was the lesson of the aguardiente riots of 1765, a lesson that, ignored by the reformist visitor-general in 1781, was to be repeated by the Comuneros in a still more obvious way. Thereafter, viceregal government became more sensitive to the threat of colonial insubordination. Thus, in 1803, Viceroy Pedro de Mendinueta commented upon the low level of wages paid to agricultural workers at a time when prices were rising, and observed that a time might come when the poor would force the landowners to yield a large share of their wealth. He also testified to the continuing existence of that strong undercurrent of popular animosity toward the tax collector, and warned the crown against imposing additional fiscal burdens on the colony, for fear that this might provoke a rebellious response.

When the refractory disposition of the New Granadan population was openly expressed, it did not take the simple form of unbridled vandalism. Among the features shared by the disturbances described above were those elements of structured and discriminating behavior that historians have frequently found in the actions of rioters and rebels in other parts of colonial America and in contemporary Europe. From the incidents described above it seems, first, that defiance of authority was rarely a simply spontaneous outburst of collective anger. Tumults often took place during hours of darkness, perhaps because this made it easier for the participants to conceal their identities. At times, crowds were brought together by some signal, such as the tolling of church bells or the beating of a drum, both of which were commonly used to gather people together for normal social functions. The use of signals and the cover of darkness suggest that there was an element of preparation behind some incidents of civil disorder, though others—like that which occurred in Tunja in 1727—arose as a spontaneous response to the actions of the authorities. There were, in addition, occasions on which disturbances merged with, or developed from, public gatherings, particularly public festivities.

The relationship between civil disorders and communal festivities has often been noted by students of popular protest and popular culture. In his study of rebellions in colonial Mexican villages, William B. Taylor has drawn attention to the similarities of behavior in riots and fiestas, and the tendency for riots to turn into celebrations. For early modern Europe, the relationship of festivals and riots has been more closely defined: there, historians have found that public festivities were occasions on which the revelry and ritual of traditional celebrations might sometimes spill over into riot and rebellion. There is some evidence, which we will now consider, that preparation for and participation in public events of the kind were also related to the phenomenon of civil disorder in eighteenth-century New Granada.

Unfortunately, we know little about the calendar and customs of festivals in colonial New Granada; nonetheless, at a general level, some of the main events for public celebration and some of the customs involved can be identified. The most important moments for public celebrations were the major feast days of the Roman calendar. These included New Year's Day, Epiphany, Carnival at the beginning of Lent and Holy Week at its end. These were followed by Whitsunday, Ascension Thursday, Corpus Christi, St. John's Day, the Feast of All Saints and All Souls, the Immaculate Conception, and, finally, the celebrations of the Christmas period, moving in to the New Year once more. In addition to these feast days, there were other saints' days, such as that of St. Peter, which had widespread significance, and still others, such as those of local patron saints, which had purely local significance. There were also opportunities for celebrations of secular inspiration: the birth of a prince, a royal marriage, the arrival of a distinguished visitor or official, the election of alcaldes, and market days. On these occasions, people interrupted their work routines, sometimes gathered at the church, sometimes participated in processions organized by the clergy, and diverted themselves with eating, drinking, dancing, and, on certain occasions, specific games and rituals.

According to a recent study of the Mompós region in New Granada, such festivals were frequent occurrences. Orlando Fals Borda, in his history of the area, suggests that public festivities lasting several days were celebrated on the slightest pretext, and moved from village to village throughout the year. While they lasted, Fals Borda argues, the whole community participated, including Indian *concertados,* Black slaves, white landowners and their tenants, and even the wives and daughters of the rich, who set up stalls to distribute sweets and cane brandy. At carnival time, social barriers were temporarily swept aside; not only did all sectors of the community mix freely in the streets, but rules of deference were violated in more direct ways, as "by means of disguises, dance and so-called *pullas,* corrosively critical stories in verse form . . . the entire society was brought to the same level." Such verses provided a means for the populace to make and to hear open criticism of the rich, the powerful, and the governing members of their society. During Holy Week in Mompós—as in other major cities in New Granada—members of all social classes were again brought together, especially in the organizations of hooded *nazarenos* who carried the ceremonial floats, and who were drawn from the cofradías ("lay brotherhoods") that organized the processions. In Mompós, there were ten cofradías and one archicofradía, and they included the sons of the principal landowners as well as common fishermen, peasants, and poor artisans. Entry was open to all, their mayordomos were chosen by election, and it was these bodies rather than the civil or ecclesiastical authorities that organized and controlled the Holy Week celebrations. The leveling of social barriers in such organizations might also be paralleled by games and rituals that inverted social positions and created a "world turned upside down" in the manner of some European carnivals. In Mompós, for example, Spaniards dressed up as Indians to take part in their festivities. In Cartagena, mock cabildos were organized by the city's barrios during carnival. These elected a king, sometimes a queen, who was surrounded with princesses, ministers, and courtiers, a complete mockery of the panoply of royal government. The "king" exercised absolute authority for the duration of his "reign" and everyone involved dressed in appropriate costume. Alliances were made, mock wars fought between neighboring barrios, and prisoners taken before mock judges to be sentenced to some forfeit, such as a ducking, or walking with shoes on the wrong feet. These "punishments" could be avoided only by payment of a fine, which then went to help finance the celebrations.

Until we know more about the character of popular festivals in New Granada, it would be hazardous to generalize about their role in the social and political life of the colony's communities. It must be noted, however, that attention to the incidence and nature of festivals may help to explain the timing of disturbances and the manner in which tumultuous crowds were mobilized and how they behaved. Festivals brought communities together in public gatherings, permitted and encouraged the relaxation of normal rules of behavior, and sometimes allowed the use of disguise and the public expression of criticism through ritual forms. It is not, then, difficult to see how they might provide the occasion for civil disturbances. In some cases of attacks on officials, the use of curious disguises by assailants indicates a connection with festive activities. The incidents of this kind that took place in Purificación in 1776 and in Moniquirá in 1802 both occurred in the festive period between Christmas and New Year, a time also charged with political significance as it heralded a change of alcaldes. Here, then, it is plausible to see a nexus between festival frolics and political action. Furthermore, action of this sort may have been an elaboration of other, more muted forms of political and social criticism permissible at this time of year. In Mompós, at least, December 31 was the time for posting pasquinades through which a secret accuser might attack the misdeeds that another person had committed during the preceding year.

Several of the other cases of riot and tumult that we have considered also coincided with important feast days, times when gatherings of community members for public and private amusement might merge into, perhaps legitimate, collective protests. The riots that took place in Vélez in 1740 started on the even of Palm Sunday and continued into Palm Sunday itself; the disturbances in Ocaña in 1755 were first reported in late March and so may also have been connected with preparations for Easter festivities. The major riot that occurred in Ocaña took place in a different season, but here, too, there was a possible connection with local festivities; for the riot occurred within two days of the feast of the Immaculate Conception, an important religious holiday in the Catholic Hispanic world and one that still attracts special celebration in some areas of contemporary Colombia. The riots in Cali in 1765 happened at a similar time, reaching a peak on December 10, two days after this feast day. Similar coincidences may also be found in the major rebellions of Quito in 1765 and of the Comuneros in 1781. The first riot in Quito took place on May 22, a week before the beginning of Holy Week and so conceivably within the period of preparation for the major festival of Semana Santa. The correlation is much clearer in the case of the second riot: it occurred on the night of St. John's Day, June 24, a day when the city attracted villagers from the surrounding countryside and the traditional moment for a half-yearly payment of tithes. The riots that sparked off the Comuneros' rebellion began in Socorro on March 16, 1781, a market day in the town. They then spread through the surrounding villages in the month leading up to Easter, with the third and last of the riots in Socorro itself taking place on April 16, Easter Monday.

If festivals may sometimes have provided the occasion for civil disorder, they may also be important to an analysis of popular protest in a more general sense. As important moments of local social concourse, in which the community could indulge in a collective experience organized by and for its members, the major festivals of the year also brought an element of organization and purpose into community life. The members of the cofradías—whose main function was the organization of religious festivals and whose membership usually crossed class lines—were mobilized; the clergy might mingle with the laity, and the rich with the poor. On most such occasions, social tensions could be released through celebration and symbolic conflict, allowing the community thereby to reaffirm a sense of common identity that transcended divisions between social groups. Moreover, while such practices may have palliated antagonisms among social groups in the local community, they may also have redirected latent animosities toward outsiders and officials who were often not of the local community or were imperfectly integrated into it.

While in some cases tumults may have been shaped by collective activities associated with festivals, the structured character of action in civil disorders seems to have been typical of all the incidents described. Where violence was used, it was purposeful and selective. The incidence of human casualties was very low, and when injuries occurred, they were rarely fatal. This was not simply because crowds went unarmed; reports of riots often refer to the presence of swords, clubs, and more rudimentary weapons, such as stones. But there was an apparent reluctance to use arms as more than instruments of threat. Only in the large-scale rebellions, of Quito in 1765 and the Comuneros in 1781, are there any signs of organized armed conflict or quasi-military organization. Even in these cases, armed conflict had an unpremeditated and improvised air. In Quito, the crowd used mortars against their opponents only after these weapons had been used against the crowd, and had been captured in defensive actions. The Comuneros' movement assumed a militaristic structure, with men from different areas under separate commands, but the rebellion never took on the aspect of war. In both cases, casualties were few relative to the large numbers of insurgents, and were less often the victims of rebel action than of violence used by the authorities in their efforts to restore order. In none of the smaller incidents described, such as those of Vélez, Ocaña, Tunja, and Cali, did the crowd's action result in any fatalities. A few people on opposing sides may have been wounded in the frays, but attacks on persons aimed to intimidate and humiliate rather than to kill or maim. In several cases, the individuals who were targets of the crowd's animosity received no more than threats or some rough treatment in actions designed to frighten or expel them from the community. As a sanction imposed by the community, expulsion was more common than serious physical violence or murder, and was an interesting imitation of a sanction used by the government itself: punishment by banishment.

Damage was much more likely to be inflicted on buildings than on persons. As historians of the Comunero rebellion have invariably observed, the Comunero rebels generally exercised great restraint in their actions. They tended simply to attack the symbols of hated taxes, taking over the *estanco* offices and stores, and destroying their contents. This restraint also marked the anti-*estanco* riots of 1765. It was particularly noticeable in the May riot in Quito, where, having emptied the *estanco* office and put its administrator to flight, the crowd then embarked on a painstaking demolition of the building, stone by stone. In smaller incidents, such as that of Tunja or Cali, we hear of attacks on the town jail and the destruction of a gibbet; in Sogamoso, of an attack on the house and mill of a vecino; and in El Plato, of the despoiling of a building used as a courtroom.

The extent of community participation is difficult to measure and compare. At times, it might be large, as in the Vélez, Ocaña, and Quito riots, where a substantial proportion of the townspeople joined in action. At other times, it was relatively small, measured in tens rather than in hundreds. In many cases, the documentation is vague on numbers, referring only to "many people," to "a multitude," or to some such ill-defined quantity. Generally, however, we may assume that crowds were small, reflecting the small size of the communities from which they were drawn.

The kinds of people who participated in civil disorders also varied with the local setting, depending on the size of the community and its ethnic composition. In most of the disturbances discussed, participants included people of different social rank, though the documentation is invariably uninformative about the occupations or economic positions of those involved. The documentation does convey, though, the impression that disturbances engaged a cross-section of the community, or, in incidents in villages such as El Plato or Chinú, virtually the entire community acting in concert. In the disturbances in Vélez, Ocaña, Zaragoza, and El Plato, as well as in the incidents of nocturnal attacks on officials, municipal officers, local clerics, and leading citizens played prominent roles in promoting action against government officials, with the support of undifferentiated crowds and gangs loosely described by some general term like the *plebe,* or "people of inferior quality." It seems, then, that participants in such collective actions mirrored the structure of local society, with leading parts played by prominent vecinos backed by their social inferiors. At times, such men may have been coopted as leaders without their full consent. Some years after the riot in Chinú in 1798, a witness confessed on his deathbed that a Catalan vecino who had been imprisoned for leading the disturbances in the village had been forced to accept a position of leadership by threats to his land and property. Such cooptation—on pain of death or damage to property—was also used by Comunero rebels to coerce men of local standing to take positions of command in the movement. By this means, the rebels showed their concern to present their protest as that of the community as a whole, represented through the traditional medium of its leading citizens, and thereby to help legitimate their actions. Apart from the case of Chinú, there are traces of this behavior in tumults that took place in Tunja, where the *maestre de campo* was called upon to champion lower-class rioters, and in Vélez, where the *alférez real* was acclaimed the "King of Vélez."

Evidently the civil disorders of late colonial New Granada were neither inspired nor guided by any specific or explicitly elaborated political ideas, they rarely had repercussions outside their immediate localities, and they left no permanent forms of political organization. Nevertheless, they were not entirely innocent of political ideas or significance. In the structured forms of collective protest and acts of defiance against government and its agents, we may dimly detect attitudes and beliefs that were normally unstated, and rarely expressed in written or explicit form. In their reactions to the fiscal and economic impositions of government, to the appointment of officials opposed by members of a local community, or to perceived abuses of authority by incumbent officials, the small and highly localized disturbances described herein throw back some reflections of popular attitudes and values, especially with respect to the relations of government to its subjects. These attitudes are similar to those encountered in other precapitalist agrarian societies: a belief in a right to land and the use of its products; a belief in the right to produce and consume essential items of consumption (foodstuffs, tobacco, and aguardiente) without arbitrary taxation; the idea that local customs should be respected and that justice fairly administered. These attitudes implicitly defined a basic notion of freedom: the right to resist arbitrary intrusions by government and its agents. This minimal and residual notion of freedom was nurtured by the colonial experience of government. Despite its imposing structure of law and bureaucracy, Spanish government in New Granada, as in other colonies, held only loose control over the mass of the population. In this sense, the society of New Granada shared in that freedom Mario Góngora has described as "peculiar to the Americas—a form of liberty existing outside the framework of the state . . . not based on any well-defined notion or any new concept of the state . . . [but] . . . rooted in laxity."[1]

This popular outlook, expressed in the minor civil disorders discussed, also played an important part in the emergence and development of the Comunero rebellion. In his analysis of the rhetoric and ideas of the Comuneros, Phelan argued that the movement was informed by beliefs about the common good of the community, the right of the community to express its interests to government and to resist unjust laws, by force if necessary. Phelan observed that these ideas were remarkably similar to those of sixteenth- and seventeenth-century Spanish political thinkers, and he suggested that they had been conveyed to the colonial context through the practices of Hapsburg government. Comunero leaders were not conversant with Spanish political theory; their acquaintance with such ideas came from experience of Hapsburg political practices that had established and observed an "unwritten constitution" in New Granada, a set of conventions and customary procedures that symbolized a pact between the monarch and his subjects. While Phelan's emphasis on the influence of Hapsburg paternalism is well placed, it must be stressed, however, that these ideas were not confined to the creole patriciate or derived solely from its conception of government. Just as the ideas of sixteenth-century Spanish political thinkers were in part a distillation of popular beliefs and attitudes, so the ideas of the Comu-

1 Mario Góngora, *Studies in the Colonial History of Spanish America*, trans. by Richard Southern (Cambridge, 1975), p. 125.

neros in eighteenth-century New Granada reflected popular attitudes that arose from local experience. In an isolated and backward agrarian society, where the writ of metropolitan government ran thin outside the main cities, local experience nurtured a belief in the community outside the state, with its own customs and conventions, and the right to defy governmental authority and to oppose the exercise of power when it collided with local interests. It is this outlook that is periodically reflected in civil disorders and that also informed the Comunero rebellion. The distinctive feature of the Comunero rebellion was that it brought popular agitation under creole leadership, molding the diffuse actions and attitudes of lower-class rioters into an explicit and coherent program of demands. But at the heart of the movement was that same defiance of arbitrary government and taxation that lay behind other, lesser civil disorders.

So, despite the special characteristics of the Comunero rebellion, it may be seen as another expression of a tradition of popular actions undertaken in defense of the customary arrangements and practices of local community life. Expressed in sporadic, multifarious actions rather than in precise arguments, revealed in criminal proceedings rather than political treatises, this tradition is inarticulate and elusive; but the ability of the populace to act collectively, in pursuit of common goals and against prescribed targets, suggests that, even in this backward and isolated colonial society, there existed a popular conception of the proper functions and limits of government that constituted a significant, if neglected, dimension of social life.

Suggested Further Reading

Campbell, Leon G. "Recent Research on Andean Peasant Revolts, 1750–1820." *Latin American Research Review* 14:1 (Spring 1979).

Klein, Herbert S. "Peasant Communities in Revolt: The Tzeltal Republic of 1712." *Pacific Historical Review* 35:3 (August 1966).

Loy, Jane M. "Forgotten Comuneros: The 1781 Revolt in the Llanos of Casanare." *Hispanic American Historical Review* 61:2 (May 1981).

Maxwell, Kenneth. *Conflicts and Conspiracies: Brazil and Portugal 1750–1808.* Cambridge, 1973.

Phelan, John Leddy. *The People and the King: The Comunero Revolt in Colombia, 1781.* Madison, 1978.

Taylor, William B. *Drinking, Homicide, and Rebellion in Colonial Mexican Villages.* Stanford, 1979.

17 ☀

The Problem of the Roots of Revolution:
Society and Intellectual Ferment in Mexico
on the Eve of Independence

PEGGY K. LISS

Causation is never easy to ascertain; yet the urge to understand the "why" of an event remains irresistible. So it is with the Mexican revolution of 1810. Historians have long recognized the need for a clearer explanation of the origins of that bloody uprising. Some have gone beyond a simple listing of background conditions, such as the external ones of Spanish weakness and involvement in European wars and the internal introduction of revolutionary ideas, in an attempt to assign priority to one or another set of these causes. Most recently, however, dissatisfied with the inadequacies of past evaluations, a number of scholars have been concerned with gaining a better understanding of the *interrelationships* of the numerous roots of revolution.

Within this trend, studies of social change and intellectual ferment in Mexico in the latter part of the eighteenth century have provided some important, if tentative, answers to longstanding questions concerning the origins of the revolution of 1810. These works give evidence that there existed within Mexico a set of conditions tending to undermine previously established notions of how society should be ordered and to promote the setting of revolutionary goals. Certainly these studies lay to rest the old assertion that all Mexicans were somnolent until pressures built up by the French Revolution and Napoleon's invasion of Spain set off an explosive chain reaction in that part of Spanish America. Historians now know that before active political revolt, certain small but influential segments of Mexican society ardently sought social and economic reform,

From *Latin American History: Select Problems,* edited by Fredrick B. Pike, © 1969 by Harcourt Brace Jovanovich, Inc. Reprinted by permission of the publisher.

became increasingly alienated from the existing regime, and came to serve as heralds of the revolution.

Although a more intricate picture of the Mexican milieu is now presented, it is at the same time a far clearer one than heretofore. For our purposes, two aspects of this scene are particularly important. First, there is evidence of a gradually evolving intellectual ambience within Mexico that welcomed change and ensured a ready but selective adaptation of enlightened and revolutionary ideas as they arrived from Europe and from other regions of the Western Hemisphere. Second, and contrary to a number of older accounts, there is a newer view of Mexican society that makes obsolete the assertion that an absolute dichotomy existed between a class of European Spaniards supporting governmental policies and a class of creoles[1] intent on subverting them; factional groupings are now recognized to have been much more complex.

The readings in this chapter, dated from the 1770s to 1811, corroborate the newer viewpoints. Two were written by creoles, two by European Spaniards. The viewpoints expressed in them may be considered representative of the states of mind of four influential, elite segments of society in Mexico. All express dissatisfaction with the existing state of affairs, all criticize current economic and social arrangements, all criticize the government, and all appear certain that the existing order is moribund. Yet, while some insist that government policies are destroying the traditional order, others complain that these same policies are perpetuating it. Thus, while some object to measures that they feel subvert the old order, others demand action designed to do just that. There is little agreement on the nature of the fundamental principles of the political system. No two of these readings reveal identical concepts of the Spanish role in Mexico.

The attitudes of the creoles and the European Spaniards who wrote these papers tend to cross class lines. Even when the authors discuss Americans and European Spaniards as if they were cohesive and distinct classes, what they say is often modified by the divergent attitudes they exhibit. For example, the majority of the *regidores* ("councilmen") of the cabildo or ayuntamiento of Mexico City who drew up Reading 1 were creoles who declared themselves proud of their Spanish ancestry, while, as we shall see, the author of Reading 2, José Antonio Alzate y Ramírez, was a creole who took pride in a different heritage.

1 While the term "creole" as used in Spanish America is often defined as a native American of Spanish descent, as used in Mexico in this period it also included Mexicans of (usually unacknowledged) mixed Spanish and Indian descent.

The *regidores* reveal themselves as men of aristocratic mien and vast pretension. The Mexican historian Lucas Alamán observed that fifteen of the councilmen held perpetual and inherited positions originally purchased by their fathers from the crown. He wrote, "They were old *mayorazgos* [propertyholders in perpetuity] of very little education in general, and the majority of them of ruined fortunes." Six additional, honorary *regidores,* however, were chosen biennially from among the distinguished merchants, landowners, and lawyers of the capital. Thus, the ayuntamiento in this period represented both propertied and professional elements of creole society. The combination is discernible in its Representation, included here.

This document exudes a strong sense of criollismo, a feeling of pride in Spanish heritage compounded with a sense of belonging to the soil of Mexico (and of it belonging to them). It was an outlook they shared with many of the wealthier, landed creoles, the hacendados referred to by another Mexican historian, Manuel Orozco y Berra, as "the semi-feudal *señores.*" Many of the *regidores* and hacendados claimed descent through pure Spanish bloodlines from the conquistadores. It was an improbable ancestry for most of them, since, as the conquistador-historian Bernal Díaz del Castillo, among others, had made clear, and as the anticreole authors of Reading 4 pointedly reiterated, the legitimate offspring of the first Spaniards in Mexico were few and not prolific. Nevertheless, these creoles would insist (in 1808) that the fruits of the conquest were theirs by right of inheritance, that their conquistador forebears had left to them the legacy of a right to preeminence over the other cabildos of Mexico. The old order venerated by the *regidores* was static, hierarchical, and regulated by creole aristocrats, the natural nobility of the Kingdom of New Spain.

A sense of pride also permeated the writings of José Antonio Alzate y Ramírez, although his pride in the main stemmed from an outsized esteem of his own intellectual ability. Alexander von Humboldt, the European savant and scientist who visited New Spain in 1803, did not entirely concur in Alzate's self-evaluation. Humboldt, an astute commentator, wrote that, while Alzate was one of the three distinguished creoles who by their astronomical observations "did honor to their country towards the end of the last century," he was also "the least informed of them. Alzate, [although] a correspondent of the Academy of Sciences of Paris, was an observer of little accuracy. Of a frequently impetuous temperament, he devoted himself to too many pursuits at one time."

Humboldt judged Alzate's enthusiasm and his influence on his fellow Mexicans to have been much greater than his mental rigor: "He had the very genuine merit of having excited his compatriots to the study of the physical sciences. The *Gaceta de Literatura,* which he published for a long time in Mexico, contributed singularly to give encouragement and stimulation to Mexican youth." Alzate is significant here because, in seeking to awaken young creoles to new ways of considering old problems, he attempted to revolutionize current habits of thought.

Such scientifically minded creoles were few in Mexico, but they grew more numerous and very much more articulate throughout the latter part of the eighteenth century. As early as the 1740s, a handful of young Mexican-born Jesuits had voiced concerns and views of the kind evidenced in Alzate's writings. By the 1760s, similar sentiments and interests were common to a number of creoles engaged in the professions, among them teachers, lawyers, journalists, secular and regular clergymen, doctors of medicine, and lesser bureaucrats. In general, these men were more educated and less propertied than the semifeudal señores. They also differed from most of the *regidores* in that they lacked assured positions. Within this group, then, were to be found the creoles whose plight was described by the councilmen of Mexico City: raised and educated as an elite, trained to be leaders in their own society, they were frustrated by exclusion from high state and church positions.

Yet Alzate and other intellectuals went beyond the concern with governmental appointments expressed by the ayuntamiento to a serious consideration of the broader economic and social problems of Mexico. Alzate, like his enlightened contemporaries in Europe, was enamored of the idea of abetting material progress by disseminating principles and pieces of useful knowledge. In his literary gazette he included notes from all over on economics, the physical sciences, mathematics, medicine, agriculture, history, and jurisprudence. He sought to provide his fellow Mexicans with factual and practical information that, once assimilated and properly applied, he felt would ensure the creation of a paradise on earth. Thus, while the *regidores* invoked a golden past, Alzate looked to an idyllic future.

He insisted that dependence on ancient authorities, especially on Aristotle, was responsible for "that profound and shameful lethargy that holds [Mexicans] deadened in perpetual inactivity," that education by the still-prevalent scholastic method was at the root of all Mexico's afflictions. Alzate, who had been ordained a priest, found his true calling as a missionary to the unenlightened. He appeared certain that he need only rout the forces of obscurantism in order to allow Mexicans through their own efforts to return their land to its natural state of abundance and health.

Alzate was critical of the state of affairs at present and in the recent—the Spanish—past. Condemning the old order, he looked back to a still older order. He was prominent among those creoles who found in the greatest of the pre-Hispanic Indian civilizations their own classical antiquity. In eulogizing the achievement of high states of culture by the ancient indigenous peoples, he implicitly denied the validity of the civilizing mission of the Spaniards. Thus he opened to question the legitimacy of Spanish rule in America, which, as the writers of Reading 4 take for granted, was based on an early shouldering by Spain of the white man's burden. In short, the past, present, and future that were of interest to Alzate were Mexican. He did not state where the Indians of his own day fit into his utopian expectations. Yet consideration of the faith he expresses in the natural goodness of human nature, at least within Mexico, leads to the conclusion that he considered the Indians, too, capable of being educated to the point of entering national life at some future time.

He urged activism upon creoles and stressed the need for change, positive that it would be for the better. In one sense, Alzate's faith in the salutary effects of change was not far removed from that of the Bourbon government. Changes that took place in eighteenth-century Spain, many of them under governmental aegis, have been described as revolutionary. Although these changes were carried out within the fabric of the old order, they may also have been an element in undermining the state of mind supporting the old order. Revolution or no, economic and political institutions had in fact undergone considerable redirection. For example, in order to strengthen central government the crown had striven to abbreviate the authority of the old, semiautonomous corporations, including that of the church and of the merchant guilds. It is not surprising, therefore, that the two remaining documents in this chapter, written by European Spaniards in Mexico by members of these corporations, include criticisms of innovations made by the government.

Reading 3 was written in 1799 by a priest, Manuel Abad y Quiepo, then vicar to Bishop Antonio de San Miguel of Michoacán, later bishop-elect of that province. In his Representation, Abad y Queipo warned the crown against enforcing royal ordinances placing a direct tax on clerical investments and restricting clerical fueros ("corporate privileges") in general. Social unrest was increasing, he argued; the church must remain strong in order to continue to function successfully as the one institution capable of mediating between the government and the people.

While Abad y Queipo as a priest opposed certain innovations, especially the taxing of the clergy, as an enlightened and objective observer he desired others. He urged general political reform: "America," he wrote elsewhere, "can no longer be governed by the maxims of Philip II." Furthermore, much like Alzate, he expressed confidence in Mexican potential. To realize this potential, the crown must institute economic and social reforms. Unlike the creole journalist, Abad y Queipo looked to the Spanish government to remedy Mexican ills. He urged that a new order be imposed from above. His was a faith in enlightened monarchy buttressed by the traditional Spanish reliance on the fair-mindedness of the law-giving king. This self-styled Montesquieu of Mexico was certain that good laws would bring wealth, health, and happiness to New Spain, as well as increased revenue to the Spanish treasury.

Other European Spaniards, the merchants of the consulado of Mexico City, were just as certain a decade later that such liberal notions were subverting the empire. In Reading 4, they demand retreat from reform. In direct opposition to the dictum of Abad y Queipo, they counsel a return to the principles of His Most Catholic Majesty, arguing that only a show of imperial force would avert the loss of the colonies. They looked back with longing to their particular view of the old order, to the golden age of Hapsburg imperialism. Spain, they insisted, had an unfulfilled civilizing mission in America.

If the consulado looked with a jaundiced eye on the political abilities of Americans, its vision was unimpaired when it observed a new spirit of self-sufficiency among creoles. Even Mexicans such as the *regidores* of the capital, seeking high position *within* the Spanish administration, evinced a new spirit of self-consciousness, compounded of pride in the expanse and growing population of Mexico, optimism concerning its future, recognition of the depopulated and decadent state of the metropolis, and perhaps above all a desire to demonstrate that "We are a nation as great as any in the world. Even this is to claim too little; permit us, Your Majesty, to say that we [the creoles] have distinguished ourselves above all."

In short, self-proclaimed creole intellectuals, officeholders, and semifeudal señores, whatever their differences, expressed in common a sense of *conciencia de sí,* of Mexican particularism. Though they differed in their views of the proper place in society of the other inhabitants of

Mexico (Indians, Blacks, and castes, or mestizos), though the ayuntamiento wanted only to dominate them and Alzate apparently wanted to educate them, yet they acknowledged these people as fellow inhabitants of Mexico.

It is interesting to note that the readings also reveal transition in the creole concept of "nation." The ayuntamiento used the word "nation" in a somewhat traditional sense: the Mexican creoles, they implied, constituted a nation within the Spanish empire. Yet in the same period, ministers of Charles III disavowed this old notion of imperial identity. Members of the Royal Council declared that they hoped to integrate the Indies into the Spanish nation-state. Henceforth Mexico was to be neither kingdom nor colony, but an intrinsic part of a *"solo cuerpo de Nación."*

This idea of the nation as the natural polity was in vogue among the European philosophes; Alzate and other creoles followed the fashion, thereby intensifying and restricting the concept of nation entertained by the ayuntamiento. Their nation, too, was composed solely of men born on the soil of Mexico, but their national feeling could not, like the older sense of imperial identity, be made to cross the ocean.

"Nation" was but part of a larger political vocabulary coming into use and boding ill for Spanish domination. Even the *regidores* appealed to such an antiimperial governing principle as that of "right reason" and placed a new emphasis on the right of native peoples (by which they meant creoles) according to "the law of nations." Alzate was more radical, as early as 1768 sprinkling his short-lived *Diario Literario* with such dangerous catchwords as "tyranny" and "liberty." The viceroy, in suspending the periodical for containing "propositions offensive to the Law and the Nation," aired additional notions associated with theories tending, at the least, to limit monarchy and silenced Alzate only temporarily. In his *Gaceta de Literatura,* published from 1788 to 1795, Alzate combined potentially revolutionary notions with the new sense of national identity. For example, he declared public utility to be the supreme law, individual reason to be the ultimate authority, and the duty of the individual to be to engage in all forms of civic activity. It was but a step to the logical conclusion, reached by some creoles in 1810, that the nation was the supreme political entity and that sovereignty resided solely in its citizens. As the consulado predicted in 1811, rebellious Mexicans would assume "the airs and trappings of a sovereign people."

Reading 1. A Representation of the
Ayuntamiento of Mexico City (1771)

In the following document, the councilmen inform the crown that they speak for the Kingdom of New Spain and desire to defend Spanish Americans against the slanderous report, made by an unidentified peninsular Spanish official serving in New Spain, that creoles are inferior to Europeans and incapable of holding public office.

We have reflected for days, not without the greatest grief, that the kind gestures and provisions of Your Majesty in favor of the Spanish Americans have become rarer than ever, not only in secular positions but in ecclesiastic, where until now we have received attention. We have observed this but contained our sorrow within the most respectful silence, and we would never have broken it even if we had never received another benefice from Your Majesty, who is incomparable in recognizing us, your vassals. [Yet we have news that some minister or prelate has slandered the Spanish Americans, and so we are now compelled to present a rejoinder.[2]]

This is not the first time that malevolence has attacked the reputation of the Americans in order to make them appear inept for all types of honors. Since the discovery of America, a war has been waged against the native Indians. In spite of the evidence, even their rationality is questioned. With no less injustice, it is claimed that those of us born of European parents on this soil scarcely have sufficient powers of reason to be considered men.

. . .

He who made the report proposed to obtain Your Majesty's assent that Spanish Americans not attain any but lower government posts in order to make sure that Europeans will always be placed in the highest positions of honor. This is to say that we shall be excluded, in the ecclesiastical realm, from being bishops and high dignitaries of the church and, in the secular sphere, from being military officers and governors and from holding the highest positions in town councils. This is to try to overturn the law of nations! It is the road not only to the loss of America but also to the ruin of the state. It is, in a word, the greatest and most enormous injustice, one that a person with less animosity would not have dared propose to Your Majesty.

2 Bracketed summaries of omitted material have been supplied by the author.

.   .   .

In regard to the provision of honorific posts, the European Spaniards have to be considered foreigners in these parts. . . . This is what
the Europeans are by birth, but not by civil right, in America. But civil
right has not the power of natural inclinations, and we have to be aware
of these inclinations in the sons of Old Spain, no matter how they think
of themselves as civilly no strangers in New Spain. Among natural inclinations are included, with good reason, the love that men have for the
soil on which they were born and the lack of affection for all other.
These two motives are the most solid principles that argue for the employment of the native and against that of the foreigner.

.   .   .

Even if they do not consider themselves civilly foreigners in the
Indies, it is obvious that they were not born here. In Old Spain they
have their houses, their parents, their brothers, and whatever is capable
of arousing ambition in a man. When they are exiled to this distance to
fill a public office, their nature does not change, and their impulses do
not deaden. For these reasons, in these regions they do not forget their
own. They consider how to help their families (if not to enrich them).
They think of themselves as transients in America. Their only concern
is to return as rich men to the quietude of their land and homes.

So experience teaches each day. It is inevitable if the public offices
are conferred on those who were not born in the regions where they serve.

.   .   .

There are public offices, such as [those of] all the alcaldes mayores
of the kingdom, that have no pay assigned to them. How, then, will these
men repay the onerous financial obligations incurred in taking office? . . . The Indies are very abundant in gold and silver for ambitious
men unscrupulous in acquiring them. They will be urged on by necessity,
annoyed by creditors, and besieged by the judge, to whom people have
come to make them pay. They will see that they can frequently find
means to escape the pinch. They will grant favors that shortly decline
into bribes. They will sell justice. Their concern for their own interest
will lead to the ruin of all that the public entrusted to them.

It is also inevitable that merit is exaggerated when seen through
the spectacles of greater affection. From this it follows that a prelate
with many European familiars [relatives and friends], however numerous, considers them deserving above many others the first benefices that
are within his power to bestow. Our students moan, oppressed by the

weight of years and by the burdens of the academy and of clerical administration. They obtain the highest qualification in their studies, the best degrees in the university. They distinguish themselves in instructing the villagers. They do not cease to strive for better positions, nor do they avoid competition. Yet, after all, they finish the contest with no other reward than praise for their performance, and the awards go to a familiar. Many of these Europeans are just starting out. They have not proved their fitness in any public contest. They have not taught in the Indies or served in any of the churches. In some cases (and it is the rule), they have never before entered a contest.

.   .   .

The European comes to govern people he does not know, to administer laws he has not studied, to regulate customs he does not understand, and to treat with people whom he has never seen, and to do these he usually comes surrounded by retainers equally inexpert. He comes full of European principles inadaptable to these lands. Here, we Spaniards do not set ourselves apart from the Europeans; the miserable Indians are of another condition. On one hand, they are a group weaker and worthier of attention, and on the other, they are the ones making up the bulk of the kingdom and all the sinews of it. They are the object of the pious concern of Your Majesty's government. They require different rules from those prescribed for Spaniards. Nevertheless, the new arrival tries to implant his ideas, to establish his principles. In this endeavor, he miserably loses time until disillusionment opens his eyes. What can be expected of his government but errors and prejudices, one after another?

.   .   .

The Spanish Americans are capable of the highest offices. They do not yield in intelligence, application, conduct, or honor to any of the other nations of the world. So impartial authors whose criticism the literary world respects have confessed. So experience proves each day, except to those who willfully close their eyes to plain truths. But hopeful, capable, useful, and worthy men of this kind are nevertheless reported to be dissuaded from improvement, abased, and abandoned. So says the informant, who claims that "they are worthy of nothing else than to be submissive and subjugated. They are serfs, detested by foreigners."

[Americans will decrease in number if they have no way of supporting families. Ordinary commercial jobs are not for them, for trade nearly always has to be transacted from Europe by Europeans. Manual labor is incompatible with the luster of their birth, nor does it suffice in the Indies for a decent subsistence; for, since the best manufactures are carried from Europe, where they are made cheaper than the Americans can make them, we can never support ourselves by manufacturing in the Indies.]

The principal basis on which we Spanish Americans can count to meet our obligations is the rents or salaries of public office. If the door to them is closed to us, we must live an obscure life. Unable to contract illustrious alliances, the sons that we shall have will augment the common people, or we will find ourselves reduced to the necessity of celibacy and perhaps forced to embrace the religious or secular ecclesiastical state, in order to rely on charity from a mass. Gone will be the principle of increasing, or even of honestly conserving, the population of America.

Nor will the fate of Europe be better. Many European nations have already reflected on the depopulation experienced by Spain since the conquest of America. It is so harmful that the greatest political theorists have urged means to remedy it—and these are certainly not to employ European Spaniards in the public posts of the Indies. This practice is the origin of the great depopulation of Spain. . . . This adverse effect on Spain, although lamented by our best political thinkers, seems an enjoyable spectacle to malevolent foreigners.

We have always considered ourselves sons of Your Majesty, just like the natives of Old Spain. Old and New Spain are like two estates. They are two wives of Your Majesty. Each one has her dowry in the honorific posts of your government, paid with the income produced by both. We have never complained that the sons of Old Spain take advantage of the dowry of their mother, but it seems fitting that ours be left to us.

.   .   .

It is indispensable that we be sent some ministers from Europe. But must all those who come be given the highest positions? Must all the governors who Your Majesty places in the provinces and towns of this region of America be born and raised in Old Spain as today they are? Are we never to have, as at present we do not have in all the continent of this kingdom, an archbishop or bishop that was born here? Is it necessary that the magistrates of these lands be, as they are today, mostly Europeans? That even the chairs of the choirs of our cathedrals be scarcely occupied by our natives? That in the management of the income that this New Spain produces for Your Majesty, only rarely do we see among many employees one of our country? That in the military offices our requests are paid so little attention that only in the militias do our volunteers generally secure a placc? Even then their positions are not the best.

. . .

It does not seem that either the equity or the attention that we, your vassals of these regions, owe Your Majesty can tolerate this. . . . Our crime must be very grave for us to suffer the punishment of eternal ignominy by being excluded from the highest offices and by receiving little attention in the others. What then is this crime that, contaminating such vast regions as those of America, has called down such an enormous punishment on all these individuals? . . .

What will the rest of the world say of America? What concept will the nations form from the attention Your Majesty pays to the cultivation of the Spanish Americans? Will they not conclude that these most ample domains of Your Majesty are full of carcasses useless to society and think them more a burden than an adornment to the state? . . . Show the world that we are not useless carcasses, but men suited for all offices, even the highest, that in nothing are the men of the Old World superior to us, that Your Majesty exceeds the other monarchs not only in the vast cxtension of lands and in the number of individuals inhabiting them, but also in the abundance of vassals who are as loyal, as generous, as able, and as useful as those gloried in by the most cultured state of the world. Let the world know that we of the Indies are apt for counsel, useful for war, experienced in the management of finances, fit for governing churches, towns, provinces, and even entire kingdoms. . . .

Thus will Your Majesty be more glorious, for the honor of children is the glory of their parents. Thus your dominion over these regions will be even more secure. Enemies would not hesitate to invade them, knowing them to be full only of pasteboard men. But they would give it much thought if they concluded from the prodigious multitude of subjects Your Majesty has in these lands that they would find here many generous vassals, all capable of resisting any foreign encroachment with decision, tenacity, loyalty, and their lives.

. . .

It is understood that we do not speak of the Indians taken in war or of those whose ancestors were conquered by our arms, but of the Spaniards, of us who are born in these lands. We originate pure in all lines from men who came from Old Spain to these regions to conquer, to settle, to do business, or to serve in some government post. The Indians, whether by descent, by divine punishment, by their condition as individuals of a subjugated nation, or perhaps by their lack of culture, even after two centuries of conquest are born in misery, raised in rusticity, and driven by punishment, and they can support themselves only by the hardest work. They live without shame, without honor, and without hope. Degraded and fallen in spirit, they are abased in character. All judicious authors say so; after long observation and much travel they have given the Indians the epithet in their books of "defeated ones." A poor understanding or perhaps a too hasty reading of these writings has caused errors in copying these expressions by men wanting to apply them to the Spanish Americans as well as to the Indians. In order to commit such injustice, one must refuse to give ear to the cries of reason. . . .

America has a large number of Spaniards, all as pure as those of Old Spain. . . . Interbreeding has been claimed of the early Spanish settlers in order to deny our purity of lineage. There were very strong arguments against it. Interbreeding did not occur except because of the attraction of beauty or other natural gifts, because of wealth, or because of the desire for honor. None of these motives has been strong enough to drag down Spanish settlers into mating with Indian women and producing mestizo sons. Generally speaking, and with only rare exceptions, the mestizos are positively of a disagreeable aspect, very bad color, rough features, and notable slovenliness of dress when not naked, and none are clean. They lack culture and rationality, have great aversion to Spaniards, and even refuse to talk to them. They are very poor and live in huts with walls of mud or branches, roofs of straw, and floors of nothing but what the soil naturally provides. They eat in the greatest misery and slovenliness. If they dress, it is no better than the way in which they eat. They have no beds to rest in, but cover themselves with a palm mat or animal skin. The little they need for such poor furnishings, they get by very hard work; a description of it would touch the limits of hyperbole.

Above all, the Spaniard, had he interbred with an Indian woman, would see his sons lacking the honor of being Spaniards and even excluded from enjoying the privileges conceded to Indians. The same thing, and with greater reason, could be said of interbreeding with Blacks, mulattoes, or the other castes originating from them. Thus, there is no way mixed bloods may be considered equal. These mixtures are much less common than malevolence paints them.

There was some interbreeding of Spaniards with Indians in the

early days of the conquest, but it was with the royal families of the indigenous nations, and their descendants are among the highest grandees
of Spain. They are considered Spanish citizens of pure blood.

.   .   .

But what if Spanish Americans are to be perpetually subordinated
to Europeans? It would be as if humanity, the law of nations, and right
reason permitted this absolute and perpetual subordination of native
peoples, this entire exclusion from the highest honors, and this subjugation to foreigners. It is indeed a cunning misrepresentation of the sentiments of humanity and of tenderness of heart that advocates so inhuman
a principle. It is pernicious to society and contrary to the interests and
honor or a nation making up the greater part of the monarchy.

.   .   .

Spain has needed no army to maintain loyalty in these dominions,
whose extension is sufficient to embrace many of the greatest kingdoms
of Europe.

.   .   .

When has the loyalty of the Spanish Americans faltered, weakened,
flagged, or wavered? In this region of America there has never been a
rebellion offending the fidelity owed to Your Majesty. It is true that
sometimes some movements of the common people have been noted.
These risings are always very reprehensible and are directed against the
ministers of Your Majesty. But they have never been undertaken to break
the yoke of obedience to the sovereign. And, after all, these were popular movements; no nation of the world has been without them. In America they have been very rare compared to Europe. They have been solely
of the lowest common people. The Spaniards of this kingdom have participated in none of them. . . .

Rather, there has been scarcely any project of magnitude conducive to the government, felicity, and quietude of the public and to the
authority of Your Majesty in these lands that was not due to our zeal
and solicitude. [We have raised militias, held a *cabildo abierto,* or municipal council open to all notables of the city, and offered personal help
and housing when troops arrived from abroad. The Mexican militias
were of help in "the commotions attending the expulsion of the Jesuits"
(1767). Now that war with Britain threatens, even artisans volunteer
for military service.]

In loyalty and service we are distinguished. We are a nation as
great as any in the world. Even this is to claim too little; permit us, Your

Majesty, to say that we have distinguished ourselves above all. To the merit of other peoples has been added the attraction of reward. Without it, has the generous impulse of our obligation alone moved us? Without reward? Yes, Sire. . . . It cannot be your wish to allow the honor of an entire nation such as America to be trampled underfoot. . . .

May God guard the Royal Catholic Person of Your Majesty for many years.

Reading 2. Excerpts from the Gaceta de Literatura of José Antonio Alzate y Ramírez

José Antonio Alzate y Ramírez (1738–99) was a first-generation creole on his father's side and a great-nephew of Sor Juana Inés de la Cruz, the poet and prodigy of Mexico's baroque era, on his mother's side. He attended the Jesuit Colegio de San Ildefonso in Mexico City. From 1788 to 1795 he edited 115 issues of the *Gaceta de Literatura,* a monthly of six to eight pages that, though not widely read, was influential.

The outpouring of periodical literary productions is so great that if they were to be categorized in terms of the cities in which they are published, the simple alphabet could not contain them. With such abundance elsewhere, is it not strange that in the metropolis of the New World, where rare talents—the particular productions of the three kingdoms—are found, a vacuum exists that a Mexican spokesman could fill with brilliance? . . .[3]

One sees the well-justified esteem that the *Gaceta de México* acquires from day to day because its author, complying with the requirements of exactitude, tells us about happenings of the time that would remain in obscurity if he did not publish them. The palpable utility of this enterprise, in which its author has experienced inexplicable fatigue, mutterings, and the other inconveniences that are felt by an author and that do not come to the notice of readers, has moved me to publish the present gazette, restricted to literature. Through it I will attempt to disseminate reports and dissertations concerning the progress of trade and navigation by extracting, copying, or translating what is useful. The progress of the arts will not be the least appreciable object to which my

3   That is, New Spain, New Galicia, and Guatemala, all under the jurisdiction of the viceroy of Mexico.

ideas are directed. Natural history, which holds such portents for our America, will be a major concern.

The lives and deeds of men who have shed glory on our Hispano-American nation—ought they to remain in obscurity? Not at all. They will be spoken of with ingenuity, without hiding what is useful in their accomplishments, but perhaps glossing over or remaining silent concerning that which men should ignore.

The geography of New Spain is so unknown that one scarcely recognizes the true relationship of its principal places to one another. It will become clear when they are discussed in documents that, if not admitting of a geometric demonstration, will be approximately correct. Not the least of the objects of my efforts will be the diaries of voyages, which are so instructive either about the customs of inhabitants or about natural products.

Shall I omit the discoveries that have taken place in Europe in experimental physics, mathematics, medicine, chemistry, and agriculture? Objects of such interest ought to be my first concern, since my duty is to be useful to my native land. Jurisprudence, designed to conserve the rights of men, to conserve their tranquility (inestimable treasure), will be found among my investigations. Those deeds worthy of serving as a model, those determinations of our wise tribunals, will be expounded upon to enlighten those whose profession obliges them to be so informed. What utility has not resulted from the periodical of jurisprudence published in Paris? How many, recognizing its transactions comparable or similar to those they intend to engage in, will abstain from a risky business when they see the outcome has been decided upon beforehand?

The few antiquities of the Mexican nation that remain will be described, and, if the costs of printing allow, illustrations will be published.

It is certain that few documents about the history of the Mexicans remain. This scarcity makes it necessary to conserve them. If not, in the short space of a century documents will seldom be found. Destruction is quick; loss of memory of deeds done is even quicker, especially since it cannot be verified that anyone is dedicated to conserving in writing the irreplaceable documents that serve as an index to discovering the genius, the character, and the customs of the Mexican nation. The writings of the learned Torquemada, of the great Sigüenza, of the collector Boturini, and of the renowned Clavijero are the only ones that in the past and present centuries supply us with historic accounts of what the Mexicans were. . . .[4]

Health and its restoration, those two poles of medicine, in Europe attain great advantage by means of the gazettes of health, welfare, and medicine circulated in various lands. They present to the public those particular cures, those methods, that are ordinarily a mystery to the members of a family, a town, and even some physicians. Thus they gain great advantages or much fame, because a resulting cure would remain forgotten if it were not publicized in such a work.

If we consider the utility to wealth: How great it will be when the present value of comestibles and other goods traded in each province is pointed out in a printed work! Then will the merchants have a sure guide to buying those things sold cheaply. And in this does not the public receive great benefit? This part of my plan is very vast, and, although it appears difficult of execution, I am confident of help from the person whose destiny and love for humanity will ensure all the necessary means. I dare to engulf myself in an occupation that is greeted with a regard varying according to self-esteem and to the greatest motivation, the love of wealth.

To give news of works published in New Spain and to form an analysis and expound a short criticism so that readers may know in advance the character of the work is an annoying, inconvenient occupation, scarcely fitting for those who dedicate themselves to publishing their own productions; but if a judicious criticism is considered in Europe to be most useful for limiting the printing of useless works and for avoiding the loss of precious time to readers, why in America would it not be most advantageous?

. . .

I do not confide in my weak forces in order to sustain the level that I have proposed. I am satisfied that other people, whose humility is greater than their opinion of their own literature, will contribute to ensuring it, on seeing that a licit means to expound their ideas is presented to them. A work of the character of this one supplies them with an innocent conveyance to divulge that which they judge useful and would not be able to divulge in any other way. . . .

Available to them now is a means to send their productions to the

---

4   Carlos de Sigüenza y Góngora and Juan de Torquemada wrote in the seventeenth century, Benaduci Boturini and Francisco Javier Mariano Clavijero in the eighteenth. Alzate probably knew the first three through Clavijero's *Storia Antica del Messico* (Cesena, 1780–81), wherein he praises their work.

editor without more expense, without more fatigue. These will be printed under their own names or as they desire, with the understanding that the *Gaceta de Literatura de México* is not begun in order to publish productions satisfying self-esteem, irreligion, vengeance, etc., etc. The characteristics that will enable the projected work to be carried out are submission to the authorities and the obligation to be useful to one's fellow men.

Happy will I be if the plan that I propose attains the innocent effect to which it is directed! Most happy if I am able to abandon the enterprise to other persons of greater wisdom and of felicitous execution, if I succeed in being one of their readers who is able to say: *Vires acquirit eundo* (It gains strength as it goes).

Alzate dedicated this essay to the members of the Spanish politicoscientific expedition to America led by Alejandro Malaspina that was ostensibly engaged in discovering the secrets of nature, including the nature of the organization of Spanish American society, but was secretly gathering material on which to base political reform.

The variety of terms in which up to now the Mexican Indians have been described, the excessive scorn with which some people, even our own [creoles], are accustomed to look upon them, and especially the black and vile colors with which foreign authors usually paint them to us moved me some years ago to investigate their origin and their habits and customs, and, in a word, everything concerning their arts, sciences, and so on. I desired to appraise the diverse judgments of the first mentioned, to rectify the injustice of the second, and ultimately to show all the world the ignorance and calumny of the last.

To this effect, in the *Gaceta de Literatura* Number 11, I treated of their origin. . . . In other issues, as occasion has permitted, I have tried to impart some competent reflections, according to my judgment, to persuade readers that the Mexican nation was not so little civilized as is commonly believed. Nevertheless, as these reflections could only make an impression on perfectly impartial men, I considered that it was necessary to add to them other more convincing and persuasive products, taken from old monuments left to us by this celebrated nation. Accordingly, I went to Xochicalco, where I had heard that one could find the ruins of an old palace.[5] I found in them a work of such precious archi-

5 Xochicalco, in present-day southern Morelos, was probably built about A.D. 900 and was a fortress town covering more than six hundred acres. The "old

tecture that I decided to give a complete description of it to the public. This is the subject of the present article.

For thousands of reasons I have thought, gentlemen, that it should be dedicated to you. Of these the principal ones are, first, your profound and fine education, which puts you in a position to judge their true merit; and second, the object of your expedition, which is not limited to surprising nature in the formation of its most admirable and portentous effects or to the vast extension of the natural sciences, but which also endeavors to collect all that information relative to the habits, customs, and arts of the towns through which you pass. Fortunate will I be if this short and informal *memoria* I publish will come to dissipate the false impressions that the sinister information that foreigners are generally accustomed to give in their works has created among literate men concerning the old Mexican Indians!

May the Lord protect for many years your lives, so important to the utility and progress of the natural sciences.

News from Querétaro, 1791

Some time ago a paper was sent to me by post from Querétaro. I would have enjoyed publishing it immediately, if certain circumstances had not obliged me to defer its publication until now.

It states that in the house of don Marcos Ijar de Arenaza, four learned men—a secular ecclesiastic, a religious, a captain, and another gentleman named Don Antonio—met in order to divert themselves. The subject of their conversations, always informal and spontaneous, had long been either political news or some matter of erudition. But at the end of April of last year, one of these gentlemen proposed to the others the idea that the five of them should form a group or an academy to treat solely of one branch of literature. The idea appeared so fine to all of them that from then on they gave serious thought to the establishment of such a group. Naming a director, a secretary, and so on, these men resolved to busy themselves with poetry.

· · ·

I cannot allow to pass in silence or fail to note that these gentlemen deserve much praise for the particular noble enterprise whereby they strive to fulfill their function as academicians and for having chosen to

---

palace" was undoubtedly what remained of the imposing fort, complete with walls and moats, built on a steep hill.

divert themselves by so pleasant and innocent a subject. It would be desirable in a court like Mexico,[6] where so many and such fertile talents abound, to arouse them by the influence of such a praiseworthy example from that profound and shameful lethargy that holds them deadened in perpetual inactivity. The most celebrated academies have originated in this type of private group. Since men are naturally inclined to imitation, it is incredible what utility this type of useful and agreeable occupation brings to the republic of letters.

Reading 3. Manuel Abad y Queipo, "Representation Concerning the Personal Immunity of the Clergy" (1799)

On behalf of the bishop and cathedral chapter of Michoacán, Abad y Queipo wrote to the crown to point out the importance of the clergy to royal government and, thus, the disservice done by the recent law limiting ecclesiastical privileges. This excerpt includes his report on the state of society in New Spain and his suggestions for laws "that would form the principal base of a liberal and beneficial government."

The population of New Spain is composed of approximately four and a half million inhabitants, who can be divided into three classes: Spaniards [including Spanish Americans], Indians, and "castes."[7] The Spaniards compose a tenth of the total population. They alone have nearly all the property and wealth of the kingdom. The other two classes, who compose nine-tenths, can be divided into thirds: two of castes and one of pure Indians.[8] Indians and castes are employed in domestic service, agricultural work, the ordinary tasks in commerce, and the arts and crafts. That is to say, they are employees, servants, or day laborers for

6 Alzate here refers to Mexico City as the capital, or court, of the viceroyalty.
7 The census of 1793 estimated the population of New Spain at "5,200,000 souls." At the end of 1803, Humboldt estimated "5,800,000 inhabitants for the Kingdom of Mexico," adding that he thought his figure low. Of these, more than one million were creoles and seventy to eighty thousand were gachupines. "Castes," as used here, includes Blacks, mulattoes, and all peoples of mixed Spanish, Indian, and Black descent. There is some evidence that Abad y Queipo overestimated the number of "pure Indians" and underestimated the number of castes.
8 Humboldt found more than two and a half million Indians and he discovered that the castes were almost as numerous as the Indians, rather than twice as numerous. In 1810, Navarro y Noriega stated that the Indians made up 60 percent of the population, castes only 22 percent. Work remains to be done before we shall arrive at reliable population estimates for New Spain on the eve of independence.

the Spanish class. Consequently, there results between the Indians and castes and the Spaniards that opposition of interests and feelings that is common in those who have nothing and in those who have everything, between workers and masters. There is envy, robbery, poor service on the part of some; scorn, usury, hardheartedness on the part of the others. These results are common to a degree everywhere. But in America they are more intense, because there are no gradations nor medians; all are rich or miserable, noble or worthless.

In effect, the two classes of Indians and castes are found in the greatest abasement and degradation. The skin color, ignorance, and misery of the Indians put them at an infinite distance from a Spaniard. The privileges conceded by law to the former benefit them little and in general harm them greatly. These people are forced by the law to live in a community circumscribed by a circle that forms a radius of 1,680 feet. They have no individual property; they cultivate communal lands by compulsion and without immediate return. It is undoubtedly a heavy burden, made more hateful to them as the difficulty of availing themselves of urgently needed products increases from day to day. Their difficulties have become insuperable because of the new form of administration, the system of intendancies. Now no one is able to settle any matter without recourse to the *junta superior* of the royal treasury in Mexico City.

Legally prevented from cohabiting and intermixing with the castes, the Indians are deprived of the education and help they should receive through communication and contact with them and with other peoples. Isolated by their language and by their most useless and tyrannical native government, the customs, uses, and gross superstitions are perpetuated that mysteriously maintain in each pueblo eight or ten old Indians living lazily at the expense of the sweat of the others and dominating them with the hardest despotism. Unable by law to make a lasting agreement, to go into debt for more than five pesos, and to treat and contract, it is impossible for them to advance in that instruction that betters fortunes or to take a step forward to lift themselves from their misery. . . . This concurrence of causes maintains the Indians in a state truly apathetic, inert, and indifferent to the future and to nearly everything that does not arouse the gross passions of the moment.

As descendants of Black slaves, the castes are declared scoundrels by law. They pay tribute, and, as the head count is so exact, the payment of tribute has come to be an indelible mark of their servitude. Time cannot efface it, nor can the mixture of races in subsequent generations. There are many who by their color, physiognomy, and conduct could be elevated to the class of Spaniards, if there were not this impediment keeping them abased in the same class. This class, then, is worthless according to law. Its members are poor and dependent. They have no proper education, only retaining traces of habits and customs ascribable to their origin. In such circumstances, they should be abased in mind and dragged down by the strong passions of their impetuous and robust temperament. They are, indeed, guilty of excess. But it is a marvel that they are not much more guilty, that there are in this class good customs observable in many individuals.

Thus, the Indians and castes are governed directly by the territorial justices, who are more than a little responsible for the condition of these groups, Formerly, the alcaldes mayores were considered not so much judges as merchants with an exclusive privilege to trade in their province. As officials, they had the power to enforce their monopolies. In a five-year period they often accrued from thirty thousand to two hundred thousand pesos. Their usurious and forced transactions caused great vexation. Yet despite all this, there were usually two favorable results: one, they administered justice with disinterest and rectitude in cases to which they were not party; the other, they promoted industry and agriculture where they deemed it important. The abuses of the alcaldes mayores were to be remedied by the subdelegates, who were forbidden to engage in all commerce. But as they were assigned no annual salary, the remedy was infinitely more harmful than the original evil. If they were to confine themselves to the business of adjudicating among miserable people who only litigate when a crime is committed, the subdelegates would perish of hunger. Necessity forces them to prostitute their offices, swindle the poor, and do business with criminals. For the same reason, it is extremely difficult for the intendants to find men suited to these posts. Only the unsuccessful or those who by their conduct and lack of talent cannot find other means to subsist seek these positions. In such circumstances, what beneficence, what protection can these ministers of the law dispense to the Indians and castes? By what means can these officials gain their good opinion and respect, when extortion and injustice are necessary to maintain themselves?

Rather, it is the priests and their assistants, dedicated only to the spiritual service and temporal aid of these miserable classes, who can gain by those ministrations and services their affection, gratitude, and respect. The clergy visit and counsel them in sickness and at work. They act as doctors . . . and as lawyers and intercessors with the justices and with those who bring suit against them. They also favor the poor when they are oppressed by the justices and the more powerful townsmen. In a word, the people do not, and cannot, have confidence in anyone but the priest or the superior magistrates, to whom appeal is very difficult.

In this state of affairs, what interest can unite these two classes with the first class and bind all three to the laws and the government? The first class has the greatest interest in the observance of the laws, for the laws assure it and protect its life, honor, property, and wealth against the insults of envy and the assaults of misery. But the other two classes have no belongings or honor or anything that can be envied. If a member of one of them be attacked, what appreciation has he of laws that only mete out punishments? What affection, what good will can these people have for the ministers of the law, whose authority is exercised only to send them to jail, to the pillory, to the frontier garrison, or to the gallows? What claims can bind these classes to the government, whose beneficent protection they are not capable of comprehending?

Can the fear of punishment suffice to keep the people in subordination to the laws and the government? Two classes, says a politician, make this resort useless: the powerful break the net; the miserable are caught in its mesh. If this maxim is true of Europe, it is much truer of America, where the people live in the open, without permanent domicile, nearly as vagabonds. Then let modern legislators come and point out a means, if they can find one, to hold these classes in subordination to the laws and the government, other than that of a religion preserved in the depth of their hearts by ministers preaching and advising from the pulpit and in the confessional. Therefore, they [the ministers] are the true custodians of the laws and the guarantors of their observance.

It appears opportune and in accord with the charge of the laws to suggest, for the supreme consideration of Your Majesty, remedies for these ills. After profound meditation based on a practical understanding of the character, temper, habits, and customs of these peoples, we think it most appropriate to raise them from their misery, suppress their vices, and tie them to the government by obedience and subordination to the laws. We do not intend to preempt the sovereign judgments of Your Majesty or the wise advice of your zealous ministers. We only wish to point out a state of affairs that is perhaps not as well known there as, naturally, it is here. If such measures as we propose should now be under consideration or adopted, we shall have the satisfaction of thinking as does Your Majesty. If they should not be adopted now, but are adopted sometime, it will double our future pleasure in having contributed to so important a step. . . . And in any case we give, Sire, a testimony of our good wishes for a felicitous outcome in this glorious enterprise of Your Majesty's.

We say, then, that of major importance is, first, general abolition of tributes in the two classes of Indians and castes. The second measure is abolition of the legal infamy affecting these castes; they should be declared honest and honored, capable of obtaining civil positions that do not require noble rank, if they should merit them for their good demeanor. The third is free division of all the unappropriated lands between Indians and castes. The fourth is free division of the communal lands of the Indians among the inhabitants of each village. The fifth is an agrarian law similar to that of Asturias and Galicia. There, by means of leases and transfers of twenty to thirty years and exemption from the royal alcabala or sales tax, the people will be permitted to work the uncultivated lands of the great proprietors. There will be just charges in adjudicating cases of discord. The reclaimed land must be enclosed. Everything will be done in order to keep intact the rights of private property. Over all these proceedings the intendants of the province will judge in the first instance; appeal will be to the audiencia of the district, as it is in all other civil business.

The sixth measure is free permission to all classes of Spaniards, castes, and Indians of other pueblos to live in Indian villages, to buy land in them, and to construct houses and buildings. The seventh is a sufficient salary for all the territorial judges, with the exception of the alcaldes ordinarios, who ought to fill their posts gratuitously as public obligations. If to these is added the free operation of the ordinary cotton and wool workshops, it will increase the impact of the other measures, which should allow people to take the first step toward happiness. Wholesale workshops are now permitted with special license of the viceroys or governors; but this licensing is an insuperable obstacle to the poor and ought to be stopped. So should all other tax burdens, except the charge of alcabala in the importation and exportation of articles.

We know that a proposition to abolish tributes in the present urgent circumstances of the crown will cause surprise. But if in the arithmetic of royal finances there are cases in which three and two are not five, this is certainly one of them. And by close calculation it can be proved that the abolition of tributes and the other mentioned proposals, far from diminishing the royal finances, will augment them in fewer than ten years to triple or quadruple what the tributes produce today.

Reading 4. Report of the Consulado of Mexico (1811)

In this report, the merchant guild protests the decree of the Spanish Cortes of Cádiz of February 9, 1811, which declared equality between Spaniards and Americans in obtaining government office and in representation in the Cortes. It attempts to prove that the inhabitants of New Spain are incapable of fulfilling these political responsibilities.

Sire,

The Royal Tribunal of the Consulado of Mexico reports to Your Majesty with much detail and judgment the state of the diverse castes of inhabitants of New Spain, their quantity, civilization, disposition, customs, passions, desires, and patriotism. From this analysis it deduces the bitter truth concerning these remote provinces: they are not even nearly ready to equal the metropolis in order, form, and number of national representation. After discussing the injustice, grievances, dangers, and uselessness of allowing them the proposed representation, it indicates the easiest, most simple, and appropriate plan, perhaps the only sure one, to reconcile American representation with the conservation of the Americas.

.　　.　　.

What then was the New World, its empires and its inhabitants? Half of the terraqueous globe, the New World was a frightful desert, or a land barely occupied, unproductive and uncultured, in the hands of diverse tribes, wandering, barbarous, and employed in hunting and in war, without peace, serenity, communication, commerce, roads, agriculture, stock raising, industry, or arts. They were preoccupied with the most rabid superstition, with rites and ceremonies insulting to reason and to nature, with laws malevolent, absurd, and mad, and with practices adding up to an abominable composite of all the errors and atrocities committed by peoples in every land and time.

Such, Sire, were the Indians, their empires, and the miserable beings that occupied them, submerged in a tender infancy, with all the appearances of vile automata, so that even respectable theologians whose opinion was very honored in the sixteenth century were persuaded that these beings had no rationality and that the Omnipotent had denied them qualities essential to man.

Such were the natives of the America . . . whom Divine Providence put under the protection of the magnanimous Spaniards, then the most powerful and illustrious nation of the cultured world. In vain do some foreigners, infatuated with the fanatic and hypocrite Las Casas, emulate him slavishly and bitterly accuse us of brutality in the conquest.

.   .   .

By the most marvelous metamorphosis that the centuries have known, the orangutan settlers [the Indians] of America were suddenly transformed, Sire, into domesticated men, subject to a mild government.

.   .   .

If happiness depended on following the exigencies of temper and inclination, nothing would compare with the pleasures and delights of the Indian. He is gifted with laziness and languor that cannot be described. His greatest gift is an absolutely frugal inclination concerning physical necessities. Removed from the superfluities, he sacrifices only a few days of resting a year and would never move if hunger or vice did not prod him. Stupid by constitution, without inventive talent or force of thought, abhorring the arts and trades, he does not lack a way of life. A drunkard by instinct, he satisfies this passion at little cost with very cheap beverages, and this depravity takes up a third of his life. Carnal, with a vice-ridden imagination, devoid of pure ideas about continence, chastity, or incest, he provides for his fleeting desires with the women whom he encounters closest to hand. He is as uncaring in Christian virtue as he is insensible to religious truths, so remorse does not disturb his soul or restrain his sinful appetites. Undiscerning about his duties to society and indifferent to all his fellow beings, he does not economize in the crimes that can bring him an immediate punishment. . . .

If this being, corrupted by the feebleness of his own powers, by his own inertia, by attachment to custom, or by the violent propensity to pleasure, has not perfected even his morals, it would be very unjust to blame legislation or the government. The government and legislation influence or work very slowly on morality and even more slowly on the emotions. . . .

The Indian does not at present carry his ideas, thought, interests, and will beyond his own reach or the range of his eyes. Uninterested in patriotic sentiments and in all social activity, he asks of public authority only an indulgent priest and a lazy subdelegate. He pays no attention to the doings of the intendant, the viceroy, the monarch, or even the nation. In his mind, all are simply a jumble of names. Three million Indians in this condition live presently in New Spain. . . .

There are two million castes; their lazy arms are employed in peonage, domestic service, trades, crafts, and the military. They are of the same condition, character, temperament, and negligence as the Indian, in spite of being reared and living in the shade of cities where they form the lowest class of the populace. With more opportunity to acquire money, with more money to pursue their vices, with more vices to destroy themselves, it is no wonder that they can be most lost and miserable. Incontinent inebriates, indolent, without shame, pleasantness, or fidelity, without notions of religion, morality, luxury, cleanliness, or decency, they appear more mechanical and slovenly than even the Indian himself. They are governed by the common law of the land. No direct imposition weighs on them; they are indirectly taxed only on what they drink! Their foodstuffs are not taxed. Their clothing is rags and the sun. They feign humility to the police. They pay no attention to the government; in turn, it counts on them neither for the immediate advantage of the state nor even for the perpetration of robberies. If the vigilance of the authorities and the exaction of tribute hinder the prosperity and civilization of the Indian, how is it that emancipation from this oppressive authority and exemption from contributions have the same effect on the castes? Is it through a defect of physical constitution caused by the climate, the food they eat, their general laxity, or their education, or is it because of another, unknown cause? The final result, at any rate, is that the castes have none of the qualities of the dignified citizen, none of the properties of vassals, none of the virtues demanded of townsmen, and none of the attributes signifying the civil and religious man.

A million whites, called Spanish Americans, show their superiority to the other five million natives more by their hereditary wealth, their careers, their luxury, their manners, and their refinement in vices than by substantial differences of temperament, sentiments, and propensities. According to experience, the multitude of whites sink themselves into the populace by squandering their patrimony. Spanish Americans occupy themselves in ruining the paternal house. They study when young under the direction of their elders and are placed in all the offices, public posts, and salaried positions of the state. They swell the professions and arts and console themselves, in the absence of wealth, with dreams and schemes of independence that would give them domination of the Americas. Destitute, adept at dreaming of the future, without reflection or judgment, with more indolence than ability, with more attachment to hypocrisy than to religion, with extreme ardor for all the delights, and without the restraint to stop themselves, the indigenous whites gamble, make love, and drink. In a few days they dissipate inheritances, dowries, and property that should support them all their lives. Later they curse at fortune, envy the thrifty, get angry at the denial of their pretensions, and sigh for a new order of things that will do them justice. . . .

In these six million inhabitants the European Spaniards do not bulk very large. Some of these seventy-five thousand men also degenerate because of the force of bad example, because of their way of life, or because of the rudeness of the country; nevertheless, this small and ill-bred family is the soul of the prosperity and opulence of the kingdom because of its undertakings in agriculture, mining, factories, and commerce. It enjoys the management of it nearly exclusively, not so much because of its energy or greed as because of the lack of interest of the creoles. Man is a very incomprehensible being. The Europeans, knowing that they work for their ungrateful, spendthrift, and alienated sons, do not shirk financial anxieties, severe privations, or self-sacrifice in order to increase a patrimony that cost half a century and will be squandered in days. In the end this blindness, this show of fatherly affection, can be reproved neither for its origin nor for its consequences, for it always benefits the state and bestows on the European Spaniard the reputation of a loyal vassal, inseparably united to the metropolis by chains of nature, of recognition, and even of egoism.

Yes, Sire, egoism is part of this notable fidelity, because the European runs the risk of losing his life at the first cry of American insubordination. In the New World, "patrimony" is understood as "the love of the land in which one has been born." This truncated and mistaken definition causes hard feelings and resentment between Spaniards from overseas and natives. It is the root of the loyalty of some men and the aversion of others to the mother country.

．　　．　　．

New Spain is a remote province, seduced by the sum of its population and by its riches, made haughty by the abasement of the metropolis, pushed toward anarchy by corruption, stupidity, and imbecility, denuded of all decent sentiments, of all generous passions, of all political combinations, of all rational foresight. It is the abode of five million automatons, a million intractable vassals, and a hundred thousand citizens addicted to order.

．　　．　　．

It was proposed in the sovereign congress to grant the colonies of the conquest a representation proportionate to that of the conquering nation. This decision, a product of the talents and patriotism of the creoles, was sustained ardently by a faction and by its influence. What blindness hurls the white Americans into such straits? Is it their haste to die, their imprudence, their ill will toward the human species, or their dreams of self-government?

The Cortes would enfranchise five million drunkards, friends of robbery, bloodshed, and evildoing, susceptible to all emotions of hate, libertinage, and looseness, dragged along mechanically by the furor of vengeance, and without an idea of shame or religion. Five million of these barbarians, united in bands spread over the area of New Spain, would take on the airs and trappings of sovereign people. They would be presided over by most perfidious chiefs, the men most excited and sanguine about independence, the fiercest, the greatest enemies of the motherland. These leaders would be assisted, urged on, and ordered about by a million lost whites, who are extremely vicious, superficial, artificial, and divorced from Christian piety and from political, moral, and natural notions of social welfare. What a cruel perspective! What road so short and so conducive to insurrection! Is this what the creole deputies seek? No, Sire, far from desiring it, they would not dare to live in the capital of the viceroyalty, anticipating such evil days, such scenes of death, horror, and weeping, expecting the victims to be of their own color and class.

. . .

What is there in common? What comparison fits, or what analogy may be found in the laws, situation, spirit, manners, exigencies, interests, institutions, habits, and regions of conquering Spain and of the conquered colonies? Would not the parallel between the Spaniard and the Indian be a comparison between a crowd of gibbon monkeys and an association or republic of urbane men?

Conclusion

In the late eighteenth century, a new spirit was abroad in Mexico, made manifest by the *regidores* of Mexico City *within* the old framework of thought concerning the relation of Mexico to the peninsula. Although blown up with creole pride, they spoke of "we Spaniards." In 1778, however, Alzate expressed himself within another ideological framework. He combined creole pride with concern for the populace of all New Spain and wrote of "we Mexicans."

Alzate served not only as an example of intellectual ferment, but also as a champion of it. He was prominent among those who raised the cry for liberty of opinion that presaged the cry raised for political liberty in 1810 by members of that same Querétaro Literary Academy he so admired. One of them, Miguel Hidalgo y Costilla, when asked by what right he had taken upon himself the destiny of Mexico, revealed to what lengths civic activity may go when he replied that he was exercising the right that any citizen has when he sees his native land in danger. Hidalgo gave an eminently popular cast to current liberal notions. He declared slaves free, abolished tribute payments, and restored lands to the Indians—measures advocated earlier by his one-time friend and fellow cleric, Abad y Queipo. Hidalgo went beyond Alzate's concept of the nation to explicitly include as fellow citizens men of all ethnic backgrounds born in Mexico.

Dissatisfaction with existing governmental policy was voiced by members of the group that should have been its staunchest adherents, the European Spaniards. Conflict was evident not only among members of the governing group, but also within the mind of the individual Spaniard. Abad y Queipo represented the dilemma of the enlightened peninsular who wanted to preserve certain privileges, notably those of the church, and abolish others in the interest of economic, social, and political reform.

If Abad y Queipo was a product of the eighteenth-century revolution in the Spanish climate of opinion, the consulado exemplified the conservative reaction to it. That previously powerful corporation blamed liberals such as Abad y Queipo for overturning the old imperial order and thus ensuring the loss of America. They insisted that liberal Spaniards share responsibility for the rejection of Spanish imperialism and the exaltation of Mexican nationality that permeated the creole revolt of 1810.

Further, these documents reveal that enlightened creoles, unlike enlightened gachupines, could not reconcile their desire for economic and social reform with the Spanish drain of Mexican wealth and with government imposed from overseas. They also shed light on related historical problems. For example, in 1778, eleven years *before* the French Revolution, Alzate used a vocabulary often attributed to the influence of that revolution. His writings, and others, indicate that an internal development of ideas occurred within Mexico in the latter part of the eighteenth century, that creoles had prepared for themselves an ambience receptive to concepts of Mexican liberty.

In short, these documents show how attitudes that undermined Spanish authority developed among widely varying segments of society in Mexico. They also indicate how intellectual ferment (initially directed against traditional methods of education) gave rise to concern with social and economic reform and, finally, to political activity. When revolution came, creoles had a ready-made ideology: the concept of a nation to call to arms. While creole society, like gachupín society, was far from monolithic in outlook, the *regidores* of the capital, the journalist Alzate, and the revolutionaries of 1810 had one thing in common: a concept of Mexican nationality, a patriotic attachment to the soil on which they were born.

Hidalgo and a small group of fellow creoles rose in the name of the nation, calling on all men born on Mexican soil to join them. For a brief period, the possibility existed that all Mexicans could unite, as Abad y Queipo had warned they might, in the cause of freedom from oppression by European Spaniards. The hope of unity died as Hidalgo's undisciplined mass of followers increasingly indulged in looting and bloodshed. The riotous nature of the revolt repelled the majority of creoles, including many of those adhering to Alzate-like liberal principles. They would neither join the rebels nor continue to look to Spain. The blandishments proffered to them by the Spanish Cortes in the form of American representation in that body and the liberal Constitution of 1812 they took instead as guides to the formulation of a Mexican congress and constitution.

Small bands of insurgents carried on the revolution. Hidalgo's successor as leader, the mestizo priest José María Morelos, declared Mexico independent in 1813, yet not until a new and more elitist unity was effected among elements of Mexican society was independence in fact achieved. In 1821, Vicente Guerrero, an insurgent leader, joined Agustín Iturbide, an army officer representing the military, the hacendados, the mineowners, and the church and, with the blessing of the liberal Spanish viceroy, Juan O'Donojú, formed a government that was to be dominated by elitist creole interests, liberal and conservative, for the greater part of a century. The continuance of a consulado-like outlook among Spaniards helped to bring about the expulsion of all Spaniards from Mexico in 1828. No sector of influential society worked to include the Indian in the nation proper until the second decade of the twentieth century, when revolution again proposed to solve old problems while at the same time posing new ones.

Suggested Further Reading

Collier, Simon. *Ideas and Politics of Chilean Independence, 1808–1833.* Cambridge, 1967.

Domínguez, Jorge I. *Insurrection or Loyalty: The Breakdown of the Spanish American Empire.* Cambridge, Mass., 1980.

Góngora, Mario. *Studies in the Colonial History of Spanish America.* Cambridge, 1975. Especially chapter 5.

Griffin, Charles C. "Economic and Social Aspects of the Era of Spanish American Independence." *Hispanic American Historical Review* 29:2 (May 1949).

———. "The Enlightenment and Latin American Independence." In *Latin America and the Enlightenment,* edited by Arthur P. Whitaker. 2d ed. Ithaca, 1961.

Humphreys, R. A., and John Lynch, eds. *The Origins of the Latin American Revolutions, 1808–1826.* New York, 1966.

Phelan, John Leddy. *The People and the King: The Comunero Revolution in Colombia, 1781.* Madison, 1978.

Russell-Wood, A. J. R., ed. *From Colony to Nation: Essays on the Independence of Brazil.* Baltimore, 1975.

Part Four ❈ Political Independence

18 ☀

The Last Viceroys of New Spain
and Peru: An Appraisal

TIMOTHY E. ANNA

The bibliography of the Spanish American wars of independence (1810–
24) is, to understate the obvious, vast. It is also, and this has apparently
not been so obvious, one-sided. It concentrates almost entirely on the
rebels, on the American side, on their aspirations, their objectives, and
their military and political campaigns. The literature on the royalist side
is very incomplete. There are, of course, many valuable studies in what
might be called the "background" to the movements for independence,
studies concentrating on the eighteenth century and on the progressive
decline of Spain's world system, on what was wrong with that system and
why Americans perceived it to be unsuited to them. This background
material, however, leaves a major gap in our understanding, for, although it tells us what Spanish Americans themselves thought to be
grievances in the imperial system, it does not, as is sometimes assumed,
automatically tell us how that system collapsed. Much less does it tell us
what the royalists were thinking, or their objectives in the war itself, or
the mistakes they made in the war. Given the fact that, as Hugh M.
Hamill, Jr., has pointed out in the case of Mexico, most Spanish Americans were not decided on the question of independence,[1] exclusive concentration on the fundamental weaknesses of the royal system and on
American objections to it, important though these were, does not tell the
whole story. It may explain, for example, why the royal system "de-

[1] Hugh M. Hamill, Jr., *The Hidalgo Revolt: Prelude to Mexican Independence*
(Gainesville, Fla., 1966), p. 151.

Reprinted by permission of the American Historical Association and published
originally in the *American Historical Review,* 81:1 (February 1976). The research
support of the Canada Council is gratefully acknowledged.

served" to be overthrown or why Americans perceived it to deserve that fate, but it does not explain how it was overthrown. Similarly, a thousand studies of military campaigns tell only how battles were won and lost. One might even go so far as to say that a thousand biographies of Simón Bolívar, José de San Martín, Miguel Hidalgo, José María Morelos, and Agustín de Iturbide only tell how they won, not how Spain lost. As C. H. Haring long ago pointed out, Spain's imperial system in America may not have been the world's best government, but it was not the world's worst.[2] It may not have made room for or fulfilled the aspirations of Americans, but it was no mere house of cards.

It is well past time, then, that Latin American historians specializing in the emancipation focus a proportionate amount of attention on the royalists. Furthermore, that focus should be concentrated, not in the eighteenth century, much less in the sixteenth, not at the time Spain's imperial institutions were created, or even at the moment of their most important institutional reform under the Bourbons, but during the wars of independence. No matter how widespread the radical ideas of the French and North American philosophers were, no matter how corroded Spain's ability to govern may have been, the obvious and automatic answer to what Americans saw wrong in the empire was not independence. It would have been, rather, reform, accommodation, and compromise. Even when the uprisings actually began, as, for example, in the case of the Hidalgo insurrection, independence was not the logical or automatic objective. It was not until 1813 in Mexico, 1816 in Río de la Plata, and 1821 in Lima that rebels formally proclaimed independence. Something must have got in the way, something must have acted after 1810 to convert the insurgent cry of "Death to bad government" into "Long live independence."

One of the fundamental mistakes the historian could make in reviewing the royal government during the wars of independence would be to think of it as functioning the way the law required it to. It did not, because it could not. Three centuries of restrictions and controls over the exercise of the crown's power by its agents in America had not prepared them for the catastrophe of 1808. During most of the wars of independence, the royal power in America functioned virtually on its own, because from 1808 to 1814 the monarch was a captive in France and from 1820 to 1823 he was a captive of the liberal Spanish constitution. Thus, while in theory major policy decisions came exclusively from

2 C. H. Haring, *The Spanish Empire in America* (New York, 1947), p. 113.

Spain—and many of them did—in practice throughout this era an extraordinary amount of major policy was made by the viceroys, and almost in spite of their natural absolutist inclinations. This is not to deny that the intransigence of peninsular Spain on the question of American autonomy also played a great role in provoking American desires for total separation. But the focus should first be on Lima and Mexico City.

The thesis of this article is that the viceroys themselves, unwittingly and without recognizing it, disproved the myths upon which Spanish imperial absolutism was based. To put it another way, they proved Spanish imperialism unsuited to America. Actual circumstances and events forced them to contradict their stated principles and the principles on which imperial political institutions were grounded. And since this was a complex time not suited to analysis by use of clear-cut extremes, the reader will be presented a second—and long overdue—thesis: that the viceroys were not incompetent, but on the contrary, extraordinarily competent politicians and military leaders. A myriad of forthright actions and forceful decisions taken by the viceroys to solve actual problems facing them ultimately proved to uncommitted Americans that Spanish imperialism was no longer valid, that it was false authority. Mere inaction could not have accomplished that, nor could mere rebel propaganda, nor could even the remarkably clearheaded political analyses of Bolívar himself. Independence was more than a coup d'état, though it was also something less than true revolution if that term be taken to require social, economic, and even intellectual revolution. It was the rejection of a three-hundred-year-old political tradition and of a previously held identity. Opposition alone could not have produced such a profound political change; established authority must first have proved itself invalid, and the viceroys were the principal agents of established authority.

The subjects of this article are the men who in their role as "alter ego," literally "vice-king," of King Ferdinand VII, represented in their persons the authority of the sovereign and the imperialism of Spain in the two chief American colonies. For New Spain they were Francisco Xavier Venegas, Marqués de la Reunión de Nueva España (1810–13); Félix María Calleja del Rey, Conde de Calderón (1813–16); and Juan Ruiz de Apodaca, Conde del Venadito (1816–21). For Peru they were José Abascal, Marqués de la Concordia (1806–16); Joaquín de la Pezuela, Marqués de Viluma (1816–21); and José de la Serna, Conde de los Andes (1821–24). In order to view them properly we must remember that emotionally inspired antipathies have long obscured the record of their remarkable accomplishments. Together they provided the strongest leadership the American kingdoms ever had with the exception of the great sixteenth-century founder-viceroys. In every sense of the word, they actually ruled America. Their strength of purpose and loyalty help explain why independence took so long to achieve and why it cannot be assumed to have been inevitable. By definition they were imperialists, by training absolutists, and as wartime leaders they were responsible, as were the rebel leaders, for the destruction of the wars. Having said this about them, we have merely reaffirmed that they were effective servants of their sovereign. It is no more valid to dismiss Calleja from study because he was viewed by his enemies as a bloody butcher than it would be to ignore Hidalgo because of the atrocities committed by his followers. It is no more valid to dismiss Abascal as a mere reactionary than it would be to forget that Bolívar was no democrat. And yet, traditionally in Latin American historiography they have been viewed as the blundering, bloody-minded, and unthinking agents of an outmoded despotism that, as the cliché about the royal dynasty they served would have it, never learned anything and never forgot anything. This is surely a disservice to history, for to view them as stereotypes is, among other things, to deny the full impact of the movement for independence and to lessen the stature of the liberators who met and defeated them in a contest whose outcome was by no means preordained. It is to ignore the political opinions of that significant number of Spanish Americans who did not want independence and to whom the viceroys were saviors—it still remains to be demonstrated whether they were a minority or a majority, for the victory of independence does not constitute automatic proof. Above all, the traditional view of the viceroys denies rationality to Spain's imperial ethos.

How did the viceroys conceive of themselves and of their role? Each, of course, was very different, and the frequent disagreements among them were one source of their ultimate failure. What united them was chiefly the fact that they faced the task of reviving viceregal authority in the face of universal assault from both America and Spain. All served the unworthy Ferdinand VII, who never failed to reward them (each was granted his title of nobility on the grounds of service as viceroy), but whose weakness and vacillation seriously undercut their authority. The extent of their love for Ferdinand himself is impossible to discover and not important anyway, as it was rather to the king as a symbol that they were loyal. Although each was a professional servant of the king, and therefore predisposed toward the defense of the king's prerogatives, which were also the viceroy's, each was genuinely dedicated to what they all conceived of as the only possible and correct foundation for the state—the absolute monarchy as represented by Ferdinand's grandfather Charles III (though they disagreed on the extent to which reform within the structure was desirable). More than that, they were also dedicated to their definition of Spain and of its role in the world, to Hispanism. Their proclamations referring to the brotherhood of Spaniards and the unity of the empire were not empty rhetoric. They believed that the brilliant civilizing mission of Spain in America was still alive. The noble titles they were granted—Concordia, Reunión—often reflected this mission. They embodied Spain's imperial ethos—absolutism, the sovereign, and the mission to spread and preserve true Christianity and true civilization.

The reader will already have scoffed, perhaps, wondering on what grounds he shall take these viceroys seriously if this was genuinely their concept of their role in America. Surely they could see that it was a concept belonging to the sixteenth century; surely they could see the illogic in it. No, in fact, they did not, or only partially at any rate, for they still genuinely believed it. They were, after all, imperialists, whose world view included belief in the rationality of their nation's history and their own actions. They could not grasp the point of view that Bolívar personified, the idea that Spain's mission in America was over and that the child had outgrown the parent. At any rate, to assume that in 1810, or even in 1820, most Americans recognized the invalidity of Spain's civilizing mission in America is to anticipate. Its validity was proven, as Spaniards viewed it, by three hundred years of history.[3] Inertia, time,

3 For studies illustrating the extraordinary staying power of Hispanism after independence, see Mark J. Van Aken, *Pan-Hispanism: Its Origin and Development to 1866* (Berkeley, 1959), and Fredrick B. Pike, *Hispanismo, 1898–1936: Spanish Conservatives and Liberals and Their Relations with Spanish America* (Notre Dame, 1971). The basic emotion, which Pike succinctly defines as "an unassailable faith in the existence of a transatlantic Hispanic family, community or *raza* (race)" (p. 1), is not, after all, very different from the fundamental principle of the British Commonwealth, but its political, social, and philosophical meanings are very different. Since Hispanism is conservative, antimodern, antidemocratic, sometimes ultrareligious, and sometimes anticapitalistic, North Americans often find it incomprehensible. This does not alter the fact that it is very real and has answered the needs of countless Spanish American philosophers since independence. In the period under consideration here, it was just beginning to be challenged. Throughout the remainder of the nineteenth century, Hispanism in Spanish America was at its ebb, because of the bitterness caused by the wars of independence, but it revived after 1898, when Spain was no longer a threat to American safety.

upbringing, and tradition were all on the royalists' side. The rebels did not win unanimous agreement when they declared that Spain's hour had passed. It had to be proved, and only the chief agents of Spain could prove it.

That is exactly what they did, for the fundamental circumstance that would destroy them, which they did not and could not recognize, was that the values upon which their authority and the crown's authority were based were rapidly becoming irrelevant. On a wider spectrum, of course, world events disproved the divinity of the monarchy, the Napoleonic wars showed that Spain was no longer Europe's foremost power, and North American independence suggested that America could function independently of its founders. But within the empire itself events were showing the viceroys to be, unknown to themselves, defenders of a glorious irrelevancy. The things they claimed and thought they represented no longer corresponded to what they actually represented in the minds of Americans. The reality was a king who had overthrown his own father (it was the first time this had happened in the history of the unified monarchy); a war-torn Spain either subjected to Napoleonic rule or divided between constitutionalism and absolutism; and for many Americans, especially the nonelite, a very real oppression. The Napoleonic conquest of Spain and the questioning of the nation's fundamental traditions exemplified by the Constitution of Cádiz together contradicted or disproved the political values Americans had previously been taught to believe. The viceroys sensed this crisis of confidence and responded to it in different ways, but they never fully understood it. It was a fault in the system, not in themselves, but they were the agents of the system and therefore of its failure.

I

José Abascal, who governed the Peruvian viceroyalty for ten years, was the most absolutistic in his response to the rebellion. Perhaps he best understood the authority that the viceroy traditionally personified. He was convinced that standing firm, not moving an inch, was the best defense against the crises he faced on all sides. Indeed rebellion provoked in him greater adherence to absolutism. In a report to Spain in 1815, he accused even the Lima Inquisition of weakening his authority by daring to criticize him. As a witness to the revolution, he testified, "I know that nothing has so prejudiced the king's cause as the lack of resolution, or the imbecility, of those who have held power" in America. In

1814, he had a disagreement with his own audiencia (high court of appeal), which he accused of being too easy on a rebel sent for trial from Arequipa. When the audiencia referred to their disagreement as a "conflict," the viceroy replied, "I urge you next time to avoid using the word 'conflict' with me, because either you do not understand its significance, or you forget where I come from and what I represent." To him a conflict between the two arms of royal authority in Peru was a contradiction in terms. This was the tone adopted by the viceroys who were in office when the insurrections broke out, for maintaining Spain's imperial power undiminished was the viceroys' appointed task.

Viceroy Félix María Calleja of Mexico was also a genuine absolutist who, unlike every other viceroy, spoke and wrote with a stunning frankness about the royal government's troubles. He came closest to understanding what was actually happening. Following the nullification of the constitution upon Ferdinand's restoration in 1814, Calleja wrote a remarkable letter in which he explained to the peninsula that "the ancient illusions" of the Americans about the authority of the crown and its agents had received a death blow from the liberalization and confusion of authority that the constitution entailed. With remarkable political perceptiveness, he pointed out that what was important was not so much the defeat of one or another rebel chieftain, but the restoration of what he frankly recognized to be the great myths that had cemented the state. The restoration of calm sufficient to allow a return to normality was also vital, "for even if the arms of the rebels prove unsuccessful . . . still misery, and a growing consumption, will do that which neither force nor intrigue may be able to effect."

Abascal and Calleja, then, had the clearest and coldest understanding of authority and its employment, which is power. Almost as a direct adjunct, they were the most successful of the viceroys in fighting the insurrection. In Peru, Abascal was able virtually to prevent the insurrection from spreading into the viceroyalty itself, while he raised money and dispatched troops to help restore royal governments in Montevideo, Upper Peru, Chile, and Quito. Calleja, the military genius who took office at the high point of rebel fortunes in Mexico, was able in three years to break the rebellion's back, to capture Morelos and destroy his forces, and to pacify almost all of the country, so that the year after Calleja left office his successor, Apodaca, could claim that the rebellion in Mexico was over. All this was accomplished even though, as Calleja wrote, "The war strengthens and propagates the desire for Independence, holding out a constant hope of our destruction, a longing desire which . . . is general amongst all classes, and has penetrated into every corner of the kingdom." He recognized the hollowness of his military victories and insisted that the only salvation from destruction was "to reanimate the authority of the government."

Slightly less cynical, but still undeniably absolutist, was Francisco Xavier Venegas, Calleja's predecessor in Mexico. It was he who had to face the shock of Hidalgo's uprising in 1810, the bloody first round of the Mexican war. Within days after his reception in the capital in September 1810, there appeared a pasquinade on the walls of the viceregal palace mocking his personal appearance and style of dress. In typically direct fashion, he is said to have ordered an answering pasquinade to be affixed next to the offending original with the words:

> My face is not that of an Excellency
> nor my clothes of a Viceroy
> but I represent the King.
> This simple advice
> I give you for what it is worth:
> The law must be the north star
> that guides my actions.
> Look out for treacheries
> done in this court.

It was Venegas's sagacity, especially his ability to choose extremely competent officers like Calleja, who was commander of the army of the center and later military governor of the capital, that allowed him to resist the terrifying uprising of the Indian masses under Hidalgo and the guerrilla war under Morelos that followed. In 1811, he faced two direct plots by dissidents in the capital to kidnap or assassinate him. He organized new militia groups, firmly resisted the more radical requirements of the constitution after 1812, opened new sources of revenue in the face of genuine financial crisis, and ended the dangerous lack of direction the government had suffered from since the shocks of 1808. In 1810 and 1811, he created a special police force for the capital city and special tribunals to deal with treason and rebellion throughout the nation. He denied charges by the city council of Mexico that these agencies were indistinguishable from those of the French tyrant in Spain, and he ignored orders from the Cortes to disband them.

The greatest danger, however, to the authority of all three of these viceroys came from Spain, not from the American insurgents. In 1812, the erosion of the fundamental principles of the empire reached its peak in the publication of the constitution written by the Spanish Cortes of Cádiz. The constitution, which the viceroys had to declare in America if only because it was the work of the single commonly accepted legitimate government, lowered the viceroys to the status of "superior political chiefs" of their kingdoms, created elected provincial deputations to share power with viceroys, reduced audiencias to mere courts of law, and established elected city governments. Most startling, it declared national sovereignty vested in the Cortes rather than the absent king, a direct contradiction of the fundamental principle of the Spanish state. For two years the constitution remained in effect until the restoration of Ferdinand nullified it, and for two years Viceroy Absacal in Peru and Viceroys Venegas and Calleja in Mexico agonized over the delicate task of appearing to execute its provisions while ignoring those they perceived to be destructive of their authority. They were in the altogether extraordinary position—and one that the true absolutist would not have expected to encounter—of serving a metropolitan government that spoke for the king, but that was controlled by a philosophy inimical, as they viewed it, to the true interests of the king. In Peru, Abascal nullified the constitution's provision for the freedom of the press, paid only nominal attention to the provincial deputations, and struggled to neutralize the revolutionary effects of a freely elected Lima city council, which he thought represented creole dissidents. In Mexico, Venegas faced the same problems, nullifying elections that came too close to threatening royal prerogatives and first implementing, then nullifying, the freedom of the press. Venegas and Calleja publicly quarreled over what Calleja viewed as the viceroy's insufficiently hostile attitude toward the constitution and his unwillingness to prosecute the war militarily. Mexican reactionaries bombarded Spain with requests for Venegas's replacement by Calleja, and in March 1813 Calleja took office. Promising to implement the constitution fully in his first proclamation to the people as viceroy, Calleja nonetheless took no action to implement the free press, even in the face of fierce complaints from every level of the moderate faction in the country. Charges and countercharges were dispatched to Spain in bewildering numbers. All three viceroys had occasion to accuse dissidents of engineering local elections, while creoles and liberals in both countries charged them with tyranny and illegal acts.

Viceroy Abascal in Peru could afford to be less heavy-handed in his efforts to neutralize the constitution, largely because the kingdom was not itself a theater of war except in 1814, following the uprising at Cuzco.[4] He attempted instead to direct the actions of the various constitutional agencies by actually giving the appearance of participation. The constitution made the viceroy titular head or president of the city council of his capital and of the provincial deputation of the capital-province, and Abascal actually filled those chairs, something his Mexican colleagues refused to do. In this way he could supervise the actions of the council. In the provincial deputation, for example, he personally appointed the secretary, while a year later he intervened in the electoral junta that was choosing a Cortes delegate from Lima. In 1813, he disqualified the elector chosen by Lima from participating in the vote to elect the Cortes delegate and provincial deputation on the grounds that the man chosen was a magistrate, and yet he was actually thought to be too well disposed toward the dissidents. In 1813, he disqualified one of the men chosen as a city councillor in Lima. He ordered the Lima city council to inform him whenever it expected to discuss a matter of major importance so that he could preside over the debate, and he demanded that it not write directly to the government in Spain without his approval, although it firmly refused to obey. He even refused to let the newly elected Lima city council for 1814 take the traditional paseo through the streets on the day of its inauguration. Abascal's real object was to allow the liberal provisions of the constitution to draw dissidents out in the open so they could be identified. As early as mid-1813, meetings of his junta of war were able to discuss with remarkable accuracy the status of prominent citizens throughout the country who in the years ahead would remain leaders of the underground in favor of independence.

Venegas and Calleja were more direct in their opposition to the constitution and consequently caused far greater public reaction, but they viewed their opposition as necessary, for the years of the constitution corresponded with the high point of Morelos's campaign. Venegas actually annulled the first elections that took place in Mexico City on November 29, 1812, claiming they had been improperly conducted. The night of the elections there were widespread popular demonstrations of support for the constitution in the capital, which both Venegas and General Calleja called riots in their reports to Spain. After allowing the free

4   As J. R. Fisher has shown, however, the constitution itself and Abascal's refusal to implement it fully were central causes of the Cuzco uprising, which we name after its Indian leader, Pumacahua: J. R. Fisher, *Government and Society in Colonial Peru: The Intendant System, 1784–1814* (London, 1970), p. 227.

press provision to go into effect for two months, Venegas annulled it as well, on the grounds that it gave cover to rebel propaganda. The fact that in a series of elections in the capital city hardly any peninsular Spaniards were ever elected conclusively showed the direction of popular feeling, and it explains Venegas's hostility.

On March 4, 1813, in the midst of the constitutional era, Calleja became viceroy. Speaking words of sweet reasonableness, he permitted the long-overdue elections of Mexico City's council and provincial deputation, but he delegated the reactionary intendant-corregidor of the province to serve as president of both. Promising everything, he simply neglected to do anything about restoring the free press, ignoring several direct orders from the Cortes to do so. He, too, was able to draw out dissidents by pretending to permit constitutional provisions. The elections were perfectly suited to that purpose. At one point, he even negotiated with the famous underground rebel group called the Guadalupes as a means of discovering the loyalties of prominent residents of the capital. The rebels of the Guadalupes wrote to Morelos the day after Calleja's assumption of office and paid him the supreme compliment of warning that the viceroy was their greatest opponent, for, they said, "he is a great politician."

Calleja now commenced a military, political, and propaganda campaign against the insurgents that clearly defines him as the fiercest, most competent, most ruthless, and, from the royalists' point of view, best viceroy of the era. He publicly promised "to dedicate myself exclusively to the destruction of Morelos." In 1814, he swore to the king that he would not let Mexico go while he remained in power even if he had to march at the head of the whole army across the country, laying it waste with fire and sword until every rebel was destroyed. Special courts-martial of the most dubious legality were set up in the provinces to deal with treason, and they were ordered to ignore the immunity of clerics from civil prosecution and to execute rebel priests without ado. By June 1814, even before he had heard of the king's nullification of the constitution, Calleja was sufficiently powerful to exult in a public decree, "Nothing can now stand in the way of the execution of my ideas." He reacted "with unspeakable joy," as he wrote himself, upon hearing of the king's restoration. With icy hauteur he commanded the dissolution of the various constitutional bodies as order after order arrived from Spain. When the constitutional city council of Mexico wrote him what he considered to be an insufficiently warm letter of thanksgiving following announcement of the restoration, he ordered it to write to him again within four hours making it clear "whether or not you are disposed to guard, obey, and execute on your part everything touched on by His Majesty in his decree . . . annulling the Cortes and the Constitution." Several months later the king wrote to Calleja approving of all his previous actions, including his refusal to obey the constitution, and authorizing him to take whatever measures necessary to stop the insurrection. Having now a fairly complete list of secret traitors among the upper classes of Mexico City, throughout 1815 Calleja ordered a series of arrests of prominent nobles and gentlemen, city councillors, lawyers, and priests, which virtually destroyed the rebel fifth column in the capital. Meanwhile Morelos was captured and executed. Calleja was triumphant; his admirers called him the "Reconqueror," the "Second Cortés."

II

The constitution was gone. But both Abascal and Calleja knew that its effects were far more widespread than their contemporaries, or even their successors Pezuela, La Serna, and Apodaca, suspected. The damage lay not in any temporary advantage the creoles or dissidents had achieved, not in the confusion and chaos that had reigned, not in the fury of liberals and moderates alike who had seen their opportunity for a government of laws trampled underfoot by self-willed men. The chief damage lay in what the constitution had done to the foundations upon which viceregal and royal authority rested. The Mexican audiencia called it a loss of Spain's "moral force." In a letter dated August 18, 1814, Calleja affirmed that the constitution had removed from the viceroy every vestige of authority he had possessed outside the use of plain force, and it could never be recovered. "The insurrection is now so deeply impressed and rooted in the heart of every American," he wrote, "that nothing but the most energetic measures, supported by an imposing force, can ever eradicate it." The constitution had exposed the ministers and magistrates to ridicule. "They have lost their *prestige,* and even their respectability." It was now too late; the mere defeat of the insurgents, he said, would not end the rebellion. This was so because continued warfare "acts against us in two ways: by open force, and by increasing distress; the first will always be repelled, the second will reduce us gradually to death's door." Calleja, the "Second Cortés," the most astute and ruthless of the last viceroys, recognized that he was trapped, for the only way to retain power was to use force, and force, he knew, was counterproductive. The more battles Spain won the fewer supporters it had, the more power the viceroys amassed the less true authority remained to the agents of Spain.

This replacement of authority by force was manifest in a remarkable exchange of letters between Calleja and the liberal bishop of Puebla, Dr. Antonio Joaquín Pérez. The bishop wrote the viceroy in April 1816, complaining about the cruelty of royal troops and the destructiveness of the war in general, and Calleja replied justifying his government's and army's actions. Calleja did not deny the excesses of the royal troops, but justified them by citing the excesses of the rebels. Pérez said farms and factories of those suspected of treason were destroyed needlessly; Calleja said the government had been too soft. Pérez accused royal troops of demanding excessive supplies; Calleja replied it was the duty of the countryside to supply a marching army. Pérez complained that the army was guilty of capricious and unwarranted bloodletting when capturing rebel towns; Calleja replied that he could not restrain successful and victorious troops. The laws of war permitted every excess. Pérez alleged the royal government had published false accounts of battles; Calleja said falsifying news from the battlefields was justified on the grounds of political expediency. In all the history of colonial Spanish America there is hardly another instance, outside of the initial conquest phase, of so unashamed a dependence on naked force. Calleja knew that any other defense of his actions would be hypocritical. Indeed, to him even compromise was hypocritical.

In Peru, meanwhile, the aging Abascal also sensed the turning point in the war had arrived. While the world witnessed royal armies sweep triumphantly across the entire continent, so that by 1816 all South America except the Río de la Plata was again reduced to royal control, he sensed that sheer force was the only thing left, for authority had evaporated. Whether he recognized it clearly or not, it was only a matter of time before simple force could no longer sustain the regime. The viceroy begged Spain to let him retire, while Spanish ministries were flooded with complaints against him and his arbitrary use of power. Most of the Peruvian complainants were unaware that it was only Abascal and his arbitrary use of power that had stanched the flood of rebellion.

Simultaneously, however, the practical problems of the royal govenment were becoming acute. Contrary to its silver-inspired popular image, Peru had always been poor, and its cost of living had for centuries been one of the highest in the world—the result, of course, of an excess of silver and a shortage of everything else. Now bread was selling for fifty cents a loaf and would rise to a dollar by 1821, while the government staggered under an unbearable cumulative deficit of 12,000,000 pesos and a yearly deficit by 1814 of 1,500,000 pesos, and 150,000 artisans were out of work. Spanish economic precepts were rapidly being disproved as well. No exertion, no force, no intransigence on the viceroy's part could rescue Peru from this inexorable plunge toward bankruptcy as long as rebellion existed anywhere on the continent. But Peru could not defeat the insurrection everywhere. Its resources were becoming overstrained, and its population could not bear such exertions much longer. And all these financial difficulties existed before the final rush to independence of Peru's neighbors.

Is it really any wonder, then, that Bolívar, writing from exile in Jamaica in 1815 at the nadir of his career, could declare that although the rebellion had been crushed almost everywhere in America, "success will crown our efforts, because the destiny of America has been irrevocably decided; the tie that bound her to Spain has been severed. Only a concept maintained that tie and kept the parts of that immense monarchy together. That which formerly bound them now divides them." The tie that bound consisted, in his own words, of "the habit of obedience; a community of interest, of understanding, of religion; mutual goodwill; a tender regard for the birthplace and good name of our forefathers." The concept that maintained that tie was Spanish authority. All that had disappeared, and Spain was now reduced to "an aged serpent, bent only on satisfying its venomous rage."

This well-known quotation of the liberator, read and remembered by later generations with the most intense affection and pride, was certainly part prophecy, but it was also a foresight of what was soon to be manifest. The liberator was predicting that the back of the royalist cause was broken, and at the very moment that royal power seemed most ascendant. How can this apparent contradiction be explained? Simply by remembering that the possession of territory by armies, especially in a civil war, is not the same thing as loyalty. In fact, there were two wars going on: one a struggle for territory, the second a struggle for men's minds. While the first was important, the second was decisive. The Spaniards were winning the first but losing the second. Bolívar knew, if only intuitively, that the authoritarianism of both Abascal and Calleja and their cynical refusal to conform to the empire's fundamental law code had broken both the chain of affection upon which loyalty depended and the habit of obedience that was the foundation of royal power. The very ground rules by which loyalty was conceived had been altered by the viceroys' responses to insurrection, converting the delicate strands of loyalty into hatred. This is more than saying simply that royal military operations provoked hatred. That those operations were conducted by men who in the name of loyalty refused to obey the fundamental law as set forth in the constitution was the fact that was so critical. This converted absolutism into true tyranny. Spanish political philosophy had always recognized a difference between absolutism and firm government, on the one hand, and tyranny on the other. Ferdinand VII himself, in his decree of May 4, 1814, annulling the constitution, could declare that he and his predecessors had never been tyrants. By definition the king could not be a tyrant because by definition he reflected and was the ultimate culmination of the wishes and aspirations of his people. But in America that definition was now collapsing, for this government was not working, which made it "bad government," and it did not adhere to the law, which made it tyranny. Even the most apathetic Spanish American was bound to notice this contradiction between theory and practice because Spain and Spanish America had always worshiped the law.

Why were the royal authorities unable to build a new affection, a new or revived habit of obedience, on the basis of their military victories? The chief reason is that once Calleja and Abascal had made unalterable and immovable authoritarianism the foundation of royal power, authoritarianism had to be maintained. Any attempt by their successors to diversify the foundations of loyalty stood little chance of success. Once the iron fist was uncovered, any attempt to glove it would appear to be either hypocrisy or weakness; both would encourage further resistance. Authority, once corroded, can never be reestablished by force. It might, however, be maintained for an indefinite period of time by force, but that force had to be constant and unremitting, and such force would require resources Spain no longer had at its disposal. Over and over again the next viceroys appealed to Spain for troops and warships. One need only read the diary of Pezuela in Peru, as he daily assessed the chances of this or that expedition being gathered and making it to Lima, to witness an unparalleled exercise in frustration. And besides, peninsular Spanish intransigence toward any reform in the years 1816–21 paralyzed the several viceregal initiatives toward compromise that were attempted. American reform was still possible in this period if only because Spain once again controlled most of the territory of America. But if the liberals who wrote the constitution and governed Spain amid the chaos of 1808–14 were unwilling to accept the reforms in trade, taxation, and government proposed by their supposedly equal American colleagues in the Cortes, the councillors of the Indies who replaced them in 1814 were certainly even less well disposed. After 1820, when reform was once again feasible on Spain's part, it was too late on America's. Independence became the logical answer because either Spain refused to consider reform or its agents in America made a mockery of it.

Both Abascal and Calleja retired from their American viceroyalties in 1816, officially hailed as saviors, positively adored by conservatives, but despised by radical and moderate Americans alike. Calleja privately urged Spain to maintain the terror in Mexico, for it was the only means of completing the destruction of the rebels, and in letter after letter written in retirement, Abascal urged maintenance of every aspect of the absolutism in Peru. But the new viceroys never received this advice directly from their predecessors (neither Abascal nor Calleja left the usual detailed instructions to their successors that earlier viceroys wrote), and besides, as witnesses to the post-1808 Spain, neither of the new viceroys would have been inclined to take it. There was a certain time lag at work here in regard to successive viceroys' attitudes toward major political questions. One of the fundamental paradoxes of the wars of independence is that Abascal and Calleja, who governed during the first constitutional era, had left Spain to take up foreign assignments in the period before the traditions of absolutism had begun to collapse. Reform was to them inconceivable. But the viceroys who governed in the time of the restored post-1814 absolutism—Pezuela and Apodaca—had experienced the formative years of their careers during the Napoleonic struggle, when Spain changed at such a dizzying rate that reform became a way of life, indeed a necessity for defeat of the usurper. They were not, unlike their predecessors, terrified of reform, even if they did not actively seek it. Both "generations" were thus somewhat out of step with the politics they were required to enforce.

In New Spain, Juan Ruiz de Apodaca, a naval commander, former ambassador to London, and former captain general of Cuba, pursued a policy of limited military activity and widespread granting of amnesties to former rebels. He hoped to rebuild Mexico by making use of the military gains of his predecessor. Even in northern Europe, it was noted that Apodaca's policy was one of trying to regain American affection rather than one of government through fear. On several occasions Apodaca criticized Calleja for his "fire-and-sword" policy and his extraordinary special war taxes. Between 1816 and 1820, he repealed four fundamental taxes Calleja had created to meet the cost of the war—a property tax, a forced contribution based on incomes, a forced lottery (all three had been new and nearly revolutionary when first introduced), and a group of taxes on horses and carriages. Based on the assumption that Calleja had broken the back of rebel resistance, Apodaca's program was a conscious attempt to ingratiate himself to the Mexicans. But by sheer contrast it helped to weaken the public image of the regime, for, while Calleja had ended the military aspect of the insurrection, he had not quashed the desire for independence. It was a time of high intensity and great drama—no lull at all, as existing historiography would have it—for it would show whether a policy of reason could solidify the gains won by relentless force. It would show whether Spain still had a right to govern.

In Peru, Joaquín de la Pezuela, former commander of the army in Upper Peru, became viceroy. He, too, made only limited use of the militia and army his predecessor had built up, even though he was very close to the troops and staunchly defended their rights in every way, as for instance in his policy of giving them preference in civil employment. He, too, criticized his predecessor publicly and privately, in this case for Abascal's authoritarianism and his refusal to permit foreign traders to land on Peruvian shores. He, too, was more flexible, more concerned with establishing popular support than with maintaining the iron fist. As in Mexico, it was too late. Confidence could not be restored, and flexibility appeared to be weakness, encouraging dedicated rebels to hold out for another day, while the extreme Right chafed at what appeared to be viceregal inactivity. Both Pezuela and Apodaca got caught in this trap, and with identical results.

When the historian focuses on the chief agents of Spain rather than on the leading rebels or on the rebellion itself, one previously unnoted characteristic of the wars of independence begins to suggest itself. It may well be that 1816 was the true turning point in the movement, the point at which Spain's power had faltered beyond the ability of its agents to restore it. This was chiefly because those agents, and indeed most of the rebels, did not recognize that the loyalties of Americans could not necessarily be measured by which army controlled which territories. In 1816, royal armies were everywhere victorious. It may have been, therefore, a lull in the rebels' fortunes, but it was not a lull in the story of the deterioration of Spain's power, because those victories had come at an excessive price. To reconquer America had required destroying its haciendas, communications, factories, and even some of its cities. It led, on the one hand, to such privation that, as Calleja had predicted, the imperial system's ability to feed and house Americans was destroyed, and on the other, to a loss of confidence that the mere presentation by the rebels of an alternative to royal government could never have accomplished. As Bolívar said, Spain was reduced to an object of hatred, and its very victories accomplished that. The viceroys who took power in 1816 did not understand this, just as their predecessors had not realized that they themselves were doing it. To oversimplify, the equation would be this: in the years 1810–16, when America might have been saved for Spain by compromise and flexibility, it was governed by force and absolutism contrary to the fundamental laws; in the years 1816–21, when force and absolutism had become the only source of strength, America was governed by men who sought alternatives.

It may be protested that well over half the story has yet to be considered. What about the resurgence of the rebels, the victory of San Martín in Chile, the heroic gathering together of Bolívar's forces and the magnificent tale of their struggles, and the reappearance of rebellion in Mexico under the leadership of Iturbide? The reply is that, of course, that is the second and greater half of the story of how the rebels won, but it may perhaps be no more than the denouement, although with a few surprises, of how the Spanish lost. Precipitating agents were still required to begin the final process in each country, and they were not long in coming. In Peru it was economic confusion and disintegration, while in Mexico it was political confusion.

III

Pezuela's final crisis was the result of the overextension of Peru's resources that was already acute when he took office. The countdown began with the final loss of Chile in 1818 at the battle of Maipo. Pezuela's major preoccupation thereafter was his attempt to open Peru to free trade with Europe, North America, and Asia, an attempt that lost him the support of Peruvian merchants, the soldiers, and the homeland. A remarkable letter from Manuel Vidaurre, former minister of the Cuzco audiencia, clarifies the economic catastrophe that was sweeping Peru and that made Pezuela's commercial reforms necessary. Writing in 1817, Vidaurre told the king, quite simply, that the excessive harshness of the royal commanders in Peru was driving the population to prefer death. Endless oppression led to unwillingness or inability to work the land, and so to hunger. In Cuzco Province wheat was then selling for twenty-seven pesos the fanega, at La Paz it was forty pesos. Entire towns had died of hunger, he said. In Moquegua war taxes on its chief product,

brandy, had quadrupled its price; in La Paz war taxes on its chief product, coca, had quadrupled its price; in Lima war taxes on bread and
grains and real estate had the same effect; while the loss of the Chilean
wheat supply after 1817 forced the capital to depend on its own poor
and unpopulated countryside. "When a man has nothing," concluded
Vidaurre, "then he becomes a rebel, because in order to survive no other
recourse remains to him but a resort to arms." In May 1818, Pezuela
convoked a junta of prominent individuals to find new sources of revenue. He told them that they needed an additional 200,000 pesos immediately for urgent expenses and an additional 117,000 pesos every
month to cover deficits. This money had to come from foreign trade,
since no domestic sources remained, and so sudden an increase in customs revenues and indirect taxes from trade could only be accomplished
by throwing Lima open to every passing vessel no matter what its nationality.

That was the rub, for every time Pezuela asked Spain for permission to allow free trade, the consulado, the chief monopoly of Lima
merchants that controlled foreign trade, resisted, as did Spain itself. As
early as 1817, Pezuela was making occasional requests to Spain to allow
individual foreign ships to land at Lima. By 1819, he made a request for
total freedom of trade, even proposing regulations by which it would be
controlled, and in 1820 he repeated the request. In opposition, the consulado claimed that foreign trade, especially British, would destroy
Peru's industry and economy, while a report drafted by the former viceroy Abascal in Spain concurred, reminding the king that the English
never withdrew once they gained a foothold in foreign ports and that
their presence was always "very dangerous." On another occasion Abascal had declared that free trade "would be tantamount to decreeing the
separation of [America] from the mother country since, once direct trade
with foreigners was established . . . Spain would matter little to them."
The demand for free trade, indeed, had long been a chief objective of
the rebels. The consulado promised to make up the treasury deficits out
of its own funds, but failed to make good its promise. In 1820, the
crown promised to appoint a commission to study the matter, but meantime Pezuela allowed almost every foreign ship that presented itself to
enter and discharge its cargo at Callao and even at the lesser ports.

Thus Peruvians were presented with the extraordinary picture of
the representative of royal authority publicly proclaiming the necessity of
rejecting the commercial exclusiveness that had been the fundamental
principle of Spanish American economics and a major grievance of the

creoles, while a former viceroy and the chief merchants opposed it. We cannot resist the conclusion that Pezuela was right, but the nation's greatest economic powers put their own interests first. The old regime could not survive when the very corporations upon which royal power depended perceived their interests to be opposed by the royal power. In the economic sphere, too, the royal system was disproving itself. By July 1819, the royal troops in Lima were on half salary, and by mid-1820, Pezuela knew that San Martín and the Chilean government had an expedition of twenty-eight ships and four thousand men ready to embark for assault against Peru's coasts.

The net effect of this economic crisis was that, even before the San Martín expedition landed in Peru, Pezuela could predict its success. He wrote the peninsula in 1818 that there was little confidence in the royal government left, especially among the lower classes and troops of the militia. Between the rebel victory at Maipo and the arrival of San Martín's expedition in September 1820, Pezuela's government was thoroughly discredited, and through it, the royal regime as a whole. Agents from Peru later reported to the peninsula that "the personal opinion of everyone was that Peru was being lost, not through lack of means of defense, not through the superiority of the enemy, but through the wrong system and lack of skill of Joaquín de la Pezuela." The veteran royal army remained intact, however, and desperately wanted to confront the Chilean expedition after it landed at Pisco. In the face of what the army interpreted as Pezuela's refusal to strike against the rebels, nineteen of the chief officers garrisoned near Lima forced him to resign in January 1821. The officers chose Field Marshal José de la Serna, general in chief of the armies, to become new viceroy.

La Serna's regime could do nothing but depend on military force. The incomparably subtle and complex question of a people's rejecting their past heritage and choosing a new form of government was now reduced to the arbitrary question of which army would win at battle. If San Martín's forces had been stronger in 1821, La Serna would have been defeated quickly. In July 1821, the viceroy and the royal army abandoned Lima and fell back upon the ancient source of Peru's strength, the Andes. The weakness and confusion of the independent republic established at Lima guaranteed several more years of life to the royal power in the highlands. La Serna claimed on many occasions that his abandonment of Lima saved the rest of Peru and that the nation surely would have been lost if Pezuela had remained in command. But an army on the march was not the same thing as a royal government, and despite the valor and skill of La Serna and his commanders, the royal forces were defeated in battle by Bolívar's forces in 1824, completing the process of independence. The La Serna administration, then, should best be viewed as merely a "last-ditch stand," even though the combination of the rebels' military weakness and La Serna's inaccessibility in the high mountains permitted it to continue for four years. He might have been able to establish an enclave, but to retake the coast would have required the aid of massive reinforcements of peninsular troops and the reestablishment of Spanish naval control of the Pacific, both impossible, and would simply have constituted a military conquest anyhow.

In Mexico, Viceroy Apodaca took office in 1816. He was the most administratively skilled of the last viceroys, the most personable, and the most genuinely popular in his capital city, though as usual residents of other parts of the nation never saw him. He frequently spoke of his wife and five children, one of whom was blind. As a former ambassador, he was attuned to the importance of communication and sent monthly summary reports on the state of the kingdom to Spain. The index alone of his letters and reports in office runs to sixty volumes. Undoubtedly his most striking characteristic was his optimism and his belief that the righteousness and truth of the royal cause would prevail over the leaderless bandits who now made up the remnants of the radical revolutionaries. He never foresaw the possibility that his government would ultimately be destroyed not by the Left but by the Right. This was not necessarily naiveté, for his optimism was the natural result of his predecessor Calleja's very success at driving the rebellion underground, where not being apparent, it was more subtle, less easy to combat, and more likely to manifest itself later from a different quarter, since its earlier loci had been disrupted. When the constitution was reinstated in 1820, Apodaca appeared to make a genuine effort to implement it. In a sense he had no choice in the matter, but unlike his predecessors he did not attempt, until it was too late, to intervene in and control the operations of the constitutional system. Elections were held regularly and without intervention, while freedom of the press was implemented for one full year, until after the Iturbide uprising began. Apodaca reported to the Cortes that he thought the reimposition of the constitution had caused no unrest whatsoever in Mexico.

But it was the constitution, in fact, that ultimately destroyed Spanish authority in Mexico, not by provoking a counterrevolution, as is sometimes alleged, but by proving to Mexicans the invalidity of the imperial ethos. The stunning royal decree of April 11, 1820, in which Ferdinand

VII apologized to the American kingdoms for his error in annulling the constitution in 1814 and declared that the ancient absolutism was wrong, while begging dissidents to remember that "errors [in judgment] are not crimes," gave the final lie to the "tribal myths" that had permitted the Spanish system to function and around which Calleja had anchored his restoration of royal power. If the throne was not sacred, if it could give in so easily to internal revolt and overthrow the fundamental law to replace it with what in 1820 was Europe's most radical government, then nothing really stood in the way of an intellectual and philosophical acceptance of independence. This is exactly what was implied in a remarkable report to the peninsula from the councillor of the audiencia, José Hipólito Odoardo, in October 1820. Odoardo reported that the Cortes's radical legislation directed at restricting the power of the church, the military, and the aristocracy throughout the empire had in only seven months completely redirected the loyalties of Mexicans, so that he could predict that some new uprising was imminent, though he could not foresee from which direction it would come, and that it would be successful in overthrowing the royal regime. The viceroy himself received a similar prediction from the city councillor Francisco Manuel Sánchez de Tagle in January 1821. The long-expected overt threat to royal dominion finally came from Agustín Iturbide, a disaffected royal officer, who in early 1821 proclaimed an uprising that, because it represented a compromise of the wishes of both upper and middle class, immediately gained the support of the elite and amnestied rebels alike. In a most unusual twist of Spanish American history, the viceroy now represented reform, while the insurgents represented a much more moderate program that threatened no one's status or wealth, but simultaneously achieved national self-determination. Iturbide knew that a confused royal government that had contradicted its own principles could not survive. He told the viceroy, "Is there anyone who can undo the opinion of an entire kingdom? . . . Any country is free that wants to be free."

Apodaca had never dreamed of such a threat, and in the face of it he had no defenses whatsoever. When he announced the uprising to Spain, he admitted that "this unexpected event has filled the capital with as much surprise and consternation as it has me." He warned that Iturbide was very dangerous because of his long association with chief officers and the creole elite and because his program of independence—the Plan of Iguala—would inevitably "seduce" many of the wealthy, while it was equally attractive to genuine rebels. It is almost incredible that Apodaca's only reply to Iturbide's treason was to offer him amnesty. By May 1821,

Apodaca reported that most of the troops and many officers had already deserted and that the kingdom was on the verge of being lost. As in Peru, royal authority had been defunct since 1816 and the viceroy's apparent paralysis and inability to get his orders obeyed led the small group of die-hard veteran army officers to view him as dispensable. Consequently, in an almost exact replay of the Peruvian incident, on July 5, 1821, Apodaca was forced to resign by his officers and was replaced by a field marshal, Francisco Novella. Iturbide's control of the nation was too far advanced, however, to permit Novella to retrench on some interior location as La Serna did in Peru, and independence triumphed only two months later. It was natural, for Iturbide genuinely embodied at that moment the wishes of the nation; he possessed, in other words, the genuine authority.

In a poignant letter describing these events after he fled to Cuba, Apodaca wrote, "I had a feeling of presentiment about this misfortune in the middle of last year, 1820, but not about the terms in which it would come about or the means by which it would be effected, because they are so extraordinary that it was not possible for anyone to imagine them." This was his confession that he had sensed the loss of authority that we have traced here, but had not grasped its significance or understood it. There is no indication that any other royalist ever did either, except perhaps Abascal, who had recognized as early as 1808 that there was some indefinable core, some not quite explicable or demonstrable principle that was in danger of being lost if he gave the slightest hint of weakening his grip over all aspects of his country, and Calleja, who by 1816 knew it was already lost. That principle was Spanish authority. Once weakened, no amount of effort could have preserved the political and social institutions that were based on it.

IV

The inability to recognize that Spain's authority in America had disintegrated continued to characterize the former royal magistrates for years afterward. They never quite accepted the fact that an event so unthinkable in 1810 had come to pass only a decade later. This lack of acceptance is part of the reason for Spain's unnecessarily long refusal to recognize the independence of its former colonies. Spain continued to imagine that some sort of restoration was possible. Significantly, two former viceroys, Venegas and Apodaca, were members of the Spanish council of state that in 1828 was still debating methods by which to "pacify" the "rebellious American provinces." Indeed Spain as a whole never quite grasped what had happened until the unforeseen shocks of 1898 made its intellectuals and philosophers aware, with great pain be it remembered, that not only did they not possess a great empire, but they possessed no empire. For a nation to have the things in which it genuinely believes proved to be irrelevant, at least to the outsiders it thought it was convincing, is a terrible discovery. Before we scorn Spain for its quijotismo in this regard (and this is also a part of the Black Legend about Spain), we should remember that every other imperialist power has suffered the same delusion. The very things that make imperialism possible—the combination of a once undeniably functional economic, governmental, and philosophical system with the missionary zeal and self-righteousness that derive from delusions of divine inspiration—guarantee that imperialists will never understand why subject peoples reject their political dominion.

The greatest loss involved in the disintegration of Spanish authority in America, however, was that the independent states had no unanimously accepted authority to take its place. This was a result of the fact that when Spanish America found royal authority irrelevant—not just wrong or misguided but actually irrelevant, no longer suited to its conditions—then it also found the tradition upon which that authority was based irrevelant, at least insofar as it directly involved the political institutions. That part, at least, Spain had predicted. When the Cortes sent peace commissioners to South America in 1822 to negotiate truces and perhaps even settlements with the insurgents in Peru, Río de la Plata, and New Granada, the commissioners carried a set of secret instructions reminding them to tell Americans that independence would mean chaos, factionalism, political discord, and the loss of individual freedoms that the Cortes said its own constitution would guarantee. The chief problem America now faced, the commissioners were informed, was an absence of authority, for authority had been replaced by "a thirst for power, which is what constitutes the overseas insurrection thus far." In all the newly independent or almost independent states, Madrid promised, the lack of authority "has to produce terrifying evils." It was a fit last word of paternal advice, though no one listened.

Spain lost America because it lost its ability to prove its right to sovereignty, its ability to convince. In politics, economics, and religion it became irrelevant. The crown, the king, his agents, and Spaniards themselves were no longer perceived to be necessary. The decadence of Charles IV and Ferdinand VII, the father's forced abdication, the son's detention in France, the Napoleonic conquest, the emergence of self-made government in the regency and Cortes, and the constitution, all these did more to weaken Spanish authority, to make it—or prove it—false, than did all the rebels in America, for these events contradicted and disproved the values upon which the state was built. The forces arrayed against the Spanish empire in America were mighty, but the most decisive of those forces were those that came from within, not from without.

At the center of this dilemma were the wartime viceroys, the men who bore the obligation of preserving Spanish power even as Spain changed so rapidly that the foundations upon which they attempted to anchor that power disappeared. In the only response they could conceive of to the undeniable threat posed by the outbreak of insurrection, Abascal in Peru and Venegas and especially Calleja in Mexico geared their governments, their armies, and their supporters to a do-or-die struggle between absolutism, untouched by any serious consideration of the possibility of reform, and rebellion. But this viceregal despotism occurred at the very moment that Spain claimed to be dedicated to reform. This authoritarianism converted the delicate strands of loyalty, faith in the monarch, and sense of brotherhood of all Spaniards into tyrannical government by foreigners over Americans. It enhanced the desire for independence. Then Apodaca in Mexico and Pezuela in Peru, not recognizing they were now the agents of tyranny, lost the military gains of their predecessors through confusion and a well-intentioned attempt to diversify the foundations of a system that had become dependent upon military force. Ultimately in Peru, La Serna's government that was no government held out in the mountains, protected until 1824 by the disorganization of its enemies. The viceroys could only operate on the understandings of politics and sovereignty that they possessed, of course. But since they were the living symbols of the dominion and majesty of Spain, they were also the living symbols of its confusion and, therefore, the agents by which it proved itself irrelevant to America.

American cries against the tyranny of Spain, which in 1810 were the product of a lack of restraint and propagandistic enthusiasm, became true and deeply felt by 1820 because the viceroys converted a system that was merely aged and in rare instances actually decrepit into genuine tyranny. What is perhaps worse, having done so they could not sustain it, proving to Americans the invalidity of their possession of power.

My contention, then, contradictory though it may appear, is that the wartime viceroys were one of the active forces that led Americans to reject their ancient imperial heritage, while at the same time they are the historiographical victims of that rejection. At the very least they were not the bloody-minded nonpersons of much of Spanish American historiography. At the most, they came close to preserving Spain's control of America. No one can read Calleja's candid letters to Spain and fail to recognize in him a political and military genius desperately struggling with a disintegrating situation. No one can read Pezuela's *diario* ("journal") and fail to notice his genuine concern for Peru or the personal agonies he endured when he learned the news of Maipo, or heard of the loss of his son aboard the *María Isabel* captured by the Chilean navy, or of the death of his son-in-law Mariano Osorio in Cuba on his way home to Spain in a desperate attempt to explain the failure to reconquer Chile. We have too long concentrated on Abascal's mundane accomplishments—the Lima surgical college, the royal cemetery—at the expense of his greatest one—the preservation of Peru in the face of revolution from all sides. We have only recently begun to treat of Venegas in studies of Hidalgo. We have never credited Apodaca with the rationality and administrative skill that his contemporaries greeted with sighs of relief. La Serna was the man who for four years fought so heroically that his conqueror Antonio José de Sucre treated him with genuine respect and felt real sadness at his personal humiliation at Ayacucho. Having recognized the viceroys to be well worth study, we can begin to become aware of the complexity of their impact on independence.

Suggested Further Reading

Anna, Timothy E. "Economic Causes of San Martín's Failure in Lima." *Hispanic American Historical Review* 54:4 (November 1974).

Archer, Christon I. "The Army of New Spain and the Wars of Independence, 1790–1821." *Hispanic American Historical Review* 61:4 (November 1981).

Domínguez, Jorge I. *Insurrection or Loyalty: The Breakdown of the Spanish American Empire*. Cambridge, Mass., 1980.

Fehrenbach, Charles Wentz. "Moderados and Exaltados: The Liberal Opposition to Ferdinand VII, 1814–1823." *Hispanic American Historical Review* 50:1 (February 1970).

Fisher, John. "Royalism, Regionalism, and Rebellion in Peru, 1808–1815." *Hispanic American Historical Review* 59:2 (May 1979).

Gilmore, Robert L. "The Imperial Crisis, Rebellion, and the Viceroy: Nueva Granada in 1809." *Hispanic American Historical Review* 40:1 (February 1960).

Hamill, Hugh M., Jr. "Royalist Propaganda and *La Porción Humilde del Pueblo* during Mexican Independence." *The Americas* 36:4 (April 1980).

Hamnett, Brian R. "Royalist Counterinsurgency and the Continuity of Rebellion: Guanajuato and Michoacán, 1813–20." *Hispanic American Historical Review* 62:1 (February 1982).

Lynch, John. *The Spanish American Revolutions, 1808–1826.* New York, 1973.

Reid, Paul Joseph. "The Constitution of Cádiz and the Independence of Yucatán." *The Americas* 36:1 (July 1979).

Woodward, Margaret L. "The Spanish Army and the Loss of America, 1810–1824." *Hispanic American Historical Review* 48:4 (November 1968).

19 ❂

Nationality, Nationalism, and Supranationalism in the Writings of Simón Bolívar

SIMON COLLIER

Any new discussion of more or less any feature of Simón Bolívar's life or thought runs the inevitable risk of covering ground whose most intimate topography has long since been scrutinized with care by generations of scholars. So self-evidently important was the Liberator's career to the course of Latin American history—and no invocation of "structures," or "conjunctures," or even "vast impersonal forces" can really diminish that importance—that legions of historians, good and bad, have devoted themselves with wholehearted passion to the reconstruction of its every detail. In the case of Spanish American writers, patriotic *pietas* has produced some memorable scholarship as well as examples of exaggerated hero-worship or tedious *detallismo*. The effort has been prodigious.

What, in fact, is there really left to say about Bolívar? The commemoration of his bicentenary offers an opportunity to reexamine some of the main themes of his career and to probe, through a perusal of his copious writings, the more persistent fixed ideas that exercised his extraordinarily vigorous mind. That it *was* an unusual mind—forcefully imaginative as well as acutely perceptive—is beyond dispute. Daniel O'Leary believed that "the force and activity of his imagination tormented him."[1] Even Salvador de Madariaga, a by no means sympathetic biographer, admits the quality of "supreme intelligence" to be found in Bolívar's prolific correspondence.[2] This is not to say, however, that

1 R. A. Humphreys, ed. The *"Detached Recollections" of General D. F. O'Leary* (London, 1969), p. 11.
2 Salvador de Madariaga, *Bolívar* (London, 1952), p. 472.

Published originally in the *Hispanic American Historical Review*, 63:1 (February 1983).

Bolívar was a systematic thinker: his writings, the great bulk of which were in epistolary form, reflect brilliant intuitions rather than deeply elaborate theoretical constructions. This is certainly the case with his views on the focus of this present essay, incipient nationalism and supra-nationalism. This topic was, of course, but one aspect of Bolívar's political thought, other features of which tended to be set out in more organized form in his writings.

It borders on the platitudinous, no doubt, to say that any anticolonial movement must ipso facto base its claims on the principle of preexisting (or at least potential) *nationality*. Without recourse to some such principle, the very demand for independence is a logical absurdity. The Spanish American revolutionaries of the wars of independence, by styling themselves "patriots," were well aware of this. National independence, however, is invariably influenced by its timing in history, not least in the sphere of ideological influences, foreign models of national organization, and so on. The breakdown of the Spanish American empire occurred at a time when discernibly "modern" types of nationalism were becoming established in Europe, and soon after the thirteen English colonies of North America had given striking proof that it was possible to *create* a new national polity out of an anticolonial struggle.

The modern European nation-state, as Heinz Lubasz reminds us, emerged "in the same area and during the same period as did modern capitalism, modern science and philosophy, and that specifically modern form of Christianity, Protestantism."[3] From this viewpoint, the emergence of new nation-states in Latin America was bound to be somewhat problematic; none of the phenomena mentioned by Lubasz was especially prominent in the Latin America of 1810. This does not mean, of course, that the Spanish colonial era had not laid the basis for independent nationhood *of a kind*. The geographical distribution (and isolation) of the main nuclei of Spanish settlement, the stubborn Hispanic propensity to localism (or "cantonalism," as it has sometimes been called), and, in the closing decades of empire, the reception of Enlightenment thought and the ideas of the United States and French revolutions—all these have been seen by most scholars as having contributed not merely to the gestation of independence itself, but also to the crystallization of a series of new Spanish American nationalities in its aftermath. These were certainly less than fully fledged.

The precise way in which incipient nationalism developed in later

3 Heinz Lubasz, *The Development of the Modern State* (New York, 1964), pp. 1–2.

colonial times undoubtedly merits closer study than it has so far received, but there is every reason to doubt that awareness of potential nationality was widely generalized among the colonial population. In his valuable assessment of the late colonial scene, John Lynch is surely correct in assuming that "in so far as there was a [potential] nation, it was a creole nation,"[4] and that the Indians, Blacks, and mixed castes who made up the vast majority of Latin Americans at that period did not share a real sense of belonging to it. Even among creoles, it has to be added, there is no reason whatever to suppose that the promoters of independence were more than a minority in 1810; the record of the wars of independence themselves is entirely eloquent in this respect. The ideal of separate nationhood spread, to be sure, as the struggle unfolded; few would claim that it was dominant or in any sense universal at the outset.

Thus, Bolívar and his associates were always conscious, during their campaigns, of the importance of "opinion," the strength of which, as Bolívar himself pointed out in the Jamaica Letter, had held the Spanish empire together for so long. Nationalism (and it is an important point to remember) was not, therefore, a "natural" development in Spanish America in the way it may have been in Europe; it had to be induced, nurtured, fostered. "The opinion of America," wrote Bolívar in the dark hours of 1815, "is still not settled; although all thinking people are for independence, the general mass still remains ignorant of its rights and interests." It was, in fact, the tenacity and heroism of the liberators, combined with the counterproductive policies of Spain after 1814, that finally persuaded the bulk of creole opinion to favor separate nationhood as the best course, after which the apparatus of nationality (flags, coats of arms, national anthems, and so forth) was adopted with alacrity throughout Spanish America.

The precise form the new nations were to take, how many of them there were to be, and whether the shattered unity of imperial times could be reconstructed on some new national or supranational basis—these questions were never far from Bolívar's mind and constitute an important dimension in his thought. He was not the only creole who pondered such matters. In some ways, his ideas can be seen to have reflected a fairly standard creole viewpoint, while in others the reach of his brilliant mind far exceeded the unique grasp on affairs which he enjoyed as the supreme actor in the great drama of independence. It is to an examination of Bolívar's principal ideas on these topics—with reference wherever

4 John Lynch, *The Spanish American Revolutions 1808–1826* (New York, 1973), p. 25.

possible to his own words—that the present article is devoted. Let us first see whether it is possible to identify his attitude toward the question of nationality and the form his own nationalism took.

Bolivarian Nationalism

"Legislators!"—Bolívar is addressing (on paper anyway) the founding fathers of Bolivia in 1826—"On seeing the new Bolivian Nation proclaimed, what generous and sublime considerations must fill your souls!" The note is entirely typical. Bolívar never doubted that the purpose of independence was the creation of new nations, or that this was an implicitly noble cause in itself. Both in the Jamaica Letter and in the Angostura Address (the two classic documents of the Bolivarian corpus) he drew his famous, if not altogether accurate, parallel between the breakdown of Spain's American empire and the fall of Rome, and the consequential rise, in both cases, of successor-nations. Thus the automatic framework for Spanish America's postrevolutionary political systems (to whose shape and form, as we know, he devoted much of his most coherent political thought) was to be the *nation-state*. The concept makes an inevitably frequent appearance in Bolivarian rhetoric. In Caracas, at the conclusion of the Campaña Admirable in 1813, he proclaimed that the states of Venezuela were "once again free and independent, and raised once more to the rank of Nation." New Granada, he announced in 1815, "appears before the world in the majestic attitude of a nation." In the difficult months of Haitian exile, he never lost sight of this goal. "Let us form a *patria* at any cost," he wrote to Luis Brion, "and everything else will be tolerable." With patriot armies once again in the field, he declared that peace with Spain could only be achieved if Spain recognized Venezuela as "a Free, Independent and Sovereign Nation." To cite further examples would be to labor an obvious point unnecessarily. After 1819, as we shall see, Bolívar transferred his fundamental national allegiance to the newly created republic of Colombia— "this nascent nation," as he described it in 1821. He accepted, and indeed assumed, that other sections of the dissolving Spanish empire were passing through transitions to nationhood similar to those in which he himself was engaged. Peru, so he flattered San Martín in 1821, was "the third *patria* which owes its existence to you." And to Bernardo O'Higgins in distant Chile he wrote: "You are the man to whom that beautiful nation will owe, to remotest posterity, its political creation."

Allegiance to, and positive affection for, the nation was, for Bolívar, the indispensable concomitant of the true citizen's obedience to the institutions of the state. As he said at Angostura, "a national spirit is required as the basis for a stable government." Indeed, the *patria* had a natural claim on its inhabitants: fulfillment of "the duty of loving their *patria*," he claimed in 1813, was the reason why Venezuelans were being persecuted by Spaniards. In an often quoted letter to General Santa Cruz (October 1826) Bolívar expressed this patriotic faith in lyrical tones: "our native soil . . . arouses tender feelings and delightful memories; it was the setting of our innocence and first loves, of our first sensations and of everything that has made us. What claims on love and dedication could be greater?" In 1817, writing to friends who were living in exile, the Liberator urged: "Come, dear friends, and die for your country or at least die *in* it. . . . I tell you . . . it is preferable to live for the *patria*, even in chains, than to exist in sad inactivity outside it." Occasionally, Bolívar was spurred to indignation when the patriotic enthusiasm of his followers was impugned. When, in 1818, the United States agent in Venezuela took an evidently flippant attitude toward certain minor operations of the patriot army, he was stiffly reproved: "These enterprises," wrote Bolívar, "were guided by love of the *patria* and of glory; far from being laughable, they merit the admiration and applause of all who have a *patria* and who love their liberty." The sincerity of Bolívar's patriotism can never be doubted. He himself set the best of possible examples.

It would be fruitless to search for a concise, academic definition of nationality in Bolívar's writings; he was not that kind of thinker. Possibly the closest he came to providing such a definition (though indirectly) was in a proclamation to his fellow Venezuelans in 1818: "You are all Venezuelans, children of the same *patria*, members of the same society, citizens of the same Republic." There is a sense, in my view, in which terms such as "nation," *"patria,"* "state," and "republic" were almost, if not quite, interchangeable in the Liberator's various pronouncements; he himself rarely if ever drew distinctions between such concepts. Aside from its semiautomatic acceptance of the inescapable criteria of birth and geography, Bolivarian nationalism cannot easily be viewed as a narrow or exclusive conception; it was not tied to closely defined ethnic, cultural, linguistic, or religious moorings. The proclamation of *guerra a muerte* in 1813, or Bolívar's resonant statement two years later that "No American can be my enemy even when fighting against me under the banners of tyrants," might seem to be clear evidence to the contrary; and plainly all his pronouncements have to be judged against the background of shifting tactical circumstances. But the general drift of his ideas is in a quite opposite direction. "For us," he declared in 1821, "all are Colombians; even our invaders, when they so wish. . . ." The ultimate criterion of nationality expressed here is, in fact, political in nature. Thus, Spaniards who accepted the revolution were welcomed as, in effect, new nationals. "If you want to be Colombians, you shall be Colombians," Bolívar told the Spaniards of Pasto in 1822, "because we want brothers who will increase our family." Defecting Spaniards such as General Mariano Renovales were urged to attract other, like-minded Spanish officers "who might wish to adopt a free *patria* in the American hemisphere." The net was spread even wider than this. As early as 1813 Bolívar issued a general invitation to foreigners to settle in Venezuela, and declared that any foreigner who fought for the country's freedom would automatically acquire citizenship. (In general, and although this does not form a conspicuous strand in his thought, he was enthusiastically in favor of immigration.) Nationality, in short, was open to all who accepted certain political principles. "For a man of honor there can only be one *patria*—and that is where citizens' rights are protected and the sacred character of humanity respected. Ours is the mother of all free and just men, without discrimination as to background or condition." It might be observed here, in passing, that the language used in this context is revealing in its own right. Bolívar's standard metaphor (insofar as he had one) for the nation-as-collection-of-people was the family, the nation-as-abstraction being assigned definitely maternal qualities. "This is the Republic of Colombia," he proclaimed in 1821; "without doubt she will find a place in your hearts, . . . for she is Mother, and all are her children." "Colombia will be a tender mother to you," he informed the recalcitrant Pastusos in 1822. (He also told the Pastusos that he himself would be their father.)

The absence of a genuine ethnic or cultural dimension in Bolivarian nationalism is perhaps worth underlining. In Europe, this dimension developed fairly steadily during the nineteenth century. The characteristic nationalism of America—North as well as South—was altogether more open and flexible. Bolívar was naturally (and sometimes uneasily) aware of the ethnic mixture that underlay Latin American life, and even suggested, in his Angostura speech, that a continuing dose of miscegenation was desirable for the future: "our fathers [are] different in their origin and blood, . . . and their skins differ visibly. . . . The blood of our citizens varies; let us mix it in order to unite it." Yet there is no suggestion, in this hint of a future *raza cósmica,* that race of itself is a necessary badge of national identity. Ethnicity was in no sense the touchstone of nationality; other factors, especially political factors, counted, too. Moreover, Bolívar never really speculated at any length, as he might have done, and as later nationalists (notably in Europe) *were* to do, on distinctions of national character. In the heat of battle, to be sure, he could refer to "the magnanimous character of our nation," or to "the natural ferocity of the Spanish character," but these were rhetorical flourishes rather than analytical comments. Spaniards, he told Santander in 1824, were "stubborn for tyranny and injustice, without possessing these qualities in support of liberal principles." It is interesting, here, to see how political considerations dominate an observation, however indirect, on "national character."

When it came to the emerging nations of America, Bolívar had little to say in this connection. The famous conspectus contained in the Jamaica Letter, for instance, is almost silent on the subject. It refers to "the character of the Mexicans" but nowhere explains what this actually is. Indeed, Bolívar's assessment of the likely prospects of the different states of America is based entirely on social, political, or geographical factors—Chile's isolation, for example, or Peru's potential corruption by "gold and slaves." Bolívar's most devastating generalizations about "national character" are applied to Spanish America as a whole, are often colorfully pejorative, and invariably reflect an extremely jaundiced view of the colonial past:

> Our being has the most impure of origins: everything that preceded us is covered with the black mantle of crime. We are the abominable product of those predatory tigers who came to America to shed its blood and to interbreed with their victims before sacrificing them—afterward mixing the dubious fruit of such unions with the offspring of slaves uprooted from Africa.

Those few historians who have studied the incipient creole nationalism of the independence period tend to see certain common features as manifesting themselves throughout Spanish America. The Chilean scholar Gonzalo Vial, in an interesting survey, notes three characteristics as cardinal: patriotic pride; the idealized exaltation of the Indian background as a suitable patriotic myth; and an emphasis on divisions between (and sometimes within) the new nations—a resurgence of traditional "cantonalism" accompanying the thrust toward national freedom. The Mexican historian Luis González y González (confining himself to his own country's independence, though the phenomenon is certainly to be found more universally) has identified a further feature, which he labels "nationalist optimism": visions of a bright future, based on optimistic (perhaps overly optimistic) assessments of national potential in certain late colonial writings.

Bolívar's high valuation of patriotism has already been sufficiently illustrated; but he does not conform to Vial's scheme in other respects. He does not seem to have shared, to any marked extent, other creoles' mythicization of the Amerindian tradition. In part, no doubt, this can be accounted for by the absence of a "usable" Indian past in his native Venezuela. It was easier for Mexican intellectuals to glory in the Aztec record, or for their counterparts in Chile to pay homage to Araucanian resistance to Iberian oppression. Venezuela had had neither Aztecs nor Araucanians. Bolívar's vision of Indians, past or present, tended to be rather stereotyped; no serious analysis of Indian problems, no serious understanding of Indian culture, is to be found in his writings. "The Indian," he wrote in 1815 "is of so tranquil a character that all he desires is repose and solitude"—hardly a remark that betrayed a close acquaintance with the real world of Indians. Though he was moved to pity by the condition of the indigenous population of the Andes, his reaction to the Inca ruins he saw on his triumphant passage through the Peruvian highlands in 1825 was strangely literary, in the manner of the "enlightened" eighteenth century: "Everything here inspires in me high ideas and profound thoughts; . . . the monuments of stone, the grand, straight highways, the innocent customs and genuine tradition, give us witness of a social creation of which we can have no idea, no model, no copy. Peru is original in the annals of man."

Nationalist optimism, however, *was* very clearly a part of Bolívar's outlook. Expressions of this in his writings are not hard to find. In the Jamaica Letter, for instance, he wrote that once freedom was attained, "we will follow a majestic course toward the great prosperity for which South America is destined." With the foundations of Colombia, he proclaimed, New Granada was summoned "to a greatness and dignity which the most brilliant imagination can scarcely perceive." And for San Martín's benefit he sketched the "remotest centuries" when Spanish America was to see "free and happy generations overwhelmed by all the gifts which heaven bestows on earth." Undoubtedly, however, the most eloquent exposition of this theme occurs in the magnificent peroration of the Angostura Address, with its lyrically imaginative retrospect from far ahead in time, with its superbly evoked glimpse of Colombia in futurity as "the center and emporium of the human family, . . . seated on the

Throne of Liberty, clasping the scepter of Justice, crowned with Glory, displaying to the Old World the majesty of the New." It is clear, however, that pronouncements such as these were more a feature of the Liberator's ascendant phase than of his later years. Somber forebodings were soon enough to replace the sanguine hopefulness of the Angostura peroration; in fact, they were never entirely absent in this earlier period. Yet the Liberator's final disillusionment, enhanced as it was by political failure and advancing sickness, should never be taken as wholly representative of his views.

In terms of those fissiparous tendencies, which Gonzalo Vial sees as fundamental to the new creole nationalism, Bolívar's stance differed notably from that of most of his contemporaries: he vehemently opposed such tendencies. His early experience, in Venezuela's First Republic and more clearly still in New Granada during the so-called Patria Boba, gave him the most adamantine of all his political opinions. "Unity, Unity, Unity should be our motto," he said at Angostura—a sentence that might well stand as the leitmotiv of his political thought.

Strongly reacting to the "federalism" that had ruined the early politics of Venezuela and New Granada, he made the creation of strong, centralist institutions the keynote of his distinctive approach to constitutional questions. But Bolívar was well aware (and became increasingly aware) of the sheer strength of regionalism in Spanish America. He accepted that each of the new nations had its own local susceptibilities and that it was ultimately impossible to override these. The point was one he came to appreciate with particular force when he left the more or less familiar terrain of Colombia and ventured into the more ambiguous lands of the South. When he told the Peruvian Congress in 1825 "I am a foreigner," he was speaking from uncomfortable experience; his earliest days in Peru had taught him that "this is not Colombia, and I am not a Peruvian." The swiftness with which he acquiesced in the formation of Bolivia was in part due to a correct perception of the strength of local feelings; the Upper Peruvian provinces simply did "not wish to be Peruvian or Argentine." Back in Venezuela in 1827, addressing himself to the problem of how long Sucre should continue as president of Bolivia, he advised: "In your position, I would not stay on in the South, for in the long term we will always have the defect of being Venezuelans, just as we were Colombians in Peru." Newly crystallizing national sentiment (even if it was crystallizing in a relatively small segment of the population) was, therefore, something to be reckoned with; it could not easily be forgotten or ignored.

As to the political boundaries of the new nation-states, Bolívar's ideas were logical and pragmatic; they were to be "the limits of the former viceroyalties, captaincies-general, and presidencies." The practical application of this principle—the principle later known as *uti possidetis, ita possideatis*—sometimes conflicted with the doctrine of popular sovereignty to which Bolívar consistently appealed in his general political philosophy. This is illustrated in the well-known cases of the annexation of Guayaquil and the creation of Bolivia. The port of Guayaquil, as part of the presidency of Quito, had been attached to the old Viceroyalty of New Granada, the territorial basis for the new nation of Colombia. Irrespective of the wishes of its inhabitants—who might conceivably have preferred affiliation with Peru or even the independence they had acquired in 1820—Guayaquil had to become Colombian: "a city on a river cannot form a nation," wrote Bolívar. "Quito cannot exist without the port. . . . Tumbes is the border with Peru, and in consequence nature has given us Guayaquil. . . . Anyway," he added candidly, "politics and war have their own laws." Upper Peru, the future Bolivia, presented a similar problem. Historically the province had been dependent since 1776 on the Viceroyalty of the River Plate; its creole elite now wanted separate nationhood. Bolívar, at least for a time, and maybe not altogether sincerely, expressed aversion to allowing a new republic to form, thought that Upper Peru's position exactly paralleled Quito's, and told Sucre, the prime mover in the affair, that he had no wish to give the Argentines the impression of "interference in their *national business.*" In other words, he did not wish to break the territorial rule he had previously enunciated so clearly.

Yet while Bolívar certainly accepted the emergence of a series of nation-states from the wreck of the Spanish empire, it seems equally clear that he did not regard this as something wholly fixed, in all its details, by nature or historical precedent. Human will—his own not least—could, he felt, play a part in determining the eventual political shape of postcolonial Spanish America. In his own region, northern South America, he succeeded in fusing three potentially (and in the end actual) national units into what he hoped would become the new nation of Colombia. And over and above this, he ardently and sincerely hoped for a measure of political association among the newly independent nations of the area. In other words, his ideals went well beyond the sphere of nationalism pure and simple, and well into the sphere of what has come to be termed "supranationalism." Three distinctive ideas dominate the record here: (1) what might be called Bolívar's maximal supranationalist

position, embracing a vast concept of subcontinental federation or confederation; (2) the "middle-range" supranationalism implicit in the short-
lived scheme of 1826 to federate or unite the three principal republics
of the Andes; and (3) the one attempt at supranational fusion which
was translated, albeit briefly, into some sort of reality—the Colombian
experiment. Each of these schemes merits an examination, for while
Bolivarian nationalism was in some ways no more than a reflection of
the common creole nationalism of the period, Bolivarian supranationalism places the Liberator in a very select company, and in territory to
which most creoles were not, in the end, prepared to follow him.

Maximal Supranationalism

In the opinion of Gerhard Masur, "continentalism was more important
than nationalism in Bolívar's ideological make-up."[5] For John J. Johnson, "Bolívar was an American first and a Venezuelan second."[6] Even
accepting the Liberator's frequent expressions of affection for his native
land (which he clearly regarded as a nation from 1810 to 1819 and as
part of a larger national unit from 1819 to 1830), it is not difficult to
concur in these well-considered judgments. Nationalism, for Bolívar, was
never enough. Indeed, his well-known supranationalist stance has given
him a definite position of prominence as one of the pioneers of "inter-
Americanism," Latin American "solidarity," and even internationalism
more universally. The regular invocation of his name is a sine qua non
at ceremonial meetings of the Western Hemisphere republics. It is important, therefore, to disentangle historical truth from pious myth. What,
in fact, were Bolívar's main ideas? As we have seen, he accepted the fact
that various new nation-states were forming in postcolonial Latin America. In the Jamaica Letter, he explicitly repudiated the idea that the New
World could become "a single nation" on the logical enough grounds
that "different situations, opposed interests, dissimilar characters" were
simply too strong.

An underlying impulse toward unity, however, even at this ultimate
level, sometimes found expression in his writings. In 1815, for instance,
he expressed the hope—admittedly a somewhat vague hope—that "the
universal link of love should bind together the children of Columbus's
hemisphere," while in his first communications with the distant revolu-

5 Gerhard Masur, *Nationalism in Latin America* (New York, 1966), p. 26.
6 John J. Johnson, *Simón Bolívar and Spanish American Independence: 1783–
1830* (Princeton, 1968), p. 68.

tionaries of the River Plate he was more definite. In a message to the Argentine people in 1818, he indicated that, once victory was won, Venezuela would invite them "into a single society, so that our motto may be *Unity* in South America." To Juan Martín de Pueyrredón, their leader, he wrote:

> Americans should have but a single *patria* . . . ; for our part, we shall hasten . . . to initiate the American pact, which, by forming a single body of all our republics, will reveal America to the world in an aspect of majesty and greatness unexampled among older nations. United in this way, America . . . will be able to call herself the queen of nations and the mother of republics.

This was not a unique inspiration. Writing to O'Higgins in rather similar vein in January 1822, Bolívar referred to "the social pact which must form, in this hemisphere, a nation of republics." Separating meaning from rhetoric in such utterances is, obviously, rather difficult, but such words can hardly be taken as implying anything other than some kind of vision of ultimate Spanish American unity. Was this, perhaps, nationalist optimism transposed to a continental scale?

Whatever the nature of this vision (and quite how far it went is impossible to divine from the evidence), Bolívar was peculiarly emphatic that some form of close association between the new nations was both desirable and essential. Here we come to another of his great fixed ideas. "From the very beginning of the revolution," he claimed in 1826, "I have known that if ever we came to form nations in South America, federation would be the strongest link which could unite them." This claim was certainly correct: it has been plausibly argued that the roots of Americanism for Bolívar, as also for his former teacher Andrés Bello, are to be found in the time they spent in Francisco de Miranda's company in London in 1810. But whenever and however it may have begun, it remained a constant théme—confirmed, of course, by the evident community of interest which the new states acquired in the common struggle against Spain, "the virtual pact implicit in the identity of [our] cause, principles, and interests." Hence the diplomatic initiatives of 1821–22, the "federal" treaties concluded by Colombia with Peru, Chile, and Mexico, and, finally, the summoning of the Congress of Panama itself.

The precise story of these proposals and agreements is less interesting here, obviously, than the root-ideas that underlay them. The basic notion was set forth simply enough in the instructions given to Bolívar's diplomatic agents in 1821: the aim is "a league or confederation or federative convention" which, however, is to be much stronger than "an ordinary offensive and defensive alliance," for:

> ours should be a society of sister nations, separated for the time being . . . , but united, strong, and powerful in sustaining themselves against the aggression of foreign powers. . . . [We must] lay the foundation of an amphictyonic body or assembly of plenipotentiaries which can give an impulse to the common interests of the American states and settle any discords which could arise in the future.

This assembly of plenipotentiaries is to become, in effect, a permanent supranational congress, meeting at periodic intervals, able not only to represent Spanish America in matters of peace and war internationally, but capable, too, of deciding contentious intra–Spanish American issues—the creation of Bolivia, the possible liberation of Cuba, and the Argentine-Brazilian war were examples cited by Bolívar himself at one time or another—and of providing a stabilizing force among *and within* the newly independent nations. Here the federal ideal shaded into Bolívar's increasing preoccupation, as the years passed by, with the problem of order in Spanish America. Ideally, therefore, the federation was to become a "universal specific" against anarchy, "a sublime authority whose name alone can calm our tempests." Noting the growth of factiousness in Venezuela and of disorder in the River Plate provinces in the mid-1820s, Bolívar wrote: "The Porteños and the Caraqueños at opposite ends of South America are the most turbulent and seditious of all Americans. Only the American Congress can contain them. I am therefore desperate that it should be formed, so that the great mass can contain these diabolical extremes."

There can be little doubt, in my view, that Bolívar's instinct was to make the supranational framework as strong as possible; in his heart he clearly wanted something much more cohesive than a loose confederation. Internally, to be sure, as he told Hipólito Unanue, each country would be "free *in its own way,*" but at the same time the federated states would ideally appear "less as nations than as *sisters.*" On learning that Argentine opinion wished to limit the powers of the Panama Congress, he commented: "I myself believe that they should be amplified almost infinitely, to give it strength and *a truly sovereign authority.*" The concept of sovereignty invoked here is no doubt figurative rather than juridical, but the drift of Bolívar's sentiments is clear enough. The extent of his supranationalist idealism can also be inferred from the kind of language he tended to use in connection with the proposed federation—"the greatest work for the happiness of the New World," as he called it. "Every time I think about it, it entrances me," he wrote to Santander, "for *the creation of a giant* is not very common. . . . Its very shadow will save us from the abyss, or at least prolong our existence." "The association of the five great states of America," he told O'Higgins, "will . . . astonish Europe. The imagination cannot conceive without amazement the magnitude of *a colossus* whose very glance . . . will shake the world."

Bolívar was very clear in his own mind that this federal union should be restricted to the Spanish American nations. He was not, therefore, a pioneer of Pan-Americanism or even, strictly speaking, Latin American solidarity. The empire of Brazil—as his correspondence throughout 1824 and 1825 makes abundantly clear—was suspect on the grounds of its possible association with the Holy Alliance. The "heterogeneous character" of French-speaking Haiti and the English-speaking United States excluded those countries, too, from the arrangement, though Bolívar acknowledged his debt of gratitude to Haiti on several occasions, and his sincere admiration for the United States—"unique in the history of the human race," as he put it at Angostura—cannot seriously be challenged. Even within Spanish America, Bolívar somehow doubted whether the federation would be all-embracing. He tended to share San Martín's view, apparently imparted during the Guayaquil interview, that the River Plate would always remain apart. Guatemala (Central America, that is), by contrast, he saw as "by its situation the most federal people in America," a country to be welcomed into the scheme "with open arms." It seems clear that he also saw the federation as somehow improving the position of his own nation, Colombia, vis-à-vis potentially stronger American nations.

> Mexico, Guatemala, Colombia, Peru, Chile, and Upper Peru could make a superb federation. Guatemala, Chile, and Upper Peru will always do as we wish. Peru and Colombia are of one mind; and Mexico would thus be isolated in the midst of this federation, which has the advantage of being homogeneous, compact, and solid.

(That was written in May 1825.) Wider schemes of international association, with one very important exception, did not greatly appeal to the Liberator. Several such world-embracing designs were mooted during the independence period. An Argentine proposal to join Spanish America with Spain, Portugal, Greece, and the United States in a great league against the Holy Alliance drew from Bolívar the wry comment that, in the event of a conflict between Greece and Turkey, "there you would have Chimborazo at war with the Caucasus."

There was, however, one scheme of wider association that *did* persistently attract Bolívar, and this was his dream of an alliance (or some stronger link) between Spanish America and Great Britain, "the Mistress of the nations." For Bolívar, Great Britain was not merely the country which provided the best of all foreign models for Spanish American progress. It was both powerful *and* liberal, and was bound therefore to see the justice of the American cause. "Nobody doubts," Bolívar affirmed in 1814, "that the powerful Nation which has defended . . . the Independence of Europe, would not equally defend that of America, were it attacked." During his months of exile, he was beside himself with eagerness to secure positive British support for the independence movements, to the extent of suggesting an actual concession to Great Britain of Spanish American territory in exchange for aid. The rise of British world power as a consequence of the Napoleonic wars enormously impressed the Liberator: "Her omnipotence is absolute and sovereign," he wrote, comparing England's "ascendant progress" to that of Rome "at the end of the Republic and beginning of the Empire." The chief factors in America's destiny, he observed on another occasion, were "God, London, and ourselves." Taking his writings as a whole, it would be permissible to argue that he had rather more faith in London than in God or his Spanish American compatriots. After Waterloo, the British were clearly a convincing counterweight to the real or imaginary threats posed by the Holy Alliance. "Do not fear the Allies," Bolívar wrote in 1823, "for the ditch is large, and the English fleet still larger."

Bolívar viewed an association with Great Britain as a useful reinforcement of his scheme for Spanish American federal union, "which cannot," he wrote, "be achieved unless the English protect it body and soul"—were they to decide to do so, on the other hand, this would be a "guarantee against Spain, the Holy Alliance and anarchy." In his stray "Thought on the Congress of Panama," published by Vicente Lecuna in 1916, Bolívar actually went so far as to visualize "the union of the new states with the British Empire" in what would obviously become "the most vast, most extraordinary, and most powerful league ever to have appeared on earth." (The reader of Bolívar's writings can hardly fail to be struck by how often he summons up images of power, vastness, and grandeur—there is something deep in his psychology here.) This may have been an unrealistic scheme, and indeed was—for Great Britain neither wanted nor needed it—but it was not altogether naïve or ill-considered.

Bolívar certainly cannot be accused of having ignored the dangers and disadvantages that an arrangement with Great Britain might bring. On balance, however, he *did* believe that these were likely to be out-weighed by positive gains. In June 1824 he made the following comment to Santander:

> Our American federation cannot survive unless England takes it under her protection. . . . The first thing is to exist, the second the means of existing: if we link ourselves to England we shall exist, and if we do not, we shall infallibly be lost. Therefore, the first course of action is preferable. And while it lasts, we shall grow up, we shall become stronger, and we shall become *truly national,* against the day when our ally might involve us in harmful commitments. Were that to happen, our own strength and the relationships we could then form with other European nations would place us beyond the reach of our tutors and allies. Let us even suppose that we suffer as a result of England's superiority: this suffering will be a proof that we exist, and by existing we shall preserve the hope of freeing ourselves from the suffering.

The root-idea at work here, as is indicated in the use of the words "our tutors" in the above passage, is of a British connection serving as a mechanism by which Spanish America can further its own progress. Indeed, the "Thought on the Congress of Panama," more specifically, sees British influence bolstering social reform, and British "character and customs" becoming the normative basis of "future existence" in Spanish America. Beyond this, in distant centuries, Bolívar dimly perceives "a single, federal, nation covering the world," to which, by implication, the union of Great Britain and Spanish America might lead. With this suggestion we undoubtedly reach the outer edge of Bolivarian speculation. Supranationalism can go no farther.

Middle-Range Supranationalism

Bolívar's maximal schemes of federal union for Spanish America sprang fairly clearly from genuine Americanist idealism. It seems likely that his "middle-range" supranational proposal, canvassed without any real prospect of success in 1826–27, stemmed much more from immediate circumstances. A full description of these is redundant here, but it will be remembered that in 1825–26 Bolívar was at the very peak of his prestige in South America. "I have loved glory and freedom," he wrote in April 1826. "Both have been achieved, and so I have no further desires." The Liberator was clearly fooling himself. The political stabilization of Spanish America remained a problem that he pondered incessantly—his idée fixe from 1826 onward being that the Bolivian Constitution was the solution. He was acutely conscious also of his own personal aura of power: this was the time when he contemplated expeditions to dislodge the baleful tyrant of Paraguay or to impose order on the turbulent Argentines—"the demon of glory must carry us to Tierra del Fuego." At one point, indeed, Bolívar even suggested that he might become a kind of peripatetic supreme arbiter of South American affairs, almost, one might say, a personal supranational guarantor of the region's stability:

> By remaining outside [Colombia] at the head of a great army . . . I menace [its] criminal factions with a formidable force. . . . Caesar in Gaul threatened Rome, and I in Bolivia threaten all the conspirators in America and thus save all the republics. If I lose my positions in the South, the Panama Congress will avail us nothing, and the emperor of Brazil will gobble up the River Plate and Bolivia.

The Liberator's followers and associates were prolific at this period with suggestions as to further uses that might be made of his great authority. Páez in Venezuela wanted him to create a Napoleonic monarchy or empire, others wished him to become the "absolute chief of the South" as protector of the Southern Cone; still others indicated that the River Plate and Bolivia might unite—under the name of Bolivia—in a single state: "If we listened to these gentlemen," Bolívar commented, "there would only be two republics, Colombia and Bolivia." What can perhaps be deduced fairly easily from the abundant evidence here is that in 1826, intuitively foreseeing the modest outcome of the Panama Congress, agreeably cushioned by Peruvian flattery, and spurred on by dreams of continued glory, Bolívar concluded that the political state of Spanish America was more fluid than it really was. A vigorous initiative at this point, he seems to have thought, might secure stability over a wide area, if not the whole of South America.

The scheme eventually taken up, evidently suggested by some of Bolívar's Peruvian advisers, was for "a federation of the three sister republics, but a positive federation, to replace the general American one, which they say is nominal and up-in-the-air." The only serious outline of this scheme from Bolívar's pen is to be found in parallel letters to Sucre and to General Gutiérrez de la Fuente composed in May 1826. Colombia, Peru, and Bolivia are to combine in a supranational entity, possibly under the name of Bolivian Federation; each constituent state is to adopt the Bolivian Constitution, suitably adapted; the federation itself is to be ruled by a congress and a vice-president, while the president himself, as "supreme chief," will spend his time touring the provinces, visiting each of the component sections at least once a year. As part of the arrangement, Colombia will be redivided into its original three states, while Peru also is possibly divisible into two parts, Arequipa becoming the capital of a new state. Thus, Venezuela is to enjoy equivalent status to Bolivia. The capital of the federation can be Quito or Guayaquil. As with the maximal American federation, Bolívar's impulse with this "middle-range" plan was to strengthen the supranational element. The federation, he wrote, was to be "tighter than that of the United States," enjoying "the most perfect unity possible under a federal form," with "one flag, one army, and a single nation." To Sucre, soon afterward, he wrote: "We should not use the word federation, but union. . . . I say *union* because later on people will demand federal forms, as has happened in Guayaquil, where, the moment they heard 'federation,' they began thinking of the former *republiquita*."

There is little need here to recount the rapid failure of Bolívar's maneuvers in favor of the Federation of the Andes. Within only a few months, in point of fact, it was politically dead, and Bolívar was advising Santa Cruz, for whom he had envisaged a key role in the scheme, to abandon "American plans" in favor of "purely Peruvian" policies. There for all practical purposes the matter ended. It is possible, however, that Bolívar never fully abandoned a residual belief in the Andean union. As late as June 1829 we find him writing—once again to Santa Cruz, who by now was in the ascendant in Bolivia—that "the league of Colombia, Peru, and Bolivia is more necessary every day, in order to cure the gangrene of revolution." By that time, of course, Bolívar was well into his final, fruitless struggle against the fissiparous tendencies he had striven so hard to overcome—this time, within the confines of his personal supranational creation: Colombia. But a distant after-echo of the Andean union can perhaps be detected: since the withdrawal of Chile in 1977, the modern Andean Pact, the most promising of more recent supranational experiments in Latin America, covers precisely those countries that would have been included in Bolívar's plan.

The Colombian Experiment

"I shall serve for as long as Colombia—or my life—endures," wrote Bolívar in May 1821. He spoke more truly than he could have known at the time. Colombia, the reconstitution of the old Viceroyalty of New Granada, was nothing if not the Liberator's personal creation. It was the only serious attempt to fuse incipient Latin American nationalities into a common national whole. This was perhaps less a supranational project than an experiment in creating a new nationality altogether. Though himself a Venezuelan, Bolívar was brought into early and increasingly intimate contact with New Granada and Granadinos—"this sister nation" of "beloved compatriots"—by the twists and turns of the first phase of the war of independence. The two territories were clearly interdependent in military and strategic terms. The project of uniting them crystallized very early in Bolívar's mind. The basic reasoning was set out in a letter to General Mariño in December 1813. What northern South America needed, according to Bolívar, was a national unit of sufficient size and strength to figure convincingly on the political map: "two different nations . . . will appear ridiculous. Even if Venezuela and New Granada *were* united, this would only just make a nation capable of inspiring due and decorous consideration in others." Colombia was born, therefore, out of military and diplomatic necessity, and "the creation of a new Republic composed of these two nations" became a basic part of the Bolivarian program, actualized as a consequence of military triumph. Although the Fundamental Law of Colombia (December 17, 1819) did not use the term "nation" to describe the newly created entity, Bolívar himself obviously regarded it as such, and regarded it as *his* nation from that point onward. He never really stopped regarding it in that light. Whatever his reservations about the 1821 (Cúcuta) Constitution, he nonetheless described it resonantly as "the pact of union which has presented the world with a new nation composed of Venezuela and New Granada." To those who pleaded with him to concentrate on governing Venezuela, he insisted: "I now belong to the family of Colombia and not to the family of Bolívar, not to Caracas alone but to the whole nation which my constancy and my companions have created."

The prime argument in favor of Colombia remained, for Bolívar, practical and what might almost be called geopolitical. Europe in particular would not pay attention if Spanish America were divided into a "multiplicity of sovereignties." It is less often noted, perhaps, that Bolívar also had a strong desire for Colombia to cut something of a dash in the newly forming panorama of Western Hemisphere politics. He was never altogether sanguine on this score. His underlying fears in this were revealed in an interesting letter to Santander in December 1822, in the course of which he elaborated one of those international political conspectuses of which he was so fond.

> When I fix my gaze on America, I see her surrounded by the maritime power of Europe, by floating fortresses of foreigners, which is to say enemies. I then observe that at the top of the continent there is a most powerful nation, rich, very bellicose, and capable of anything. . . . Then I notice the vast and powerful Mexican empire which . . . is in a position to throw itself advantageously upon Colombia. . . . Facing us we have the rich and beautiful Spanish islands, which can never be other than enemies. At our backs we have ambitious Portugal with her immense Brazilian colony, and to the South, Peru, with its many millions of pesos, its rivalry with Colombia, its connections with Chile and Buenos Aires. . . . We are inferior to our brothers in the South, to the Mexicans, to the [North] Americans, to the English, and indeed to all the Europeans. . . . We have two and a half million inhabitants spread out across an extensive wilderness. Some of them are savages, some slaves, most enemies among themselves, and all vitiated by despotism and superstition. What a contrast to put against the nations of the world! That is our position. That is Colombia. And they wish to divide her!

Thus the union—and it is inaccurate to speak, as many historians do, of a Colombian federation—was not merely a condition of survival, but of *successful* survival. At times, particularly as he made his way southward—it is tempting to say the farther he got from Bogotá—Bolívar seems to have believed for a while that Colombia's position was, in fact, distinctly promising as compared with that of other emergent states. In May 1823, for instance, he told Santander that government propaganda should stress the difference between Colombia, "with its heroes and generals," and the ridiculous spectacle of "the rest of independent America, with its governments both absolute and dissolute, its . . . three-guaranteers, emperors, directors, protectors, delegates, regents, admirals, etc."

And yet, not the least interesting aspect of Bolívar's attitude to his own creation was a persistent intuition that it would simply not work. His doubts began early. Venezuelans in New Granada, he had occasion to suggest in 1820, should not be given public jobs in that territory—"all they are good for is quarreling." Soon afterward he complained that dissensions within the new union made him "suffer the agonies of torture." (These dissensions he once described as an "astonishing chaos of *patriots, royalists, egoists, blancos, pardos, Venezuelans, Cundinamarcans, federalists, centralists, republicans, aristocrats, good and bad.*") He was invariably conscious of the sheer effort needed to keep Colombia united, even playing (though not very seriously) with the idea of allowing the royalists to retain Peru so as to provide Colombia with "fearsome neighbors" to concentrate its mind. To Santander he confessed his growing conviction that Colombia needed "an army of occupation" to keep it free, and later concluded that he himself was the only force that could keep the union together. "Colombia is the sacred word, the magic word for all virtuous citizens," he told General Urdaneta as he made his way homeward in 1826, "and *I myself am the rallying point* for all who love national glory and the rights of the people."

Bolívar's perception of the obstacles to unity in northern South America was as acute as anybody's. "There is no cohesion in this republic," he told the faithful O'Leary. Time and time again in his letters he refers to the persistent force of local antipathy, undermining the very foundations of the union: "the South does not like the North. The coasts do not like the sierra. Venezuela does not like Cundinamarca. Cundinamarca suffers the disorders of Venezuela." It was all very well to tell the Caraqueños, after Carabobo, that their city was no longer "the capital of a Republic" but would henceforth become "the capital of a vast department governed in a manner worthy of its importance." Not all Venezuelans were convinced that this gave them much in the way of importance, and it was no doubt galling to some to hear Bolívar describing their country as "these departments of the Former Venezuela." New Granada, too, had its susceptibilities. "Venezuelans," Bolívar wrote in 1829, "cannot govern in New Granada. . . . This factor of implacable hatred has fixed my destiny, and that of Colombia." To Sucre he made the same point in wrier tones: "We shall always be of reprehensible birth: Venezuelan and white. Guilty of this offense, we can never rule in these regions." The human materials to bridge the great divide between Venezuela and New Granada were simply lacking—though Bolívar was delighted when Pedro Gual, a Venezuelan, married a New Granadan lady: "That is the way to make Colombians," he commented to Santander.

It is doubtless true that with Páez's rebellion in 1826 and Bolívar's subsequent rift with Santander (who, despite his own New Granadan sensitivities, had done all that was humanly possible to make a going concern of the union), the break-up of Colombia was only a matter of time. Bolívar's solution to the Venezuelan problem merely delayed the moment of truth. The ups and downs of the increasingly tragic story of the next four years do not concern us here, but it is worth noting, perhaps, that Bolívar himself never ceased to hope that some dramatic constitutional innovation might rescue his political creation from disaster. The Ocaña Convention—"Colombia's last chance"—failed to provide the required constitution, or any constitution at all. Bolívar's clear rejection of a monarchical or "imperial" solution left him with few further ideas beyond the summoning of yet another constituent assembly, which, he continued to hope, might adopt his own frequently expounded political ideas—the concentration of "republican forms under the direction of a monocracy," in other words, something rather like the Bolivian Constitution. Such proposals as the creation of a new department straddling the border between New Granada and Venezuela to eliminate "this division . . . which is killing us," or the suggestion that he himself might become a roving generalissimo while someone else exercised the presidency—"I would run around the government like a bull round its herd of cows"—came too late to be of use, and in any case were never properly developed.

Bolívar very clearly foresaw the impending dissolution of Colombia; he was well aware that local pressures were building up to just such an outcome. "The day this act is sealed," he wrote, "the active part (*parte agente*) of the population will be filled with joy." "We had better carry out what the caudillos of these peoples want," he opined in January 1830, just before hearing of the successful breakaway movement in Venezuela. It seems clear that beyond the fear of Colombia splitting up into its natural component parts there lay a worse fear—the fear that dissolution would be followed by still greater dissolution. The model was the River Plate, an example that instilled deep foreboding in Bolívar: "Buenos Aires is in the vanguard," he told Santa Cruz in September 1830, "and we are following her." To forestall such an eventuality, Bolívar finally thought it preferable to "divide [Colombia] with legality, in peace and good harmony," and perhaps "an international pact" could link the newly separated states; "time, which is prodigal in resources, will do the rest."

Even in the bitter months that followed the disintegration, the last months of his life, Bolívar could never entirely bring himself to accept what had occurred. The hope of Colombian reunification remained: if necessary, he was prepared to use force to bring it about. "If they give me an army, I shall accept it," he wrote from Cartagena in September 1830. "If they send me to Venezuela, I shall go." But to Santa Cruz, at around the same time, he wrote: "Although the best party, the party of national integrity, is the strongest . . . I have my doubts about the final reestablishment of order." By the end of October 1830 he evidently felt that the "restoration of Colombia" was beyond his—or anyone's—reach. Yet it is no doubt significant that at the very end, if only for the historical record, Bolívar still enunciated his hope. In his will, drawn up on December 10, 1830—seven days before he died—he described himself not as a Venezuelan, but as "a native of the city of Caracas, in the department of Venezuela," and the last of his many proclamations contained an ultimate appeal for the preservation of Colombia: "If my death helps . . . to consolidate the Union, I shall go in peace to the grave." With these words, so very well known, the Liberator closed his public career. It is fair to say that they fell on empty air, and, in every important respect, have done so ever since.

"From every perspective except the Bolivarian," writes the author of a recent general history of Venezuela, "the Colombian consolidation was a colossal mistake." Gerhard Masur invokes the example of Scandinavia to suggest that "South America visualized its destiny more clearly than Bolívar" by splitting into different nationalities. It is easy to be wise after the event. In hindsight, of course, we can clearly see that Latin America's antecedent colonial experience, and the circumstances of the revolutions for independence, were factors that only superhuman effort could have neutralized. Colonial administrative divisions had created, in Hugh Seton-Watson's phrase, "separate hierarchies of interest and ambition" in Spanish America. Independence confirmed these tendencies to division and separateness, or, rather, they *were* confirmed, as Rudolf Rocker puts it, in an undeservedly neglected classic on the theme of nationalism, by "the power lust of small minorities and dictatorially inclined individuals." The genuine Americanists, among whom Bolívar stood supreme, were never more than a minority, however active, within the creole elites who decided Spanish America's subsequent fate.

And yet, when all has been said, and when all the difficulties have been neatly cataloged, it is still somehow difficult to restrain a feeling that the independence of Spanish America, like other historical moments, such as the end of World War I in Europe, offered opportunities that were somehow missed. Was Bolívar simply too visionary? Was he, in the overworked phrase, a man before his time? Time, as he himself said, is prodigal in its resources, but these do not necessarily favor unity. Latin American moves toward supranational integration in recent decades have not been especially encouraging; indeed, they have been markedly less so than Western Europe's moves in that direction. Supranationalism, as Europeans have discovered in the quarter-century since the Treaty of Rome, is certainly no panacea, and yet it does seem to offer solid advantages of a commercial and social kind, and it even has its political uses. Many Latin Americans nowadays consider a degree of unity to be indispensable in the quest for greater prosperity and autonomy. Simón Bolívar's efforts must always, therefore, remain an inspiration in his own continent. As the wise Dr. Rafael Caldera has written, "Why should we not recognize in Bolívar, a Spanish American creole, the evidence that we are capable of sustained and tenacious effort?" And as for Bolívar's ultimate speculation—"a single, federal, nation covering the world"—few would deny its relevance to a divided planet whose very survival is a matter for serious debate. That phrase alone is sufficient to place the great hero of Spanish American independence in the ranks of those who have expressed, however fleetingly, one of the noblest ideals of modern mankind.

Suggested Further Reading

Halperin-Donghi, Tulio. *The Aftermath of Revolution in Latin America*. New York, 1973.

———. *Politics, Economics and Society in Argentina in the Revolutionary Period*. London, 1975.

Humphreys, R. A., and John Lynch, eds. *The Origins of the Latin American Revolutions, 1808–1826*. New York, 1965.

Johnson, John J., with the collaboration of Doris M. Ladd. *Simón Bolívar and Spanish American Independence: 1783–1830*. Princeton, 1968.

Masur, Gerhard. *Simón Bolívar*. Albuquerque, 1948.

Robertson, William Spence. *Rise of the Spanish-American Republics, as told in the Lives of their Liberators*. New York, 1961.

Claims of Political Tradition

RICHARD M. MORSE

The Transfer of Political Institutions

Many think of the Spanish colonization of America as the work of free-acting conquistadors and their followers, avid for products of soil and subsoil, in particular gold and silver, and for the servile labor to be used in extracting them. Others, who applaud the "individualism" of the self-reliant settlements of Anglo America, criticize Spain for having stifled colonial development with statism, bureaucracy, and discrimination against the early settlers. First off, then, we must distinguish the roles played by private and public initiative and appreciate the connotations of each in the Spanish American context.

Mario Góngora reminds us that although the Spanish state had acquired a strong administrative nucleus by the sixteenth century, it was not yet, as it later became, "a unitary and rationalized whole, dominated by the 'monism of sovereignty.' " Political jurisdiction and other rights brought together in the king were exercised through the bureaucracy; but these might be conceded as privileges that could be defended juridically against the king himself. The categories of the public and private spheres, established under revived Roman law, were still in process of elaboration. Thus, for example, the conquistador was not a "free" entrepreneur under a private contract. He was under continuing obligation to ask the crown for privileges, such as grants of Indian labor. His contract (*capitulación*) linked freely assembled social forces with the power of the state, converting them into political elements.

The state, then, was a colonizing state (*estado poblador*), operating through laws, customs, and judicial and administrative decisions. Grants of soil and subsoil were founded in royal concession, not in pri-

---

Reprinted by permission of the author.

vate law. Colonization implied the organizing of a congeries of civil and ecclesiastical jurisdictions and hierarchies; a regime of defense, taxation, and tribute; and systems of schools and universities. Not only did economic life and claims to land have their origin in the state, but also the whole colonizing process was conceived as having the "civilizing" function of transmitting Western Christian culture. For sixteenth-century Spaniards the state was an institutional equivalent to temporal human life in all its fullness. It contained only in embryo such possibilities as the rationalist state of seventeenth-century mercantilism, the free-enterprise state envisioned in the eighteenth century, or the "imperialist" state of the nineteenth.

From Columbus onward, the conquistadors took possession of new lands and oceans in the name of the crown. Although the crown's resources were insufficient to underwrite the vast colonizing adventure, neither conquest nor settlement was a private enterprise undertaken at the margin of the Castilian state. Apart from a few important voyages subsidized by the crown (Columbus, Pedrarias Dávila, Magellan), recruitment and financing of most expeditions were left to private initiative. Such undertakings were sanctioned, however, only if they conformed to the broad policies of the state. An expeditionary leader might be given a liberal contract for life, or for two or more generations, to distribute and settle land, found towns, engage in commerce, and use Indian labor. But as the Indians were considered vassals to be protected and Christianized—and also taxed—his retinue included officials and ecclesiastics who represented the political, fiscal, and spiritual interests of the crown.

Gradually there emerged as an embedding context for the *capitulaciones:* (1) an elaborate juridical and theological casuistry that justified the Spanish title to the Indies and set down principles for treatment of the natives, and (2) a series of civil and ecclesiastical hierarchies that exhibited both functional overlap among agencies and coalescence of function (especially administrative and judicial) within given agencies. These hierarchies culminated in the arbitrating crown, which delegated its power hesitantly and erratically. The legal apparatus for empire betrayed its medieval origins. It was informed by the broad Christian principles of theologians and jurists, but frequently took the form of trifling administrative detail. Legal codifications such as the 1573 colonizing ordinances and the 1680 Laws of the Indies were essentially compilations that failed to work natural-law principles and administrative decrees into a coherent whole.

That such government signified deprivation of autonomy for Spanish America and meager preparation for independent nationhood is widely accepted. Nonetheless, the theoretical premise for centralization was not colonial subjection of the Indies, but the assumption that the New World viceroyalties were coequal with the realms of Spain, having equal claims to redress from the crown. The Council of the Indies was not a colonial office but had ministerial status. The viceroy of New Spain or Peru was the king's proxy. He and lesser royal officials were under elaborate regulations not to acquire private interests, economic or domestic, in their jurisdictions, and they underwent judicial review at the end of their terms. In the case of both Spanish America and Brazil, one can argue that it was only under the "enlightened" peninsular monarchies of the eighteenth century that a status, "colonial" in the modern sense, was adumbrated. The differences between Hapsburg rule, under which Spanish American institutions were established, and Bourbon rule, which tried somewhat ineffectually to reform them, has been called by apologists for the former the difference between absolutism and despotism.

The insistence on the neomedievalism of Spanish American colonial institutions reflects no intent to romanticize them. It looks toward identifying a design that the formative period of Spanish rule left implanted in the Indies. This design, which had roots in outlook as well as institutional arrangement, was to conflict with many administrative directives of the Bourbon period. It was to conflict even more sharply with the ideas and ideals, constitutions and reforms, that swept in on the independent Spanish American nations after 1830. It continues to conflict at many points with modern programs of "development"—political, social, and economic.

There was of course practical motivation for the Spanish monarchs' concern with Christian treatment of the Indians and for the sixteenth-century debates as to their rationality and the propriety of enslaving them. This was the threat to the crown's income and political control posed by the conquistadors once they were established in their new domains. The centrifugal movement of settlers into farm, ranch, and mining lands, far removed from seaports and administrative centers (with these in turn distant from Spain by an arduous sea voyage), created the danger of sovereign satrapies, each enjoying absolute control of Indian workers who, in the Mexican and Andean highlands, and in Paraguay, could not combine for effective resistance to their new masters. As a result, and "in the face of the excessive privileges granted by the monarchs themselves to the first discoverers and their descendants, the officials of the Court and the *Audiencias* reacted by retrieving all the grants of the Crown in the discovered lands, through long suits, tenaciously sustained."

Since Tocqueville, the growth of the centralized state in Western Europe has been described as a process that undermines local autonomy and initiative and, by equalizing all citizens before the law and the state bureaucracy, weakens the protection afforded them by community ties and customs. In Spanish America under the Hapsburgs, the role of the state was in some respects the opposite. Central to its function was the preservation or creation of Indian communities that would maintain their own way of life, be protected against crushing exploitation, and have independent access to royal justice and to spiritual guidance and consolation. The Laws of the Indies contained extensive tutelary legislation that respected the Indians' cultural identity. Some have called them the most comprehensive code ever devised by an important colonizing power. None would deny, however, that their enforcement was greatly wanting. As occasion demanded and circumstances permitted, ways were found to exact grueling labor of Indians, notably in the mines and *obrajes* ("textile factories"). Corregidors of Indian towns regularly exploited their wards for personal gain, often in conspiracy with priests and Indian caciques.

It serves little purpose, however, to assess out of context the Spaniards' cruelty toward or exploitation of the native population. In an age that saw the predatory forces of commercial capitalism unleashed, and the face of Europe ravaged by religious persecution and the havoc of the Thirty Years' War, it would be fatuous to expect the conquest of a new continent and its millions of pagans to have lacked ferocity and trauma. Recent historiography shelves the question of the Spanish "Black Legend" and examines forms of Indian defiance and accommodation, the mentality and institutions born of the conquest that contributed to form an enduring "creole" culture. What concerns us here is to define the European tradition that set the mold for this culture.

I suggested that the rationale of the Spanish state had medieval accents. Yet one conspicuous feature of the medieval European polity, a system of "estates," in the sense of social orders having rights of representation, was not reproduced in the Indies because no Cortes, or parliamentary body, was established.

In a period when the granting of subsidies or pecuniary assistance to the King and the accompanying request for privileges was at the heart of the internal life of the State, the Indies—relatively free of tribute and paying the King the royal fifths and other perquisites which did not require consent—did not exhibit the political density and the pronounced King-Kingdom dualism characteristic of Europe in this era.

Only in the broad sense of groups having common jurisdictional privileges can estates be said to have existed in Spanish America. The state had a corporate character. Within it there were independently defined privileges and jurisdictions for general groups (Indians, Blacks, Europeans, ecclesiastics) and for subgroups, such as Indians in missions, *pueblos de indios,* Indians on encomiendas; African slaves, colored freedmen; merchants, university students, artisans; regular clergy, secular clergy, Inquisitorial officials, and so forth. The medieval imprint that the system as a whole bore was not parliamentary representation, but pluralistic, compartmented privilege and administrative paternalism.

Claudio Sánchez-Albornoz claimed that the classic institutions of feudalism never developed fully in Spain itself. In summary his argument runs as follows. During the reconquest of the central tableland from the Moors, roughly A.D. 850–1200, cities and castles served as advance points of resettlement. From these nuclei colonization was undertaken only with clear guarantees of personal liberty and freedom of movement. Few colonists were tied permanently to the soil or to a lord. Society had, relatively speaking, a fluidity that precluded a complex net of vassalic relations or the emergence of a stable, conservative bourgeoisie. The commoner who could equip himself with arms and a steed was valuable to the crown and could become a lesser knight or, in the paradoxical phrase, a *caballero villano.* He might even owe fealty directly to the king rather than to a blood noble.

The importance of central authority to the reconquest meant that the strength of the crown and the organization of the state never faded out, as in the Carolingian realm. Even when the centralizing process was temporarily checked in the tenth century, the crown never recognized usurpations by nobles. The flood of feudal ideas and practices that entered Spain in the eleventh century with warrior or pilgrim knights from northern Europe, and with royal marriages to French princesses, was not accompanied by the juridical formulae of feudalism. The advancing frontier periodically renewed the spoils and prebends that the crown could distribute, thus renewing its economic and military potential. Towns were strong and numerous, and not merely islands dispersed in a feudal sea. They were an active counterweight to the church and the nobility; to keep pace, nobles were forced to beg additional lands, honors, and prebends from the crown. When in the thirteenth century a struggle developed between crown and nobles, it was not one by which the crown strove to break feudal power (as in France) or by which the knights strove to restrict royal power (as in Germany), but a contest by both to control an extant state apparatus.

With respect to economic as distinct from sociopolitical organization, the following considerations should be borne in mind as militating against the emergence of a manorial regime in the Spanish Indies:

(1) Spain itself never witnessed a flowering of the classic manorial pattern of other parts of Europe because of the seven centuries' strife between Christians and Moors and because of the privileges, prejudicial to agriculture, acquired by the medieval sheep raisers' guild.

(2) A manorial system implies that lord and worker share a common culture and a traditional regime of mutual obligation. Clearly, such a context was lacking for Spaniard and Indian, to say nothing of Spaniard and African. Here the tutelary state and the "universal" church (usually through its regular orders) were more protective of Indian workers than was the local agrarian unit.

(3) Manorialism takes form in a vegetative, decentralized fashion in a nonurban economy, perpetuated by local tradition, reflecting stability both social and ecological. The initial settlement of America was accomplished by a mere handful of men, not simply avid for gold as is sometimes said, but certainly in quest of status and fame as these might be embodied in specie (however fleetingly retained), land, and a situation of authority free of manual toil. In vast areas possessing immeasurable resources along with native labor, honor, status, and possession were inevitably factored out of the medieval social complex. Here, for example, status might be acquired through land, rather than control of land being a function of status. Or, honor and status might be achieved through heroism, rather than heroism being assumed as an attribute of status.

Because the New World encomienda, or allocation of Indian labor, bore only limited resemblance to the medieval manor, Góngora prefers the term "patrimonialism" to "feudalism" or "manorialism" for describing the system it represented. His reason is that the conquistadors in their urgency to acquire lands and sources of wealth were at the same time bearers of royal authority. They conceived of the state as a mass of lands, tributes, benefices, grants, and honors belonging to the royal patrimony, but legitimately claimed by those who had made them available to the crown.

> The specifically vassalic relation of loyalty evaporated before general loyalty of subjects to the King; the link between conquistadors and King assumes a new aspect, not through a personal bond distinct from what they have as subjects, but through the relation they have with the lands, won for the royal domain.

Ideological Implications

Discussion of the transatlantic institutional legacy leads to its ideological rationale. Was it the case that Spain implanted archaic and authoritarian political precepts that its overseas realms would one day expunge in a primal act of "liberation"? Or did it leave behind an adaptable political culture that would condition political and social life for an indefinite future? Nineteenth-century ideologists of the newly independent Spanish American nations, unless they had clerical, authoritarian sympathies, replied "yes" to the first question and dismissed the second. In a longer-term "anthropological" perspective, however, the second query deserves consideration. Religion, after all, takes hold in many realms, one of them being a shared instinct for behavior. In other words, we may take religion not simply as an ideological bulwark for a political structure, but also as a pliant set of beliefs, social as well as theological, entertained by common folk. There is, in short, a sociology of Catholicism.

Because our recollection of seventeenth-century Protestantism tends to be more positive than of sixteenth-century Catholicism—given the "success" of the Anglo American enterprise—it is helpful to remember how closely religion and social process were entwined in the north. For conveying the logic of Protestant colonization there is no more revealing statement than that of Martin Luther in his *Open Letter to the Christian Nobility:*

> If a little group of pious Christian laymen were taken captive and set down in a wilderness, and had among them no priest consecrated by a bishop, and if there in the wilderness they were to agree in choosing one of themselves, married or unmarried, and were to charge him with the office of baptizing, saying mass, absolving and preaching, such a man would be as truly a priest as though all bishops and popes had consecrated him.

This passage contains two revealing clues. The first is that a land uninhabited, or inhabited by heathen, is a "wilderness," a no-man's-land outside the pale of society, civilization, and church. The second is that the world is composed not of *one highly differentiated society* for which common forms, acts, and ceremonies are a needed binding force, but of a *multitude of unrelated societies,* each of them a congregation of similar persons, which is finite in time and place and ordered by the declarative terms of a compact rather than by common symbolic observances. As Kenneth Burke puts it:

> [In] contrast with the church's "organic" theory, whereby one put a going social concern together by the toleration of *differences,* the Protestant sects stressed the value of *complete uniformity.* Each time this uniformity was impaired, the sect itself tended to split, with a new "uncompromising" offshoot reaffirming the need for a homogeneous community, all members alike in status.

If, then, Christendom was for the Spaniard "universal," this meant that his overseas settlements were not truly "colonies," whether orthodox or heterodox, that had been spun off from the mother country into a "wilderness." Nor was Spanish expansion properly a "conquest" insofar as this means the acquisition of alien lands and peoples. In fact the word itself, which Father Las Casas called "tyrannical, Mohammedan, abusive, improper, and infernal," was banned from official use in favor of "pacification" or "settlement" (*población*). The term frequently used to designate the extension of Spanish political rule to America was "incorporation," as for example "the incorporation of the Indies to the crown of Castile." What is implied is not annexation of terra incognita, but the bringing together of what should rightfully be joined.

To say this much is not to idealize the motives of those who erected the Spanish empire in America. Fortune seeking, aggrandizement, fanaticism, escapism, cruelty were all in evidence. Economically and otherwise the Spanish Indies were exploited. The point is that they were incorporated into Christendom, directly under the Spanish crown, by a carefully legitimized patrimonial state apparatus. Oppression certainly occurs within such a realm, but subjects tend to attribute it to bad information, misunderstanding, incompetence, and selfishness originating at lower administrative levels. The system itself is not seriously challenged, nor is the authority of the symbolic and irreplaceable crown.

These principles of society and government help us not only to understand Hapsburg rule in America, but also to assess the reception of the Enlightenment, to analyze the process by which the Spanish American nations became independent, and to interpret their subsequent careers. Scholars have debated whether neo-Scholastic thought kept its hold throughout the eighteenth century to provide justification for Spanish American independence or whether the patriots of liberation took up the liberal and rationalist program of the Enlightenment. Evidence can be adduced either way, and in any case, once one begins tracing the causes of independence, ideology yields ground to other factors. The question here has less to do with the history of ideas than with political sociology. If we accept that the design for Spanish American governance was established by about 1570, and if two centuries passed before spokesmen began issuing discreet challenges to the premises whereon it rested, one can imagine that an enduring political culture had been set in place. The logic of that culture found expression in Spanish neo-Thomist thought of the sixteenth and seventeenth centuries, not because philosophers dictate ground rules for political behavior but because certain thinkers become "influential" for being attuned to that very behavior.

Francisco Suárez (1548–1617) is generally recognized as the leading synthesizer of neo-Thomist political thought in Spain's baroque age of Scholasticism. His recapitulation was far from being a mere disinterment of thirteenth-century Thomism; for in recasting the Thomist argument he devised a metaphysics that found acceptance even in northern, Protestant Europe. Although one can point to instances when Suárez was invoked at the start of the Spanish American independence wars, his significance for the subsequent history of the new nations does not depend on whether or not he provided a pre-Enlightenment precedent for contract and popular sovereignty. It lies, rather, in the fact that his fresh marshaling of Scholastic doctrines, in response to imperatives of time and place, encapsulated assumptions about political man and his dilemmas that survive in Spanish America to this day. The following Suárezian principles illustrate the point:

(1) *Natural law is clearly distinguished from conscience.* Natural law is a general rule; conscience is a practical application of it to specific cases. Natural law is never mistaken; conscience may be. Society and the body politic are therefore properly seen as ordered by objective and external natural-law precepts, rather than by consensus sprung from the promptings of private consciences. (Where such an assumption prevails, free elections and the ballot box are unlikely to attain the mystique they possess in Protestant countries.)

(2) *Sovereign power originates with the collectivity of men.* God is the author of civil power, but He created it as a property emanating from nature so that no society would lack the power necessary for its preservation. (This proposition allowed the view that Indians, save for recalcitrant cannibals, were not savages, but lived in societies ordered by natural law. A second implication, important at the time of independence, was that when central authority collapses, power reverts to the sovereign people.)

(3) *The people do not delegate but alienate sovereignty to their prince.* Although the people are in principle superior to the prince, they vest power in him without condition (simpliciter) that he may use it as he deems fitting. By contrast, then, the prince is superior to the people.

(4) *In certain cases the law of the prince loses its force.* Several conditions can cause a law to lose force: if it is unjust, for an unjust law is not a law; if it is too harsh; or if the majority has already ceased to obey it (even though the first to cease obeying would have sinned).

(5) *The prince is bound by his own law.* He cannot, however, be punished by himself or by his people, for he is responsible only to God or His representative.

For generations the difficulties that Spanish American peoples experience in erecting constitutional regimes based on wide popular participation have been commonly ascribed to: inadequate schooling in Western democratic principles; impoverished, unwholesome, and disorderly social conditions; and an ingrained personalistic or authoritarian psychology. Anchored in the propositions of Suárez, however, we discern precisely those seeming inconsistencies that many have attributed to environmental causes or psychic disposition. Paul Janet summarized them as follows:

Such are the Scholastic doctrines of the 16th century, incoherent doctrines in which are united . . . democratic and absolutist ideas, without the author seeing very clearly where the former or the latter lead him. He adopts in all its force the principle of popular sovereignty: he excludes the doctrine of divine law . . . and he causes not simply government but even society to rest on unanimous consent. But these principles serve only to allow him immediately to effect the absolute and unconditional alienation of popular sovereignty into the hands of one person. He denies the need for consent of the people in the formulation of law; and as guarantee against an unjust law he offers only a disobedience both seditious and disloyal. Finally, he shelters the prince under the power of the laws and sees over him only the judgment of the Church.

We need not say that Suárez himself was a decisive intellectual influence on Spanish America's institutional development (although the University of Mexico did have a Suárezian chair, and his doctrines won increasing attention in New Spain during the seventeenth century). It would seem, however, that his writings are symptomatic of a postmedieval Hispano-Catholic view of man, society, and government that is by no means superseded in modern Spanish America.

One must grasp that Spanish neo-Thomism was not a blind, obstinate reaction to the Protestant Reformation any more than it was a nostalgic revival of ethereal religious aspirations. What it did was to offer sophisticated theoretical formulation of the ideals and many sociological realities of the Spanish patrimonial state. In some ways the political philosophy of St. Thomas Aquinas was more apt for Spain and its overseas empire than for thirteenth-century feudal Europe where it was conceived. The two central principles of Thomist social thought, as Ernst Troeltsch states them, are organicism and patriarchalism. First, society is a hierarchical system in which each person or group serves a purpose larger than any one of them can encompass. Social unity is architectonic, deriving from faith in the larger *corpus mysticum* and not from rationalistic definitions of purpose and strategy at critical moments of history. To the social hierarchy corresponds a scale of inequalities and imperfections that should be corrected only when Christian justice is in jeopardy. Thus casuistry—in the technical sense of judging cases of conscience by "revealed" norms—takes precedence over contrived and mutable human law because to adjudicate is to determine whether a given case affects all of society or whether it can be dispatched by an ad hoc decision.

Second, the inequalities inherent in society imply the acquiescence of each person in his station with its attendant obligations. Such acquiescence is naturally contingent on public acceptance of a supreme authority—prince, king, or pope—who must enjoy full legitimacy to serve as the ultimate, paternal source of the casuistical decisions that resolve the incessant conflicts of function and jurisdiction throughout the realm.

Troeltsch suggests why this majestic philosophic edifice was partly inconsonant with the thirteenth century. He points out that the image of the Aristotelian city-state influenced St. Thomas more strongly than did the constitutional life of his own day. "Catholic theory is, largely, comparatively independent of feudal tenure and the feudal system; the relation between the public authority and subjective public rights is treated in a highly abstract manner." Moreover, St. Thomas displays an urban bias: "[In] contrast to the inclination of modern Catholicism towards the rural population and its specific Ethos, it is solely the city that St. Thomas takes into account. In his view man is naturally a town-dweller, and he regards rural life only as the result of misfortune or of want." Previously we stressed the weakness of the feudal tradition in Spain and the important role of the medieval Spanish city. We can therefore appreciate that it was for sociological as well as strategic ideological reasons that Thomist theory struck resonances throughout the Spanish empire in the sixteenth and seventeenth centuries.

These historically rooted precepts for governance may be generalized to an archetype that brings out more clinically their logic and implications. We speak of what Max Weber called a patrimonial state, which he distinguished as a form of "traditional" domination. The patrimonial ruler is ever alert to forestall the growth of an independent landed aristocracy enjoying inherited privileges. He awards benefices or prebends as remuneration for services; income accruing from benefices is an attribute of the office, not of the incumbent as a person. Characteristic ways for preserving the ruler's authority are limiting the tenure of royal officials; forbidding officials to acquire family and economic ties in their jurisdictions; using inspectors and spies to supervise all levels of administration; defining territorial and functional jurisdictions loosely so that they will be competitive and mutually supervisory. The authority of the rules is oriented to tradition, but allows him claim to full personal power. As he is reluctant to bind himself by law, his rule takes the form of a series of directives, each subject to supersession. Thus problems of adjudication tend to become problems of administration, with administrative and judicial functions united in many offices throughout the bureaucracy. Legal remedies are frequently regarded not as applications of law, but as a gift of grace or a privilege awarded on the merits of the case and not binding as precedent.

Selectively used, this patrimonial type describes with surprising accuracy the structure and logic of the Spanish empire in America. It also helps us to understand why chaos ensued when the ultimate authority for the system, the Spanish crown, was suddenly removed. The compatible general case, however, returns us to historical specifics, or else we are left with a category so spacious that it lumps Spanish America with ancient Egypt and the Chinese empire. Weber himself cautioned against using ideal types as description. Typology does not impart logic to a historical situation, but reveals a logic already inherent. If history yields only complex variants, combinations, and transitions among pure types, typology is merely a guide to configurations and tendencies. Although he recognized a partial "fit," the late John Leddy Phelan was wary of construing colonial Spanish American government along purely patrimonial lines and properly reminded us that the polity also bore traces of feudal, charismatic, and legal domination. Such caution was justified in a study focused on the Kingdom of Quito during a twenty-year period.[1] For this essay, however, which treats all Latin America over a span of five centuries, audacious generalization seems indispensable if we are to place it in provisional perspective as a world civilization.

Above I suggested why, for both Spain and its overseas realms, feudalism was a recessive and patrimonialism a dominant trait of the polity. In what follows we shall make the following points: First, the norms of legal or rational domination were conspicuously asserted after about 1760, and their tension with patrimonialism characterizes Latin America up to the present. Second, the fragmentation of Spanish America during the independence wars of the 1810s and 1820s caused temporary reversion to charismatic domination reminiscent of the era of European conquest. Third, the ethos of patrimonialism survived this interlude of decentralization and ruralization, and it still conditions Latin American reception of industrial capitalism and political rationality.

The Challenges of Enlightenment

For pedagogical purposes Latin American history is conventionally divided into "colonial" and "national" periods. Our present treatment requires an earlier watershed in the 1760s, when the administrative and economic reforms of the Bourbon monarchy took hold and when the promising agenda of the Anglo-French Enlightenment began to overcome the misoneism (hatred of novelty) of intellectuals and the academic establishment. Neither at the institutional nor at the ideological level, however, did full transition or supersession occur. The Ibero-Atlantic world had remained at the margin of the great modern "revolutions"—commercial, scientific, political, and religious—and had actively resisted the last of these. Precisely because Spain and Portugal had "prematurely" modernized their political institutions and renovated their scholastic ideology during Europe's early period of nation building

1   John Leddy Phelan, *The Kingdom of Quito in the Seventeenth Century: Bureaucratic Politics in the Spanish Empire* (Madison, 1967).

and overseas expansion, they resisted the full implications of the great revolutions and failed to internalize their generative force.

One implies such recalcitrance in speaking of the seventeenth century as a "baroque" age for Spain and Portugal and their overseas urban centers. The term conveys the tensions of a deeply orthodox society that is bound by determinations of the Council of Trent in an age of religious experimentalism; that acquiesces in Aristotelianism in an age when scientific inquiry is repositioning the earth and heavens; that countenances the intimate coexistence of pomp, splendor, and vanity with scenes of misery and depravity in an age when human rights are finding formulation. In this setting faith and reason are no longer wedded. Clear statements and logical progressions become elusive. Underlying themes and ideas are embroidered with ornament and allegory. Expression becomes convoluted and cryptic. As the curved line replaces the straight in art, so metaphor and paradox replace direct utterance in literature. In the popular realm the baroque eye sees the world as theater, life as farce, people as caricatures. Here expression is marked not by convolution and overrefinement, but by ridicule, "creole malice," sadism, and obsession with death.

Against a baroque outlook the Enlightenment program of rationalism, liberalism, individualism, and secularism made strategic incursions without, by and large, achieving conclusive victories. The Spanish Bourbon monarchy favored ventilation of fresh ideas, but publication of critiques by political economists might be delayed for decades; the Inquisition still made its presence felt; and the crown was quick to move against lay or religious groups of doubtful loyalty. If Bourbon rule was more rationalized and progressive than Hapsburg, it was also more centralized, more impatient with built-in checks and balances, more given to employing inspectors to spy on lesser officials, more reliant on military force. While implying Bourbon "despotism," this very description bespeaks the undercover survival of the cumbersome, paternalistic pluralism of the old Hapsburg state. The times were inconclusive, and intellectual attainments of the Spanish Enlightenment deserve the customary epithet of "eclecticism" that designates guarded coexistence rather than fusion or transcendence, an ideological mosaic rather than a system.

Against this background the energetic program of Bourbon reform in America appears not as a cluster of measures launched from lofty doctrinal commitment, but as a set of responses to demographic, economic, and political change. The main emphases were commercial, administrative, and strategic. The Spanish American population, which had hovered near ten million, rose by half from 1750 to 1800. This increase enlarged the market for both domestic and European products and, by the same token, yielded additional manpower to produce for local and foreign markets. Gradually, a regime of free trade was introduced within the Spanish empire while at the same time steps were taken to rationalize administration, to decentralize power from the old viceregal centers in Mexico and Peru (thus assuring better central control from Madrid), and to bolster defenses against rival powers in North America.

Economic reform provoked antagonism from merchants in Mexico City, Caracas, and Buenos Aires who had thrived under the old monopolistic system. One can even conclude that "while Spain evolved toward [economic] liberalism, there were interests in America which obstructed those new currents." Administrative reform, and specifically the new system of intendants, "revealed a fatal lack of integration in Spanish policy." New officials were underpaid without being allowed the traditional extralegal fees and exactions. Division of authority between intendants and viceroys was unwisely or vaguely stipulated. The activities of intendants aroused town governments to greater exertion without commensurate increase in their authority. In short, the administrative and commercial reforms of Carlos III (1759–88)—sometimes called the Diocletian of the Spanish empire—"helped to precipitate the collapse of the imperial regime they were intended to prolong."

Suggested Further Reading

Dealy, Glen C. *The Public Man: An Interpretation of Latin American and Other Catholic Countries.* Amherst, 1977.

Góngora, Mario. *Studies in the Colonial History of Spanish America.* Cambridge, 1975. Especially chapters 2, 3, 5, and 6.

Hamilton, Bernice. *Political Thought in Sixteenth-Century Spain.* New York, 1963.

Haring, Clarence H. *The Spanish Empire in America.* New York, 1947.

Johnson, H. B., Jr., ed. *From Reconquest to Empire: The Iberian Background to Latin American History.* New York, 1970.

Liss, Peggy K. *Mexico under Spain, 1521–1556.* Chicago, 1975.